Larry—

# ODE TO A TENOR TITAN

I hope you enjoy reading This sad and beautiful tale of The late Mikey B. He was a friend and hero to me. This book was my love letter to him.

All the best!

Bill Milkowski

# ODE TO A TENOR TITAN

## The Life and Times and Music of Michael Brecker

BILL MILKOWSKI

Backbeat Books

Guilford, Connecticut

*Dedicated to the memory of Chick Corea,*
*McCoy Tyner, and Ralph Peterson*

An imprint of Globe Pequot, the trade division of
The Rowman & Littlefield Publishing Group, Inc.
4501 Forbes Blvd., Ste. 200
Lanham, MD 20706
www.rowman.com

Distributed by NATIONAL BOOK NETWORK

British Library Cataloguing in Publication Information available

**Library of Congress Cataloging-in-Publication Data**

Names: Milkowski, Bill, 1954- author.
Title: Ode to a tenor titan : the life and times and music of Michael Brecker /
  Bill Milkowski.
Description: Guilford, Connecticut : Backbeat Books, 2021. | Includes index.
Identifiers: LCCN 2021017414 (print) | LCCN 2021017415 (ebook) | ISBN
  9781493053766 (cloth) | ISBN 9781493053780 (ebook)
Subjects: LCSH: Brecker, Michael. | Saxophonists--United States--Biography. |
  Jazz musicians--United States--Biography.
Classification: LCC ML419.B7424 M55 2021  (print) | LCC ML419.B7424 (ebook)
  | DDC 788.7/165092 [B]--dc23
LC record available at https://lccn.loc.gov/2021017414
LC ebook record available at https://lccn.loc.gov/2021017415

♾™ The paper used in this publication meets the minimum requirements of
American National Standard for Information Sciences—Permanence of Paper
for Printed Library Materials, ANSI/NISO Z39.48-1992

# CONTENTS

# FOREWORD

## My Brother Mike

### by Randy Brecker

Mike was indeed an iconic figure in jazz, but it was always hard for me to see him in that light. To me, he was still my kid brother in whose milk I used to spit when he wasn't looking.

Imagine, I was there when he first blew some air into a clarinet when he was eight years old. As kids, we met in the bathroom adjoining our bedrooms—Mike on clarinet, me on my first trumpet—and we'd play free jazz (pre-Ornette Coleman) because we liked the echo in that bathroom.

We played together our whole lives, so I also miss him dearly as a section mate. I recently heard both of our early '70s Dreams records, which have amazing examples of "developing Mike" on them, as well as one of the greatest horn sections ever—Mike, Barry Rogers, and me. We were in uncharted territory then, and Mike stayed there his whole life.

Always the scientist, he spent the better part of his life in basements, first at our parents' house outside Philly, where he experimented with his chemistry set until the inevitable explosion. Later in life, the chemistry lab morphed into his basement music studio, and music became his greatest experiment. He studied, studied, and studied some more, mixing different elements of melody, harmony, rhythm, and sound until he came up with a potion that was unique and one which would be copied by thousands of saxophonists and musicians the world over.

Both as a player, and later as a composer, he set the standard. He brought music and musicians from different spheres and cultures together, thus making for a better world. When he was first taken ill, he was working on a project fusing Bulgarian folk music and jazz. I thought to myself, "Well, he's really taking it too far out this time!"

*(Photo by Judy Schiller)*

Then, later down the line, I heard some of his Logic sequences in his basement, and what I heard was genius, unlike anything he had done before, unlike anything anyone had heard before. At this point he had been sick for two years, and he still had the drive to walk down the stairs into his studio to compose and play. But again, that was Mike.

His greatest playing transcended idioms or genres. When he performed his solo improvisations on tunes such as "Naima," one conjured up visions of Paganini, Caruso, Stravinsky, and Mahalia Jackson. It was an absolute marriage of incredible technique with deep feeling and soul. People came away forever transformed by those performances.

Mike always had a strong sense of humility. How many musicians do you know who waited until they were thirty-seven to record their first solo album because they "weren't ready"? That alone says volumes about his honesty and integrity.

I remember doing a session with him a few years ago. Turns out the artist had a sixteen-bar solo spot for him in a 3/4 gospel-type tune. Mike was in the studio with headphones on, and when he heard the track, he started waving his arms and saying, "No, no. You got the wrong guy!"

I had to go out, take him aside, talk him into doing the solo, and when he finally did a take, it was so soulful there wasn't a dry eye in the recording booth. Not only was he the right guy: he was the only guy.

Besides music, Mike loved his family, all of whom gave him reason to live, and they along with my sister, Emmy, and longtime manager and friend Darryl Pitt, left no stone unturned in his struggle.

A picture of Michael Brecker would not be complete if I didn't mention all the incredible things he did for thousands of people mired in substance abuse. After becoming ill with myelodysplastic syndrome (MDS), he also helped thousands more, by going public with his illness, and raising thousands upon thousands of dollars to help with donor drives. The fact that minorities are seriously under-represented in the bone marrow donor registry at marrow.org was brought to the fore by Mike's spearheading the movement.

To all of us in the music community he was a jazz titan, yet let us not forget that to many ordinary people in the rest of the world, who are deep in recovery from addiction, or who have been saved by a successful bone marrow transplant, Michael Brecker was . . . no, *is* a true hero.

# PREFACE

## Ode to a Tenor Titan

He was a generational talent. After John Coltrane, there was no more revered and profoundly influential saxophonist on the planet than Michael Brecker. For those of us coming of age in the 1970s, during that transitional decade when the boundaries between rock and jazz had begun to blur, Brecker stood as a transcendent figure. He was our Trane.

Like John Coltrane before him, Michael came out of the fertile Philadelphia jazz scene along with his older brother, trumpeter Randy. The music of Trane imprinted on him deeply as a teenager and together with Randy, they would later put their stamp on the music world—at the outset of the '70s with Dreams, the seminal jazz-rock band fueled by super drummer Billy Cobham, and by the mid-'70s as the wildly successful Brecker Brothers, an innovative group that created one of the most potent fusions of pop, funk, rock, and jazz ever. The signature Brecker Brothers sound, defined by the tight, swaggering horn lines between Mike, Randy, and "adopted" brother David Sanborn on alto sax, became the soundtrack of New York City, circa 1975–1981, and lit the fuse for the burgeoning funk-fusion movement of the '70s.

A commanding voice in jazz for four decades, Brecker possessed peerless technique (a by-product of his remarkable work ethic and relentless woodshedding) and an uncanny ability to fit into every musical situation he encountered, whether it was playing the perfectly succinct and memorable eight-bar solo on a pop tune, soaring majestically over dark, dense passages in an orchestral suite, or taking flight on some heightened post-Trane modal burn. Combining monstrous chops and a bold, authoritative tone with a passionate intensity on his instrument and boundless curiosity, Brecker pushed the envelope and expanded his palette in ways that few other saxophonists had done before him. "In terms of just pure technique and musicality, there was nobody who could touch Mike," said Sanborn. "He had so much more technical ability than any other saxophone player I've ever known or even heard about in my life."

Brecker's prowess as a tenor player was legendary among his many disciples. As one devotee put it, "There's nobody who I've ever heard who could or can touch the 'Brecker Realm,'" referring to his combination of uncanny speed, remarkable precision, nonchalant doubling of tempos, and daring leaps into the altissimo range of the horn where few ever go but where Michael often dwelled. "No matter who you are, there's always someone who can play the sax better than you," he continued. "The exception to that rule is Michael Brecker."

Or perhaps guitarist and longtime collaborator Pat Metheny put it best when he said, "The most treacherous position in jazz is being the guy on the bandstand who has to take a solo right after Mike Brecker."

Sanborn can attest to that. "I made the mistake one time of letting Mike take the first solo on a tune," he recalled. "I never made that mistake again. Because he'd finish playing, and I would step up to the mic, and it was like the stage had been napalmed. You know, there's one sad little B flat lying in the corner that I picked up. That's all that was left. How do you follow that? Well, lesson learned."

Although Michael's technical command of the instrument may have had fellow saxophonists standing in awe, it was ultimately his sheer passionate intensity that connected with listeners. "He always put everything he had into every note," said bassist Will Lee, a former member of Dreams and charter member of the Brecker Brothers. "He never was like slouching for a second. He was constantly trying to get to a new place, constantly trying to avoid cliché, constantly wrestling with his sound, trying to get that right. That's what it takes to be a Mike Brecker. You can't ever go to sleep on the job."

Added longtime friend and sax playing colleague Dave Liebman, "Mike was about virtuosity, he had amazing technique. And one thing for sure, you could never doubt his passionate feeling. Elvin Jones used to say, 'We play like there's no tomorrow,' and we all had that ethic in his band. And Mike was like that, too. He always committed himself. And he did not let up because Trane did not let up."

Embracing funk and jazz on equal footing, Michael could summon up the raw, muscular force of R&B honkers such as King Curtis and Junior Walker while also bringing John Coltrane's "sheets of sound" approach and deeply searching aesthetic to the mainstream. As San-

*(Photo by John Abbott)*

born noted, "Mike had a gift for being cross-genre or ecumenical in his playing. He did such a deep dive into John Coltrane's music, but he also genuinely loved funk music. So, you never got the feeling that he was slumming when he played a solo on a pop or rock or funk track. No way. He never looked down on that music; he was fascinated by it."

For those of us who followed Dreams, The Brecker Brothers, Steps Ahead, or his own bands through the '70s and '80s, we routinely witnessed Michael flying effortlessly through intricate heads and complex chord changes, flashing incomparable speed and a darting imagination while double-timing tempos at will. We stood in awe as he covered the full range of his horn with remarkable commitment and clarity while unleashing torrents of intense overblowing, flurries of multiphonics, and ecstatic peaks of pure cathartic abandon in the altissimo range in the heat of an inspired solo. The sheer force and fluency of Michael's kinetic lines—a unique combination of velocity, virtuosity, and *vonce*—always seemed to lift the entire bandstand and seemed superhuman. As jazz legend Dave Brubeck noted in commenting on the track "Michael Brecker Waltz," which he had penned especially for the saxophonist on *Young and Old Lions* (Telarc Jazz, 1995), "Each chorus seemed to move into a higher gear and drove until the ending, which became even more adventurous than I had anticipated."

Michael's pulse-quickening performances (the most mind-blowing were referred to by sax enthusiasts as him going into "beast mode") would invariably leave audiences and fellow saxophonists alike positively slack jawed and even the most jaded critics shaking their heads in disbelief. Michael's bandmates would often get swept up into the force of his galvanizing solos, effectively becoming part of the audience when he kicked into full beast mode. "What Michael could do on the saxophone . . . I mean, it was stunning," said Sanborn. "It's just jaw-droppingly great. And I don't think you could find a musician on Earth that would disagree with that."

Added guitarist Adam Rogers, who toured with Brecker in the late 1990s and early 2000s, "Michael wanted to create this fuckin' freight train of energy, and that meant playing on the periphery of his abilities and reaching for things that were not easily accessible. Of course, what was easy for him was impossibly difficult for any other saxophonists I've ever heard, aside from maybe a couple of people. So, Mike evinced that outlook or paradigm of using this incredible facility on his instrument to breakthrough into this level of mind-blowing, transcendent energy. It was like standing next to a fire or something."

The primacy of Michael's playing became such a powerful magnet for many aspiring players that he actually posed a problem for their development. "His influence was so pervasive, and it became so dominant that you kind of had to take a position relative to Michael," said Joshua Redman, one of the more stellar tenor saxophonists on the scene today. "Every saxophonist of my generation had to do that because his sound and his conception were so charismatic and so compelling. The gravitational pull of that was so extreme that it threatened our ability to find ourselves." Consequently, dozens of players who followed in Michael's wake wrestled with the stigma of being tagged "Brecker clones" through the '80s and '90s.

Countless other players on the scene today who have forged their own voices, from Chris Potter and Donny McCaslin to Mark Turner, Joel Frahm, Seamus Blake, and Ben Wendel, readily acknowledge a debt of gratitude to Michael Brecker, citing him as an important role model who defined a new paradigm for what the tenor saxophone could be.

As Redman put it, "His technique was, quite frankly, godly. I mean, it was untouchable. He displayed a level of technical mastery of the instrument that arguably you could say had never been shown before. That was the thing that hit people when they heard Mike for the first time, but I don't think it was in any way the greatest thing about his playing.

And it certainly wasn't the thing that influenced me the most. To me, one of Mike's great gifts was his sense of architecture, his ability to build a solo in a way that was both completely logical but also emotional and charismatic and compelling. It wasn't just this incredible facility and the amazing lines he had—the way he could just dash them off and execute them perfectly. It was the way he put everything together, and the way he used that amazing technique to create improvisational masterpieces. He could construct an improvisation over twenty choruses or over eight bars, on the grandest scale and on the smallest scale."

Fundamental to Michael's musical makeup was his inherent gift for melody, which communicated to listeners across the board. That was as evident on his memorable solo to James Taylor's hit single "Don't Let Me Be Lonely Tonight" from *One Man Dog* (1972) as it was thirty years later on his gorgeous solo reading of John Coltrane's "Naima" from *Directions in Music: Live at Massey Hall* (2002). Michael's gentle readings of Pat Metheny's "Every Day (I Thank You)" from *80/81*, Kurt Weill's "My Ship" from *Nearness of You: The Ballad Book* (2001), or Don Grolnick's melancholy masterpiece, "Cost of Living" from *Michael Brecker* (1987), further cemented his reputation as a master of melodic improvisation.

As a ubiquitous session player during the '70s, Brecker contributed to a deluge of studio recordings by such high-profile pop producers as Arif Mardin, Tommy LiPuma, Phil Ramone, and others. The breadth of Michael's output during that productive decade is astounding. His solos on Taylor's aforementioned "Don't Let Me Be Lonely Tonight" and Paul Simon's "Still Crazy After All These Years" (title track from his 1975 album) are prime examples of melodic gems that have become part of our collective consciousness. Mike also made key contributions to innumerable recordings by other prominent pop and rock artists during that decade, including James Brown (*Get on the Good Foot*, 1972), Todd Rundgren (*Something/Anything?*, 1972), John Lennon (*Mind Games*, 1973), Lou Reed (*Berlin*, 1973), Average White Band (*AWB*, 1974), Aerosmith (*Get Your Wings*, 1974), Bruce Springsteen (*Born to Run*, 1975), Laura Nyro (*Smile*, 1976), Blue Oyster Cult (*Agents of Fortune*, 1976), Parliament (*Mothership Connection*, 1975; and *Clones of Dr. Funkenstein*, 1977), Wild Cherry (*Electrified Funk*, 1977), Ringo Starr (*Ringo the 4th*, 1977), Phoebe Snow (*Against the Grain*, 1978), Carly Simon (*Boys in the Trees*, 1978), Chaka Khan (*Chaka*, 1978), Bette Midler (*Thighs and Whispers*, 1979), and Steely Dan (*Gaucho*, 1980).

This same tenor saxophonist, who could provide the perfect solo in pop settings, would turn around and deliver the kind of dazzling, virtuosic improvisations in headier contexts that rank him in the upper echelon of all-time great jazz soloists.

Consider the dichotomy: here is a cat who in the same incredibly productive year (1981) played on Chick Corea's *Three Quartets* and Chaka Khan's *What Cha' Gonna Do for Me*, Jaco Pastorius's *Word of Mouth* and Chic's smooth-grooving *Take It Off*, Mike Mainieri's beguiling *Wanderlust* and Funkadelic's nasty *Electric Spanking of War Babies*, Yoko Ono's cathartic *Season of Glass* and Diana Ross's appealing *Why Do Fools Fall in Love?* He could fit in perfectly with such imposing figures as Frank Zappa (*Zappa in New York*, 1978) and Charles Mingus (*Me Myself An Eye*, 1978), then deliver just the right motivational solo on the background music for Jane Fonda's 1984 *Prime Time Workout*. He thrived in the haunting orchestral environment of German composer-arranger Claus Ogerman's opus, *Cityscape* (1982), then would throw down with requisite swagger on the blistering funk jam "Candy," the hit single from Cameo's mega-selling album, *Word Up!* (1986).

It is precisely that kind of dichotomy that may have confused critics, as Michael's longtime friend and manager, Darryl Pitt, suggested, and ultimately lowered Brecker's standing in the jazz world. "It's because he did so much studio work in the '70s on pop and rock sessions that some people don't take him seriously as a jazz artist," he said. "And that, of course, is just foolish."

But Michael more than made up for what some perceived as his early career pop indiscretions by producing some of the most challenging, inspired, and visionary modern jazz recordings during the last twenty years of his career, bookended by his 1987 self-titled Impulse! debut and *Pilgrimage* (2007), which Metheny called "one of the great codas in modern music history."

What gave such incredible depth and expressive power to Brecker's playing throughout his celebrated career, and elevated every bandstand and session he ever played on, was his tremendous heart. It was that same heart that got him off a sick bed in 2006—after lengthy hospitalizations from a pre-leukemic bone marrow disorder and an experimental partial matching stem cell transplant from his sixteen-year-old daughter, Jessica—to record his emotionally charged swan song, *Pil-*

*grimage*, which earned Michael two posthumous Grammy Awards, pushing his lifetime total to fifteen.

And yet, in spite of all the awards and accolades, the nine hundred-plus recording sessions and innumerable concerts he played around the world, Brecker was well known among his peers for his genuine humility and wry self-deprecation. Sanborn, a charter member of The Brecker Brothers band, remembers Michael being modest to a fault: "Sometimes I couldn't believe it! His denigration of himself and his abilities was almost neurotic at times. You wanna say, 'Mike, you have to see that you're just so much better than everyone else!' But he didn't get it. When you listen to the hundreds and hundreds of recorded solos that Mike played over the course of his career, there's no let up on any tune, there is no bad day. But, of course, Mike would differ there. Every time I talked to him, he would always be like, 'Ah, I'm completely upset with my sound. It's too bright. I don't like it.' And invariably his next question would be, 'What are you playing on? What are you using?' So, he was always dissatisfied with his sound, his mouthpiece, his gear. But he was also always burning on every solo he ever played in any con-text—pop, jazz funk, ballads; everything he did was always smoking. And it wouldn't surprise me on some of those great pop solos he played if that were the fifth or sixth attempt he made in the studio that day. And I'm sure the first five were just as great. He just didn't like them."

Adam Rogers addressed this self-critical streak in Brecker: "We'd come off stage sometimes, and he'd go, 'Oh, I couldn't play tonight.' And I'd go, 'What are you talking about, man? That was fucking killing!' So, my sense of it was that Mike was an unbelievable virtuoso who was always looking for something that he hadn't heard or played before, and if he didn't reach that on a given set, he would be frustrated. But I remember one night in Seattle when he said after the set, 'You know what? I really felt like I was improvising tonight.' And he was obviously expressing having felt good about that."

Longtime friend and collaborator Mike Mainieri witnessed Mike's self-critical side too many times to even count. "In all the years that I played with him, that humility and self-deprecation was evident almost every time we played," he said. "You'd go backstage after a show, and he'd say, 'I sounded like shit tonight.' And you'd be like, 'What?!' I have this image of him trying different reeds backstage and throwing out one after the other. 'How does this sound?' 'It sounds great to me, Mike.' Eight reeds later, he's like, 'How about this one?' 'That sounds great too, Mike.' Meanwhile, the floor would be covered with reeds, and then he would go back to the reed he had the first set or the night before."

Michael's penchant for being overly self-critical was also noted by Herbie Hancock: "Every solo that Michael played was brilliant and every time I would be like, 'How does he do that?' Always exciting, always extraordinary. He would walk off the bandstand, and people would be screaming, and I'd come up to him and say, 'Michael, that was unbelievable!' And he would go, 'Oh, man, I'm sorry.' He would apologize! He'd say, 'I wasn't on the mark this time' or 'I sucked' or something like that. He was always downing himself. And I'd be like, 'What?! What are you talking about? That was incredible!' I never understood that. I'd always think, 'Why is he saying that?' And it wasn't that he was just being polite and being unassuming. No, he seriously thought he didn't do well."

Pianist Richie Beirach, who gave Michael harmony lessons shortly after he had arrived in New York, had this story about Mike's self-deprecating nature: "We were hanging out, having a couple of drinks after a recording session, and I said to him, 'Look, man. Do you know how good that take was you just played?' And he says no. So, I say, 'So, it's not just some bullshit act, right? You're not going for the humble sad artist routine to try and pick up some girl, right?' And he says, 'No, I really didn't like it.' And I say to him, 'So you really have no objectivity about your own playing, do you? You can't step back and assess it honestly.' And he says, 'Absolutely not.' And I'll tell you who else was not as vocal but was definitely in that line, was Trane. Liebs told me a story about going to the Vanguard to see Trane play. And after the set, which was amazing, of course, Liebs is waiting near the pay phone on the way to the kitchen at the Vanguard, and Trane walks by. And he overhears somebody say to Trane, 'Amazing set! How's it going?' And Trane says, 'It goes better at home.' So, they had that in common. But there's a line between wanting to always improve and never settling, and just self-hatred. I mean, that's Psychology 101, right? And Michael walked that line."

"He was beyond humble, he was self-deprecating, to a fault, I think," Beirach continued. "And I felt so bad for him because he didn't seem to enjoy it. I mean, he liked the cats, he liked hanging, but he was so really down on his own playing, even though it was obviously great playing. So, there's the Shakespearean tragedy right in there. In some kind of a way he was afraid of himself. I think he was afraid of his own talent or some very complex shit like that, but something wasn't right there. A lot of that had to do with the drug shit. Getting strung out didn't help, but he had a hard road. His father was very tough on him, and then he had Randy, who was an unbelievable talent and was the older brother who was already established. So, Mike just never felt good enough. And that's, to me, the tragedy. You know, Randy loved him to death and did everything he could to make him comfortable, but Mike was not comfortable in his own skin."

But pianist Marc Copland, who grew up with Mike as teenagers in suburban Cheltenham Township, just outside of Philadelphia, regarded Michael's self-deprecating nature as less a hindrance than a tool for self-actualization. "I think he had a pretty good idea what he was about and what he was capable of," said Copland. "But I think if you don't have a certain amount of self-doubt, then you're never going to try and look at yourself from a different perspective to see what's there. And if you don't do that, then you're shutting the door on the possibility of growing as an artist. So, yeah, I think Mike had some of that self-doubt, but I think it was entirely healthy. I think maybe in Mike's case it seemed a little surreal given his technical proficiency and his musical ideas and everything. But I think it was kind of healthy, actually."

Beirach offered this final streetwise assessment of the tenor titan: "He was a tall, very handsome motherfucker who could play. And with talent and looks like that, he could have been a real arrogant asshole. But, instead, he was very open and humble, and he never had an attitude. He always played with so much intent. Plus, he had this sound on the tenor—it was just natural to him. It was not intellectual; it was not manufactured. You could tell it was him. He was like a great soccer player, who from the very first minute they played were already at that level of excellence. He was one with the horn. There are a lot of really great musicians that are technically great, but it doesn't touch you. Why doesn't it touch you? Don't ask, I don't know. But there's a quality that's not there that if you add it, it works. And Michael had it."

A universally beloved figure among musicians, fans, and writers alike, Michael was alternately described as "sweet," "nice guy," and "gentle giant" by several of the hundred-plus people I interviewed for this book. Both tenor saxophonist Bob Franceschini and pianist David

Kikoski, the latter who toured with Michael in an all-acoustic version of The Brecker Brothers band at the outset of the new millennium, described him as "an angel." Bob Mintzer called him "a very caring soul," Jerry Bergonzi described him "one-of-a-kind," and drummer Steve Gadd summed it up by saying, "He was a good guy, he had a big heart, and he shared a lot of love with a lot of people."

That Michael Brecker—so preternaturally gifted and possessing an unequaled work ethic—would rise to such rarefied heights in his career, inspiring legions of other saxophonists along the way, is the stuff of legend. That he was able to kick a decade-long heroin addiction and later serve as an example to hordes of fellow musicians to lead clean and sober lives themselves is a great story of redemption. That he died so tragically of such a rare disease at the top of his game and in the most contented place in his life as a loving husband and devoted father is the stuff of Shakespearean tragedy.

Even in death, Michael continued to help people. Through a comprehensive, worldwide blood marrow donor campaign that was undertaken by his wife, Susan Brecker, and his longtime manager, Darryl Pitt, to find a match for a life-saving stem cell transplant, thousands of people around the world joined the bone marrow registry. Since Michael's passing, many of those same donors who registered to try to help save Michael's life have ended up providing perfect matches that have saved other lives.

In preparing to write this *Ode to a Tenor Titan*, I reflected back on the fifty or so galvanizing Michael Brecker performances I witnessed over nearly forty years of covering the jazz scene. And I fondly recalled the several interviews conducted with him through different phases of his career. He was always soft-spoken, articulate, thoughtful in his responses. But more than that, I remember the humor—the playful grin, the easy laugh, the deadpan Jack Benny-inspired takes and the distinctly Yiddish shtick he could affect at the drop of a hat. There was a touch of Mel Brooks, Myron Cohen, and Mickey Katz in this gentle, funny man, who also happened to be the baddest tenor sax player on the planet.

In a candid moment from an outdoor video interview with Michael at the 2004 Newport Jazz Festival, the filmmaker suddenly interrupts the proceedings to point out that a flock of birds had just flown into camera view, ruining his shot. As an assistant goes to chase the birds away while the camera continues to roll, Mike can be heard mumbling under his breath, "Filthy, disgusting boids," a reference to a comedic scene from Mel Brooks's *The Producers* where Max Bialystock (Zero Mostel) and Leo Bloom (Gene Wilder) inquire with the "concierge" (Madelyn Cates) of a tenement building the whereabouts of one Franz Liebkind (Kenneth Mars). Humor was always right on the surface with Michael.

I first witnessed him in concert on Joni Mitchell's 1979 *Shadows and Light* tour, which rolled into the Alpine Valley Music Theatre on August 17 that year in bucolic East Troy, Wisconsin, about thirty-five miles from where I grew up in Milwaukee. He was tall, slender, and bearded, and he blew with focused, Herculean authority on "Free Man in Paris," "The Dry Cleaner from Des Moines" and Joni's version of the melancholy Charles Mingus ballad, "Goodbye Pork Pie Hat," mixing it up with kindred spirits Jaco Pastorius, Pat Metheny, Don Alias, and Lyle Mays on the bandstand. After moving to New York City in 1980, I saw Mike more regularly, often at Seventh Avenue South, the jazz club that he and his brother, Randy, had opened in 1977. I caught Mike there on several occasions in the early '80s playing with Steps, Don Grolnick's Idiot Savant, Jaco's Word of Mouth band, and Bob Mintzer's big band.

I finally got the chance to meet Michael face-to-face in January of 1982 when I landed an assignment from a magazine to interview him about *Cityscape*, an impressive opus that had just come out on Warner Bros. Conceived by the renowned German composer-arranger-conductor Claus Ogerman, it showcased Mike stretching out with his commanding tenor voice on some dense, sometimes dissonant, and very demanding orchestral music. Conducting the interview at the Warner Bros. offices in midtown Manhattan, I found Michael to be reserved and unassuming, almost introverted. His bashful persona seemed incongruous to the towering figure emitting torrents of notes with blast furnace intensity on the tenor sax that I had witnessed before in concert. But he spoke eloquently, weighing each question before he spoke and reeling off articulate and insightful answers. I found him to be genuinely down to earth.

I caught Mike in concert numerous times after that interview. I saw him with Steps at Seventh Avenue South and with Steps Ahead at the Bottom Line. I was in attendance at the Village Vanguard in October 1985 when Michael joined John Abercrombie's group featuring bassist Marc Johnson and drummer Peter Erskine for an exhilarating set, marking his first performance at that hallowed subterranean jazz club just up the road from Seventh Avenue South since he and Randy had played there in 1977 as members of Hal Galper's quintet. I also attended Seventh Avenue South's New Year's Eve party on December 31, 1985, when Mike played with Jaco, Hiram Bullock, Kenwood Dennard, and Mitch Forman (aka The Seventh Avenue South All-Stars). And I saw Michael leading his own band with guitarist Mike Stern, pianist Joey Calderazzo, bassist Jeff Andrews, and drummer Adam Nussbaum at Fat Tuesday's and the Bottom Line.

Over the years, I saw Michael lead groups at the Blue Note, Joe's Pub, Iridium, and Birdland and caught him with Randy in Return of The Brecker Brothers gigs at the Blue Note and Town Hall. There was also his memorable appearance on June 26, 1988, at the Beacon Theater, where he appeared as special guest with Herbie Hancock's Headhunters II band, showcasing his latest jaw-dropping EWI experiments in a solo setting while blowing ferocious tenor on Herbie's "Hang Up Your Hangups."

In December 1999, I had a ringside seat at Birdland when Mike, Dave Liebman, and Joe Lovano premiered their Saxophone Summit with pianist Phil Markowitz, bassist Rufus Reid, and drummer Billy Hart. I was in the house at the "Made in America" 9/11 benefit concert held on December 5, 2001, at Town Hall, which reunited Mike and guitarist John Scofield for the first time since they had toured together in Billy Cobham's band a quarter of a century earlier in support of his 1975 album, *A Funky Thide of Sings*. I witnessed the unveiling of Brecker's fifteen-piece Quindectet at Iridium in November 2003. And I was also in attendance at Carnegie Hall the night Michael made his heroic surprise appearance at Herbie Hancock's sixty-sixth birthday gala on June 23, 2006, long after he had been sidelined by a life-threatening bone marrow disease.

Other gigs featuring Mike spring to mind: Herbie Hancock's The New Standard band at the 1997 Montreal Jazz Festival, Chick Corea's stellar *Three Quartets* ensemble at the Blue Note in 2001 commemorating the pianist's sixtieth birthday, Herbie's Directions in Music band at Avery Fisher Hall in 2001. I saw Michael alongside Ravi Coltrane, McCoy Tyner, Christian McBride, and Roy Haynes in a memorable John Coltrane tribute at the 2004 Newport Jazz Festival and also caught him in guest roles with the Elvin Jones Jazz Machine at the Blue Note in 1999 and with the Odean Pope Sax Choir at the Blue Note in 2004. Michael and Randy made a rare, unpublicized appearance with the Metropole Orchestra at the 2001 IAJE Conference in the Hilton Hotel, and I was in attendance for another rare gig—an all-acoustic edition of the Brecker Brothers at the 2001 Estoril Jazz Festival in Portugal.

I have a distinct memory of a gig of Michael's quintet making its New York City debut on May 18, 1987, at Fat Tuesday's, the Manhattan club run by Stan Getz's son Steve. A subterranean venue on 18th Street and Third Avenue, located in the historic Scheffel Hall that once housed the German-American Athletic Club, Fat Tuesday's was the home to legendary guitarist-inventor Les Paul, who played there every Monday night. The club also showcased jazz greats such as Betty Carter, Jimmy Smith, Chet Baker, Pepper Adams, Kenny Barron, and Freddie Hubbard. I lived on 29th Street just off Third Avenue at the time and was freelancing a lot for *Downbeat* magazine, so I was pretty much a regular at the club in those days. On this particular night when Michael unveiled his new band featuring guitarist Mike Stern, bassist Jeff Andrews, pianist Joey Calderazzo, and Adam Nussbaum, I was seated at a ringside table along with wives and girlfriends of the band members. And I'll never forget the sight of Michael's tall, wiry frame bobbing and weaving on the bandstand during one particularly scorching solo, his head nearly scraping the ceiling every time it jerked back in full beast mode.

But it was a performance five months after that Brecker quintet debut at Fat Tuesday's that carried the most personal meaning for me. I had just come off cancer surgery that summer and a regimen of follow-up radiation therapy at Memorial Sloan Kettering Hospital (the same place that Michael would be visiting regularly nearly twenty years later). And because, like many other freelancers at that time, I didn't have health insurance, a few kind colleagues helped organize a benefit concert for me at the old Tramps nightclub, a blues and roots venue on East 15th Street. Proprietor Terry Dunne donated the space for this Monday evening event on October 12, 1987. With fellow scribe Howard Mandel acting as emcee, several notable musicians showed up to play gratis to help raise money for my hospital bills. Mike and Leni Stern played duets, then Michael jammed with John Scofield, Mike Stern, pianist Laszlo Gardony, bassist Jeff Andrews, and drummer Danny Gottlieb on "Straight No Chaser," "Autumn Leaves," and "Alone Together." Jon Paris's blues band, featuring guest guitarists Eric Warren and Elliott Sharp, got people up and dancing while a group featuring alto saxophonist John Zorn, slide guitarist David Tronzo, bassist Ed Maguire, and drummer Bobby Previte explored the outer fringes. And my own band, The Pit Bulls, featuring alto saxophonist Steve Buchanan, bassist Ed Maguire, drummer Billy McClellan, and special guest guitarist Robert Quine, put an exclamation point on the proceedings with some edgy, blues-tinged punk-funk. What a night!

Thirty-two years later, I began the exhaustive process of writing this book. After being invited into people's homes to share their stories about Michael, I was profoundly moved to see how deeply he touched the lives of so many through his music, his humility, and his humanity. He touched my life as well.

One final analogy, which I think is apt, given Michael's lifelong love of basketball. In the heat of the writing phase for this *Ode to a Tenor Titan*, I took a break one evening to begin watching the ten-part Michael Jordan Netflix documentary, *The Last Dance*. And I found the comparison between the two Michaels to be startling: both were astounding raw talents who, through single-minded determination and hard work, became supremely gifted players who accelerated through the ranks so quickly and kept adding onto that raw talent, expanding their respective vocabularies until they were each in a league of their own. Wedding incredibly high standards to unparalleled dedication, they willed themselves to greatness. And each—no small coincidence here—competed with an older brother for his father's approval.

Michael Brecker lived a rich life—fame and accolades, universal respect and admiration from his colleagues, as well as an abundance of unconditional love from his wife and soulmate, Susan, and his two adoring children, Jessica and Sam. We all miss him and still love him madly.

—Bill Milkowski

# PROLOGUE
## One Finger Snap

One of the highlights of the 2006 JVC Jazz Festival in New York City was "Herbie's World," an all-star concert at Carnegie Hall celebrating the iconic and multidirectional pianist-composer Herbie Hancock in four distinct settings that showcased his singular virtuosity, uncanny open-mindedness, and unrelenting creativity. The June 23rd gala, which touched on different periods of Hancock's expansive career, opened with Herbie on piano, accompanied by the great bass-drums tandem of Ron Carter and Jack DeJohnette, performing "Toys" (from *Speak Like A Child*, 1968) and a radical reworking of the jazz standard "I Thought About You." Hancock then stepped up to the mic to announce their next number, "One Finger Snap" (from his classic Blue Note album, *Empyrean Isles*, 1964). "I feel kind of funny doing this tune as a trio because usually I play it with a quartet," he told the capacity crowd. After glancing off stage, he coyly added, "There must be some sax player backstage there who could sit in on this one."

And with that, out came Michael Brecker, to the utter disbelief of everyone in attendance. The Carnegie crowd leaped to its feet with cheers as Brecker slowly emerged from the wings, comedically walking backward onto the stage, cradling his golden Selmer Mark VI sax while casting a bewildered gaze about the cavernous, hallowed hall, feigning disorientation as if to say, "Where am I? How did I get here?" It was a positively Chaplinesque entrance.

There were audible gasps in the crowd, and some wept openly upon seeing Michael's familiar 6-foot, 4½-inch bespectacled visage. I confess that I, too, had tears welling up in my eyes as a frail Michael made his way over to Hancock's piano, put tenor sax to mouth, and proceeded to blow in quintessentially titanic fashion. As Ben Ratliff noted the next day in the *New York Times*: "It was the first time he had performed since his hospitalization. Mr. Brecker looked slightly tired, but otherwise gave it his all, playing long, tumultuous lines at full strength through the song."

When the tune ended, the crowd erupted into another standing ovation as Hancock and Brecker shared a big hug. Michael's surprising return to the scene, albeit brief, was easily the emotional highpoint of this evening and a potent reminder of his preternatural prowess. Hearing Michael's blistering lines again—his own personal take on John Coltrane's fabled "sheets of sound"—along with that beautiful burnished tone, the deft double-timing, and passionate intensity at the peak of an altissimo flurry filled us with hope.

People all over the world had been praying for his recovery and return to the scene. And there he was, somehow summoning up those consummate Michael Brecker powers once again in the regal company of Herbie, Ron, and Jack. It all seemed like a beautiful dream. And in that one brief moment, it made us feel like, "He's back!"

# 1

# BECOMING MICHAEL BRECKER

In raising the age-old nature versus nurture debate, one could say that Michael Brecker checked both boxes. Inherited traits and environmental factors combined to mold Mike during his formative years. Add to those fundamental qualities an uncommon work ethic, remarkable diligence and dedication to his craft, and a ceaselessly curious mind, and you have the recipe for what Michael would become—the most potent and influential saxophonist of his generation.

Regarding the genetic side of the argument, a decided gift for music in the Brecker family can be traced at least a few generations. "Music ran through the whole family," said older brother Randy Brecker. "My grandfather on my father's side was a great singer who could belt out vaudeville type songs and other popular tunes of the day. His favorite was 'I Left My Heart in San Francisco.' He was a real outgoing, cigar-smoking character named Emmanuel Brecker; we called him Manny. Both of my father's parents were immigrants—his mother was from Austria, and his father was from Russia, and they both came over to the States pretty early on in their lives. My grandfather on my mother's side was a violinist. His name was Jacob Tecosky, but we called him Pop Pop. He came over from Tykocin, Poland, escaping all the tragedy over there by settling in Philadelphia. Pop Pop's first cousin was Morton DaCosta, the famous director [of Broadway productions such as *The Music Man*, *Auntie Mame*, and *No Time for Sergeants* and who also produced and directed the film versions of *The Music Man* and *Auntie Mame*]. He was also a Tecosky from Philly before he changed his name. His nickname was Tec, but we knew him as Uncle Morty when we were kids."

Occupying another branch of the Brecker family tree was Randy and Mike's great Uncle Lou Brecker, who founded Roseland Ballroom in Philadelphia in 1916 before relocating to New York City three years later to escape blue laws that banned dancing on Sundays in the City of Brotherly Love. In its original New York City location at 51st and Broadway, Roseland was notable for presenting hot jazz stars during the 1920s and 1930s—Fletcher Henderson, Louis Armstrong, Count Basie, and the Chick Webb band featuring a young Ella Fitzgerald—as well as the popular swing era big bands of Harry James, Tommy Dorsey, and Glenn Miller during the 1940s. In 1956, the club relocated to a new venue on 52nd and Broadway and remained there for decades, persevering through the disco era and later hosting hip-hop and rock concerts in the 1990s and 2000s. Lou Brecker's daughter, Nancy Leeds, ran the famed ballroom until its final days in 2014. Roseland's nearly one-hundred-year run culminated with a seven-night engagement by headliner Lady Gaga before the doors finally closed forever on April 8 that year.

The Brecker-Tecosky gene pool deepens with the parents. Said Randy, "I was blessed to have really talented parents, and we were a pretty tight-knit musical family." The family patriarch, the irrepressible Bobby Brecker (born 1916), was a lawyer by trade but a musician at heart. A talented, semiprofessional pianist and skillful songwriter, he loved to entertain at parties and would hold regular family jam sessions at the Breckers' suburban home in Cheltenham Township, Pennsylvania. Their mother, Sylvia Tecosky (born 1920), was also artistically gifted. Widely known by her nickname, "Ticky" (a derivation of her family surname), she played piano but became more recognized as a skilled painter. One striking portrait of her sons in the heyday of the Brecker Brothers remained in Michael's Hastings-on-Hudson home for years and is still on display in the home of his widow, Susan Neustadt Brecker. "She was heavily involved in art, that was her thing," said Randy of his mother. "And she was really good at what she did. She studied her whole life and was pretty successful as a commissioned portrait artist in Philadelphia and the surrounding area. She always seemed to be working on somebody's portraits."

The third and middle sibling from the gifted Brecker family is sister Emily. A classically trained pianist, Mike often referred to her as "the most talented member of the family." Still residing in the Elkins Park section of Cheltenham Township where she grew up, Emily Brecker Greenberg is currently an accomplished pianist-harpist-arranger and president of Sharp Sounds Publishing.

Genetics aside, the nurturing aspect of Michael's development as a player was evident in the supportive musical environment fostered at home by both of his artistically inclined parents. With a piano and a Hammond organ, bass, vibes, and a set of drums in the living room, Bobby Brecker presided over family jams at their suburban home. "When I was a kid, I really thought that everybody was a musician," Mike told a roomful of students in a 1984 clinic at North Texas State University. "We had jam sessions at home all the time, and I just thought that's what every family does. I later learned that it wasn't so common. And it was a shock to me to find out that we were kind of an oddity.

"Having access to the instruments and then watching other people coming over to the house and play them had an enormous influence on us as well," he continued. "It was almost kind of a reverse family where, you know, normally parents encourage their kids to learn music, but then when it comes time to get a real job, they try and give them a light push in another direction. In our case, we were encouraged to be musicians. We were encouraged to do whatever we wanted, whatever we liked. But we ended up liking music, so we were supported for that."

On weekends, some rather high-level local musicians would come over to the Brecker household to join the family jam sessions. As Randy recalled, "There was a great trumpet player named Bobby Mojica, who eventually moved to Detroit. He was a professional player all his life, really sounded great. I was just enthralled to see him play at those sessions in our living room. In fact, I think I sound a little like him, so I guess some of Bobby's playing kind of magically rubbed off on me."

Occasionally, some bona fide stars performing in Philadelphia would fall by the Brecker house to sit in. "Jon Hendricks comes to mind," said Randy. "I actually played at that one. In fact, that's the first time I ever heard myself back because Dad had just bought a tape recorder, and I sounded pretty good on it. I had been strictly playing with records before that, but on this night, I sat in at the jam session with my Dad on piano and a good guitar player named Irv Weiner, who was also a great scat singer. Jon Hendricks was staying at Irv's house and got snowed in, so he actually spent a couple of days in Philly, and we did a lot of playing together. I distinctly remember playing on this ballad with Jon. I forget the name of the tune, but I can still hear Jon singing it and sounding so amazing.

"I was a bit older then, which is why they let me sit in," Randy continued. "But I had been a Jon Hendricks fan long before I ever met him. In fact, in fifth grade our music class teacher picked one student a week to bring in his or her favorite record. This was 1955, during Elvis Presley's incubation period and the beginnings of rock 'n' roll, and I brought in Jon Hendricks singing 'Cloudburst' with the Dave Lambert Singers. I had the whole thing memorized at ten years old."

The elder Brecker brother was born on November 27, 1945, in a New York City hospital but shortly after went home to Cheltenham Township's Elkins Park, a northern suburb located just five miles or four station stops on the Septa Regional Rail from Philadelphia's City Center. Randy lived at 8244 New Second St. until the third grade. (Interesting footnote: in 1983, comedian/actor Bill Cosby bought the 8,940 square foot home at 8210 New Second St. in Elkins Park, just down the block from Randy's childhood home.)

Michael was born on March 29, 1949, in a Philadelphia hospital and lived in Elkins Park before the Brecker family moved to a bigger house a mile away in the Melrose Park section of Cheltenham Township at 1005 Valley Rd. As Randy explained, "Melrose Park was technically in the suburbs but only a block out of the Philadelphia city limits, which made for maybe a better education in general but not a better music education. Philadelphia had some pretty highly developed music programs in the schools, particularly in Northeast Philadelphia. Some of the trade schools and high schools there, like Mastbaum Technical High School and Walter George Smith School, produced all these great Philly musicians like Lee Morgan, the Heath Brothers, Billy Root and my trumpet teacher, Tony Marchione, who also taught Lee Morgan. So, the Philly school system was a famous spawning ground for some pretty great musicians."

Although Randy, Emily, and Mike got a good education growing up in Cheltenham Township, the music programs there were indeed lacking. "They didn't have a lot of instruments," Randy recalled. "We didn't even have a dance band until I was in eleventh grade. So, in terms of music education, we probably would've been better off one block over in the Philadelphia school system. So, we were unlucky in that respect but lucky that we got so much music at home."

The brothers and sister Emily attended B. R. Myers Elementary School in Elkins Park and later attended Cheltenham High School, where the future prime minister of Israel, Benjamin Netanyahu, also attended from 1963 to 1967. Michael and Benjy, a star on the high school soccer team, were both part of Cheltenham High's graduating class of 1967.

4

Another key element of Michael's nurturing was Camp Onibar, a Jewish summer camp on Lake Como, Pennsylvania, in the Poconos that he and his siblings attended each year. A long-standing Brecker family tradition, their parents, Bobby and Ticky, had even met there as teenagers in the 1930s. "The name of the camp was the family name, Rabino, spelled backwards," explained Randy. "It was probably an abbreviation of Rabinowitz. [Actually, the camp was opened in the 1920s by Michael Rabbino and carried on under the same family for decades until it was sold in 1968.] They put on a lot of really professionally done shows at Onibar. That was Dad's background—writing songs and playing for the shows at the camp. He was competing with a bunch of other songwriters to get their songs in the camp productions. All of these guys went on to achieve some fame as songwriters, and Dad was right up there with them. He could've been a professional songwriter. In fact, when I was there twenty-some years later, they were still singing all of Dad's tunes at Camp Onibar. They were really good."

(Indeed, Bobby Brecker penned the enduring camp anthem, "Dear Onibar.")

As a young man at Camp Onibar, Bobby Brecker's competitors included such aspiring songwriters as "Moose" Charlap (Morris Isaac Charlap, who wrote the 1954 Broadway musical *Peter Pan* and is the father of jazz pianist Bill Charlap), Irvin Graham (who wrote the 1953 hit song for Frankie Laine, "I Believe," later covered by everyone from Perry Como and Andy Williams to Louis Armstrong, Barbra Streisand, and Elvis Presley, and who also penned "You Better Go Now," covered by Billie Holiday in 1945), and Bobby Troup (of "Route 66" fame, who also wrote "The Girl Can't Help It" for Little Richard and "The Meaning of the Blues" for his wife, singer Julie London).

While Randy and Michael attended the boys camp, Onibar, Emily attended the nearby girls camp, Geneva. Randy was not exactly a happy camper at Onibar, dropping out after one summer. "I didn't take to it," he said. "It was mostly sports with some music. I ended up hanging out a lot with a guy named Gary Pace. He was kind of a bebop pianist, and we had a little quartet together at camp. That's mostly what I did at Onibar. I wasn't that interested in camp, so I only went one year."

Michael, however, spent three summers at Onibar, from 1962 to 1965, and seemed to thrive in the sports atmosphere of the camp. Randy recalled that some of the young counselors and staff at Onibar later went on to fabulous careers in the arts. "When I went there, the guy who was music director at the girls camp was Marvin Hamlisch. He was just a kid out of Juilliard, maybe seventeen or eighteen years old. And James Caan of acting fame was my brother's counselor. I remember his nickname at camp was Superman because he had such a great body." The late actor-director Penny Marshall (of *Laverne & Shirley* and director of *A League of Their Own* fame) also worked one summer as a waitress at Camp Geneva.

Emily Brecker ended up meeting her future husband, Howard Greenberg, at Camp Onibar-Geneva. "He was part of the Rabino family, and he eventually worked in my father's law firm," said Randy. "My dad ended up doing the legal work at a company called J. G. Hook [a subsidiary of Morgan Raab], which was a blouse manufacturing company run by a pretty well-known guy named Max Raab, who was also an entrepreneur who put on jazz concerts in Philly. Dad and Max Raab both had some kind of interest in the first music tent that started up in area—the Valley Forge Music Fair, just outside Philly in suburban Devon. There were three main guys behind that enterprise: Eddie Felbin, whose broadcast radio name was Frank Ford; nightclub owner and theater impresario Lee Guber, who was married to Barbara Walters; and television news anchor Shelly Gross. They started the first theater-in-the-round at Valley Forge Music Fair [its inaugural season was in 1955], and Dad was part of that somehow. They would have jazz nights on Monday, so I would go there quite a bit with Dad to hear Dave Brubeck, Gerry Mulligan, Maynard Ferguson's big band, and watch the stage slowly go around. After Valley Forge, they opened Westbury Music Fair on Long Island, which opened the following year. So, my dad was pretty involved in the music scene around Philadelphia as well as being a lawyer."

By all accounts, Bobby Brecker, the ringleader for all of those family jam sessions that took place in the Brecker family living room in suburban Cheltenham Township, was quite a character. Born in 1916, he endured blatant acts of anti-Semitism as young man growing up in North Philly but that didn't deter him from becoming a successful self-made man. He attended the Wharton School in Philadelphia, graduated from the University of Pennsylvania Law School in 1938, and a year later became founding partner of Kleinbard Bell & Brecker, a law firm specializing in labor law.

"He grew up in a tough neighborhood," said Randy. "He was telling me when he was young, there weren't a lot of Jews in his neighborhood. And the other kids in the neighborhood there had a game they called Garbage, where they'd throw garbage at the Jewish kids. So, he had a tough life, and he had a temper. When he got mad, he would get pretty hot under the collar. But he was also a colorful character, by far the most outgoing of all of us. He was never shy about playing music and later on, when Mike and I started getting popular, he'd go up to anybody and say, 'Hi, I'm The Brecker Brothers' father.'

"I remember once he went up to Oscar Peterson, and I was trying to hold him back, saying, 'Dad, don't do it.' But he wanted to meet Oscar, so he walked right up to him and introduced himself. He was a pretty interesting character, a great guy. He probably would've loved music first, but his parents were immigrants, and they insisted on him getting into a more solid profession. So, he became a lawyer. But music was always first with him anyway. He loved horn players, especially trumpeters. And being from Philly, he was naturally a big Clifford Brown fan. Clifford was the talk of the town, so my Dad had all his records."

To celebrate the birth of his firstborn son in 1945, Bobby Brecker wrote a song for a two-week-old Randy called "The Hottest Man in Town." The lyrics go: *You're gonna be the hottest man in town/You're gonna get the girls from all around/You're gonna love music, maybe play a hot fife/Play a horn and love music even more than your wife.*

Fifty-two years later, Randy would recruit Bobby, at age seventy-nine, to reprise that song in the studio, which he then excerpted for the opening of an autobiographical four-part suite that closed out his 1997 album, *Into the Sun.* Randy wrote in the liner notes of that album, which won a Grammy Award for Best Contemporary Jazz Performance the following year: "In closing the album, the seeds of my life are presented by my Dad, Bobby Brecker, who was my biggest fan and influence. I was happy that he was able to hear the tune inspired by him and his own performance before he passed away shortly after the album was completed. I thank him for his everlasting inspiration. This is for you, Dad."

When it came time for Michael to begin playing an instrument at the age of six, he chose clarinet. "I didn't want to play the same instrument that my brother was playing, and I liked the way the clarinet looked," he recalled. His brother, three years and four months older, had already been playing trumpet from age five. "Randy kind of set the tone, and the rest of us followed suit," Mike told KCRW's Tom Schnabel in a 1997 interview.

Early in his development on clarinet, Mike began taking lessons with Leon Lester, principal clarinetist with the Philadelphia Orchestra. "I started on clarinet at a very young age and played it not too well," he told students in a 1984 clinic at North Texas State. "I was more interested in sports, really." Randy confirmed that his younger brother didn't seem to embrace music with the same passion that he did, at first. "Music was everything for me," said Randy. "I tried to get interested in other things. I liked to write and, like my mother, I was a pretty good artist. But I let all that go at some point. It was only music for me."

Aside from music, Michael had varied interests, the main one being basketball. "He was tall, thin, and he really liked to play, and he was good," recalled Randy. "He was on the basketball team at school as a junior. So, basketball was really first for him. Science was second for him. He was serious about his chemistry set, and he was downstairs all the time working with that [young Michael also had a subscription to *Scientific American*]. Music, I think, was third for Mike. And interestingly, he approached music like a scientist, in a way."

"I had a lab at home and I was interested in chemistry and biology," Mike told Canadian TV talk show host Lorne Frohman in a 2004 segment from Toronto's *Distinguished Artists*. "But I was also bitten by the music bug when I was a kid. And that was also a good way, I think, to really get my father's attention."

Michael's studies with Leon Lester would go on for five years, and as he developed some technique on the instrument, he began copying clarinet solos off of Jimmy Giuffre records. As Randy recalled, "The record we both played along with at home was Shorty Rogers's *Martians Come Back!* [Atlantic Records, 1956] because Jimmy Giuffre's clarinet was on that record. Mike couldn't find clarinet players that he could really identify with until he found that record in Dad's collection."

"I didn't really gravitate towards players like Benny Goodman," Michael told John Robert Brown in a 1973 *Downbeat* interview. "But I loved Jimmy Giuffre's approach to the instrument. I loved his dark sound, the fact that he played in the low register, and he had a kind of soulful approach. I remember taking Jimmy Giuffre solos off of records when I was ten years old, and I can still remember some of those solos today. I used to play them into a garbage can for reverb. I had a little

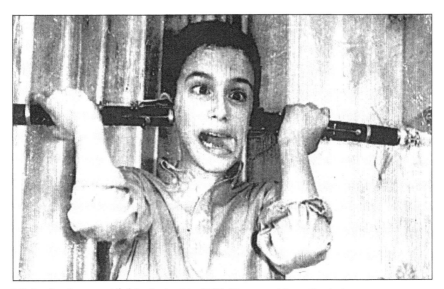

Michael at home with his clarinet in 1958 *(Courtesy of Susan Brecker)*

gold wastebasket and that's where I practiced. And to this day I still love reverb."

Recalling those youthful days in Cheltenham Township, Randy added, "We eventually started playing some duets, just improvising together. We had a kind of a suite connected by a bathroom, and we liked to play in the bathroom because of the echo and the resonance. We were playing tunes like 'Pop Goes the Weasel' and stuff, and it was kind of a cute thing because we were just little kids. But we were actually really good at playing together, even from an early age. We always had some kind of musical connection playing duets in the bathroom like that. And we did a little tribute to that time on my first record, *Score* [Solid State, 1969], where we did a duo piece called 'The Weasel Goes Out To Lunch.' It's a two-minute completely improvised duet, but there's really a close connection between the two of us. You can easily tell because the parts fit great. I relistened to it a few months ago and said, 'Man! That was pretty damn good!'"

Bobby Brecker took fatherly pride in bringing both his sons to see live jazz in Philly nightclubs. "Instead of taking us to the baseball game or football game, my dad took us to hear live jazz concerts," Michael recalled in a 1998 backstage interview at the Newport Jazz Festival. "So, by the time I was thirteen, I had already heard Miles Davis a couple of times, I heard Thelonious Monk, Dave Brubeck, Duke Ellington, Woody Herman's band, Count Basie's band . . . on and on and on. I have a lot of fond memories of these concerts. And those are really kind of my roots as far as music."

One revelation came from a memorable Thelonious Monk performance he attended early on. As Michael told students at the 1984 NTS clinic, "I must've been eleven or twelve years old, and this was a concert featuring a bunch of different pianists. And as Thelonious was about to come on stage, my dad leaned over to me, and he said that Thelonious could somehow create sounds on the piano that nobody else could. I thought that he meant that he could make a piano sound like a chicken or something. I had no idea what he was talking about. But when I sat and then listened to Monk from that perspective, I could hear it. And that was an important lesson for me."

Though Michael initially chose clarinet because he liked the way it looked, he never really fell in love with the instrument. "There was just something about the clarinet that he didn't like," said Randy. "Maybe it was the sound. Years later when we were playing at the Buddy DeFranco Jazz Festival in Missoula, Montana, there was this moment when Buddy was playing so great, and Mike leaned over on the bandstand and whispered in my ear, 'I don't care how good he is; I still hate the clarinet.'"

Michael eventually began gravitating toward the alto saxophone. "I was playing clarinet and feeling frustrated with the instrument because I liked saxophone and trumpet, and I couldn't quite get the same freedom on the clarinet," he told Frohman. "And I remember falling in love with a Dave Brubeck record in my father's collection called 'Look for the Silver Lining' [10" 78 rpm single b/w "This Can't Be Love," released in 1952 on the Fantasy label] with Paul Desmond. I just loved the sound of Desmond's alto. But then when my brother gave me a Cannonball Adderley record for my birthday, *Jazz Workshop Revisited*, that was it! I wanted to be able to play like Cannonball, with that kind of freedom. So, I asked my parents for an alto and I started trying to learn his solos from records. Those were some hard solos to learn, but it was a good way for me to begin to really learn the language of jazz. So, I began to take it seriously then, while still playing basketball, which was my major pastime. Music and basketball were the only things I

Switching to alto saxophone in 1960 *(Courtesy of Susan Brecker)*

was interested in at that point. But when I switched to alto sax in ninth grade, music really started to grab me."

Shortly after obtaining his first alto saxophone, Michael had a brief encounter with another young budding alto sax player in the Cheltenham Township area named Marc Cohen (who later became the renowned jazz pianist Marc Copland). "This was around 1963," recalled Copland, "and I was playing alto sax in a Top 40 band with two guitars, electric bass, and drums. We did all the popular tunes of the day, like 'Louie, Louie,' 'Gloria,' 'Secret Agent Man,' 'Walk, Don't Run,' all that stuff. And at some point, we were looking to add a piece, so I said to the guys in the group, 'Well, Mike Brecker's really supposed to be good.' I had heard about him in school. So, Mike comes to a rehearsal with his alto, and he's all over the horn. I mean, he's playing great stuff, but it wasn't what the band was looking for. They just wanted somebody to play simple parts behind the singers. And, so, I had to be the one to call Mike later and tell him, 'I don't think it's gonna work out.' So, I'm going to go down in history as the only guy ever to give Michael Brecker a pink slip!"

Copland would eventually become close friends with Michael and the entire Brecker family, participating in jam sessions in their living room and even rehearsing his own pieces there. "Bobby treated me like his third son, and he was like my musical dad, in a way," he recalled. "We'd talk about music and so forth, and if I needed to have a rehearsal, he'd say, 'You can come rehearse your bands here anytime.' I had a couple of things where their sister, Emmy, played piano. I sat next to Emily in French class at school, so I was close to all three of the Brecker kids."

To Copland, who lived a five-minute drive away, the Breckers' musical household was "a cultural island in a suburban wasteland." As he explained, "In my house there was nothing—a couple of Frank Sinatra LPs, that was about it. And you walk into Mike's house, and it's like a history of jazz right there in Bobby's record collection. And they had drums and vibes and a bass in the living room. So, Mike had a lot to draw on. It was kind of ingrained in him early on."

Copland recalled a particularly eventful summer afternoon in '63 when Michael came over to check out his new sound system and ended up getting more than an earful. "I had just gotten a KLH model 11 portable stereo turntable, and I said to Mike, 'You've got to check this out.' So, he came over, and I put on John Coltrane's *Impressions*, which had just come out. And Mike is listening to this and running from one speaker to the other, because I had them in different corners of the room. He's standing right in front of one speaker, and then he runs to the other speaker. And at some point, he looks at me and says very excitedly, 'Marky, I don't know whether to listen to Elvin or to Trane!' I had just bought that record, and he hadn't heard it yet. And he flipped out."

"We were basically listening to records a lot and learning saxophone together," Copland continued. "I was a year older, but he was definitely some notches above me in terms of playing. Michael was really sounding like a saxophone player at the time, and I was still trying to figure it out. He certainly had a facility, that's for damn sure. He was playing these long lines, and he was always lightning fast, even from the get-go. Mike could play lines all over the place, but he needed me to explain the chord changes to him, which I just kind of knew from sitting at the piano, even though I was a saxophone player. So, I'd listen to him and say, 'OK, that's nice. Now, how are you playing those lines?' And he'd giggle and shrug his shoulders and say, 'I don't know, Marky!' He was just playing what he heard. He was a natural."

After his initial encounter with John Coltrane's *Impressions* on Copland's turntable, Michael's appreciation of the saxophone master only deepened. As he recalled in a 2004 interview at the Newport Jazz Festival, "The first Coltrane album that I bought was *Live at Birdland*, which was a pretty bizarre record for a fledgling listener because the music was so intense and absolutely riveting. A lot of it was modal music with long solos. And I'd never heard drums play with that kind of intensity and crashing. And Coltrane was playing in a style and with a sound that I was not accustomed to. I didn't like the record at first, but I began listening to it every day until finally, after listening to it over a period of probably months, I began to understand what was going on. From there, I started buying other Coltrane records and became really interested in his music, to the degree that it became an enormous influence in the direction that I chose for a life's endeavor. Coltrane's music was both spiritual and certainly intellectual, technically highly developed, emotional and immensely creative and courageous. Put all those things together, plus the phenomenon quartet, which was one of those groups where the sum is greater than the whole, and the power of that group literally kind of propelled me into choosing music as a livelihood."

By late 1964, Michael began taking lessons with a local saxophonist named Vince Trombetta. A veteran on the Philadelphia scene, Trombetta had once shared a billing with a young John Coltrane at the Rave Bar on Columbia Avenue (aka The Golden Strip) when they were both playing in R&B/jump blues bands. As Vince recalled, "I was in a band called the Three Sharps and a Flat. I was sixteen years old. We were low band on the billing. The headliner was Daisy Mae & Her Hep Cats, and Trane was in that band. It was a good rhythm and blues band. They copped a lot of stuff from the Earl Bostic band. Trane only did a couple of weeks with them, but I got to know him a little bit then."

At the time Trombetta took on young Michael Brecker as a sax student, he had also begun working in the house band for a Philadelphia-based daytime television talk show, *The Mike Douglas Show*. Michael, still in ninth grade at the time, had to take two buses from his home in Melrose Park to get to Trombetta's place in Port Richmond for lessons every Saturday afternoon. It was an hour schlep each way, but Mike never missed a lesson, showing a newfound dedication toward getting serious about his instrument. Vince, who kept meticulous records about all of his private lessons and still has the ledgers to prove it, confirmed that Michael's first saxophone lesson was on December 12, 1964, just three and a half months shy of his sixteenth birthday.

"I met his mother at a club called the Proscenium on Walnut Street in Philadelphia," Vince recalled. "She came to me and said, 'Do you accept students?' And I said, 'Yeah, I do teach.' The next thing I knew, here he was at the door—tall, lanky, with an alto saxophone. And we started doing my procedure, my pedagogy on how the saxophone worked for me and for my teachers."

After four months, Trombetta suggested that his new student consider switching instruments once again. "I said, 'Michael, you should be playing a tenor. Not because you're six foot three at your age, but because everything you do doesn't sound like Phil Woods or Gene Quill or Bird or any of the great alto players. It sounds more like you're playing Trane.'"

Trombetta then helped track down a new Selmer Mark VI 87,000 series tenor saxophone, for which Michael's parents paid $375. And from that point on, he was off to the races. "Michael went through the Labanchi studies and the Bossi studies, the old-fashioned clarinet and oboe studies transcribed for saxophone," Vince recalled. "I also worked with him on the usual ii-V-I [two-five-one progression] exercises and different patterns and going through all the twelve keys and all like that. Then we dealt with these Italian etudes and *The Universal Method for Saxophone* [Paul De Ville's book commonly referred to as the "saxophone bible"]. I believed in turning pages, just to get that repertoire in your brain. And he went through it all like a hot knife going through butter. There seemed to be no effort for him."

Michael soon became Trombetta's prized pupil. "I wrote a piece when he was studying with me called 'Four Ives,' which was based on a lot of fourths and the traditional New England kind of folk songs that

Charles Ives frequently used, like 'Columbia, The Gem of the Ocean' and the like. And he just took to it so quickly. He was just very advanced for a sixteen-year-old. In fact, I had another saxophone student at the same time who was a very gifted player himself. His name was Bill Zaccagni, and he happened to be my first cousin and my godchild. He took his lessons right after Michael on Saturday, and one day he said to me, 'Could we switch my lesson to another time?' And said, 'Oh, you can't make it at noon?' And he said, 'No, I just don't want to go after him.' That's how good Michael was. They were the same age, but Michael just had acrobatic skills on the saxophone that were beyond anybody."

During the summer of 1966, between Michael's junior and senior years at Cheltenham High, Trombetta recommended that his star pupil attend the Ramblerny music camp in New Hope, Pennsylvania, which was directed by his good friend alto sax great Phil Woods. Michael did indeed attend that summer and was part of the Ramblerny Big Band horn section alongside fellow campers Richie Cole on alto sax and Roger Rosenberg on baritone sax. Together they studied with Woods, rehearsed challenging big band arrangements, and played concerts for the fellow campers. That group ended up documenting their progress on the album *Ramblerny '66: New Hope for Jazz*, on which Michael appears as featured soloist on Woods's composition, "Summer '66," as well as on Don Sebesky's "The Swinger."

"Phil Woods once told me that he could see right away that Mike was burning very bright for a young guy," said saxophonist-educator David Demsey, professor of music and coordinator of jazz studies at William Paterson University and curator of the Michael Brecker Archive there. "He said Mike didn't quite have a handle on it yet, but he really was a bright light. And that piece he wrote was basically a chart that featured Mike doing his thing. You listen to that *Ramblerny '66* recording today and you say, 'Who the hell is that on tenor sax? Somebody's really got some stuff going on.' Michael is still in high school then, but it's apparent that something very special is happening, although the language is not yet codified."

Following his summer at Phil Woods's Ramblerny music camp, Michael returned to Cheltenham High for the fall semester of 1966. He resumed his lessons with Trombetta and joined the Cheltenham High jazz band on tenor, in the sax section alongside his close friend Marc Cohen (Marc Copland) on alto sax. A couple of months into the new semester came a life-changing event on November 11, 1966, when Michael attended a John Coltrane concert at Temple University. Hearing Trane in full flight, with his wife, Alice Coltrane, on piano, Pharaoh Sanders on tenor saxophone, Sonny Johnson on bass, and Rashied Ali on drums, was an overwhelming experience for the young Brecker. "His playing was highly emotional; it had a large spiritual, mystical quality to it and a gorgeous sound," he told author Michael Segell for his 2005 book, *The Devil's Horn: The Story of the Saxophone, From Noisy Novelty to King of Cool*. "His tone was unique—mysterious, dark, hard, yet lushly beautiful. It took some getting used to. Every note of a Coltrane tune had weight and meaning. From a technical viewpoint it was outrageous; from an intellectual view it was deep, full of exciting, innovative ideas that hadn't been done before . . . For me, as a high school musician, it was just outrageous and compelling. Through the music of John Coltrane, I had found a calling. And I remember feeling so grateful that I was playing the tenor saxophone."

Years later, Coltrane's sax-playing son, Ravi Coltrane, had given Michael a bootleg copy of the fabled 1966 Temple concert to trigger his memory of that transformative day. (Nearly 50 years after the event, and seven years after Michael Brecker had passed, Zev Feldman and Resonance Records would team with Impulse!—Trane's label in the latter part of his career—to release it commercially in 2014 as *Offering: Live at Temple University*.)

After the galvanizing experience of seeing John Coltrane in concert, Michael returned to his lessons with Trombetta. And at some point, the student reached out to the teacher for some career advice. "He said, 'I don't know what to do as far as my music career,' and I told him, 'Well, Michael, there's nothing in Philadelphia other than the Philadelphia Orchestra and *The Mike Douglas Show*, and I don't intend to die soon. And we only augment the band about four times a year. That's no way to make a living. You don't want to be like these guys that live in Philly that bebop around for $25 a gig. That's not what you deserve.' So, the next thing I knew, he went off to college at Indiana University and then on to New York, and the rest is history."

Regarding his contribution to Michael's musical development, Trombetta said, "People say, 'A good root helps the plant grow properly.' I think if I had to say anything about my contribution, I rooted him deeply in studies that required practicing. If you didn't practice, you weren't going to be playing some of these things. And if that excited you to listen carefully to recordings and transcriptions and stuff, then hallelujah. Then the mission was accomplished."

Trombetta, a bona fide jazz warrior who had been in the trenches since the mid '50s, seemed genuinely touched years later when Michael acknowledged his teacher from the stage during a gig at Catalina Jazz Club in Hollywood. "I was there with my wife and my two sons, Nick and Adam, and we're sitting very close to the stage. Michael opened up with a fast standard and then, when it was over, he said to the audience, 'Ladies and gentlemen, there's only two reasons why I'm up here playing saxophone for you all. One is John Coltrane, and the other is my teacher, Vince Trombetta, sitting there with his family.' You know, that blew me totally away. It was the biggest compliment I ever got. And then afterwards, outside the club, the actors Ray Liotta and Michael Keaton are just standing there talking as I walked by with my family to get our car. And Ray yelled out, 'Hey professor, you taking any students?' I had to laugh. Bottom line: that was a memorable night, and very personal to me."

Michael playing tenor sax in the Cheltenham High Jazz Band in 1966 (sitting next to Marc Cohen/Copland on alto sax) *(Courtesy of Susan Brecker)*

Michael's last lesson with Trombetta was on May 4, 1967. He graduated from Cheltenham High in June, then enrolled in a five-week summer course at the Berklee College of Music in Boston, where he studied with saxophone guru Joe Viola, whose groundbreaking, three-volume method book from that period, *The Technique of the Saxophone*, remains part of Berklee's curriculum. Shortly after enrolling in that summer program at Berklee, Michael's musical North Star, John Coltrane, passed away on July 17, 1967. It was the fabled Summer of Love in Haight-Ashbury, and Michael Brecker, now charged with an even deeper commitment to the saxophone, was poised on the brink of bigger and better things.

Randy, meanwhile, missed out on his younger brother's rapid development. As he recalled, "Unfortunately, because of the age difference, I wasn't around when he made that transition to alto sax and really started to get serious about music. I was away at Indiana University, and I also had a steady gig during the summer in the Catskills or the Poconos, so I wasn't home much. But I would copy some of my lessons with Dave Baker—he wasn't at Indiana University yet, so I would drive from Bloomington to his home in Indianapolis to study privately with him—and I would send them to Mike.

"Dave helped me with jazz harmony," Randy continued. "We'd study Monk and get into half-tone, whole-tone, and diminished scales. He was also a big proponent of George Russell's book, *The Lydian Chromatic Concept of Tonal Organization*. And Dave was also a "lickmeister." He'd write out a bunch of licks that I had been hearing, some of which I had been playing, and I'd copy them and send them to Mike, who had just started playing alto. But that's as close as I got to his development on that instrument."

As Michael told Herb Nolan in a 1973 *Downbeat* interview, "By the time I actually became interested in music, my brother was already away in school at Indiana. In some ways, that enabled me to play—it took the pressure off."

Fueled by the inspiration of having seen John Coltrane in concert at Temple University during his senior year in high school and armed with a mountain of information that his sax teacher, Vince Trombetta, had given him over the course of their two and a half years together, Michael was primed to make an incremental leap in his development at Indiana University, which his older brother had previously attended.

As he was preparing to follow in Randy's footsteps, the two Brecker brothers were still a couple of years away from teaming up together and making a significant impact on the scene. In fact, by the time Michael had entered IU as a freshman in the fall of '67, the older Brecker brother had yet to hear his younger brother play the saxophone. "I don't have a memory, really, of even hearing him play alto, let alone tenor," said Randy. "But by the time I finally saw Mike play the saxophone, he was flying."

# 2

# IU AND A NIGHTMARE IN CHI-TOWN

When Michael enrolled at Indiana University in Bloomington for the fall semester of 1967, he did not declare the expected major. As he told *Downbeat* in a 1973 interview, "Weirdly enough, I intended to enroll as a music major and then at the last minute I had a short-lived rebellion and switched to premed, since I had always been interested in science as well. But I ended up at the music school every day anyway, just practicing and playing with the guys who were music majors. And from there I ended up falling into music."

Michael expounded on that decision eleven years later in a clinic at North Texas State University in 1984: "I realized that I had been playing music half my life partially to compete for my parents' approval. Because that's the way my family was. So, I switched my major at the last minute to premed. That wasn't working too well, so I tried fine arts. I had some talent in drawing, and I became friends with the fine arts teacher, who kept dropping subtle hints that I should just move to New York." But Michael would remain at IU for three semesters before finally committing to the Big Apple.

As Michael was getting acclimated to freshman life at Indiana University, Randy was busy forging a career as an in-demand trumpeter. He had already made a big splash two years earlier at the 1965 Notre Dame Collegiate Jazz Festival. Not only did the nineteen-piece Indiana University Jazz Ensemble, led by Jerry Coker, win the competition, but Randy also won the prize as Most Promising Instrumentalist, presented to him by Clark Terry, one of the judges of that year's competition. As an added perk of their winning first place at the Notre Dame festival, the IU Jazz Ensemble embarked on a State Department-sponsored tour of the Middle East and Asia. Commencing on January 29, 1966, the 109-day tour took them to Ceylon (today's Sri Lanka), India, Pakistan, Iran, Iraq, Afghanistan, Syria, Jordan, Egypt, Lebanon, Israel, and

Greece before concluding on May 17 in Nicosia, Cyprus. "It was a first-class big band, and it was a tough tour—nearly four months of being constantly on the road," Randy recalled. "It was just an eye-opening experience for us."

Following that whirlwind collegiate tour, Randy decided to forgo his final year at IU and a chance of repeating as Notre Dame Collegiate Jazz Festival winners in favor of participating in the prestigious Vienna International Jazz Competition held in May of 1966. "We finished our State Department tour in Cyprus, and then some of us took a train to Vienna," he said. "In fact, my parents came over to Vienna because they hadn't seen me in so long at that point."

Directed by pianist and famous jazz-classical impresario Friedrich Gulda, the two-week competition featured a distinguished panel of judges in J. J. Johnson, Art Farmer, Cannonball Adderley, Ron Carter, Joe Zawinul, and Mel Lewis. Randy went through the first week of semifinal competition, then made it to the finals, ultimately losing by a tenth of a point to the eventual first-place winner, Swiss trumpeter Franco Ambrosetti, who would later become a lifelong friend to both Brecker brothers. "Randy was about nineteen at the time, and I was twenty-four," recalled Ambrosetti. "They ran the final competition in alphabetical order, so I was the one to go first and then Randy. There were about thirty people that made it to the finals, including Claudio Roditi and Tomasz Stanko, and we all had to play the same three songs we had played in the previous competition in getting to the finals. And they had a big clock that ticked down the time because you had a maximum of fifteen minutes to play the three songs. It was a bit nerve-racking, so Randy and I shared a bottle of whiskey to relax us before playing. I think we drank half the bottle between us before going out to play. And at the end, I got 98 out of 100 and Randy got 97 out of 100. So really, who won?"

Upon returning to the States during that summer of 1966, while seventeen-year-old Michael was being mentored by Phil Woods at Ramblerny jazz camp in New Hope, Pennsylvania, Randy moved to New York City at age twenty and immediately picked up work with Clark Terry's big band. Through that year he also gigged around town with the Thad Jones-Mel Lewis Orchestra and with pianist-composer Duke Pearson's big band, recording with the latter on December 15, 1967, at

Rudy Van Gelder's Studio in Englewood Cliffs, New Jersey, for the Blue Note album *Introducing Duke Pearson's Big Band*, released in April 1968.

Concurrent with his intermittent appearances in Duke Pearson big band, Randy fell into another unlikely situation that would thrust the aspiring hard bop and big band trumpeter into a whole different spotlight. In October of 1967, Randy was recruited by keyboardist-singer-composer Al Kooper to join his innovative new band, Blood, Sweat & Tears. Kooper had already made a name for himself for his organ work on Bob Dylan's 1965 hit, "Like a Rolling Stone," and for playing keyboards behind the folk icon at his notorious Dylan Goes Electric concert at the Newport Folk Festival on July 25 that summer of '65. Kooper was also coming off a run with The Blues Project, which he had joined in late 1965, appearing on the group's March 1966 debut album, *Live at the Cafe Au Go Go*, as well as playing their last hurrah at the Monterey International Pop Festival during the summer of 1967. By the fall of that year, Kooper got the radical notion of forming a rock band with a horn section and brought in fellow New Yorkers Dick Halligan on trombone, Fred Lipsius on alto sax, Jerry Weiss on trumpet, and transplanted New Yorker Randy Brecker on second trumpet. On November 11, they recorded a six-track demo for Columbia Records at the CBS 30th Street Studio. They were signed to the label on November 16 and the following day made their auspicious debut by kicking off a three-night run (Friday, November 17–Sunday, November 19) at the Cafe Au Go Go on Bleecker Street in the heart of Greenwich Village.

BS&T later shared the bill with the Chambers Brothers and Tiny Tim for a Thanksgiving Blues Jam at Steve Paul's The Scene in midtown Manhattan, then went into CBS Studio from December 11–20 to record their first official album for Columbia Records, *Child Is Father to the Man*. Released on February 21, 1968, it was instantly hailed as one of the most potent post-*Sgt. Pepper's* statements in pop music. *Rolling Stone* called it a major breakthrough.

Randy's presence is felt throughout *Child Is Father to the Man*, and his high-spirited trading with saxophonist Fred Lipsius on a smooth bossa nova rendition of Harry Nilsson's "Without Her" is a precursor of the tightly arranged horn work and near-telepathic call-and-response exchanges he would engage in with brother Michael just a few years later in the bands Dreams and The Brecker Brothers.

BS&T's debut was followed by a string of high-profile gigs on the burgeoning rock concert circuit, which found them sharing the bill with Big Brother & The Holding Company at the Psychedelic Supermarket in Boston on February 23; with the James Cotton Blues Band at La Cave in Cleveland March 1–3; with Iggy Pop & The Stooges at the Grande Ballroom in Detroit on March 3; with Cream and Jeremy & The Satyrs at the Fillmore Auditorium in San Francisco on March 7, then three nights (March 8–10) at Winterland with Cream and the James Cotton Blues Band. Back on the East Coast, BS&T played two nights (March 26 and 28) at The Electric Circus in the East Village on a bill with Judy Collins, Taj Mahal, and Elephant's Memory (later to become known as John Lennon and Yoko Ono's backing band).

Blood, Sweat & Tears's last gigs together in that original incarnation were April 11–14, 1968, at the Garrick Theatre upstairs from the Cafe Au Go Go. Kooper left the band after that three-night engagement over artistic differences with founding members Steve Katz and Bobby Colomby. Whether he quit or was ousted is a matter of debate. Although Katz and Colomby openly admired Kooper's songwriting ability, they had doubts about his vocal ability and wanted to hire a singer to front the band. Kooper walked after that April 14th gig, and Randy Brecker immediately followed suit. "I left the same night Al did, saying, 'You guys'll never make it without Al!,' recalled Randy. "The next day I had a rehearsal with Joe Henderson's big band, and I was sitting next to (trumpeter) Lew Soloff and talked him into taking my place in Blood, Sweat & Tears. He didn't really want to do it." Soloff would tour with BS&T through the summer and fall and in December recorded his memorable solo on the group's 1968 hit single, "Spinning Wheel," from their self-titled second album. He ended up remaining with Blood, Sweat & Tears through 1973.

A week after Randy left BS&T, he joined Horace Silver's quintet at The Showboat in Philadelphia. "That was my first gig with him," he recalled. "I distinctly remember that first gig since my parents lived near the club in Philly, and I smashed my head on the clear glass front door to their apartment house walking into the building and cut my forehead open. I was so nervous about that first night."

While Randy's career was rapidly ascending, Michael's was just getting started. As a freshman at Indiana University, he hung out with a small group of aspiring musicians on campus. "We all lived in the same dorm called Willkie Quad," said trumpeter Randy Sandke, "and there were several rooms that we could congregate in. If somebody had a new record that was of interest, we would show up in that person's dorm room and listen to it. And that record, of course, made the rounds. Mike had a small record collection with him, but he seemed to really hone in on those records and knew them intimately. He was listening to a lot of Coltrane back then and taking things off the records. I was trying to get Mike to listen to some classical music, but he wasn't really that interested in it, though he always seemed laser-focused on what he did like.

"I remember he was up in my room one time, going through my records, looking for something to borrow to play on his machine and take apart [transcribe]," continued Sandke. "And the only thing that he found that he was interested in was some Maynard Ferguson records with Joe Farrell on them. He really wanted to check out Joe Farrell."

Sandke was already in his second year at IU when he met Mike, though they were the same age. "I had been playing in the first band with David Baker," he recalled. "My first year was also David Baker's first year as a professor at Indiana University and heading up the jazz department there, though it was pretty minimal back then. You couldn't major in jazz, but David presided over several courses in addition to three big bands. I was playing in the first band, and I assumed that Michael would be in the first band, too. But when he did his audition, David mentioned that Mike couldn't read note one. So, because of that, he felt compelled to put Mike in the second band."

But Sandke, and Baker himself, would soon discover that Michael had a special talent that went beyond the notes on a page. "I remember going to hear a concert by the second band, and it was all very kind of bland, not-so-challenging big band charts," Sandke recalled. "But then Mike stood up to take a solo, and he just blew the roof off the place. It was like going into hyperspace. Suddenly, we were just transported into a whole other realm. And Mike was typically like that when he soloed. He could just reach an incredible peak in his solos. He was clearly the best jazz player of all the sax players at Indiana. Michael stood out from the beginning, and he just improved on that over the years."

(Michael would shine as a guest soloist with Jazz Ensemble I, conducted by David Baker, at a February 21, 1968, concert, blowing with signature authority on Sandke's composition, "Hyde Park.")

While certainly a genetic gift was at work here, Michael's astounding ability on the saxophone was also a by-product of plain hard work and constant woodshedding with his instrument. "He really worked on his rhythm and his sense of metronomic time," noted Sandke. "And he played drums as well. That's why his sense of time is just so great and so strong, even on ballads. Mike's time was always good, but it got much better because he was very focused on improving himself."

Sandke added, "I also remember that Michael kind of idolized his brother, Randy. He thought of Randy as being way ahead of him and that he would have to really work his ass off to keep up with him. And, so, he always had this mentality, it seemed, that he was kind of coming from behind and had to work really hard to catch up."

Sandke distinctly remembers a particular poster hanging on the wall in Mike's Willke Quad dorm room that promoted racial harmony. "It was a poster of this little black kid and this little white kid together, each with an arm around the other, and it said, 'The blind are also color blind.' That was the first thing you would see when you walked into Mike's dorm room."

Another aspect of Mike's character was revealed in the compassionate way he treated his roommate during that first semester at IU. "This guy had been in a very bad fire that had disfigured his face," Sandke recalled. "So, he was very scarred, and it was a little hard to look at him, but I remember Mike was really nice to him and really tried to help him out. And he would always speak well of this guy to try to encourage other people to be his friend, too."

The atmosphere on campus at Indiana University during Michael's time there had changed radically from just three years earlier when Randy enrolled at IU, reflecting the cultural shift that took place in the country in the wake of Timothy Leary's countercultural manifesto "turn on, tune in, drop out" and the fallout from Haight-Ashbury's Summer of Love. "When I was at IU, it was strictly straight ahead; no pot, no nothing," Randy recalled. "You'd go out and have a beer, and that was about it. We were jazz guys. We hadn't really thought of jazz-rock yet. We were really more closely connected to hard boppers than hippies. But when Mike was there, you'd see people with long hair laying around stoned as hell. And they had Be-Ins and all this stuff that people did back then. It was a different time."

Sandke, who hails from Chicago, remembers Michael coming home with him for Thanksgiving break during that first fall semester of 1967. "I lived in Hyde Park, and the AACM [Association for the Advancement of Creative Musicians] had its beginnings in that neighborhood as well. That's where they all lived. In fact, Joseph Jarman [alto saxophonist who cofounded the Art Ensemble of Chicago in 1969] was sharing an apartment with my brother at that time. Their other roommate was this guy named Jeff Carp, a blues harp player and singer who was later on *The London Howlin' Wolf Sessions* [Chess Records, 1971] with Eric Clapton and two guys from the Rolling Stones [bassist Bill Wyman and drummer Charlie Watts]. And Janis Joplin was kind of hanging out with him. So, it was this crazy apartment on the South Side of Chicago with my brother, Joseph Jarman, Jeff Carp, and Janis Joplin.

"In any case, Michael came down and stayed with me for Thanksgiving that year, and we went out and heard some of these guys from the AACM play a concert. Mike was into that stuff, too. He seemed to enjoy the rawness and the emotional intensity of that music. And I remember there was this tenor player named Fred Anderson who was so intense that he was playing and drooling at the same time. Michael was fascinated by that. There was so much going on to plug into. It was a very alive time musically, and Michael just soaked it all in."

By late fall of '67, Michael joined Sandke's septet, which included second tenor saxophonist Bruce Nifong, keyboardist Shelby Janes, bassist Brent McKesson, and drummer Jim Nelson. Quickly forging a tight sound through rehearsals and gigs around campus, Sandke's septet went on to represent Indiana University at the 1968 Notre Dame Collegiate Jazz Festival held on March 8 and 9 and were considered to be runaway favorites at the tenth annual competition in South Bend, Indiana. As *Chicago Daily News* writer Buck Walmsley noted in his review of the event, "From the preliminary hearings held Friday and Saturday afternoon, the Randy Sandke Septet of Indiana University sounded much, much better than any of the seven other combos entered in the competition—more exciting and inventive than any of the nine big bands competing too. The group's performance electrified the crowd and earned three of its members top soloists' awards—Sandke on trumpet; saxophonist Mike Brecker was cited as the festival's outstanding instrumentalist, and James Nelson was named the best combo drummer."

In his scorecard for that preliminary round, judge Gerald Wilson rated Sandke's septet highly: "A very fine group showing much imagination," he wrote. "All members played with technical knowledge and feeling. Excellent in all categories." Judge Ray Brown added, "Very creative group. Excellent tenor sax soloist and good trumpet player and bassist. Good structure to the music and good style."

Seemingly a shoo-in to take the top prize at the collegiate festival, things took a sudden detour on finals night. As Walmsley reported in the second part of his *Chicago Daily News* story, "In the finals, the septet chose to break out of the jazz idiom and perform a rock version of Duke Ellington's 'Warm Valley.' As rock, it sounded great. As jazz, it didn't meet the judges' standards, so they (Wilson and Brown along with Oliver Nelson, Robert Share and *Downbeat* editor Dan Morgenstern) decided that the group had not performed in the finals to the extent of its ability. Nor had the other two combo finalists."

Walmsley summarized: "To give the award to Sandke's men would be to set a precedent in rewarding rock music in a jazz festival, the judges said. To give the prize to one of the other two finalists would be, in effect, rewarding mediocrity, they said. So, there was no award."

Sandke's septet did indeed begin its finals presentation in fairly straightforward fashion by covering Ellington's "Warm Valley," a slow, sensual tone poem with a haunting melody performed by alto saxophonist Johnny Hodges on the original 1940 Victor recording. Saxophonist Nifong played the lush melody at Notre Dame as the band stayed close to the original arrangement through the first 1:50 minutes of their performance, before segueing to a spacey rubato interlude lasting two minutes. And then, to the judges' collective horror, the septet launched into a wildly bombastic percussion jam with the twin tenors wailing in gnarly "New Thing" style over a two-chord vamp for four and a half minutes. But what must've irked the judges most was that they culminated their sprawling free-blowing jam by segueing into a spot-on re-creation of The Doors' "Light My Fire" for the last 3:11 of their performance. That defiant act did not sit well with the august panel of judges. And while their decision was not popular with the audience, it remained steadfast.

Sandke recalled their subversive set: "It started out with this kind of straight reading of Duke Ellington's 'Warm Valley,' and then it just kind of devolved into this series of sounds. Mike started chirping in his upper register while other players were adding in random sounds. Then that morphed into this kind of Art Ensemble of Chicago free-for-all sort of semi-humorous, quasi-march sort of thing. And then that went into this rock vamp, which turned into the riff from 'Light My Fire' with the two saxophones going crazy on it. And that was that."

Sandke was privy to the judges' written comments following their audacious finals set. "That's where Ray Brown said, 'I didn't like any of it.' And that became a kind of inside joke for the band. On stage, after playing a tune, we'd get on mic and say, 'I didn't like any of it . . . Ray Brown.'"

Writing about the 1968 Notre Dame Collegiate Jazz Festival in his May 2 *Downbeat* story, "Jazz Goes to College," Dan Morgenstern described the performance of the Sandke septet as "the most original, creative and stimulating combo-jazz heard at the festival, avant-garde but together," and singled out the leader as "a trumpeter with great promise combining a fine, bright tone and flawless execution with real musical intelligence."

Notre Dame's *Dome*, the campus yearbook, covered it this way: "One thing can be said definitely about the 10th annual Collegiate Jazz Festival: It was different. While jazz fans turned out in record numbers for the Friday and Saturday night concerts, the CJF judges elected not to present a Best Combo Award. This decision of the judges, five outstanding jazz authorities, was not very popular with the audience. Many felt that the Indiana Septet deserved the award because they demonstrated an obvious superiority to the other two finalists in the Friday performance. However, the judges based their awards only on the Saturday night finals, without consideration of the semi-finals. Saturday night, the Indiana Septet played a quasi-rock program which the judges found musically interesting, but not jazz. On the other hand, the remaining two finalists did not display the talent evident in the Indiana Septet. On this basis, the judges could not single out one of them for excellence in the jazz combo category. John Noel, CJF's chairman, supported the judges. 'As far as I know, this is the first time at any festival that the judges have withheld a combo award,' he said. "Groups have been presenting thinly disguised rock and calling it jazz. This decision may limit our scope but does give the festival, and jazz itself, some definition."

In the 1969 Notre Dame Collegiate Jazz Festival program, the festival redefined its take on jazz: "Last year's CJF was somewhat controversial in that no Best Combo award was given out, on the basis that the combo in line for the award, the Randy Sandke Septet from Indiana University, played what the judges felt was not true jazz. It was quite obvious to anyone in the audience that they were deliberately playing in a rock idiom, something unprecedented at the CJF. Clearly, times have changed. And so has the CJF judging policy. Even on last year's judging panel, there was the opinion voiced (notably from Dan Morgenstern, editor of *Down Beat*) that rock is no longer equivalent to bad music. Since he took over as editor, *Down Beat* has been covering the best of rock, as well as jazz. Jazz and rock are distinct musical forms, and one is not to be confused with the other. But there is a growing *rapprochement* between the two forms that involves each form borrowing certain techniques from the other. So, what now for the groups at the CJF? The 1968 Festival marked a watershed in the style of music to be performed there. Randy Sandke did some un-jazz things, things that had never been done here before. The judges felt that he did not perform according to the standards of the past ten Collegiate Jazz Festivals, and thus could not be given the award. After the festival, in consultation with Dan Morgenstern (once again chairman of the judges), it was decided to make a policy statement regarding CJF performances. That statement reads, in part: 'There will be no prejudice toward any styles or effects used by the participants, so long as the element of creative improvisation is present, and the musicianship is of high quality.' In other words, rock effects are legal. Consequently, we are likely to hear some different types of things from this year's groups."

Some seven hundred miles away, at roughly the same time, adventurous new groups in New York's Greenwich Village such as The Free Spirits (guitarist Larry Coryell, saxophonist Jim Pepper, guitarist Chip Baker, bassist Chris Hills, and drummer Bob Moses) and Jeremy & The Satyrs (flutist Jeremy Steig, guitarist Adrian Guillery, keyboardist Warren Bernhardt, bassist Eddie Gomez, and Donald McDonald) were seamlessly combining rock and jazz elements with groundbreaking results. Sandke's septet was solidly in that same trailblazing spirit in early March of 1968, nearly two months before Sly & The Family Stone's breakthrough album, *Dance to the Music*, a full year before Chicago's inaugural album, *Chicago Transit Authority*, and just around the same time that Blood, Sweat & Tears released its debut album, *Child Is Father to the Man*. And Michael was eagerly down with this new direction in music, foreshadowing his own future experiments in fusing rock and jazz with Dreams, Billy Cobham, and The Brecker Brothers.

Meanwhile, Sandke and Brecker were intent on taking things a step further by starting up an electric ensemble that reflected a burgeoning new movement in jazz. "I remember Mike and I talking about how jazz had once been this kind of avant-garde thing, but we were both feeling that it had become something from another era, and that this electric direction was where it needed to go," Sandke recalled. "We definitely felt the excitement that came from making this kind of music and just trying to synthesize all these different elements, so we started rehearsing on a regular basis. And I remember our first rehearsal. Something happened with the electric guitar and the electric bass and the electric organ . . . when we switched it on it was like all that electricity translated into a sound that really gave us all a jolt."

The group was christened Mrs. Seaman's Sound Band as a tongue-in-cheek tribute to an unpopular lunch lady at Willkie Quad. As Sandke explained, "She hated the kids, the ones that look like hippies, which we were all starting to look like. That was probably the first year we started growing our hair long and started dressing a little different. Mike used to wear these striped pants and a blazer and boots. I wouldn't say he ever looked like a full-fledged hippie, but he did let his hair grow long. And, so, Mrs. Seaman used to give us a hard time because she sort of figured that we were probably unsanitary, too. You know, the long hair, the sandals. I don't remember any of us wearing sandals, but there were people on campus that did. And Mrs. Seaman would throw them out and make them put shoes on. So, she was always this stern, disapproving, authoritarian figure there. And we thought that we would stick it to her by naming the band after her."

The personnel for Mrs. Seaman's Sound Band were Mike and Bruce Nifong on tenor saxes, Sandke on trumpet, Marc Thorman on keyboards, Bruce Anderson on guitar, Brent McKesson on electric bass, and Eric Long on drums. Aside from playing his usual tenor sax, Michael also played the crumhorn, a Renaissance-era double-reed instrument. "I don't know where he got it from," said Sandke, "but he said he wanted to be the first jazz crumhorn player."

A key member in the renegade genre-hopping ensemble was drummer Long, whom Sandke described as "a guiding light for all of us and kind of a mysterious but real charismatic figure." As he explained,

"Eric was somebody we were all drawn to. He lived in Willkie Quad with us, too, and he had a very strong interest in jazz, especially Elvin Jones, and he listened to a lot of classical music as well as contemporary pop music and rock. So, he fit right into what we were trying to do, which was synthesizing all these elements from these different kinds of music that we were listening to."

Mrs. Seaman's Sound Band began performing around campus, gradually building up a fan base. But they leaped to a whole new level of popularity after playing at a campaign rally in April 1968 for Democratic presidential hopeful Eugene McCarthy held outdoors at Dunn Meadow, a twenty-acre grassy expanse on the IU campus that was a prime spot for students to relax, study, or play. Because the Minnesota senator was running on an anti–Vietnam War platform, and most of the male population of Indiana University was draft age, Dunn Meadow was brimming with antiwar demonstrators for McCarthy's political rally that afternoon. It was a high-visibility gig for the group at a

Mrs. Seaman's Sound Band gig poster, 1968 *(Courtesy of Randy Sandke)*

time when America was experiencing cultural and political upheaval. Though McCarthy would ultimately lose the Democratic nomination to fellow Minnesota senator Hubert Humphrey, Mrs. Seaman's Sound Band would win over hordes of new fans introduced to their sound at the rally that April afternoon.

"It was kind of amazing to see the reaction to the band, because people really responded to it," Sandke recalled. "And that's something that we weren't used to. You know, with jazz, usually you play for smaller audiences who tend to be more on the staid side. No matter how much they like it, they're not that demonstrative about it, except for applauding solos maybe. But to get this sea of people that were really responding and really loving the band, it was a kick for all of us. And I think that's the first time Mike experienced that. Probably one of the last times I experienced that as well."

Shortly after playing at the McCarthy rally, Sandke received a mysterious telegram from an admirer. "I think it was the first telegram I ever received in my life," he recalled. "It read: 'This is Buck Walmsley. My wife Ashley wants to manage the band. Please contact us at this number.'"

It turns out that Walmsley, who had written the rave review of Sandke's septet in the *Chicago Daily News*, was married to Ashley Simmons, a photographer who had aspirations of becoming a manager. She had shot Sandke's septet during their notorious performance at the Notre Dame Collegiate Jazz Festival a month earlier. Sandke remembered Simmons prowling in front of the stage during their finals' performance, camera in hand. "She was this very sexy looking older woman—meaning she was about twenty-four . . . you know, we were like eighteen. She had on a miniskirt, and she'd be like kneeling down in front of the band taking photos during our entire set. Buck must have been in his mid-forties, and she was his second wife, I believe. They were kind of the odd couple."

Sandke ended up making the trip to Chicago on spring break to meet and talk business with Ashley Simmons. "I took the Illinois Central train, and this was shortly after Martin Luther King had been shot [on April 4, 1968]," he recalled. "So, it was a very tense time. I remember all these people were throwing rocks at the train as we pulled into Chicago, and the whole station was filled with people with shopping bags who had been looting. It was a weird scene because it was kind of like a party atmosphere but in the context of this huge national tragedy. I was the only white face there, and I was feeling pretty nervous about the whole thing, so I pulled out my trumpet and I started to play Louis Armstrong solos as I waited for the subway to come along."

At their meeting, Simmons laid out her master plan for the band. She proposed bringing the band to Chicago after IU's spring session ended in May, renting a place for them to rehearse, booking time at Chess Studios, and recording a demo. By the end of his spring semester in early May 1968, Mike joined Sandke and the rest of the guys in Mrs. Seaman's Sound Band on that trip from Bloomington to Chicago to chase what appeared to be a golden opportunity. Hyped on visions of a record deal and counterculture pop stardom, they followed Ashley Simmons's plan to the letter. As Sandke recalled, "She paid for the demo we made, and she ended up getting us this large two-floor apartment in the Old Town section of Chicago above a jazz club called The Midas Touch [at 1520 North Wells St.]. At that time, Wells Street was the bohemian strip in Chicago, like Telegraph Hill in San Francisco or West Eighth Street in New York. It was hippie central, but it was also a kind of a tourist attraction. The Ripley's Believe It or Not Museum was there, Second City Theater was a little further up the street from us, and the famous Plugged Nickel jazz club was just across the street."

Coincidentally, Michael's brother, Randy, who had been touring with the Horace Silver quintet during this time, rolled into Chicago that summer for a two-week engagement at the Plugged Nickel with Horace. "Mike was living right across the street from the club in a place that he had with Randy Sandke and the other guys in their band," Randy recalled. "It was a dyed-in-the-wool hippie crash pad with chicks laying around and people stoned and the whole thing. They were heavily into psilocybin and other things. The whole band was pretty stoned out. I actually was pretty far out myself, in a way, for a jazz guy. But this was a little too far out for me, though I eventually took some. One day Mike and I went out really early to Lake Michigan and just meditated, stoned on psilocybin."

During his run at the Plugged Nickel with Horace Silver, Randy brought bandmates Billy Cobham and Bennie Maupin over to the crash pad one day to jam with Mike's band. "That's the first time I heard Mike play saxophone," he said. "And I just remembered our jaws dropped because Mike had so much technique, and he had already combined the Coltrane, Junior Walker, King Curtis elements . . . all players who had been hugely influential for him. I had entirely missed Mike's evolution because I had been away, first at Indiana University and then on the road with Horace. So, really, my first recollection of hearing Mike on tenor was at this jam session we played in the summer of 1968. And all I can say is, Mike already had his own thing going. I'll just never forget the look on everyone's face, especially Bennie's."

Later that summer, things started deteriorating between the band members and manager Simmons. "It quickly turned into this kind of trap we felt we couldn't get out of," said Sandke.

At some point, it became obvious that the married Simmons had developed an uncomfortable attraction to drummer Long. As Sandke recalled, "These were the kind of free love days and she was definitely interested in Eric, who had this kind of magnetic personality—just very striking features and very striking light blue eyes. So, one day, we were fixing up the place to make it nicer for us to live in. And we all took a trip to the Goodwill or Salvation Army to buy used mattresses, which fortunately the board of health doesn't permit anymore, because we all ended up getting crabs from them. Anyway, while we were gone, Eric remained behind in the place with Charles, a gay friend of our organ player. Being a real free-spirited person, Eric thought that to be free you should be able to love men as well as women. In any case, he was up there tripping on LSD with Charles when Ashley came in. And Ashley wore a lot of makeup for some reason, maybe personal insecurity. Because she was a very attractive looking woman, but for some reason she would just cake her face with this kind of muck and wear a lot of eyeliner and eyeshadow, all that kind of stuff. And, so, Ashley wanted to get into something with Eric, but he was tripping so hard that when he looked at her face it looked so artificial that it freaked him out, and he immediately kind of grabbed onto Charles for refuge. Ashley became furious and stormed out.

"So suddenly we were in this weird position where Ashley had done all of this work for us, but now she was all pissed off and she wouldn't communicate, and there was this tension between her and the band. And one of the other tensions was that she didn't like the fact we'd let people crash at the place. That was pretty typical of that era, trying to be open to humanity in all its forms. So, we clashed about that. Meanwhile, we were having a problem with the lock downstairs so that we couldn't really lock the door at night. I remember coming home one night, and there were all these strange people sleeping on the floor, and some of them looked a little menacing. So, the situation was getting a little bit out of hand."

The tensions with their manager and the overcrowding at their crash pad finally led to Nifong and McKesson suddenly leaving the band. "We were then in this position where we couldn't really function as a band, so we started auditioning bass players," said Sandke. "But again, it was like a real '60s kind of dynamic where this wasn't just getting somebody to do a gig, it was recruiting somebody to join our little family. Also, it was difficult to find somebody who played Fender bass who could read and play both jazz and rock, which was almost impossible at that time."

McKesson was eventually replaced on bass by Donald Beggs, while Nifong, who went on to join the Airmen of Note jazz ensemble, was replaced by saxophonist Dennis Lansing. "Finding replacements took a long time," said Sandke. "Meanwhile, we weren't making any money on gigs or getting any money from home, and we were practically starving."

Eventually, Sandke, too, threw in the towel. "One day I said, 'Look, I just got to get out of here. This is really getting to me.' So, I left the place on Wells Street and went back to live with my parents in Hyde Park."

By that time, a childhood friend of the band's organist named Lucy, who had been staying at the crash pad on Wells Street, invited her sister Bridgette back home in Indianapolis to come stay for a few weeks in Chicago before they both headed to a commune outside of Denver. "So, Bridgette moved in, and this created even more tension with Ashley, who was barely in touch with us at that point," said Sandke. "Ashley kept saying, 'You've got to get these people out of here. I don't want to deal with any people that aren't in the band.' Bridgette got wind of that and felt very unwelcome there. Meanwhile, she and Lucy had gotten word that the guy who had founded this commune in Denver had taken ill and that the whole thing was not going to happen. So, they were stuck in Chicago, living in our place, not knowing what their next move was. And in the midst of all this, I bailed and went back home."

Late in the evening of July 22, Sandke got a phone call at his parents' home in Hyde Park explaining that there had been a terrible accident back at the crash pad on Wells Street. "Eric and Bridgette were on the top floor of the building, and everybody had taken acid, which Lucy had given out to everybody," he explained. "She had gotten it to sell and make a little money for their trip out West. But now that was canceled, so they all took the acid themselves. I don't know whether Mike took anything, but he could sense that things were off that night, and he just left the apartment, which was an incredibly smart thing to do. Also, his tenor was being worked on, so it was in the shop at the time this whole mess went down."

Apparently, something happened between Eric and Bridgette that night to upset her so much that she jumped from the third-floor window of the apartment, ending up in the street, later dying from the fall. Chaos ensued. As Sandke recalled, "After Bridgette jumped, then Eric went downstairs to the second floor and tried to jump out a window himself. But we had soundproofing around that window, because that's where the band used to rehearse, and it prevented him from falling through. But he did break glass that fell on the street below. An ambulance showed up for Bridgette and took her away. Then the police showed up and got everybody together on one floor and ended up arresting everybody that was there because they found marijuana and the LSD that Lucy had been planning to sell. They took everybody to jail.

"And the cops were very sadistic," he continued. "This was the summer of '68. A month later was the Democratic Convention in Chicago. So, I think the cops and everybody really had it out for hippies at the time, and they were just going to teach them a lesson they wouldn't forget. So, what they did is they took all the people that were arrested and put them in separate jails, some of them with these hardened gang members. Two of the guys were raped in their jail cells, one of them being Eric. So, you can imagine what he went through. Here he was tripping, Bridgette jumps out the window to her death, he tries to jump out another window, he's arrested, taken to Cook County Jail, and he's raped, probably repeatedly."

The next day, July 23, 1968, the headline in the afternoon daily, *Chicago's American*, read "Cops Raid Hippie Pad After Woman's Plunge."

The story went on to say:

"Police arrested five youths in the apartment at 1520 N. Wells Street after finding what appeared to be marijuana and several hundred pills. A girl, 16, was turned over to juvenile authorities. The victim, Miss Bridgette Gwin, 21, was unconscious in Henrotin Hospital. Doctors said she suffered a skull fracture. Detectives said it appeared she dived thru a screen covering the open window during what apparently was a party in the apartment. Miss Gwin was found lying on the sidewalk several feet from the building. Police went to the apartment and found the girl and five young men. The six were questioned at the Chicago Avenue police station where one policeman termed them 'uncooperative.' They said they all lived in the apartment but declined to say who their landlord was or who had signed the rental lease. The five-room apartment was described by police as dirty and littered with debris. All six denied seeing Miss Gwin plunge, but one reportedly said she had been despondent. The youths were charged with possession of narcotics."

Two photos splashed across the front page of that paper, showing the aftermath of Gwin's horrifying plunge, carried the damning headline, "Girl's Tragic Plunge from Old Town Pad, Round Up Hippie Pals."

As the local newspapers played up the sensational angle, an ambitious prosecutor pressed for a case of premeditated murder. "The attitude was, 'Maybe they had forced her to take the drugs or influenced her in some way,'" said Sandke. "But later on, the case was thrown out on a technicality, thanks to the efforts of a legal scholar from the University of Chicago that my mother got to represent some of the accused. And the reason everybody got off is because there were two levels to the apartment, and legally those are two separate apartments, but the police only found drugs in one of them. Legally, they would've had to show who was where at the time of the arrest. But by corralling everybody into one room and then arresting everybody, they basically destroyed their own case."

In the aftermath of the whole nightmarish scene that played out that summer night in the hippie crash pad on Wells Street, the investigating officers had left the front door to the building unlocked. "It was hanging wide open," said Sandke. "We later heard that vans pulled up that night, possibly from the police department . . . because this was a pretty corrupt time in Chicago. There was a saying then that Chicago police were the best money can buy. At any rate, all our instruments were taken—the organ, my trumpet and flugelhorn, Mike's crumhorn, the electric bass and guitars, amplifiers, microphones, tape recorder . . . all our stuff was taken out from our place. Then after that, street people came in and completely cleaned it out—our record collections, clothes, bedding, blankets, furniture, everything was missing, even the alarm clock. And the place just looked like a battle zone. One of the daily papers came in and took pictures of it and had an article saying, 'This is the kind of squalor that these hippies live in. No wonder this girl committed suicide, having to live in this place.'"

All charges were eventually dismissed on August 1, 1968. And as Sandke explained, "The other thing that became evident was that the drugs the police found were in the possession of Bridgette's sister, Lucy. And I guess they decided not to prosecute Lucy because Bridgette had just died. So, the whole thing ended up kind of going out with a whimper. But there was plenty of damage that had already been done. Everyone who had gotten arrested and taken to the Cook County jail was traumatized. Mike and I were the lucky ones who weren't there that night to witness what went down and get arrested and thrown in jail. Nevertheless, we were both traumatized as well by the events that happened that night. I remember coming out of it just feeling totally emotionally numb, to the point where I couldn't even really listen to music. It just meant nothing to me, like I had no emotional connection to it after that night. I don't know exactly how it affected Mike, but I suspect that he was affected as deeply and in his own way. As a result of this thing that happened in the summer of '68, Mike and I both ended up back in Indiana University. But our hearts were really not in that whole scene."

For the fall semester at IU, both Sandke and Brecker transferred to fine arts majors. "Somehow the idea of just drawing boxes or something in class seemed relaxing after what we had been through," said Randy. "And we tried to get the band back together, which we eventually did in a slightly different configuration."

Mike was living off campus that semester with drummer Eric Long as his roommate. They enjoyed a close musical connection and often played duets together at The Owl, a basement club in a Methodist church located in downtown Bloomington that hosted local jazz, folk, and blues bands and the occasional experimental theater group such as The Pocket Players featuring IU theater majors Michael Bourne (later to become the longtime award-winning on-air jazz DJ at radio station WBGO in Newark, New Jersey) and Kevin Kline (Oscar and Tony Award-winning actor of *Sophie's Choice*, *The Big Chill*, *Pirates of Penzance*, and *A Fish Called Wanda* fame). In the Michael Brecker Archive at William Paterson University is a rare audio document of a nineteen-year-old Michael wailing with signature intensity and remarkable facility on Dizzy Gillespie's "Night in Tunisia" and John Coltrane's "Resolution" from *A Love Supreme*, accompanied by the freewheeling, Elvin Jones–inspired drummer Long and an unknown bassist. As archive curator Demsey said of Brecker's tenor playing in those formative years, "You can hear that familiar Brecker voice in there—a little rough around the edges, but so powerful."

Unfortunately, Long would never recover from his horrific night of being raped repeatedly in jail while tripping on LSD. Still haunted by those tragic events from the summer, he made two suicide attempts in the building he shared with Michael. As Sandke said, "He would always relive what had happened that night in Chicago. Sometimes he would take some psychedelic or something, and he would just go through it all over again. He twice tried to jump out of the window there where he and Mike lived. And of course, living with Eric at the time must have been very traumatic for Mike. I think that was really the worm eating at his soul that caused him to get into hard drugs and all these things he did later on in New York."

Sandke maintains that while he and Mike never touched narcotics during their term at IU, they did indulge in other recreational drugs. "He was drinking heavily at Indiana and was definitely just trying to anesthetize himself in different ways," Sandke recalled. "He did get into psychedelics, and he would smoke some grass, but I don't remember him being really habitual with anything. I remember our drug of choice at the time was psilocybin or psilocin, which is the synthetic version of psilocybin mushrooms. It was a milder thing, and it gave you a kind of a spiritual high. It was like you take it, and you'd feel very connected to each other and the world and all living things. You know, it was an almost quasi-religious experience. But I don't remember Mike as being constantly on it. It's something that we would do on a weekend as a special treat  kind of thing. But I didn't see any interest in him doing anything beyond that. I mean, even cocaine wasn't around at that time. We didn't try it. But it just seemed like all those things were not some-thing that we were going to mess with. No hard drugs for us. That was off our radar and something that we disapproved of."

After that fall semester at Indiana University concluded in late December of '68, Sandke returned home to Chicago to treat a hernia in his throat (an affliction that would also plague Michael a couple of years later) that had greatly affected his playing. "I was having problems," he said. "And it got to the point where it was so painful to play that I was wrapping gauze around my neck just so I could continue. So, I went back to Chicago and had an operation." Because of his condi-tion, Sandke turned down an offer to play in Janis Joplin's band and, in fact, stopped playing trumpet for most of a decade, focusing instead on piano and guitar until returning to trumpet in 1979.

Michael never finished that fall semester. Whether he flunked out or just stopped going to classes, he suddenly left IU and traveled to Mexico City on an ill-fated adventure with alto saxophonist David Alan Gross. The two landed some kind of month-long engagement there, though they ended up not getting paid for their services. A by-product of Mike's trip to Mexico was a bad case of hepatitis, which landed him in a Philadelphia hospital for a couple of weeks near the end of 1968.

Upon getting out of the hospital, Michael resumed playing around the Philadelphia area. "I had the opportunity and good fortune to be around great local musicians there," he said in a 1973 *Downbeat* interview. "It was a wonderful time to be a young musician learning how to play. There was a kind of community feeling among the musicians in Philly who were into playing and trying to improve and were willing to help you. You could go to a session and there would be 10 saxophone players waiting their turn. And I had the chance to play with guys who were far better than me. So, it was a good training ground. It wasn't New York City but it still had sort of that same kind of urban immediacy to it. And the gentleman that really helped me along the way was a guy named Eric Gravatt. He was a tremendous influence on me. He exposed me to a lot of things I hadn't heard, and to different ways of playing."

Gravatt, who would later go on to play with Weather Report in the early '70s and with Philadelphia hometown hero McCoy Tyner in the '80s, did a lot of duet playing together with Brecker; just tenor sax and drums summoning up the ferocious power of their respective heroes, John Coltrane and Elvin Jones. As Mike told *Downbeat*'s Ted Panken, "He used to set an alarm clock for an hour and we'd improvise straight through—killin'!"

For a brief period, Gravatt, Brecker, and pianist Mark Kramer backed local Philly soul singer Billy Paul, four years before his hit single "Me & Mrs. Jones" (1972) made him a national name. "It was a good place to learn how to play," Mike told a French interviewer. "I have wonderful memories of Philly."

With Indiana University in his rearview mirror, and Philadelphia having served him well, nineteen-year-old Michael was ready to take a bite out of the Big Apple.

# 3

# LOFT SCENES AND BIG APPLE DREAMS

Two momentous events happened in 1969: Man landed on the moon, and Michael Brecker landed in Manhattan. After being away at Indiana University for the better part of three semesters, Michael finally made his move to the Big Apple, initially occupying a modest one-bedroom apartment on Manhattan's Upper West Side at 340 West End Ave. at 76th Street. As he told *Distinguished Artists*' Lorne Frohman in a 2004 interview: "My father gave me money for a couple of months' rent and said, 'After that, you're on your own.' And I was very lucky because my brother Randy had already been living in New York for a couple of years at that point, pursuing music as a livelihood. He had already kind of made a name for himself. He did very well very quickly and he was really kind and gracious to me when I came to town. He introduced me to everybody he knew, so I started working fairly early. I immediately started making rehearsals and whatever gigs I could get, learning whatever I could. So after the two, three months' rent that my parents gave me ran out, I didn't really need any more money from them. I started making enough money to support myself."

Added alto saxophonist and Brecker colleague Steve Slagle: "Being a few years older, Randy really set up a scene with the studios in New York that Mike could just step into without having to do any of the social business connection thing that it usually takes to break into that. I mean, you can be a great player, but you gotta make social connections to get work. So, Randy set it all up in that sense, business-wise, and just got his younger brother in on it. Of course, once anyone heard Mike, it was obvious just how great he was. But that whole thing was set up by Randy, and I think Mike really didn't at all take that for granted. Mike was very fortunate—and he'd be the first to say it—to have Randy as an older brother."

Shortly after settling into his new digs, Michael made the trip across the Hudson River to Rudy Van Gelder's famous studio in Englewood Cliffs, New Jersey, on January 21, 1969, to play on brother Randy's debut album as a leader, *Score*. Van Gelder Studio had been the site of countless classic Prestige, Blue Note, and Impulse! recordings, including a succession of John Coltrane albums, from *Ballads* (1962) to *Impressions* (1963), *Crescent* (1964), his 1965 masterwork, *A Love Supreme*, and beyond. For a young Trane devotee such as Michael, it was like standing on hallowed ground.

Though Michael was fairly inexperienced with professional studios at the time, Randy was confident that his younger brother would deliver the goods. "Mike sounded so great the one time I heard him at that jam we had in Chicago the previous summer, so I invited him to come in for this session," he said. "And to be called for his first record date at age nineteen, his first time recording in New York, he must've been nervous as hell. But you can hear on that record . . . the Mike that we all know was there; his style was just not fully developed. He was a diamond in the rough. He wasn't Michael Brecker yet, but all the pieces were there."

Produced by Randy's mentor, pianist-composer Duke Pearson, whose big band Randy continued to play in sporadically, *Score* was released on Solid State, a label founded by Sonny Lester, Phil Ramone, and Manny Albam as the jazz division of United Artists. Following on the heels of Chick Corea's *Now He Sings, Now He Sobs* and the Mike Mainieri Quartet's *Insight*, both of which had come out on Solid State in December 1968, *Score* captured a moment in time when the music was changing and stylistic boundaries were being blurred. Although The Free Spirits (guitarist Larry Coryell, tenor saxophonist Jim Pepper, guitarist-singer Chip Baker, bassist-singer Chris Hills, and drummer Bob Moses) may have led the way with their 1967 ABC Records debut, *Out of Sight and Sound*, and Jeremy & The Satyrs (flutist Jeremy Steig, guitarist-vocalist Adrian Guillery, electric pianist Warren Bernhardt, upright bassist Eddie Gomez, and drummer Donald McDonald) followed suit with their self-titled debut released on Reprise Records in February 1968, Randy's ambitious debut, released in late 1969, explored the relatively uncharted territory of jazz-rock a full year before the release of Miles Davis's groundbreaking *Bitches Brew*.

In his four-star review of *Score* from the February 19, 1970, issue of *Downbeat*, editor Dan Morgenstern wrote: "Randy Brecker is, at 24, one of the best equipped all-round young trumpeters on the scene. His younger brother Michael, who here makes his recording debut, has fire and guts plus fine command of his horn. I was much impressed with him at the Notre Dame Collegiate Jazz Festival in early 1968, and his outing here sustains the feeling that he will become a player to reckon with. Not unexpectedly, the brothers work together with great empathy, and one hopes they'll have the chance to pursue this promising musical relationship further."

Just a week before the *Score* sessions commenced on January 21, 1969, Randy had participated in another potent session at Van Gelder Studio as a member of Horace Silver's hard bop quintet, along with tenor saxophonist Bennie Maupin, bassist John B. Williams, and drummer Billy Cobham, who had just been honorably discharged from the army, where he picked up his slick drum and bugle corps snare drum skills playing in the 179th Army Band at Fort Dix, New Jersey. Although Horace's *You Gotta Take a Little Love*, released on Blue Note in June that year, was a fairly straight-ahead affair, with the typical Silverian touches of funk and Latin thrown into the mix, Randy's own project found him with one foot in old school swing while striding forward with the other into an emerging new world of sound.

This dichotomy is played out on the eight tracks to *Score*, where Brecker jumps comfortably between the disparate worlds of hard bop and jazz-rock, using separate rhythm tandems to represent each style authentically. For Randy's swinging, hard boppish "Bangalore" and his lightly swinging jazz waltz "Pipe Dream," he recruited upright bassist Eddie Gomez and veteran drummer Mickey Roker alongside swinging pianist Hal Galper, who was fresh in from Boston after having played in Chet Baker's band. The more hard-hitting, pocket-oriented, rock-tinged numbers like Galper's groovy title track and his electric boogaloo, "The Vamp," are handled with aplomb by consummate session aces Bernard Purdie on drums and Chuck Rainey on electric bass, with Galper switching to electric piano. Musical chameleon Larry Coryell seamlessly bridges both settings, offering hip, Wes Montgomery influenced comping and soloing on the jazzier numbers while rocking in raw, cathartic fashion and laying down funky rhythm guitar parts on the more urgent jazz-rock numbers. The two Brecker brothers are equally at home in either camp, showcasing their remarkable versatility while documenting for the first time the uncanny connection they shared on the front line.

Whether it's their close trumpet-tenor harmonies on Randy's swinging opener, "Bangalore," and his buoyant bossa nova-flavored "The Morning Sea" or on Galper's "with it" title track, the tight, near-telepathic hookup of the brothers is evident. This is the template that would later serve them so well in future bands such as Dreams and The Brecker Brothers.

On "Bangalore," a modal number somewhat reminiscent of Miles Davis's "Paraphernalia" from *Miles in the Sky* (1968), Michael's tenor sax solo is flowing, rhythmically assured, and harmonically adventurous—just a hint of things to come. Randy delivers a high-note bravura solo here, and Hal Galper also turns in an outstanding, McCoy Tyner-inspired piano solo on this progressive modern jazz number. Shifting gears on "Score," Galper switches to electric piano while the rhythm tandem of Rainey and Purdie fuels the track with tight pocket playing. Michael digs deep into his King Curtis bag here, unleashing gutsy tenor licks that build to upper register squeals. He reveals a more introspective, probing side of his playing on Galper's haunting "Name Game," a gentle, misterioso number with allusions to Herbie Hancock's "Maiden Voyage." And on Galper's "The Vamp," an earthy boogaloo framed by a funky Eddie Harris–styled line, Michael brings his brusque King Curtis/Junior Walker tone and raw abandon back to the table, along with the kind of outré "New Thing" excursions he had been experimenting with at IU in his free-blowing jams at The Owl with drummer Eric Long. Nothing is at all tentative about any of Michael's soloing on *Score*, yet the signature Brecker authority and jaw-dropping virtuosity are still a few years off.

Perhaps one of the more interesting tunes on the record, at least historically, is also the shortest. At just 1:19, "The Weasel Goes Out To Lunch" is an improvised duet between the brothers that highlights their spontaneous contrapuntal interplay, re-creating the natural chemistry they shared as kids playing together in their tiled bathroom back home in Cheltenham Township.

Having wrapped up his work on *Score* on February 3, 1969, Michael cast about the Big Apple to make his next move. While picking up some session work and playing with various rehearsals band at Lynn Oliver's studio at 89th and Broadway or at Charles Colin's studio on 53rd Street between Eighth and Ninth Avenues, he also took the time during his early phase in New York to study and improve upon his already prodigious saxophone skills. He thoroughly checked out the Schillinger System of Musical Composition, then studied for a time with Juilliard saxophone instructor Joe Allard.

As he told Nathan Kline in a 1987 master class at the Berklee College of Music, "Joe was constantly on my case telling me I was working too hard to create the sound and he started getting me to relax. In fact, he used to use me as an example to his students of what not to do. And he used to do crazy things—take out his teeth, put my hand into his mouth to feel. That sounds ridiculous but it was very instructive. He knew every muscle and he really had a pretty incredible understanding of the whole larynx and how it effects the sound. And he got me to be aware of my Adam's apple and exactly where my tongue was when I was playing, all that kind of stuff. I used to play with my tongue too low and he got me not to drop my jaw, which I still occasionally do when I am hitting low notes or sub-toning. That was the kind of stuff I learned from Joe. He was amazing, and a great teacher."

By May of 1969, Michael left his tiny Upper West Side pad and moved to a more spacious loft downtown in Chelsea, an area bordered by 14th Street to the south, 13th Street to the north, Sixth Avenue to the east, and the Hudson River to the west. As Randy recalled of the place, "It was a terrible dumpy loft on 18th Street between Sixth and Seventh Avenues. He had trouble with the upstairs neighbor, who was a painter. The guy hated Mike's constant practicing and would blast his radio on the floor of his loft when he was out, just to bug Mike. So, Mike only lived there for a few months before he finally got out."

The West Side neighborhood that Mike moved into contained several huge loft spaces, in some cases up to 3,000–5,000 square feet, that once housed manufacturing businesses and sweatshops. Long since abandoned, these raw spaces were taken over by painters, sculptors, jazz musicians, and other bohemians of the emerging counterculture. A fertile jamming scene developed during the late '60s among young aspiring jazz musicians who lived in those gutted industrial spaces. As Michael explained to Frohman, "A lot of the musicians had lofts simply because it was possible to play in them. They were terrible for living but great for noise because they were surrounded by other abandoned factories, and you could play all night, make any amount of noise and not have to suffer complaints from the neighbors. I worked out a lot of things in these loft jam sessions, mostly just how to communicate with other musicians musically. We took those experiences and let it kind of subconsciously dictate who we became. I know that my basic musical leanings were really shaped in those early loft days."

Dave Liebman was a pioneer of that loft scene. As the Brooklyn native recalled, "I got a degree in history in '68 from New York University, and then I went away for three or four months to practice up in Woodstock. And when I came back to town, around Thanksgiving of '68, I knew I had to live in a loft. I had already been hanging out with Bob Moses and Jim Pepper in their lofts, and I saw that this was, for me, the way to learn. Because I didn't get any formal training, the way to learn was to play a lot, and I knew if I played a lot, I'd have a chance to get good at it. And having a loft would allow me to do that."

To secure his loft space at 138 W. 19th St., between Sixth and Seventh Avenues, Liebman paid $1,200 in "key money" to the landlord, whose name, ironically, was Saul Lieberman. Thereafter, his monthly rent was $125, an unbelievable steal by today's standards. "But the thing about the lofts, it was illegal to live there," he explained. "The landlord never gave me any problem, but if the fire department came up to inspect, which they did, they had to get either payoffs, or the landlord would get a citation. It was, you know . . . chancy living."

Liebman was the first musician to move into the abandoned warehouse building on 19th Street, occupying the top floor loft that would eventually become a focal point for freewheeling marathon jam sessions. "My place was formerly a shirt tie-dye factory," he explained. "The room was twelve hundred square feet. Nobody had been living there previously; it was a pretty raw industrial space. I don't think they left me any appliances. It had plumbing, but just barely. We all lived very bare bones, no question about it. You bought a refrigerator, a hot plate, you had bare lightbulbs. Not too much furniture—a table and a bed, that's it. So, it wasn't the most comfortable place to live, but the point was to be able to play all the time."

As he explained in *What It Is: The Life of a Jazz Artist* (Rowman & Littlefield), a series of conversations with pianist-composer-educator Lewis Porter: "For me, it was very clear that the way I worked, to make musical progress, I had to play, play, play. I needed hands-on playing to get better. In my case, I knew that the only way I could get better was to be on the spot 'in the coal mine,' working on it."

Liebman's first instinct after securing his place was to decorate the 19th Street loft in quintessential hippie fashion befitting the times. "The factory had left a lot of tie-dyed shirts still lying all over the floor when I moved in," he recalled, "so I just took out a staple gun and put them all up on the ceiling." He next outfitted the space with instruments to officially designate it as jam central. "I got it ready quickly because I knew that if I had drums, piano, and a bass, people would come. We weren't really supposed to play after working hours, but there was music happening in that loft at all hours of the day. The loft scene was a twenty-four-hour situation. I just threw the key down to cats on the street, they'd come up, and we'd play for three, four hours, then break and go down to Chinatown to get something to eat, come back to the loft and play some more."

He added that many of his personal relationships that continue to this day began in those early loft days. "Randy Brecker came by my loft quite a bit to jam, and we became good friends. And I can't remember the day Mike finally showed up, but I do remember Randy telling me, 'My brother's coming to town, and he's very good.'"

"I met Mike at Steve Paul's The Scene, that club on 46th Street," recalled Liebman's musical partner, pianist Richie Beirach. "I was there with Dave and Randy, we were hanging out, and Michael had just come to town. Randy said, 'This is my brother, Michael.' He was nineteen, and he looked about sixteen. Gangly motherfucker. Tall, good looking kid. And I said to him, 'Hey, man. So, you're a Brecker?' And Randy jumps in, like an older brother, and says, 'Yeah, he's great, but he's got a lot to learn.' You know, the typical big brother shit."

Randy recalled Michael's first visit to Liebman's loft on 19th Street. "He had just moved to town, so I took him by Lieb's to play. We jammed, and it sounded great, and Liebman was impressed, but I remember how nervous Mike was. His hands were shaking. I had never seen that before. Mike didn't sound as good as he could sound because he was really tense playing. It shows you how sometimes it takes a while to get acclimated to New York."

Michael soon became a fixture at many of those marathon jams at Liebman's loft. John Coltrane was the guiding light at that point for both Liebman and Brecker as well as for other Trane disciples on the scene such as Steve Grossman and Bob Berg. "All those guys were convinced that Trane was God," said drummer Lenny White, who had played on Miles Davis's seminal *Bitches Brew* sessions in 1969 and was a ubiquitous figure on the loft scene. "Every young saxophone player was channeling that. But for me, of all those guys, Michael played the least like Trane. From my perspective, when I heard Michael, his influences to me were more Stanley Turrentine and Joe Henderson than John Coltrane."

But as Beirach saw it, "Trane was central to Michael's gestalt, his makeup. So much so that it was almost painful for him to talk about. He loved Trane so much, but he also loved King Curtis . . . not making comparisons. How do you compare King Curtis to Trane? It's impossible. Trane is like Bach and Beethoven, on that level. Trane was a mountain. It was a revolution. It was something that only happens maybe every hundred years. And Michael was very aware of that at the time."

In their freewheeling loft jams, the saxophonists tended to hone in on latter day Coltrane. "That was the period of Trane that we were most affected by and were emulating," said Liebman. "And us being young guys, as is always the case, you want to emulate what you hear around your environment. And *Ascension* is the record that stands out as 'Let's do that!' Meaning, play group improv with as many horns as possible at the same time, even with a couple drummers . . . no basic heads, no melodies, no chords, just completely free association and a lot of energy, which, of course, is a big component of it. And Michael was very much a part of that."

Liebman added, "If you were a young musician in New York at that time, you had to deal with Trane; you couldn't avoid it. Why would you? You had to deal with Coltrane's oeuvre, his work and his language. So, we were all enamored by that and really affected by it. Trane was everywhere, and the immensity of what he did was on everybody's mind. And when you hear tapes of some of our jams from back then, you really hear the personalities coming out between me and Michael and Steve Grossman and Bob Berg. It was the beginnings of what would become our way of being stylistic; playing a vernacular that's known and putting it together in your own way."

As drummer Bob Moses told Robert Mike Mahaffay for his audio documentary, *Free Life Loft Jazz, Snapshot of a Movement*, "For me, those sessions were almost like, you could say . . . prayer meeting. And if we're going to be honest about it, too, we have to recognize that many times there was a sacrament being taken, like perhaps mescaline or

LSD or mind-altering agents. And I think it was in a sense like a prayer circle—get out of the mind, get out of the self. You put away all the form and all the pre-composed and everything that you've learned and practiced and just meet in the zero. It's like getting to see your true soul in the mirror, and the beauty and the ugly and all of it is right there. I think it's a very valuable process for artists, for visionaries. And in those years, there were a lot of musicians experimenting in that direction."

Randy confirmed that the sessions at Liebman's and other lofts around New York at that time were, indeed, happening around the clock. "There were sometimes three sessions going on at once in that building on 19th Street on each floor, as well as other lofts around town where cats would go to play at any hour. Liebman's loft became a main focal point mostly for free jazz jams. The bebop and Miles-infused fusion jams were over at Gene Perla's loft, who shared a space with Jan Hammer and Don Alias in Lower Manhattan on Jefferson Street near the Fulton Street Fish Market just off the East River. I had gone to Berklee with Gene one summer and met Jan at the Vienna Jazz Competition in 1966, so I was over there jamming quite a bit, too, along with a lot of people who were under the electric Miles wing.

"And then you had the big band rehearsal spaces like Lynn Oliver's uptown on 89th and Broadway and downtown at Tom DiPietro's place Upsurge on 19th between Fifth and Sixth Avenues, where the Chuck Israels [Jazz] Orchestra and Joe Henderson Big Band used to rehearse. I went to those places as well. There were so many places to play then."

(Marc Copland also had a loft downtown at 77 Warren St. that was frequented by guitarists John Abercrombie and Ralph Towner, bassist Glenn Moore, and drummer Jeff Williams; drummer Bob Moses ran sessions at his loft just off the Bowery at 7 Bleecker St.; drummer Bruce Ditmas hosted jams at his loft on Greene Street in Soho; and New Zealand pianist Mike Nock hosted jams at his nearby loft in the East Village on Bleecker and Third Avenue.)

Meanwhile, Randy had moved from his West Village apartment at 21 Jones St., where he was paying all of $90 a month rent, into his own sixteen-hundred-square-foot loft on the Bowery, where his rent was a whopping $175. "It was easier living in New York back then because rates for musicians really haven't gone up that much, and yet the rents have gone up twentyfold," he said. "So now it's nearly impossible to live in the city."

Following Liebman into the building at 138 W. 19th St. was bassist Dave Holland, who moved into the second-floor loft vacated by drummer-pianist Howie Wyeth (grandson of the famed illustrator N. C. Wyeth and nephew of the great painter Andrew Wyeth and who would later tour in 1975 as a member of Bob Dylan's Rolling Thunder Revue). Liebman had met Holland in London a couple of years earlier and ended up jamming with him at Ronnie Scott's nightclub. "My parents believed in travel, so in '67, when I was twenty-one years old, they gave me a thousand dollars, the book *Europe on Five Dollars a Day*, and a ticket to London and back out of London two months later. The bassist Cameron Brown had given me a couple of phone numbers over there from when he had been living in Europe. And on the first night over I called Dave Holland, who was living with John Surman at the time. I heard the guys at Ronnie Scott's and sat in with them there. Afterwards, they let me crash at their place, and I ended up staying for three weeks. For the remaining five weeks of my trip, I went around Europe with my horn and a duffel bag and just sat in here and there."

Holland, who had arrived in the States in August of '68 to play with Miles Davis, was eager to move into the spacious second-floor loft at 138 W. 19th St. And when another loft space later opened up on the first floor of that same building, he encouraged pianist Chick Corea to move in. (Corea and Holland were bandmates in Miles Davis's exploratory electric ensemble at the time, both later appearing on such fusion landmarks as *In A Silent Way* [1969] and *Bitches Brew* [1970] and subsequently forming the free jazz group Circle with drummer Barry Altschul and alto saxophonist Anthony Braxton.)

"So, there were three of us in that building—me, Dave Holland, Chick Corea—baking bread every night, being very strictly macrobiotic for a year or year and a half," Liebman recalled. "And there was also LSD and mescaline and stand-on-your-head and Swami Vivekananda and Hare Krishna. I mean, we went through everything. It was a laboratory for living."

Holland remembered twenty-year-old Michael Brecker as being a fresh-faced figure on the loft scene: "He was just out of college, and he moved into a place which was backed onto mine. In other words, he was on 18th Street, and there was a roof connecting the two buildings—mine on 19th, his on 18th. So, you could climb out of his kitchen window and then walk across the roof and climb into my kitchen window. And

Mike, who was a young man living pretty much on his own at the time, would make that walk and climb into our kitchen window to visit me and my wife, Clare. Soon after moving into his place on 18th Street, he discovered her cooking was wonderful, and the company wasn't too bad either. So, he used to come over and climb through our window and hang out, eat dinner, jam a little bit, listen to records, not just jazz but often contemporary classical music."

In one of their late-night listening sessions together, Holland turned Michael onto the music of the Canadian-born, London-based trumpeter-composer Kenny Wheeler. As he recalled, "I had done a record with Kenny just a short while before I came to New York called *Windmill Tilter*. It's an extraordinary piece of writing that Kenny did, commissioned by John Dankworth, the big band leader and composer in England that Kenny worked with for quite some time. I brought this recording with me to New York, and I was so taken by the recording and by Kenny's writing that I played it for many people. I played it for Dave Liebman, I took it to Miles's house on one of my visits and played it to him, and I played it to Mike. And as everybody else was, Mike was amazed by the beauty of this music. [Holland and Brecker would later play together on Wheeler's 1983 ECM album, *Double, Double You*, alongside pianist John Taylor and drummer Jack DeJohnette.]

"Mike was always very interested in all of these things," Holland continued. "So, I took him to be somebody that was really serious about his work and was letting the music speak for him rather than talking up his abilities. He wasn't the sort of brash 'Here I am, check this out' kind of person. He was always looking to learn, and he was always aware that there was more to learn. This is what made him a great musician. I think this is a quality you see in musicians that continue to grow throughout their career and throughout their life. They're open to new things and learning, and they always realize that there's more to know and more to learn. And I felt that about Mike. He was always curious."

Holland reacted the same way that most musicians did after jamming with Michael for the first time up at Liebman's loft. "He was an extraordinary saxophone player even at that point in his life," the bassist recalled. "He had worked very, very hard and absorbed a lot of information and a lot of understanding of the history of the music. But he grew up at a time when the boundaries between different musics were being ignored quite a bit, and there was a crossover happening between rhythm and blues and rock and roll and jazz. We didn't see these different musics as being in opposition to each other. Some of the more traditional jazz players that were perhaps less open-minded felt like jazz should be a more isolated form of music and it shouldn't dip into these other forms. But we saw them as all being related. I think our generation was just drawing on different sources for putting our music together. And there was a lot of really interesting mixtures that came up from that, which, of course, Miles was aware of as well and worked with in his direction that he was taking. So, Mike was checking out all these different things that were going on—free improvisation, the traditions of Coltrane, Joe Henderson, as far as the tenor was concerned. And this was all coming together in his playing and synthesized eventually into his own personal style of playing."

"It was a special time to be in New York," Michael told Frohman. "That's when the so-called boundaries between what was then pop music and jazz were becoming very blurry. And those of us who experimented with combining R&B rhythms with jazz harmony began to develop a music that was a fusion, if you'll excuse the word, of various elements. The music was fresh, exciting, powerful, and exhilarating. We really had no word for it; at the time it was loosely referred to as jazz-jock."

By the fall of 1969, a few months after the release of *You Gotta Take a Little Love*, Horace Silver decided to disband his quintet, leaving Randy Brecker, Billy Cobham, Bennie Maupin, and John B. Williams suddenly unemployed. "Horace broke up the band in California," Randy recalled. "We had been together almost two years. He wanted to resettle in California. He had gotten married around that time and wanted to move out to Malibu, which is where he spent the rest of his life. But we had a band meeting, and he gave us two weeks' notice. That was typical Horace—professional, but two weeks instead of a month. So, Billy and I came back to New York. This was around the time that Mike met trombonist Barry Rogers. And Barry, in turn, had met two singer-songwriters, Jeff Kent and Doug Lubahn, who wanted to start a band called Dreams. And by pure happenstance, they needed a trumpet player and a drummer. I remember I was at the Village Vanguard talking to Mike . . . I think Barry might've been there as well . . . and I said, 'Well, guess what? Horace just broke up the band, so me and Billy are back in town.' So it was just an amazing coincidence that we were free."

Cobham remembered Michael as "this scrawny, tall kid" he had jammed with during the summer of '68 in Chicago when Horace Silver's quintet had that two-week engagement in the Windy City at The Plugged Nickel. But before they would all join the band that Kent and Lubahn were putting together, Michael, Randy, Rogers, and Cobham would play seven nights at Ungano's on 70th Street between Broadway and West End Avenue (not far from where Mike was living on the Upper West Side when he first moved to Manhattan earlier that year) with Birdsong, an R&B/funk group led by singer-songwriter-keyboardist Edwin Birdsong, who would later land a contract with Polydor Records and become more well known as a producer for vibraphonist and funk-soul-jazz pioneer Roy Ayers. "It was like James Brown styled stuff," Randy recalled. "And that horn section of me, Michael, and Barry just clicked. There were no charts, but we were just great at jamming up parts together on the spot. We never wrote anything down. We basically worked off cues that would allow the music to go from section to section with a lot of group improvising in between, a la Charles Mingus's group. Barry just fit like a glove between the two of us, jamming up stuff that way. And we would develop that even further in Dreams."

Rogers was a veteran of the salsa scene of New York and a key member of Eddie Palmieri's innovative La Perfecta band of the early 1960s. An imaginative improviser and gifted arranger, he would become an important mentor for Michael during those early Dreams days. "He was older than me and he took me under his wing, helped me feel comfortable living in New York," Michael recalled in a 1973 *Downbeat* interview. "He was the first to play me African music . . . out of Guinea, to be exact. And I was smitten by it. He was the first to play me Cajun music and Latin music. Barry could take music apart and analyze it very well, and he experienced it on a very deep level, spiritually and emotionally, with tremendous excitement—a very basic instinct that I was attracted to. We have certain similarities. I definitely don't have his ability to communicate excitement, but we were excited by the same things—a certain rhythmic and harmonic tension and release that gets my skin going, that reaches me, as it reached Barry, in a deep emotional-spiritual place."

In a 2006 interview with the trombonist's son, trumpeter Chris Rogers, Michael expounded on Rogers's profound influence on him: "Barry early on took an interest in me and in the way I played. And somehow his constant positive feedback gave me an extra confidence that I didn't have at the time, which was very valuable for me. It gave me a platform to work off of. Because at that time I was probably my worst enemy, as most musicians are. We're often our own worst judges. And Barry gave me a lot of positive feedback and would genuinely get excited by what I was doing, and it was enormously helpful to me. Often if I was too judgmental of myself, I had Barry's voice as an important part of the committee that we all have in the back of our heads, offering a very positive kind of life affirming message that enabled me to play. And I'm always indebted to him for that."

Rogers's home in the Bronx contained an incredibly eclectic record collection that other members of Dreams, especially Michael, would periodically check out. "He had all the Miles, Monk, Coltrane, and J. J. Johnson records," recalled Chris Rogers. "But he also had Irish music, Arabic music; of course, all the Latin American music, especially the Cuban, Peruvian, and Afro-Caribbean. And he had African field record-ings from the Smithsonian Folkways and Nonesuch labels. He was excited by all of this stuff and got deeply into it, like an ethnomusicolo-gist. And some of that curiosity about different musical cultures rubbed off on Michael. I just felt like they were kindred spirits in a certain way. They shared a certain energy. They were both intrepid explorers, each searching in his own way."

By 1970, more and more players began committing to full-time gigs and branching out from the unruly loft jam scene. As Mike and Randy began formulating plans for Dreams, Liebman hooked up with the innovative horn-driven rock band Ten Wheel Drive, which featured the charismatic, Janis Joplin–esque singer Genya Ravan. "That was the year that jazz-rock was ascendant," said Liebman. "Straight-ahead jazz was at its lowest ebb in its history. A lot of the black guys went to Europe because of personal and musical reasons, because they had gigs, and they were treated like human beings there. Meanwhile, in the States, the jazz-rock thing was coming in strong. Nobody called it fusion then. But suddenly a bunch of horn players who really couldn't find work started playing in these rock bands with horn sections, like Dreams, Ten Wheel Drive, Blood, Sweat & Tears, Chicago, Chase, and others. It was new music, it was popular, and we were all happy about it. Of course, by the '80s it had gotten watered down. But during the '70s, it was definitely happening."

The Dreams horn line of Michael Brecker, Randy Brecker, and Barry Rogers, 1970
*(Courtesy of Jeff Kent Estate)*

While the Dreams songwriting team of Kent and Lubahn tapped into the zeitgeist of the late '60s with thoughtful, socially conscious lyrics, their memorable melodies and catchy hooks, fueled by punchy horns and Cobham's thunderous beats, scored big with young listeners. "Dreams was a rock band with horns, much like Blood, Sweat & Tears and Chicago, but the only difference was we were really pretty much jazz musicians in this group," Michael told Herb Nolan in *Downbeat.* "But we were jazz musicians that had grown up listening to rock and playing R&B, and we made up the horn parts every night. We improvised them. They weren't written out, which was quite different for that time."

Adding Cobham's muscular drumming to the potent mix gave the band unlimited firepower. "Billy could create this kind of pyrotechnic thing on the drum kit that people had never heard before," said Kent. "And then when Michael soloed, it was just so far ahead, so superior to what was going on in other bands at the time."

"Nobody played like Billy," Randy concurred. "He had bulked up by then, was lifting weights all the time, and he added a bunch of tom toms, so his set became huge. He set a new standard back then for drumming."

(Cobham was later recruited by Miles Davis to play on the August 19–21, 1969, studio sessions that produced such landmark fusion outings as 1970's *Bitches Brew* and the April 7, 1970, sessions that yielded *Jack Johnson, Live-Evil, Get Up with It, Big Fun,* and *Circle in the Round*.)

With Cobham's power precision drumming and the impeccably tight, intertwining horn lines of Rogers and the two Brecker brothers, Dreams quickly developed a cult following in 1969 through regular appearances at the Fillmore East, where they opened for Canned Heat and the Allman Brothers; and the Electric Circus, where they opened for Ike & Tina Turner. The group also enjoyed a residency at the Village Gate in the heart of Greenwich Village, where they caught the eye of Columbia Records executive Clive Davis, who eventually signed them to the label. "And the next thing you know, we went to the Columbia Record Convention in the Bahamas that year," Randy recalled. "Chick Corea was there, Miles Davis was there, and a whole bunch of pop stars on the label were there. And everything you've read about the music business was happening there. On the whole second floor of the hotel there were hookers that the label had flown in. And a lot more was going on. It was a wild scene."

Aside from Clive Davis, Randy also recalls seeing another familiar figure attending their celebrated gigs at Art D'Lugoff's Village Gate on the corner of Thompson and Bleecker Streets in the heart of Greenwich Village. "Miles would come and hear us all the time," he said. "He'd always be sitting in the back, listening intently. I was playing my trumpet through a wah-wah pedal a lot at those Village Gate shows, and Miles really took notice."

(Davis used wah-wah for the first time on a June 3, 1970, studio recording of "Little High People," though that track wasn't released until 2003 when it was included in the sprawling five-CD boxed set, *The Complete Jack Johnson Sessions*. Davis's use of wah-wah pedal was later documented on a December 19, 1970, performance at the Cellar Door in Washington, D.C., portions of which appear on 1971's *Live-Evil* and later appeared on the 2005 six-CD boxed set, *The Cellar Door Sessions, 1970*.)

While Dreams was acknowledged as a quintessential NYC band (they even had an anthem titled "New York," which carried the urgent vocal refrain: *You work all day, you work all day, you work all . . . day*), the band ended up recording its debut album in Chicago.

Cobham remembers Dreams playing a gig at Soldier's Field on the bill with Sly & The Family Stone and Parliament-Funkadelic during the stretch of time they spent in the Windy City recording their first album that summer of 1970.

"Fred Weinberg, who was a famed engineer in the Latin world and a friend of Barry Rogers's, produced that first Dreams recording," Randy recalled. "And we did it mostly live. That's why it sounds so raw and open. We were intent on not just laying down the tracks and doing overdubs; we really wanted that live vibe that we got on gigs. And because we had been gigging a lot then, all our chops were up. And since there wasn't anybody from the label telling us, 'Don't do that,' we decided to stretch out on that record."

A cursory listen to the nearly fifteen-minute "Dream Suite" was enough to show that Dreams was into something completely different on that first album. As Jeff Kent put it, "There was the rock world and the jazz world, and this was kind of the point where they joined." Rather than being a band of jazzers checking out the visceral power of rock, or a band of rockers making a feeble attempt at improvising, Dreams was a balanced act—rock and jazz musicians bringing their influences to bear, creating together, melding their disparate sensibilities into a wholly unique hybrid.

"There was really no term for what we were doing back then," said Michael in the liner notes for Columbia/Legacy's 1992 CD reissue of *Dreams*. "Nobody called it fusion. We were just searching for new ways to break down barriers. It was a very fertile period. People were experimenting, trying different things. It was an exciting time to be in New York."

And in Michael, Dreams had the ultimate secret weapon—a soloist of unparalleled skill and imagination who was well versed in the John Coltrane-Joe Henderson-Wayne Shorter tenor sax tradition but who was also intimately aware of the grittier King Curtis-Junior Walker-Maceo Parker tradition. Although Chicago and BS&T and even Tower of Power may have been cultivating tight, punchy horn sections, none had a soloist to rank with the sheer incandescence and authority of Michael Brecker. Randy and Barry Rogers were no slouches either in the improvisational department. Indeed, Randy stretches with abandon on "Holli Be Home," the ambitious "Dream Suite" and the anthemic "New York," a driving number that opens with a burst of fusillades on the kit from Cobham and also features a pulse-quickening tenor solo from Michael.

The rock element of Dreams was provided by Jeff Kent and Doug Lubahn, two songwriters with loose connections to Stephen Stills of Crosby, Stills, Nash & Young fame. As Kent recalled, "For a while we were staying at his house on Long Island. The way that came about was through Dallas Taylor, who was in CSN&Y at the time and was the drummer in Doug's first band, Clear Light. Stephen had this incredible A-frame home out in Sag Harbor but was never there. Dallas ended up staying there a lot, and we'd come out to visit him. The place had a B-3 organ, some Leslie speakers, and a set of drums, so we ended up playing continuously in this house, just jamming up material."

In the beginning stages of Dreams, Lubahn and Kent sang lead vocals exclusively. They eventually auditioned several singers and ended up recruiting Edward Vernon to front the band. Guitarist John Abercrombie was later added to the mix. "He was just out of Berklee and had met Randy somehow," recalled Michael. "At that time, I had never heard anybody play guitar like him. He had his own style even back then."

(Sixteen years later, Michael was a part of the John Abercrombie group, featuring bassist Marc Johnson and drummer Peter Erskine, that performed at the Village Vanguard, documented on VHS/later on DVD.)

While Abercrombie's Hendrixian, wah-wah-infused guitar solos and Cobham's muscular displays on the kit grabbed rock ears, fans who flocked to Dreams concerts invariably got introduced to jazz through the accomplished improvising of Randy, Michael, and Barry. This cross-fertilization formula clicked on the college campus circuit, where Dreams scored big with young crowds in the wake of their self-titled debut in November 1970. The band's funkier side is presented on that album by "Devil Lady" while a decided prog-rock influence emerges on "The Maryanne." Regarding the hippie hitchhiker saga, "15 Miles to Provo," think The Band's anthemic "The Weight" with horns.

"Holli Be Home" features some sophisticated, jazzy horn arrangements by Randy and showcases his beautiful muted trumpet playing. "Try Me" is powered by Cobham's crisp, rapid-fire drum fills while the tight, funky horn arrangement here serves as a prototype for the signature Brecker Brothers sound that was still five years off. Abercrombie's dissonant, distortion-laced guitar solo on this track can only be described as "otherwordly" by rock standards.

The standout track on Dreams' debut is the three-movement, fifteen-minute "Dream Suite." It opens with an a cappella blast of tenor sax and a display of the uncanny note-bending technique that Michael picked up from emulating Albert King and other blues guitarists he admired. That first movement, "Asset Stop," segues to some grinding funk-rock colored by Abercrombie's mesmerizing wah-wah rhythm guitar work. Cobham's intense fills and slamming backbeat here foreshadow things to come with the Mahavishnu Orchestra. As that opening movement develops, the three horns float and interact freely in a kind of urban Dixieland vibe that opens up to more avant terrain at the tag. No other horn section of the day stretched so freely and yet cohesively as the Breckers and Rogers did on this first movement to "Dream Suite."

A quirky Nino Rota flavored waltz then sets up the second movement, the balladic "Jane." And the ambitious suite closes on a high-energy note with "Crunchy Granola," an ode to the health-conscious Rogers's favorite snack. Michael blows ferociously on the vamp section here as Abercrombie unleashes a flood of ominous wah-wah guitar, predating Pete Cosey's wah-wah wailing with Miles Davis's wild, mid-'70s electric band by at least a few years.

With David Wilcox's trippy, René Magritte-styled album cover art depicting graphic illustrations of the eight band members in long trench coats and bowler hats raining down from the sky, that first Dreams album was a striking introduction to record buyers. And the accompanying full-page ads in various music magazines of the day gave a strong indication that the label was solidly backing this exciting new group on the burgeoning jazz-rock scene.

The original lineup of Dreams continued to play together through the end of 1970, at which point founding members Lubahn and Kent were replaced by a new keyboardist and bassist. As Randy recalled,

"Doug and Jeff, the original songwriters, were really rock guys, and they couldn't keep up with the way the band was going, as far as improvising. Because it just went in different directions every night, and their playing wasn't up to the writing. So eventually we replaced them at Barry's urging . . . he was a pretty strong-willed individual. Then we auditioned guys, and we found an unknown pianist named Don Grolnick. I knew him, however, because I had gone to Stan Kenton band camp with him when we were both fifteen. No one else had heard of Don before, but he worked out great."

Bassist Will Lee was the next new recruit in Dreams. As Randy recalled, "I was talking to a friend of mine named Gary Campbell, a wonderful saxophonist who lives in Florida who I had gone to Indiana University with, and I told him that we were looking for a bass player. He said, 'Well, the son of the dean of music at the University of Miami is only seventeen, but he plays real good. And he sings his ass off. Why don't you try him? His name is Will Lee.' So, we flew Will up to New York for an audition, and inside of ten seconds he got the gig."

(That lineup of Michael and Randy with Grolnick and Lee would later become the core of The Brecker Brothers band.)

Will Lee had been the ultimate Dreams fan when he got the call from Randy to audition. As he recalled, "It was hilarious because my musical focus and the thing I was getting the most enjoyment out of listening to at that time was that first Dreams album. And I wasn't the only one. All my peers at UM were focused on *Dreams*. Because it was just mind-blowing, changing-the-course-of-music stuff—super-innovative playing and just some of the tightest, greatest playing of all the horn bands. You had Chicago and Blood, Sweat & Tears on one level, but then, on a whole other level, was Dreams. And those of us that were lucky enough to have a copy of *Dreams* didn't just listen to it once; we would wear out many copies and use it as an excuse to get together and play that album for each other in the dorms."

The multitalented Lee was actually booked solid with gigs around the Miami area at the time Randy called and hadn't really thought about leaving town. But an offer to join Dreams was one he couldn't refuse. "I was working steady, playing six nights a week, six sets a night until 4 a.m., and my first class the next morning, a theory class, was at 8 a.m.," he recalled with a laugh. "I was in eight different bands at the time, and as far as I was concerned, I would've been content to stay there for the rest of my life. I was kind of a goofy guy, you know . . . just happy to get the next toke and get the next buzz. I didn't have my sights set on leaving Miami or anything, and I certainly never thought that my future would have New York in it. But Dreams was like the perfect music to me because it was right in the middle of all the stuff I was working on. Here's jazz, here's rock, and here's a pop element, too, with the vocals. So, for a person with my values, these were the next Beatles, in a way. And they were that popular among my peers, too. So, of course, it was thrilling to get the call to come up to New York to audition."

First, Dreams laid out a proposition to Will. "They said, 'Look, you fly yourself up. If you get the gig, we'll pay you back for the flight.' And I didn't care if I paid or who paid because this was like the most amazing thing that ever happened to me."

Lee recalled his first encounter with Dreams in great detail: "The whole scene was really intimidating. It was in a building on Crosby Street in Soho. To get to the rehearsal room, I had to take a beat-up elevator that a guy operated by pulling a rope. I had never seen anything so funky in all my life. The rehearsal space was in the basement. So, you go down in this funky elevator, and now you're in the basement, and you're walking down the hallway surrounded by anvil cases that have stenciled on it: Johnny Winter, Santana, Miles Davis. And I'm like, 'What is this place?! This is just too bizarre! This can't be happening to me!' But here I am in New York City, and the band of my dreams, Dreams, is asking me to audition!

"So, I walk into the rehearsal room, and there's my heroes standing there—there's Mike Brecker, there's Randy Brecker, there's Billy Cobham. And Randy says, 'OK, here's some music,' and he puts a big score of the Dreams music on a stand in front of my chair so I could read it down and play along with them. And I said, 'Guys, I can read, but I don't think I'm going to need this. Let's just count it off.' Because I noticed that they were all songs from that first Dreams album, which I knew backwards and forwards. So, we started running down one of the tunes, and for the most part I had never really played with a drummer that I didn't have to feel like I was the timekeeper in the band. But I'd never felt anything as strong as this guy Billy Cobham. He counts the tune off and lays down the groove, and suddenly I'm not having to do anything, really. I no longer have to be the timekeeper in the band; I can just play bass for the first time ever. And it was just like floating. It was the coolest thing. And then when they found out that I sang, they hired me on the spot."

The newest member of Dreams, still a teenager, quickly had to figure out how to deal in the Big Apple. "So now I'm in New York, and I don't know anybody, and I don't have any money, and I don't have a place to stay," Lee recalled. "So, Mike Brecker generously offers to let me stay in his loft on 19th Street until I start sussing things out, which was a huge step. And for a guy who grew up in Huntsville, Texas, and then lived in Coral Gables during my time at University of Miami, I had never seen buildings like this in New York City where they all look the same. You know, I grew up with houses. And I have no sense of direction. Still don't. So, trying to find my way back home after I had left Mike's loft to go out anywhere—to get groceries or do anything—would've been impossible if it weren't for the sound of Mike practicing. I couldn't tell one building from the other, so I'd just follow my ears back to his loft because he was always going to be practicing. Guaranteed. He was so dedicated that he would practice like a fiend around the clock. So, you could just listen your way home at night."

Lee remembers waking up one morning after a drugged-out drunken night to the strains of Michael practicing his horn. "He had a little mattress on the floor where I slept, and it was right in the wide-open room where he'd always be practicing. So, I wake up out of my Quaalude stupor, and he notices me stirring, so he stops playing for a second. And I go, 'Hey, man, how long you been practicing?' He says, 'Four hours.' I was so gone, I slept through the whole thing! But Mike was always practicing. He just worked his ass off all the time. That's something you could always count on."

Meanwhile, Columbia Records' head honcho, Clive Davis, had been pressuring Dreams to take a more commercial direction on their second record. "Basically, he wanted this innovative jazz-rock band to be a Top 40 group," said Lee. "What he wanted was hits. And what's funny is, history would repeat itself five years later when the same guy pressured The Brecker Brothers to come up with some hit singles at Arista Records."

For their second album, *Imagine My Surprise* (1971), Columbia flew the band down to Nashville to record new material with guitarist Steve Cropper of Booker T. & the MGs fame producing. "Mike told me that they had a meeting with the label, and it was determined that they had to start acting more like a rock band or a popular band than a jazz

Michael Brecker and Barry Rogers, 1971
*(Courtesy of Jeff Kent Estate)*

band," said Barry Rogers's son Chris. "Columbia laid out certain rules. The guys in Dreams had to start referring to the music as songs instead of tunes. And on the bandstand, they had to look like they were really digging it . . . put on a happy face, so to speak. My dad didn't take too well to that particular new rule. And Mike told me this hilarious story about looking around the bandstand at a gig one night, and Don was grooving on keyboard, and Randy was looking like he was into it. Then he looks over at Barry, and he was shaving on the bandstand! He was definitely the rebel of the group."

*Imagine My Surprise* was not nearly as well received, at least by fellow musicians, as Dreams' self-titled debut in 1970. A blatant attempt at reining in some of that raw, renegade energy that defined the group at its best, their sophomore effort was more commercially viable though less compelling than the first album. Middle of the road, Chicago-ish fare such as "Calico Baby," "Just Be Ourselves," and "Why Can't I Find a Home" was clearly aiming at the Top 40 market, as was their punchy take on Traffic's "Medicated Goo." Still, *Imagine My Surprise* had some bright moments, including Michael's raspy tenor solo on "Child of Wisdom" and his brief call-and-response exchanges with Rogers's trombone on the Gerry Goffin/Carole King song "I Can't Hear You." Randy contributes a tasty muted trumpet solo on his title track, which also has him singing lead vocals. "I wrote that after hearing Jimi Hendrix's 'Up from the Skies,' which was one of his most jazz-influenced songs," he recalled. "That was one of the few times, in fact, that I wrote something with only one influence and song in mind. But Jimi's playing was an influence in general on me. Whenever I plugged into my effects [wah-wah pedals and delays], I always had him in mind, along with my various jazz influences like Clifford Brown and Lee Morgan."

Will Lee acquits himself nicely with some soulful vocals on "Here She Comes Now." And although the stretching factor is diminished on this second Dreams album, Michael's tenor does shine on the pop ballad "Don't Cry My Lady," foreshadowing his memorable work a year later on James Taylor's pop gem "Don't Let Me Be Lonely Tonight."

Ultimately, Randy concluded that Dreams' second outing fell well short of the mark. "There's some nice stuff on there, but it wasn't cohesive enough," he said. "We all started writing for that project, and the writing styles were all a little different from each other. The band kind of lost the core sound without Doug and Jeff there. That first record did pretty well, especially among musicians. It just didn't sell that much right away but enough for Columbia to fund a second record."

Added Cobham, "The one thing that Dreams really lacked was leadership. It was too much of a cooperative band at that point, and I kept getting myself in the middle of things that I couldn't get myself out of. The guy who really was the leader of the band, even though he didn't want to be, was Barry Rogers. He'd say, 'No, I don't want to make any decisions,' and then he'd make the decisions. Or he'd say, 'You're not telling me what to do.' Yet, he didn't want to say what we should be doing. So, the decisions came too slowly. The fabric of the band got frayed. Everything just fell apart, and that was a drag. And at some point, I thought, 'Oh, man, it's too much for me. I'm not ready for this.' From my perspective, I needed to move on. So, I found myself drifting away."

"Billy was already leaving the band; that was kind of in the cards," said Randy. "And when Billy was finally snapped up by John

McLaughlin for the Mahavishnu Orchestra, that was basically the end of the band."

After Cobham left Dreams, the band scrambled to find a replacement. Drummer Bruce Ditmas ended up doing a week-long tour, and they also did a couple of gigs with Rick Marotta, who would go on to become an in-demand session drummer in the '70s and '80s. Alan Schwartzberg, who would later play with The Brecker Brothers band, also filled in on a couple of Dreams gigs. "We auditioned like sixty drummers, including Steve Gadd," said Randy. "He had just moved to town from Rochester and was still more of a jazz drummer, but we were looking for someone with some R&B roots in him, too. We couldn't find anyone to play like Billy. He stood alone in inventing that style."

Regarding the ultimate demise of Dreams, Randy said, "In the end, there weren't enough gigs since the second record didn't sell well. And we were all busy in the studios anyway, so that was it."

Michael had a thoughtful take on the rise and fall of Dreams, as he expressed in a 1973 *Downbeat* interview: "I think the band was strongest at the beginning, but we got sidetracked. On the second album we tried to make something really commercial. We tried to make everything like a single because we really wanted a hit. It ended up screwing us up a lot because we devoted a considerable amount of energy to something we realized we weren't cut out to do. We sacrificed a lot of things the group was most capable of doing, like cooking and stretching out, which is what we used to do live."

Regardless of its short duration, Dreams had a major impact on a lot of young players coming up on the scene. "This band was a game-changer," said drummer and Dreams' fan Peter Erskine. "And while both albums are favorites of mine, the first album with the Magritte-inspired cover gave us—in the form of Michael Brecker and William Cobham playing in duet—a Coltrane and Elvin for our generation."

One of the unfortunate by-products of Michael's two-year stint with Dreams was a herniated larynx, which happened from blowing too forcefully over the sheer volume of electrified guitars and organs in an era when sound systems and monitors were primitive. That scenario, going back to Mrs. Seaman's Sound Band and up to Dreams, created so much tension that Mike had literally blown a hole in his throat from such forceful overblowing on his tenor sax, resulting in his neck ballooning like Dizzy Gillespie's famous cheeks when he played trumpet.

"Little air holes had formed through the muscles, which made his neck expand," explained Randy.

One doctor had advised trumpeter Randy Sandke, who experienced the same problem with his throat when he and Mike were at Indiana University, to lay off his instrument: "Without surgery, the best treatment is to stop playing, maybe for a long time . . . months not weeks . . . and come back gradually, avoiding excess air pressure, which means staying out of the high range until the neck tissue can handle the air pressure—which may be never."

"Mike eventually had surgery for it in 1973," said Randy. "And for a while, later on, he wrapped a velcro bandage around his neck to keep it from bulging out." And as David Demsey pointed out, "What he wore around his neck was not so much a bandage as a Velcro-attached support belt for his neck. Perhaps a parallel is the back supports that people wear when they're doing heavy lifting. But he soon found that it was too restrictive, especially in terms of his breathing."

Meanwhile, the NYC loft jazz scene had undergone some changes. By late 1970, Liebman and Moses formed Free Life Communication, a loosely organized association of about twenty-five creative players who had been playing uncompromising free jazz in each other's loft spaces. Patterned after the Association for the Advancement of Creative Musicians in Chicago and the Black Artists Group (BAG) collective in St. Louis, Free Life Communication was a grassroots organization with a mission. "By this time, we thought that this playing in the loft for each other thing was basically masturbating and that we needed to play for people," said Liebman. "So we decided to take it to the next level by putting on concerts at the Judson Church on Washington Square in the Village, up at Columbia on WKCR, and at museums, churches, wherever we could. And eventually it got to a point where I would call a meeting at my loft and have like fifteen, twenty cats show up."

"I'm not pulling any punches, we were quite naïve," Liebman wrote in a short history of the organization's early years that appeared on his website. "Try to imagine 15 to 20 young (ranging from 18 to late 20s) aspiring jazz musicians, mostly white and middle class, unknown and not working at the time in jazz, sitting in my loft on W. 19th St. in New York, attempting to come up with a name, principles and guidelines for a collective organization. With that much raw energy in one place, it's amazing to me that anything was accomplished. The discussions on the name of the organization were very involved with ideas ranging from Marxist-type politics to hippie-based communal axioms prevalent in the late '60s. To my mind, these first meetings were fantastic for the great discussions that took place among such a vibrant, young, diverse and naïve group of musicians."

Free Life Communication eventually became a 501 nonprofit organization with Liebman as its president and Richie Beirach as vice president. A mission statement they drew up reflected the countercultural leanings of the group: "The music we play is so filled with reality of our being/existence that it is no longer something we do; it has become something we are. Improvisation is the core of our work—spontaneous creation. Our improvised music works to produce an intensification of the present moment in order to dramatize vividly to all people everywhere that life is to be lived with as much involvement in the now as possible."

Shortly after gaining nonprofit status, Free Life Communication got a $5,000 grant from the New York State Council on the Arts as seed money for a more permanent facility than Liebman's loft. "Eventually we heard about the availability of this place on 36th Street called The Space for Innovative Development, which was a former church being renovated by the benefactor, the Rubin Foundation. And they were looking for groups to be in there. They already were housing the Nikolais Dance Theater, which was a cutting-edge company, and the experimental video artist Joe Chaikin. So, we invited them to check us out as well. The guy from the Rubin Foundation came in a limousine and was dressed to the nines—very high class. He sat on my couch with the tie-dyed shirts on the ceiling and the walls painted all crazy colors, and he listened to us play free jazz for like forty-five minutes and decided we were perfect."

Free Life Communication moved its base of operations from Liebman's 1,200-square-foot loft to the 2,500-square-foot Space for Innovative Development. "It had pristine, shiny floors, a grand piano, and I went out and bought like a hundred pillows so people would sit on the ground when we put on concerts," recalled Liebman. "In our first year, we put on three hundred concerts, all pretty much free jazz, sometimes as many as seven saxophones at once playing full-tilt and then hitting the wall before going back for more. We were just immersed in free jazz and late Coltrane. And it was an important training ground for us.

"What it did was, you got your instrument together in a different kind of way because you weren't restricted by chord changes or by steady pulse," Liebman continued. "You could just do what you wanted to do. I have a tape from those days of Michael, myself, and Steve Grossman on tenors, Randy and Terumasa Hino on trumpet, Calvin Hill on bass, and Bob Moses on drums. It's like an hour and a half . . . some of the best of what we played in that way at the time. This was chaos free jazz. This was energy jazz. Pure burn."

Michael would eventually take over Liebman's loft space in the building at 138 W. 19th St. "I sold it to him and went to a bigger loft on Warren Street," said Liebman. "Michael took it over, and he was there for quite a long time, and that's where he did a lot of his practicing to become who he became. It was always peaceful there; you had nobody bothering you, so you could practice all the time, which he did."

Guitarist and future Brecker Brothers member Steve Khan has vivid memories of Michael's new loft space on 19th Street. "It was an expansive raw space, and over on the side there'd be a mattress on the floor, maybe a sheet or two strewn over it. And all over the place were Tropicana orange juice cartons. There was one circular wood table, and on this table were a bunch of reeds and mouthpieces. I'd enter Mike's loft, and he'd look at me and say, 'I want you to listen to something.' He'd pick up his saxophone, get one of the reeds and a mouthpiece, and he'd say, 'OK, listen to this carefully.' And he'd play some amazing shit. Then he'd say, 'OK, now listen to this.' He'd change mouthpieces and play something equally ridiculous. And I would say, 'I don't know, they both sound amazing to me, Mike.' And he'd look at me frustrated and go, 'Jesus! I can't believe you can't hear the difference!' And I'd say, 'Mike, they both sound great. What do you want me to say?' So, this would go on all the time at his loft. Every time I would walk in there, we'd go through that same ritual."

Khan viewed Michael's spartan existence with mixed feelings. "In some ways, Mike was living kind of a shit life. He didn't have any furniture to speak of, he barely ate, and he didn't have any 'creature comforts,' because everything was directed at his mastering the saxophone. But it was so constantly inspiring and humbling just to watch somebody working that hard, which is all he did in that space. I've never seen anybody that dedicated to excellence."

Khan also recalled being fascinated by a new exercise that Michael had designed to develop his writing chops. "During this time, there was no *Real Book*, there were no play-along tapes, no YouTube, no instructional videos. There was nothing like that. And so, if you wanted to know all those great Blue Note tunes, or all the Miles solos, or whatever, you had to do it yourself. And, so, every guy I knew then was compiling these notebooks full of tunes and transcribed solos. When I came to New York from L.A., I had seven huge notebooks of my transcriptions of this stuff that I brought along with me. Mine was maybe a little more guitar-centric than others, mostly Wes Montgomery solos. But saxophone players like Mike, who were way more advanced than me, were transcribing solos by Trane and Sonny Rollins and Joe Henderson, all the great, great players. And it didn't matter where you were—L.A., New York, Philly, or wherever—everybody was doing the same thing. Everybody had these notebooks.

"So I was over at Mike's loft one day and noticed he had been working on something, and I asked him, 'What's in your notebook?,' which is a phrase you heard a lot in those days. And he says, 'Well, I'm trying something new, just kind of an exercise. I've been trying to write a blues a day. I figure if I do this for a year, maybe there'll be one or two good things to come from it. But I discipline myself, and I try to do it every day.' I thought that was a great idea, so I started doing a similar thing myself. I figured if it's good enough for Michael Brecker, it's got to be good enough for me."

(One of the tunes to come out of Michael's "blues-a-day" exercises was "Uptown Ed," a blazing up-tempo romp recorded six years later at the 1978 Montreux Jazz Festival by the Arista All-Stars, featuring Mike on tenor sax, Khan on guitar, Mike Mainieri on vibes, Warren Bernhardt on piano, Tony Levin on bass, and Steve Jordan on drums, for the live album *Blue Montreux II*.)

Concurrent with the loft scene, Michael and Randy also participated in weekly jam sessions that vibraphonist Mike Mainieri had been organizing uptown. A producer and arranger and president of Gnu Music, Inc., a New York City production company that supplied talent for the lucrative jingle and recording scene, Mainieri invited some of the most talented, and still unknown, studio players to come uptown and blow off some steam after business hours. The sprawling sessions began around 10 or 11 p.m. and would often last until sunrise. "Starting my own jingle company gave me access to a lot of the recording studios around town, and I started putting together these very loose jams whenever I could get a studio that was dark," Mainieri recalled. "Jingle studios in those days were pretty much dark at night, so I'd end up calling on [drummer] Donald MacDonald and [bassist] Tony Levin and whoever else was free and into experimenting that night. It might be guitarists like Hugh McCracken, David Spinozza, Bob Mann, Paul Metzke, or Sam Brown and horn players like Frank Vicari on tenor sax, George Young on alto sax, and Ronnie Cuber on bari sax. You never knew who was going to show up because some people had dates or gigs or whatever. But cats just started showing up, having fun, playing, getting high. It was a tremendous bonding experience, so guys really looked forward to coming."

Randy Brecker would often drop by to these late-night sessions with fellow studio cats and friends. One evening he brought his younger brother, Mike, to join in on the fun. "Randy had been talking about Mike, but he's not the kind of a guy who's gonna rave about somebody," said Mainieri. "He was more like, 'Yeah, my kid brother plays saxophone; he's gonna come by,' in that little offhanded kind of way of Randy's. But Michael got up and played a solo, and it was the type of thing where your head spins around three times and you go, 'What the hell was that?' He blew everyone's mind in that room, and we all knew right away that Mike was really special. Now, I was pretty much a decade older than everybody else and had seen a lot at that point. I played with Buddy Rich for years, I played opposite Trane, I had heard all those cats, and not just on records. But when I heard Mike that night—something that's so extraordinary, someone so gifted—it was like some kind of divine intervention, like he had been tapped on the head with a magic wand. And everybody's sort of looking over at Mike—the cats who hadn't heard him before like Ronnie Cuber, George Young, Frank Vicari, Lew Soloff, all guys who pretty much had heard everybody—and they were blown away, too!"

Christine Martin, who was working as Mainieri's secretary at Gnu Music at the time, remembers regularly calling Michael for jingles before finally meeting him face-to-face at one of the late-night studio jams. "That was my job. I would call up musicians and tell them when and where to report. Most of the jingles were done in the morning, and the musicians all really liked doing them because they were getting royalties through the American Federation of Labor. We had big clients—soap companies, regular national stuff—and the residuals paid pretty well. So, if you did ten jingles in the month, you were making a good living. And that's how I initially got to know Mike, by calling him to show up and play on these jingles."

She remembers her first impression of Michael upon meeting him for first time at one of the late-night jams she attended. "I thought he was gorgeous," she said. "He was like 110 pounds and had really long hair past the shoulders. And from my college days, that's the kind of guys I used to like—real tall and lanky."

Saxophonist Bob Mintzer remembers meeting Michael around the time of these fabled White Elephant jams. "Two friends of mine, trumpeter John D'Earth and the drummer Bob Jospé, had a loft on 21st Street between Sixth and Seventh. Mike lived on 19th Street between Sixth and Seventh in what was formerly Dave Liebman's loft, and he would frequently fall by this loft on 21st Street just to jam. Back then we couldn't get a whole band together, so invariably it would be a drummer and a bunch of horn players just wailing. And on this particular night, sometime in '71–'72, Mike had just flown back from this gig he had in Chicago with White Elephant, and he came by this loft to jam with us. At the time, I was really new to jazz. I had been a classical clarinet major in college, and I was working on it. So, Mike showed up, and he started to play, and I was like a deer in the headlights. I was just frozen with amazement, really, just at his fluidity and command of the instrument. And what was equally shocking was his response to his own playing. After he played for a good long while, he kind of lowered his head and shook his head as if he had done something really horrible to humanity. That was really shocking to me. It was like, 'Holy shit, man! If this guy plays like this and he feels like that, what does that mean for me?' You know, it was really striking how very hard he was on himself early on."

Eventually Mainieri's free-blowing late-night jams would evolve into full-blown rehearsals. Material was worked up, and a select few gigs were booked. "At first, there were no arrangements," he recalled. "We'd just blow on grooves. Everybody would take a solo and just find parts. Then I was introduced to a few singers like Nick Holmes, Sue Manchester, and Ann E. Sutton, and they started coming to the jams. So, I started putting together horn arrangements to play behind them. Now, instead of just blowing on one groove for half an hour, we had actual tunes to play. And we'd do some of Nick's tunes because guys like Tony Levin, Hugh McCracken, and Donald MacDonald had played on his album and already knew his stuff. And then John Pierson, who was a bass trombonist and singer in a group called Ars Nova, started coming by, so suddenly I'm writing lyrics for him. So now there's this whole other thing that was happening where it coalesced into a large ensemble, and I was writing arrangements for these vocal tunes. It was all very kind of folky with messages in the lyrics like 'Save the water, save the land' . . . sort of what we're trying to do now. Finally, I was offered a gig downtown at the Village Gate. And they asked, 'Well, what should we call it?' We called the band Red Eye for that gig [which ran five nights, September 15–20, 1970]. After that, I started getting some other offers. And for all of those gigs, it was billed as White Elephant."

Christine Martin, who would eventually become the production coordinator for White Elephant, remembers the difficulty in managing such a sprawling ensemble. "It was almost sixteen people or more, so there was no way possible for that number of people to be touring around the country," she said. "But there were a few select gigs. There was one in Cincinnati that didn't go so well, we did one in upstate New York in a blizzard, and then we did a radio show for WNEW at Avery Fisher Hall with a huge ensemble."

Randy recalled the ill-fated White Elephant gig in Cincinnati: "Mike Mainieri found an old hippie-looking bus with flowers painted all over it that he was going to drive to this gig in Ohio with a bunch of the band. Me and Jon Faddis bagged that and went to the airport and got a flight to Cincinnati. Ronnie Cuber showed up at the meeting point, but without his baritone sax, thinking he could pick one up in town when he got out there. So, Frank Vicari snapped, 'Sure Ronnie, we'll just go out to the baritone fields and pick one for you.'"

Through her White Elephant associations, Martin began working with individual musicians on doing contracts and other kinds of clerical work for them. "I realized that many of them needed help to do things that they weren't good at or didn't feel like doing, secretarial things. I saw that there was a need for somebody to help these people out because business was not their thing. So, I figured, 'OK, I can type up American Federation of Musician contracts and all of that stuff.' So that's how I started with the service bureau: Whatever you need, call me."

She became a contractor and intermediary between artists and producers or labels.

Through her associations with so many musicians from those White Elephant days, Martin eventually got into artist management. She ended up managing the group Steps (Michael Brecker, Mike Mainieri, Don Grolnick, Eddie Gomez, and Steve Gadd) in the late 1970s, doing two tours of Japan with them and executive producing their 1981 live album, *Smokin' in the Pit*, recorded at Tokyo's Pit Inn.

In 1972, Mainieri would interest producer Tommy Lipuma in putting out a double-LP set of studio recordings of White Elephant from 1969 to 1972 that featured Michael Brecker on tenor sax. It was originally released on the Just Sunshine Records label, owned and operated by concert promoter Michael Lang of Woodstock fame. "Michael Lang used to come down and see the band when we played at Joyous Lake in Woodstock," he recalled. "He loved the band."

As Mainieri wrote in the liner notes to his two-CD set reissue of *White Elephant*, which he reissued in 1995 on his own NYC Records label: "The music embodied in these volumes is a collection of recordings from rehearsals, jam session and record dates that took place at various studios in New York City, usually beginning around 10 or 11 at night and continuing until the early morning hours. They were an opportunity to exchange musical, philosophical and political concepts, and a place to hang out, get high, cool out from a day of recording sessions or gather after nightly gigs. For many of us, it became an Oasis in the middle of the City. Some nights only a few stragglers would arrive, but there were many nights 20 or 30 would play, sing and dance until we shook the '50s out of our skins. The first jams initially began in 1965 with a small circle of members from the Jeremy Steig group, The Satyrs. By 1969, it gradually grew into what became a 'tribal experience.' Our wives, husbands, friends, lovers and children were as important to the experience as the music itself. After all, it was the '60s."

Michael is captured on three tracks from the sprawling double-LP self-titled debut from White Elephant. He can be heard dipping into his gutsy King Curtis bag on the brass-fueled funk-rocker "Animal Fat," which carries the health-conscious refrain: *Animal fat ain't where it's all/ you got to chew the vegetable/bring it on back to the grape*. Fronted by raw-throated vocalist Ann E. Sutton and driven by Tony Levin's fuzz bass lines, this funky vehicle grooves hard but only hints at the harmonic extrapolation that would later become a part of Michael's arsenal. Elsewhere on *White Elephant*, he plays an expressive tenor solo on a gospel-tinged rendition of "Auld Lang Syne" (the album's first single, featuring Nick Holmes's soulful vocals), and he stretches on the blistering funk section of the suite-like title track. A marathon twelve-minute opus composed and arranged by Mainieri, "White Elephant" opens with a lush a cappella horn arrangement that segues to a romantic waltz section highlighted by Randy's lyrical trumpet solo. The piece then shifts gears to a driving funk-rock section fueled by Donald MacDonald's solid backbeat, Levin's grinding bass ostinato, David Spinozza's funky rhythm guitar playing, and Paul Metzke's stinging, bluesy guitar licks. This opens the door for Michael to flex his abundant chops, and he does precisely that over the course of an epic three-minute solo that travels from earthy King Curtis honking to Trane-inspired double-timing to Pharoah Sanders-esque multiphonics screaming; a noteworthy early showcase for the twenty-one-year-old Michael Brecker.

By the time of the original vinyl release of *White Elephant* on May 1, 1972, Dreams had already disbanded. Mainieri would head to Woodstock, where he formed the fusion group L'Image with bassist Tony Levin, drummer Steve Gadd, and keyboardist Warren Bernhardt. Mike and Randy had already been playing in pianist-composer Hal Galper's wildly adventurous jazz sextet, almost in reaction to the more blatantly commercial path music that Dreams had been pressured into taking on their second Columbia Records release.

Galper's relationship with Randy Brecker went back before *Score*, the trumpeter's 1969 solo debut that Galper had played on and contributed tunes to. As he recalled, "I had been working with Randy in a quartet at a club uptown called La Intrigue, and he had mentioned that his younger brother, who was still at Indiana University, was coming to New York. He said, 'If you think I can play, wait till you hear him.' Of course, Michael played on *Score*, and it's amazing how mature and powerful his playing was at that young age. He was only nineteen at the time! I later brought both Michael and Randy into my group, and we recorded two albums for Mainstream Records. And Michael was just unbelievable on both of them. We were playing very complex music with double rhythm sections and guitar, and Michael was just killing it. His time and his tone were so together that it was frightening."

The two Mainstream albums—1971's *Guerilla Band* (apt title for a group of jazz marauders who took no prisoners) and 1972's *Wild Bird*—were both heavily influenced by Miles Davis's landmark 1970 recording, *Bitches Brew*, which opened the fusion floodgates for a generation of young players. And though Galper's audacious experiments garnered far less attention than Miles Davis's game-changing explorations, they were no less prized among jazz musicians and aficionados who didn't shy away from electronics and the power of rock music at the time. Regarded today as twin gems of the era that fell between the cracks of history, *Guerilla Band* and *Wild Bird* represent a fascinating interim phase for both Michael and Randy between Dreams and The Brecker Brothers.

The kinetic opener from *Guerilla Band*, "Call," features a rare recorded performance of Michael on soprano sax while Randy blows aggressive trumpet licks through an Echoplex and wah-wah pedal while adding sonic tweakage via his Condor box, a strange electrical contraption made by the Hammond company that created a kind of spacey underwater sound (its limited range of sonic options caused Randy to fairly quickly discard this primitive bit of technology). Michael unleashes with pent-up intensity on tenor sax on Galper's rhythmically intricate "Figure Eight," which has the leader playing his electric piano through a Hammond Leslie speaker to odd effect. The brothers team brilliantly on the front line for Galper's ambitious arrangement of Jimmy Van Heusen's "Welcome to My Dream," playing the haunting melody in long, slow tones over a churning, African-flavored 12/8 groove fueled by the dual drumming tandem of Steven Haas and Don Alias (Alias had played drums and congas on Miles's sprawling *Bitches Brew* sessions). Randy delivers his most potent solo over the funk-jazz groove of "Point of View," which also has Mike wailing with abandon on tenor in signature Breckerian fashion. And the brothers dig into Galper's irrepressible swinger "Black Night" with gusto.

Galper and company continued their momentum on the exploratory *Wild Bird*, released on Mainstream in January 1972. Once again going with a dual drumming tandem (this time Bill Goodwin and Billy Hart) and relying on the edgy rock lines and wah-wah-laced rhythm guitar work of former Dreams' member Bob Mann, Galper leads the group through a three-part "Trilogy" that is teeming with wah-wah-infused trumpet solos from Randy and cathartic abandon from Michael on tenor. The coup de grâce for Michael on *Wild Bird* is his unrelentingly ferocious playing on the grungy, heavy-duty funk-rock closer "Change Up," a kind of throwback to Michael's Indiana days when Randy Sandke's septet concluded their lengthy set at the 1968 Notre Dame Collegiate Jazz Festival with a taste of The Doors' "Light My Fire."

By late 1972, Randy returned to Horace Silver's band and brought brother Michael with him. Together they recorded *In Pursuit of the 27th Man* at Van Gelder Studio in November of that year, joined by Bob Cranshaw on bass and Mickey Roker on drums. Following that mid-March 1973 Blue Note release, former Dreams bassist Will Lee and drummer Alvin Queen were brought in to tour behind *In Pursuit of the 27th Man*. Said a twenty-four-year-old Michael to Herb Nolan for a 1973 *Downbeat* story about playing in Silver's quintet: "Horace is the first established jazz gig I've done. With Horace, most of my energy is put into soloing and practicing things and working ideas out on the stand while I'm playing. It's really a good chance to get my shit together. This is the first time I've had a gig where I play every night and I play a lot—I get to stretch out.

"I see playing with Horace as kind of a school and I feel like a beginner in a lot of ways, but for me it's a good way to get a little maturity," he continued. "With Horace, all the tunes are different and they require different feelings. Like some R&B type tunes we do, there is a certain kind of tone and sound I hear. Then we'll play another kind of thing and I'll hear something completely different. Playing with Horace is a new experience. I enjoy it. I find it particularly demanding to play things that fit the feelings of the tunes. His tunes, to me, have a distinctive sound and I try to play things that don't sound like somebody else. I don't mind sounding like other people; that's just a way to grow. If I sound like Trane on a certain thing, or if I sound like Trane all night— screw it! That's just what I hear and I just let it come out."

In a TV interview with Lorne Frohman for Canada's *Distinguished Artists* talk show, Michael explained how he once got schooled on the bandstand by jazz elder Silver: "It was my first night on the gig with Horace, and we were playing 'Song for My Father,' which was his big hit and the song that he was identified with at the time. People in the audience always used to call out for it, and it happened to be kind of a tenor extravaganza. The tenor solo was always the last solo on that tune, and that was kind of the big climax of the song. So, on this night, I started playing my solo on 'Song for My Father,' and I had played for a while and thought that I was doing a great job. And Horace turned around to me and at the top of his lungs yelled, 'Gone!' And I thought he was saying, 'Go on!' I didn't know that 'gone' was kind of be-bop lingo for 'stop.' You know, 'You've said it, you've had enough, now stop!' But because I thought he said, 'Go on,' I thought he was enjoying what I was playing, so I beared [*sic*] down even harder.

"After another minute and half or two minutes of me soloing, he yelled, now frustrated, and said, 'Gone!' And I'm thinking, 'Great! Fantastic! I'm going to go on.' Eventually, I ended my solo probably after ten or fifteen minutes. Horace came up to me after the show, and he said, 'When I say gone, that means stop!' And that was the first inkling I had of editing myself to affect a better presentation, thanks to Horace. He was a very good teacher and a great band leader. On the one hand, he gave us an enormous amount of freedom, but he also knew how to put on a good show. So, I learned a lot in that environment and try to hold on to some of that to this day."

By 1974, Mike and Randy were reunited with their former Dreams bandmate Billy Cobham. Only this time, the drummer-composer was running the show, and Mike and Randy were the hired hands, along with trombonist Garnett Brown, former Dreams guitarist John Abercrombie, keyboardist George Duke, percussionist Lee Pastora, and bassist John B. Williams (Billy and Randy's former bandmate in the Horace Silver quintet). Cobham had already done his first solo album, the fusion classic *Spectrum* (released on October 1, 1973), while he was still a member of the Mahavishnu Orchestra. But by the beginning of 1974, he was on his own. "I thought I was going to be in Mahavishnu for one more year," Cobham said in an interview at the New York Blue Note in 2019 during his week-long engagement there with Randy Brecker for his Crosswinds Revisited Project. "And like how Horace didn't give us much notice before breaking up his quintet when he did, John McLaughlin did the same thing. At first, he told me, 'I just want to change the band, but I'd like you to stay on.' But then all of a sudden, we were all gone."

The original Mahavishnu Orchestra with McLaughlin, Cobham, Jan Hammer, Jerry Goodman, and Rick Laird played its last gig on December 30, 1973, at Detroit's Masonic Temple Auditorium. "And then . . . poof! It was over," said Cobham. "I felt like I had a marriage when I started on the road with Mahavishnu Orchestra, and then all of a sudden, I got divorced. And I had no idea what I was gonna do."

Cobham rebounded nicely with *Crossroads*, which was recorded in January 1974 at Jimi Hendrix's former home base in the heart of Greenwich Village, Electric Lady Studios. One of Michael's standout solos on that record comes on the funky "The Pleasant Pheasant," a showcase replete with signature note-bending and altissimo blowing and featuring the kind of bracing chemistry between him, Randy on trumpet, and Garnett Brown on trombone that recalled the brothers' impeccably tight front-line work with Barry Rogers in Dreams, a precursor of what would later become known as 'The Brecker Brothers sound.'"

Michael also delivers a monumental solo on the atmospheric ballad "Heather," which Cobham fondly recalled: "There was a day when I needed to have Michael come in to the studio to play on a composition of mine called 'Heather,' and he was late. When he finally arrived for the session, he was a bit stressed, so I said to him, 'Please just listen to this and play what you hear and feel from the heart.' I said this because I have always known Mike to be a very sensitive person who is always looking inside himself to understand who he is and how to project this person through the music. Well, the track is running, and he plays what to me was the best solo I had heard him play up to that point that we had worked together. It was a classic Michael Brecker solo. I was extremely happy with it and wanted to just stop there, but Michael always thought that it could be better. So, we tried it maybe three or four more times before I had to put my foot down and say, 'No mas!' He already had it nailed on the first take."

*Crosswinds*, released in April 1974, closes with the ultra-funky "Crosswind," which quickly became a cover staple for local fusion bands all over the country that summer. Guitarist John Abercrombie turns in a mind-blowing solo here to rival Tommy Bolin's (of Deep Purple fame) scintillating solo on "Stratus" from Cobham's *Spectrum*. Cobham's follow-up, *Total Eclipse*, released in December of that year, again showcased the leader's muscular drumming, the tight horn play between the Brecker brothers and trombonist Glenn Ferris, and the rampaging, distortion-laced electric guitar solos of Abercrombie. Recorded at Electric Lady Studios, Cobham's third album as a leader features a rare soprano sax solo by Mike on the title track and showcases him in full-on King Curtis mode on the swaggering, Brecker Brothers-ish funk of "Moon Germs," while his playing on the driving "Sea of Tranquility" is more in a Joe Hen-Trane bag. This potent band was documented on the live *Shabazz*, recorded during the summer of '74 at the Montreux Jazz Festival in Switzerland and at London's Rainbow Theatre. Released in June 1975, it features some audacious wah-wah trumpet playing by

Randy on the title track while Michael's intense tenor solo on an adrenalized "Taurian Matador" (a tune from *Spectrum*) is a show stopper.

By January 1975, guitarist John Scofield would replace Abercrombie in the band for the studio recording of *A Funky Thide of Sings*. As he recalled, "It was a big thing for me to get hired by Billy because it allowed me to move to New York City. So, I got a sublet in town, and when I went to the first rehearsal, Mike and Randy were there. I was already a fan of theirs because I had Randy's first record, *Score*, which Mike was killing on. And I had also listened to those really great Hal Galper records that they were on. I had heard Dreams on record, though never live, but I had seen Mike and Randy with Horace Silver at the Jazz Workshop in Boston when I was a Berklee student. I also saw them with Billy Cobham band at Paul's Mall in Boston. So, I was just thrilled to join the band. I idolized those guys. Their jazz playing was an extension of modern jazz. And as funky as Mike was, he was also this super-comprehensive jazz stylist. So, I was a total Mike fan when I joined Billy's band."

Though their time together in Billy Cobham's band lasted only a couple of months, Scofield and the Breckers got to hang out, play some gigs together, and record a few tracks on the drummer's 1975 album, *A Funky Thide of Sings*. As Scofield recalled, "Mike and Randy ended up leaving Billy's band shortly after I had joined. But during those couple of months, I got to hang with them extensively. As people, they were really nice to me because they saw me as this jazz kid who was just picking their brains all the time about what they were doing—how they were playing all those great lines and what they were into. I had been a protégé of Gary Burton and Steve Swallow at Berklee, but Mike and Randy's thing was very different, like a real New York thing. And Mike really became a friend and mentor to me during that time."

Mike and Randy's contributions to Cobham's *A Funky Thide of Sings* overlapped with the recording of their Arista Records debut, *The Brecker Brothers*. And as Scofield pointed out, they did both while maintaining a busy schedule as first-call session players. "They were the number one studio musicians in New York, so they were already making dates with rock stars like Billy Joel, Lou Reed, Todd Rundgren, and Bruce Springsteen. Plus, they were also doing a lot of jingles at the same time, so they were super-busy guys. In fact, I remember one time in Cobham's band we had a gig in Columbus, Ohio, and the next night was in Chicago. Mike and Randy split after the Columbus gig and went back to

New York, and they missed the sound check the next day in Chicago but showed up in time for the gig. And I was like, 'Where were you guys?' And they said, 'Well, we didn't tell Billy, but we had a big-paying national jingle that would mean residuals for years. So, we took the first flight out after the gig last night, made the session in New York, then flew directly to Chicago. And we knew we were gonna miss the sound check, but here we are for the gig.' They were doing stuff like that a lot. Essentially, they didn't want to tour because the jingle scene in New York was so incredibly lucrative."

Although Michael's presence is less prevalent on *A Funky Thide of Sings* than on previous Cobham outings, due to the fact that he and Randy play on just half the album, he does deliver burly, urgent tenor solos on the driving fuzoid title track and the mellow "Thinking of You," a danceable track that reflected the emerging disco craze. "We were not on that whole record because I guess we had left the band halfway through to focus on The Brecker Brothers' album," recalled Randy. "So, Billy finished his recording with Walt Fowler on trumpet and Larry Schneider on tenor sax."

*A Funky Thide of Sings* is perhaps most memorable for showcasing Randy Brecker's classic "Some Skunk Funk," a complex and punchy work that would also appear that year on the Brecker Brothers' self-titled Arista Records debut. And although Cobham's version of "Some Skunk Funk" was recorded first (January 1975), *A Funky Thide of Sings* was released later (November 11, 1975) than *The Brecker Brothers* (September 1975). Michael's extended tenor solo on the Cobham version of "Some Skunk Funk," a song that captured all the kinetic energy and tension of a packed rush-hour A-train ride hurtling uptown, is breathtaking. And his solo on *The Brecker Brothers* version of that anthemic number is etched in the collective consciousness of a generation of saxophonists.

Said Randy of that classic composition, which continues to be covered by bands today, "Herbie Hancock's tune 'Blind Man, Blind Man,' the first tune on his second Blue Note album [*My Point of View*, 1963] was a big influence on me writing 'Some Skunk Funk.' I wanted a break like Herbie's tune has, so the break in my tune started out with this in mind. Then I warped it out so it doesn't really sound too much like 'Bind Man, Blind Man.' But that was the inspiration behind it."

With Dreams, Horace Silver, and the Billy Cobham band in the rearview mirror, Michael and Randy began to focus on their own brotherly collaboration. Bigger things were just ahead for the two talented siblings.

# SNEAKIN' UP BEHIND YOU

On August 1, 1974, Mike and Randy began a week of rehearsals in New York with Yoko Ono in preparation for her first tour of Japan. Six concerts had been booked by the eccentric Japanese rock star Yuya Uchida for the much-hyped Plastic Ono Super Band Tour, which kicked off in Karyama and continued on through Osaka, Nagoya, Tokyo, and Hiroshima. Rounding out the band were keyboardist Don Grolnick, bassist Andy Muson, guitarist Steve Kahn, and the drumming tandem of Rick Marotta and Steve Gadd. Guitarist David Spinozza, who coproduced Ono's aborted 1974 album, *A Story* (eventually released in 1992 as part of the six-CD set *Onobox*), and had appeared on John Lennon's *Mind Games* and Yoko's *Feeling the Space* the year before, was supposed to make that highly anticipated tour of Japan and serve as musical director for the group. But Yoko had a last-minute change of plans.

"This was during the period when John had taken up with May Pang," recalled Randy, referring to the personal assistant and production coordinator for both Lennon and Ono, who were in the midst of an eighteen-month separation. "Meanwhile, Yoko hooked up with Spinozza, who did her charts and then did her, too. But whenever she would start to sing, he would howl like a dog. And so, she got pissed off one day and fired him. Khan came in as a last-minute replacement."

Khan remembers that Plastic Ono Super Band Tour as a total disaster. "It was an absurd tour. We were all really close friends, but we were playing horrible music, really awful. We got to open the concert with a couple of instrumentals—a tune of mine and one of Grolnick's. Then she would come out, and it all dissolved pretty quickly."

As Randy recalled, "We'd follow the charts for like a minute, then spent the rest of the gig making up funny, sarcastic parts and noises behind her. It was hard for the whole band to keep our composure since everyone started doing it. It was hilarious, but she didn't know the difference anyway."

One night Mike decided to mock one of Ono's concert rituals—throwing flowers into the audience—by striding to the front of the stage, lighting his cigarette with a match, and throwing the match into the audience. "That's how the gigs went," laughed Randy.

It was on the long flight back to New York from Japan that Randy shared with Khan that he was ready to make his next career move. "He was saying that he had all these tunes that weren't right for Dreams and that he wanted to make a record. And that was really the beginning of what became The Brecker Brothers band."

As Randy recalled, "I had an idea to start writing some new stuff for three horns—myself, Mike, and instead of Barry Rogers I wanted to use Dave Sanborn, who I had never played with professionally but had met at Stan Kenton Music Camp when we were both fifteen. And I got Don Grolnick and Will Lee, both from Dreams. We had been hanging out almost every night and we just saw things eye to eye musically. They were great jazz players, too, but they also had that one foot in R&B stuff as well. So that was the core of the band."

At roughly the same time that Randy Brecker was playing with Blood, Sweat & Tears, recording 1967's *Child Is Father to the Man* and then touring later that year with the Horace Silver Quintet, his former Stan Kenton Band Camp mate Sanborn was gigging with the Paul Butterfield Blues Band, recording 1967's *The Resurrection of Pigboy Crenshaw* and appearing at the 1967 Monterey Pop Festival on the same bill as The Who, The Byrds, The Animals, Big Brother & The Holding Company, and Jimi Hendrix.

They started rehearsing together at Grolnick's fourth-floor walk-up in the same Greenwich Village building where bassist Lee and session drummer Chris Parker also resided. As Parker recalled, "In the early '70s, I moved into 70 Carmine Street at the suggestion of Will Lee, who I had met playing a gig in Woodstock. When I moved into the building, Will and Grolnick were already there, and we pretty soon started jamming together. We actually had a group together called the Carmine Street Band, which was me, Will, Don, and Steve Khan. We were doing gigs at Mikell's on the Upper West Side, and we'd rehearse at Don's place."

When Sanborn started coming around, suddenly it was three horns and rhythm section crammed into Grolnick's place. "It was a very small apartment," Parker recalled. "We were literally elbow to elbow in that place. We'd rehearse during the day at Don's and then cross paths in the evenings at Mikell's, where I was playing with Stuff. And all those guys would sit in from time to time. So, picture Stuff with The Brecker Brothers horn section!"

As Randy explained, "Once or twice a week we'd get together and just work on new stuff we were writing—mostly me, Grolnick, and Khan. The rest of the guys, including Mike, hadn't started to write yet. And, so, it was my idea to take my tunes and do a record with that instrumentation and call it *Randy Brecker* or something . . . I hadn't thought of a title yet. But I had nine charts, including 'Some Skunk Funk' and 'Sponge' and all those things. So that was the idea. I was going to record my stuff, Grolnick was going to do a record of his stuff, using similar personnel, and Khan was writing tunes along similar lines that featured the horn section that he also wanted to record."

Added Parker, "Randy brought in all the stuff that he was writing at the time, including a lot of what ended up on that first Brecker Brothers album. His music was really difficult. There was a lot of intricate stuff going on in his tunes, and it was a big challenge for me."

Just as Randy was preparing to demo his new material, he got a call from a Steve Backer, A&R man at the newly formed Arista label headed by Clive Davis, who had previously signed Dreams to Columbia Records. As Randy recalled, "Steve said, 'Clive's heard about this music, and we know everybody in the band, and I'm sure it's great. Clive wants to sign you, but he wants to call it The Brecker Brothers.' And at first, I protested, for about a week. I said, 'Man, I've been really planning this for a long time, I wrote all the music, and I want to do it under my name.' But Clive being Clive knew what he wanted. And it was a good opportunity, so . . ."

A week later, Randy relented. "I called Backer and told him, 'OK, call it the Brecker Brothers. But it's going to look funny because Sanborn is on the front line. I suppose we could say he's a long-lost cousin or something, but he's definitely not a brother.'"

With Randy finally agreeing to call the band The Brecker Brothers, they went into the studio on January 1, 1975, and recorded everything for their first album. "So, all my tunes are down, and it all sounds great," he recalled. "Then Clive, who had come to rehearsals a couple of times, called me up to his office for another meeting. Mike wasn't really involved as any kind of a coleader of the band; he was just concerned with practicing and hadn't really thought about a solo career at that point. So, it was just me and Clive at this meeting. And he says to me, 'These tunes are great! I love everything! But you need a single.' And once again, I protested. But Clive had to have his way. He basically said he wasn't going to release it or put any money behind it unless we did a single. So, I went back to the rehearsal place and told the guys."

Putting their heads together, Randy and Mike quickly reverted back to their Dreams instincts and jammed up a tight, punchy horn line on the spot alongside Sanborn while keyboardist Grolnick came up with an idea on Fender Rhodes, and Lee contributed the sly vocals and catchy refrain to what became The Brecker Brothers' first single, "Sneakin' Up Behind You."

"Everybody contributed a little idea, and we jammed it up in one session," said Randy. "It took maybe three or four hours, and we went in and recorded it a day or two later. And Clive loved it, thankfully."

With the catchy, disco-flavored single "Sneakin' Up Behind You" cracking the Hot 100 chart, *The Brecker Bros.* became a crossover hit album in 1975. "That single got up to number two and stayed up on the charts for a long while," Randy recalled, "and that pushed the record up the pop charts. It got up into the 50s in the Top 200. Me and Grolnick would get *Billboard* and look at the charts and go, 'Holy shit!' Meanwhile, we never really thought of it as an opportunity to get a foothold in the pop business because we were all busy doing studio work, and this was kind of a hobby for us. I just figured, 'It'll sell just five thousand records, but at least I'll get my writing out there.' The next thing you know, Clive's trying to get us on the road all the time to promote the album. But we were just too busy to do that. And it was not only me . . . everybody was busy in the studios, doing really well and working every day. Clive tried his best. He could lean on me as much as he wanted, but I couldn't talk the other guys into going out on the road. We did tour some, but he could never get us on the road as much as he wanted us to. It just didn't make sense financially."

Guitarist Steve Khan, son of famed songwriter and lyricist Sammy Cahn, a frequent songwriting partner of Jules Styne and Jimmy Van

Photo for back cover of The Brecker Brothers' 1975 self-titled debut album on
Arista Records *(Photo courtesy John Paul Endress Photography)*

Heusen, was a ubiquitous figure on that lucrative Manhattan studio
scene, along with Mike and Randy. As he explained, "When I moved
here from Los Angeles in 1970, I never knew there was such a thing as a
jingle scene. At the time, I just had one goal in mind. My original dream
was to be the next Wes Montgomery. I thought I'd come to New York,
there'd be a Jimmy Smith–type organ trio on every block, I'd get myself
in one of them, and I'd learn how to play. That was what I thought

was going to happen. And of course, that's not what happened. Because fusion happened, and jingles started happening."

Khan was introduced to the jingle scene by vibraphonist David Friedman, one of two people he knew in town when he arrived on the scene. "David took me down to the Village Vanguard on a Monday night to see the Thad Jones/Mel Lewis band, and then the next day he says, 'Come on, I've got a couple of jingles today. I want you to see this.' So, I tagged along. We go to some little jingle studio, and I walk in, and there is Mel Lewis on drums, Thad Jones on trumpet . . . and I'm like in a complete state of shock. Like, this doesn't compute! I just saw these guys playing this brilliant big band jazz at the Vanguard the night before. What are they doing there playing for a toothpaste commercial? I didn't understand, and I said, 'David, what the fuck is this?' And he says, 'Everybody does this. Do you think you can support yourself playing at the Vanguard?' And he's shaking his head at me. I go in another room, and there's Chico Hamilton producing a jingle. And I'm like, 'How could this be?'

"But Randy and Mike were doing this stuff, too," Khan continued. "So was Will Lee, who had an especially lucrative situation because he could sing on those jingles. That's where the real money was. Randy and Will used to say, 'Well, I'm going out with The Brecker Brothers, and I'm losing a fortune because I'm missing all these jingles.' So, you have this conflict of, 'Hey, I'm going out here with the band, which I love, and I'm coming home with $200. Meanwhile, I pissed away twenty grand worth of jingles.' That was a very real concern for guys like Randy and Will."

Khan eventually fell into the jingle scene the way many other musicians did. "I was playing in a club, playing the music I love to play—jazz. And some guy came up to me and said, 'Hey, kid, are you in the union? Can you read? Can you be at the studio tomorrow at ten o'clock? I think you'd be great for this thing.' And I'd go and do the jingle, and they'd like me. And then the phone wouldn't stop ringing."

Although the music might not have been on the highest level, Khan said the most enjoyable part of the jingle scene was the camaraderie he felt with the other musicians going from session to session. "It was like high school for grownups, where if you looked at your daily schedule you'd say, 'OK, I have social studies at 9 a.m., then I have English class at 10 a.m.,' and there's a different group of people in each class, some of whom might be great friends. It was that same way with the jingle scene: 'I'm working at 9 a.m. in this studio, I'm doing a 10 a.m. session in this place.' And you see five, six, seven, eight musicians from session to session, some of whom you really like and enjoy playing with. So, you're constantly mingling with some fantastic musicians for an hour, then you go on to the next session and meet other musicians who are all great players and fun to be around. And for Mike, there were certain guys in the horn section he'd love to see, whether it was Jon Faddis or Lew Soloff, Joe Farrell, Howard Johnson, or whoever . . . all wonderful people and great players. So, you go from one thing to another throughout the day. And if you see one person you really like along the way, that part of it is really great."

At the height of this lucrative jingle period, Khan also recruited the brothers for his early '70s band Future Shock, with included their former Dreams keyboardist Don Grolnick along with bassist John Miller and drummer Bruce Ditmas. "We played some Future Shock gigs together at the Bitter End and Folk City on their jazz fusion nights," Khan recalled. "We made a demo together in November of 1972, which I recently resurrected. It's remarkable listening to those things again some forty years later. And what really stands out is how Mike and Randy's playing really elevated the band. They made kind of derivative and lousy music sound great somehow."

(The same combination of Mike and Randy with Grolnick, Khan, and Gadd would later emerge as the second incarnation of The Brecker Brothers band, documented on *Back to Back*, 1976.)

While "Sneakin' Up Behind You" was The Brecker Brothers' one commercial concession to Clive Davis, the rest of the material on their 1975 self-titled debut was wildly ambitious and uncompromising. Randy's complex, suite-like "A Creature of Many Faces" gets a kick from Bob Mann's stinging, rock-edged guitar work while his "Twilight" shifts back and forth from up-tempo Latin jam to eerie Mahavishnu-esque chromaticism, with Mann spiking the proceedings with some urgent Jeff Beckian six-string work. The strongest and most enduring works here are "Sponge," the fusion anthem "Some Skunk Funk," highlighted by Randy's wild wah-wah-inflected trumpet work (which he had already showcased in Dreams) and a ripping tenor solo from Michael, and the clavinet-fueled "Rocks," featuring some dizzying, rapid-fire exchanging of eights between Michael and Sanborn. Randy's atmospheric ballad "Levitate" provides a respite from all the pyrotechnics while also showcasing his more lyrical side. Randy's lone vocal number, "Oh My Stars," is a kind of giddy, lighthearted indulgence that bears the signature tight, forceful three-horn Brecker Brothers front line. An overlooked gem in Brecker Brothers lore from this debut album is the burning closer, "D.B.B.," which sounds like a highly disciplined big band chart featuring virtuosic solos from both Mike and Randy.

The slick drumming heard throughout their acclaimed debut album was done by Harvey Mason rather than Chris Parker. As Randy explained, "I had met Harvey at a jam session we played together in Boston when I was in town with Horace Silver," he recalled. "And then later when I heard him playing with Herbie Hancock's Headhunters, I thought, 'Yeah, we gotta use Harvey on this session.' So, he ended up doing the first Brecker Brothers record, as did Ralph McDonald." (Parker did play drums on the album's single, "Sneakin' Up Behind You.")

After joining Mike and Randy on the front line of The Brecker Brothers, Sanborn felt an immediate connection with his horn brethren. "At a certain point, you can't really explain chemistry," he said. "We just seemed to be, from the very beginning, on the same wavelength. We all listened to each other very intently, not that every horn section doesn't do that, but I think that what we shared that was special was an ability to catch each other's nuances—the way you shape a note, the way you attack a note, the phrasing. It just seemed to be natural. Of course, Mike and Randy had been playing all their lives together and had their own kind of telepathy going, but, somehow, I just kind of fit into that and balanced it out in terms of the sound. We filled out each other's sound. I tended to have a little bit more edge to my sound, but Mike gave it substance and body, and he really took the lead with articulation. It was a pretty amazing fit."

Added Khan, "It's in the phrasing, it's just so ridiculously tight. You hear that kind of tight staccato phrasing in Latin music, with the short notes. Mike and Randy created this style of playing together that really does involve the brother thing, where the two of them just have something where they know what to. And Sanborn just immediately got it, so they phrase beautifully together. Barry Rogers already had that kind of phrasing with Mike and Randy in Dreams, so when you put the four of them together, it's really magical [documented on percussionist Ralph MacDonald's 1978 album, The Path]. When you can all just do something together without having to talk about it, that's magic. And it's remarkable to be around that. It's this level of excellence and precision that you don't find everywhere. And I think when you've been around that, it's really hard to let that go and get back to something looser, which I think Mike wanted to have—this way of playing that's a little more elastic than precision."

Along the way, Sanborn learned an important lesson on The Brecker Brothers bandstand. "I made the mistake one time of letting Mike take the first solo on a tune," he recalled. "And I never made that mistake again. Because he'd finish playing, and it was like I stepped up to the mic, and the stage had been napalmed. You know, there's one sad little B flat lying in the corner that I picked up. You know what I mean? How the fuck do you follow that?"

Khan believes that Sanborn actually rubbed off on Mike in a positive way when they played together on The Brecker Brothers front line. "Mike and Sanborn used to drive each other crazy with their playing," he said. "Mike had everything Sanborn would give his soul to have in terms of sheer facility, and yet Mike would look at Sanborn and say, 'This guy plays two fucking notes, and they're not only equal to the ten thousand I just played, they're actually touching people in a way that is ridiculous.' And this is before Sanborn became the most imitated alto saxophonist maybe forever. But those two, Mike and Sanborn, worked so hard, apart from each other—practicing, practicing, practicing—and they ended up having a profound influence on each other. It may have taken a long time for Mike to grasp onto this more minimalist approach, but playing next to Dave all that time, it began to sink in and became really important to him."

Sanborn added that the difference between the Paul Butterfield Blues Band horn section that he came up with in the '60s and The Brecker Brothers horn section he joined in the '70s was like night and day. "Mike and Randy were jazz musicians more than the guys in the Butterfield Band were. Of course, Gene Dinwiddie, the tenor sax player from the Butterfield Band, certainly came from a jazz sensibility. But the nature of the music with the Breckers was far more complex harmonically, melodically, and rhythmically, so it gave us a chance to really explore a wide range of dynamics. And we could navigate that with a kind of ease because we had such a strong chemistry with each other.

"We just complemented each other so well, and we did so in a way that made that music seem effortless, though it certainly wasn't," he continued. "I mean, you listen to tunes like 'Some Skunk Funk' and 'Sponge' and 'Rocks' . . . these are extremely challenging charts. And I was reminded of that within the last year or so when I played a project of Randy's with the NDR Orchestra [*Rocks*, 2019]. It was The Brecker Brothers' music arranged for big band. During rehearsal I was like, 'Holy fuck! This shit is really hard!' At first, I said, 'There's no way on earth that I can play this music again.' And it really took me a minute to get it under my fingers. So, it impressed on me even more what a great period of my life that was to have the opportunity and good luck to play with those guys as long as I did. I went on to do my own stuff, but I always had a great affection for that music and do to this day."

In rapid succession, after The Brecker Brothers' self-titled debut in January 1975, that same simpatico crew of Michael, Randy, Sanborn, Grolnick, Parker, Lee, and Khan appeared in the studio in February to record David Sanborn's debut, *Taking Off*, for Warner Bros. In April, they recorded together again on Esther Phillips's *What a Diff'rence a Day Makes*, which features Michael bearing down in full-on King Curtis mode on the title track, a Dinah Washington signature, and on the gritty Lu Emerson funk tune "Hurtin' House." Phillips's disco version of Grover Washington's instrumental funk-jazz hit from earlier that year, "Mr. Magic," is replete with tight, swaggering, quintessentially Becker Brothers-ish horn lines.

Following that session for Phillips, the same copacetic crew went back into the studio to record Felix Cavaliere's *Destiny* for Warner Bros. In May, Mike went into Van Gelder Studio along with Randy, Sanborn, Barry Rogers, and Gadd to record Don Sebesky's *The Rape of El Morro* for CTI, which included a monumental, uncommonly expressive solo by Michael on the ballad "Moon Dreams."

A month after the September 1975 release of *The Brecker Bros.*, Michael appeared on the October release of Paul Simon's *Still Crazy After All These Years*, playing the memorable solo from the title track, which became a hit single for Simon later that year. As the multiple-Grammy Award-winning pop songwriter recalled of that session, "Michael did a few takes on the 'Still Crazy' solo. We put together at least two, maybe three. The distinctive first phrase was a complete thought. The second phrase comes from a second take, and the last few notes may have come from a third take. In any case, a memorable piece of improvisation from Mike."

(The cold open for the second episode of the first season of *Saturday Night Live*, airing on October 18, 1975, had Simon seated on a stool with a hand mic, singing "Still Crazy After All These Years," with the solo played not by Michael Brecker but by David Sanborn.)

Although Mike's solo on Simon's "Still Crazy After All These Years" registered deeply with the collective pop consciousness, it was his tremendous tenor solo on James Taylor's romantic ballad "Don't Let Me Be Lonely Tonight," a hit single from the singer-songwriter's 1972 album *One Man Dog* that really put him on the map. In a National Public Radio interview from 2007 reflecting on his late comrade, guitarist-composer and longtime friend Pat Metheny said of Mike's epic tenor solo on that lovely James Taylor tune, "I remember vividly hearing that solo for the first time and almost having a car accident by virtue of the fact that that was the most good notes that had ever been transmitted into everyday America's lives. I mean, this was an incredible, short, but brilliant improvisational statement. Who was that saxophone player? New guy, Michael Brecker. And I became a major fan from that point."

For The Brecker Brothers' second release, *Back to Back* (1976), Chris Parker and Steve Gadd shared drumming duties alongside the usual suspects—Mike, Randy, and Sanborn in the horn section, Grolnick on keyboards, Steve Khan on guitar, and Will Lee on bass. With an emphasis on vocals (courtesy of Luther Vandross, Patti Austin, and Lee), this sophomore outing was a more commercially minded affair than the first Brecker Brothers release and now feels somewhat dated by today's standards. That sentiment is perhaps best exemplified by the album's opener, "Keep It Steady (Brecker Bump)," which tried to cash in on a dance craze of the day, The Bump. Notwithstanding some searing solos from Sanborn and Khan, it pandered to the burgeoning disco market with cheesy background vocals, thumping bass from Lee, clavinet and synth bass funk lines by Grolnick, and a relentless disco hi-hat beat from Parker. There's even some cowbell in there!

"When we were doing the *Back to Back* album, it seemed like all the solos were going to Mike and Sanborn," recalled Khan. "And so, Randy, at a certain point, looks at all of us and says something like, 'What the fuck is going on here, man? I'm part of The Brecker Brothers, too! Where are the trumpet solos?' And Will looked at him and said kind of jokingly, 'Hey, man, you can't bump to the trump.' And, of course, that's obviously an abbreviation of trumpet, not the asshole who was in the

White House. But it was so funny because it was a play on 'the Brecker Bump.' As if to say, 'Hey, man, the trumpet's not very commercial.'"

Will's vocals on the playfully funky "If You Wanna Boogie (Forget It Baby)" are good natured and soulful, though the song is clearly dated. The danceable instrumental, "Grease Piece," driven by funky clavinet and a chorus handclaps, has both Lee and Mike playing through an envelope filter of some kind (probably a Seamoon Funk Machine pedal). Mike also unleashes on "I Love Wastin' Time with You," a funky, gospel-tinged, kind of Dr. John-ish vocal duet sung by Lee and Patti Austin.

*Back to Back* also marked the first Michael Brecker composition on record—the driving bit of funk-fusion "Night Flight," which had Mike unleashing a killer tenor solo. Khan noted that Michael was somewhat shy about sharing his tunes with the band, even though he had been locked into his "blues-a-day" initiative for a year by then. Being the younger brother of such a prolific composer as Randy may have had something to do with Michael's reluctance to write. As Randy acknowledged, "He may have felt intimidated early on because he was always . . . I guess 'insecure' is not the right word; he was just a perfectionist. And so whatever insecurities we all have were maybe just magnified a bit with him.

"We had long conversations about writing," Randy continued. "He hadn't started to write so much yet, and he thought he wasn't talented in that direction. But I was trying to explain to him that talent doesn't have that much to do with it, that it's a craft, and you just really have to spend time sitting at a keyboard and just methodically, tediously working out things. You don't wait for inspiration to hit; you just have to sit there and do the work. And I remember bringing up a Truman Capote interview where he said how much pure craft is involved in the writing process. You might make an outline, but you have to just sit there and do it. And Mike eventually took that to heart, I think, and started sitting at a keyboard. And he slowly started coming up with some nice tunes."

Randy maintains that Michael never liked his own contributions to The Brecker Brothers catalog. "He always found something that he didn't like with a tune he wrote, so we always had to kind of beg him to write. One of his first tunes was 'Night Flight' (from *Back to Back*), and by sheer coincidence he realized the first five notes of this main riff of the tune were the same as Tony Williams's 'Vashkar.' It was just subconscious or luck. So, then we had to beg him to play it. He wouldn't do that tune. He never liked his tune 'Straphangin'' either [title track of The Brecker Brothers' 1981 album]. We had to beg him to play that one as well because he thought that when it went into the kind of 'Sunny' [popular 1963 tune by Bobby Hebb] changes that it was too corny. But everyone loved that tune, so we always had to talk him into doing that one. He always found something negative in his tunes."

As Michael confessed to Lorne Frohman in a 2004 TV interview for Canada's *Distinguished Artists*: "Writing was never one of my favorite things when I first started becoming a professional musician. And the way I learned to write was out of necessity, really. I was playing in The Brecker Brothers with my brother, Randy, and we had kind of scored a hit in 1975 with our first record. And my brother had written the whole record with the exception of one tune that we all made up together. And that one particular tune became a hit ['Sneakin' Up Behind You']. And I thought that this was gonna be kind of a one-record deal, one shot, and I was just there to kind of play in the band and have fun. And all of a sudden, we were slated to record again pretty quickly. And then I felt like I needed to contribute to this thing in some way because I felt guilty that I hadn't written anything. So, I started writing in the style of my brother, Randy, which is very difficult to do because he had a very unique style of writing that's really uncopyable. He had written some unbelievably creative and interesting music. It was kind of like jazz-funk but really different from anything that had been recorded . . . different from anything I'd have ever heard.

"So, I started trying to write kind of in my brother Randy's style, and that's how I got started writing. And eventually I studied composition and struggled with it quite a bit until really the last ten years, where it's become something that I enjoy doing. Randy actually has a different technique that works for him. He kind of uses the jigsaw puzzle approach, where he'll have a great A section or five A sections that have nothing to do with each other and a bunch of other sections that could be a good bridge or a good B section or C section or chorus. And then he kind of shuffles them around, and it sometimes ends up with really startling results. And that occasionally has worked for me as well in the past. But, generally, I prefer to try and through-write something. There's less tendency for me to jump around, and I have a more consistent thought that way."

The Brecker Brothers' spring '76 tour in support of *Back to Back* took them on a whirlwind swing through the Midwest with stops in Milwaukee, Wisconsin; Saginaw, Grand Rapids, and Detroit, Michigan; Akron and Cleveland, Ohio; and Schaumburg, Illinois. Khan recalls that while most of the guys in the band at that time were doing the typical knucklehead stuff that twenty-something guys do on the road, Grolnick remained a steadying presence for the band. "Don was definitely the adult in the room," said Khan. Will Lee confirms that Grolnick's nickname among the band members was "Don Grownup."

Added Randy, "Don really helped me with keeping everybody together, calling the rehearsals, renting the cars, the stuff you needed to do. Because we couldn't really afford a tour manager. And we'd argue all the time, so Don was usually there to break things up. And if we had to rent a car, he'd usually drive. Sanborn and Mike couldn't have been less interested in the whole thing, really. Khan was cool. It was just a question of making it from gig to gig—all crammed together in a car—without going crazy."

"Don would usually drive, and sometimes Mike would leave his soprano at the hotel, and then we'd have to go back and get it," recalled Parker. Khan vividly remembers various "lost soprano" incidents on the road. "Don would always command one of the two rental cars as we went from the city to another town or to the airport. And so, periodically, Mike was always losing things. And the two things he kept losing—I guess it fits into that thing of like wanting to lose something psychologically—were his soprano sax and a flute he brought along with him for one of Randy's tunes. And so, invariably he would leave—accidentally on purpose—one of those things behind. And it could happen anywhere. We'd leave the hotel, and before we drove off, Don would say, 'OK now, everybody have everything?' And, of course, everybody's going, 'Yeah, sure.' Mike could've been asleep in the backseat or something, so he didn't speak up. And so, we're driving along, and all of a sudden, we would all hear this, 'Oh-oh!' from Mike in the backseat. And Don would roll his eyes and go, 'Big oh-oh or little oh-oh?' And Mike would go, 'Big oh-oh . . . I left my soprano at the hotel.' And Don would get so pissed. He had this saying he'd often use, 'I'm surrounded by idiots; I'm surrounded by incompetents.' And it could've applied to any one of us, but when one of us would screw up, he would break out that phrase. And we'd turn the car around, back we'd go to the hotel to retrieve Mike's soprano, always barely making the plane in time. So, Mike was either leaving his soprano back at the hotel or in the back of a cab . . . accidentally on purpose because he fucking hated the soprano."

Khan also recalled that on these lengthy road trips, Michael and Grolnick would inevitably engage in debates about who's better and why. "They would always have this thing about Trane versus Sonny. And obviously, they loved both of them, but Don would be more on the Sonny Rollins side, feeling that Sonny was more swinging than Trane; and Mike would be on the John Coltrane side, feeling that he was swinging like crazy, and it was also more spiritual. This would go on for a whole tour. Probably their whole lives they were arguing about this shit. And one of Don's great conclusions out of all these discussions was, 'I think that if you have good time, it doesn't matter what the fuck you play; it's gonna sound great.' And I think what he meant was, 'If your time is swinging, then you can be as far outside the tonality as you want. Whatever it is, you accept it because it's still swinging.' And they both agreed on that."

Khan also recalled Michael's wicked sense of humor and penchant for practical jokes on the road. "When we were in The Brecker Brothers band, Mike was fascinated by the guitar. He always wanted to ask questions about bending notes because you hear in his playing, aside from all the great saxophone influences, that he also is fascinated by mimicking the guitar. He loved Jimi Hendrix and Albert King, so there's a lot of blues guitar mannerisms in his playing. And he was able to do even better with the EWI [Electronic Wind Instrument]. But what he would do to me . . . somehow between the sound check and the gig, he'd sneak up on stage, and he'd turn the knobs on my pedals, all of them, and then we'd hit the stage and, of course, I'm not looking at him. And suddenly, the first tune starts, and I hit the first stomp box, and it explodes with all this noise, and he's sitting on my right, laughing his ass off. So as a result of that prank, I went to the stationery store and put these little dots on my pedals so even if he would mess with the settings, I could just instantly turn them back to the dots, and I'd be OK. And when I first did that, he looked at me on stage as if to say, 'Touché.' And I was like, 'I got you now, man!'"

In spite of their widespread popularity, Khan does recall at least a few Brecker Brothers concerts where the band was not so widely accepted. "Early on, we were playing huge R&B concerts for audiences of fifteen hundred people or more opposite great bands like Rufus with Chaka Khan, Graham Central Station, and the Ohio Players. And we'd always open the concerts to glazed-over stares from the audience that said, 'Who the fuck are these guys?!' I mean, we'd open up with 'Sneakin' Up Behind You,' and they'd like that. But the rest of the set it was like, 'What kind of music is that?'"

Khan recounted one unfortunate scene that happened early on in their '76 tour, at a February 18 concert at the Bijou in the Breckers' hometown, Philadelphia. "We happened to be opening for Rahsaan Roland Kirk, and I don't think he knew what the hell to make of the music we were playing. It certainly wasn't the jazz he was used to, but he should obviously have been able to hear that the guy playing the tenor saxophone in our band was really something special. But, apparently, he didn't feel that way. So, he went on a tirade on mic during his set about white musicians playing electric instruments and how that ain't jazz. And I remember he said something like, 'You know, they got bands today, they even calling themselves the Average White Band.' And, of course, the audience is uncomfortably laughing. But backstage in the upstairs dressing room, Mike and Randy's father, Bobby, is just steaming. And maybe he had a little too much to drink that night, but he was furious. And after Rahsaan's set, Bobby is waiting for Rahsaan to come up the stairs and was going to get into a fistfight with him. Luckily, Randy grabbed his father and escorted him out the door. But that's an example of how much the Brecker parents would fight for their kids. They were always super-supportive, and Bobby just went over the top that night."

As Randy recalls of that event, "Rahsaan was the headliner for this show, and everybody in his band was black, and most of the audience that came to see him was black. And here we were an all-white band playing this kind of fusion music. I was doing the talking for our band on stage, and at some point, when I was trying to introduce the band or something, I remember some guy in the audience yelling out, 'Rahsaan don't need no amplifiers!' Then when Rahsaan and his band took the stage, he made some negative, somewhat racially charged comments about us. So, Dad was mortified. He was going to go backstage and have it out with Rahsaan. I had to hold him back. We were trying to placate the situation."

By this time, drummer Chris Parker was going back and forth between playing with The Brecker Brothers and Stuff, where he held dual-drum duties with Steve Gadd. "Actually, the guys in Stuff were dogging me about, 'What are you doing playing that music?' But I was involved in The Brecker Brothers equally as much as Stuff, so they had to deal with it."

Parker eventually grew tired of the cramped quarters of his one-bedroom apartment on Carmine Street in the Village, so he moved into a more spacious loft in the Bowery at 247 Grand St. "Actually, Christine Martin found the building, so Don and I both moved in there," he recalled. "Don was on the second floor; I was on the third floor." Located above a Chinese furniture store and right across the street from the Chrystie Street basketball courts, the rent was $250 [that same space today rents for $4,000 a month]. "By late 1976 or early 1977, Don ended up selling his loft to Mike and moving to Montrose, New York," Parker continued. "I guess my future wife and I had driven poor Don bonkers with our tap dancing, drumming, and skateboarding. So, then it was Mike and me living in this building on Grand Street.

"I gave Mike a set of drums for him to play—he was an amazing drummer as well as everything else, with a heavy Elvin Jones influence—and I had my own set up on my floor. And we were playing all the time. We'd do a lot of practicing together, and I would often hear him practicing his tenor late into the night, and that would inspire me to keep practicing myself. Sometimes after jamming all night till sunrise, we would go to the corner for breakfast at a coffee shop called Moishe's. And a waitress, who had been there probably for thirty or forty years, would come to our table and say, 'Boys, take it easy on me this morning. I didn't sleep very well last night with all the drums, drums, drums!"

By then, Arista's Clive Davis had reached out to Michael on a few occasions about doing a spinoff project apart from The Brecker Brothers. "That whole six years we were with Clive, whenever there was a band meeting with me and Mike, Mike would bring up that he wanted to do a solo record," recalled Randy. "And at one of the meetings, Clive exasperatedly said, 'Well, we want you to do a solo record, Michael. Do one any time you want.' But Mike hadn't really thought through how he was going to do that. He wasn't the conceptualist yet that he would later become. Which, I think, is part of the reason he started his solo career so late. He was a perfectionist, as we all know. And it took him a while to figure out how he was gonna do it. He always wanted to do it; that's why he was never that involved in the band at first. But eventually, he started to get involved."

By the end of 1976, Mike and Randy were tapped by Frank Zappa to play four sold-out shows at New York's Palladium between Christmas and New Year's Eve. Material from those concerts was later edited into a live double album, *Zappa in New York,* released in March 1978. In March 2019, all the material from that fabled Palladium engagement was released in total on the sprawling five-CD set, *Zappa in New York: 40th Anniversary Deluxe.* Zappa encouraged individual soloists to stretch with impunity on these live performances, and the horn players responded with jazzy abandon. Michael unleashes a torrential downpour of notes in his jaw-dropping tenor solo on an epic twenty-eight-minute "Black Napkins," which also includes a bright, high-note trumpet solo from Randy and a brilliant electric violin solo from ex-Roxy Music member Eddie Jobson. On a seventeen-minute version of "The Purple Lagoon" (which also appeared on the original two-LP set), Michael delivers a pulse-quickening tenor solo and is followed, in turn, by Randy, whose eerie harmonizer effect on his trumpet pushes the envelope on electronic experimentation. The Palladium outing is also highlighted by Zappa's complex, through-composed showcase for drummer Terry Bozzio, "The Black Page #1." Bozzio would end up going on the road with The Brecker Brothers the following year.

"What I remember most about that gig is just being terrified at being able to play the parts because a lot of his music was really, really difficult," said Randy. "That's why Alan Rubin, the regular trumpeter in the *Saturday Night Live* horn section at the time, bailed after he saw the music. So, I got hired to do that Palladium gig. [Zappa appeared as a musical guest on the December 10, 1976, *SNL* show; two weeks later he played The Palladium, December 26–29.] Frank was really like a classical conductor in a hippie uniform, which was part of his comedy routine. And he was a genius at that. But the band for that *SNL* gig was first rate—Patrick O'Hearn on bass, Ronnie Cuber on bari sax, Lou Marini on sax, David Samuels on vibes, Terry Bozzio on drums—and everybody played great. That's where we met Bozzio. And what came out of that Palladium gig was *Heavy Metal Be-Bop* because Frank had some months off, and Terry was free, so we hired him to do a Brecker

David Sanborn, Mike Brecker, Randy Brecker at Ultra Sonic Studios, Long Island for WLIR Brecker Brothers broadcast, 1976 (*Photo by Steve Orlando*)

Brothers tour that culminated with that live recording from My Father's Place on Long Island.

"But I enjoyed getting to meet Zappa that week at The Palladium," Randy continued. "He seemed to be having a good time, and he had his family with him—two little kids, Moon and Dweezil. I didn't get to know him very well. In fact, I ran into him a month later in a lobby of a hotel somewhere, and he didn't remember who I was. That's the music life, I guess."

With 1977's *Don't Stop the Music*, The Brecker Brothers (now sans Sanborn, who was off touring as a successful solo act on the strength of his 1976 self-titled album and 1977's *Promise Me the Moon*) continued courting the disco crowd with two blatantly commercial offerings. The opener, "Finger Lickin' Good" (strangely, co-credited to Randy and his mother, Ticky Brecker) and the title track, written by session guitarist Jerry Friedman, both exude elements of trendy chic in their incessant disco hi-hat grooves and cheesy background vocals. On the other side of the coin, Randy's "Squids" and Michael's soulful "Funky Sea, Funky Dew" both hold up today as excellent, fully realized compositions and

Brecker Brothers classics. (Indeed, "Funky Sea, Funky Dew" received a Grammy Award nomination for Best R&B Instrumental Performance.) Randy also turns in some tasty flugelhorn work on his lovely ballad "Petals" while Michael goes scorched-earth on his rampaging tenor solo to Randy's adrenalized, chops-busting fusion closer, "Tabula Rasa." Randy follows with some fiery wah-wah-inflected trumpet work (one of the few times that following Mike wasn't a disastrous choice). Guest drummer Lenny White of Return to Forever kicks in a whirlwind drum solo at the end of this hard-charging number.

"That record was kind of an aberration of our usual path, through no one's fault," said Randy. "Mike had worked with a producer named Jack Richardson on a Joe Beck record [*Watch the Time* for Polydor, 1977], and he liked what Richardson had done and suggested that we use him on our next record. Jack was from Canada, a real pro, but he was a little overly intent on getting his own people from Canada on the record. And not only that. but trying to sell us tunes that he had publishing on. And it got kind of screwed up because he was out for himself, and we were too weak. He was pretty forceful about bringing people down from Canada, including a horn arranger, which we needed like a hole in the head."

By this time, guitarist Khan had seen the writing on the wall. "There were sort of two factions in the band," he observed. "There was Randy and Will on the one side, echoing what Clive Davis had envisioned for the band from the start. Clive smelled money and success, and so he started putting pressure on them: 'This is the direction you guys should be going in.' And because Will could sing, and Randy wanted the band to do well, financially speaking, they followed that line of thinking. And then there was the other side of things, which was Don and me and Michael, representing the artistic argument. Mike was always more the artiste. Randy was older and more experienced and had his mind on the business things as well as the playing and stuff. But the big factor was the older brother thing, where Randy could pull Mike over to the other side. So, Don and I would be there by ourselves arguing against being turned into a glorified R&B band.

"In the end, that kind of thinking perverted the direction of the band to where on *Back to Back* you start to see three, four vocal tunes mixed in there with Randy's great instrumental compositions. And it just felt strange to me. I almost at times felt embarrassed by it. I was like, 'Randy, you're too good to be doing this.' And then the last record I did with the band, *Don't Stop the Music*, was even worse, where you have these extremes. We had two amazing tunes by Randy, 'Squids' which had Steve Gadd on drums; and 'Tabula Rasa,' which is a great piece of music that had Lenny White coming in to play drums. But then there were all these other tunes that were, to me, just awful. And shortly after, I left the band. I just didn't feel it anymore."

Khan would end up recruiting the potent Brecker Brothers lineup of Mike, Randy, and Sanborn on horns with Grolnick on piano, Lee on bass, and Gadd on drums to back him on his first album as a leader for Columbia Records, *Tightrope* (1977). They also appeared on *The Blue Man* (1978) and *Arrows* (1979). "My first three records for Columbia were really like me trying to desperately hold together the sound of the original Brecker Brothers band, just playing more guitar-centric stuff," Khan said. "I tried to always have something where the three horns were playing together—Mike, Randy, and Sanborn—to keep that sound together. Because I believed in that so much, I didn't want to let it go."

(Check Michael's harmonizer-inflected tenor solo on "Some Punk Funk" from *Tightrope*, his quintessentially epic exchanges with Khan on "An Eye over Autumn" from *The Blue Man*, and his urgent tenor solo on "City Suite (For Folon)" and rare soprano solos on "Candles" and "Daily Village" from *Arrows*.)

To keep up their jazz chops during their constant session work and the increasingly commercial direction of The Brecker Brothers band, Mike and Randy gigged around town as much as they could with Hal Galper's quintet and also with guitarist Jack Wilkins. Both bandleaders put a premium on swinging while providing a platform for extended improvisation. In both acoustic jazz settings, Mike and Randy dug deep and stretched, resulting in some of their most brilliant performances of that time.

On October 31, 1977, Mike and Randy went into New York's Downtown Sound Studio with Wilkins to record *You Can't Live Without It* for the Chiaroscuro label. A quintet date featuring Phil Markowitz on piano, Jon Burr on bass, and Al Foster on drums, it's a swinging affair that has Randy and Mike both flexing their bop muscles on an up-tempo romp through Tommy Flanagan's "Freight Train." Mike's tour de force on this excellent outing is his virtuosic performance on Bronislau Kaper's "Invitation." The first two and a half minutes of this thirteen-minute marathon find Wilkins and Michael engaging in a delicate duo conversation with the guitarist showing his masterful chording and ringing harmonics skills against Michael's relaxed rubato reading of the haunting melody. As the band kicks in at the three-minute mark, Michael comes alive with an arresting solo full of electrifying double-timing and outrageous sheets of sound improvisations over the next three minutes to conclude his show-stopping solo. Wilkins follows with an astounding solo, then Randy kicks in an energized solo himself near the end of this dynamic showcase. Elsewhere on this outstanding Wilkins release, they blaze through a frenetic up-tempo romp on "What Is This Thing Called Love" and show ultimate finesse on the ballad "What's New?," with Randy blowing a tasty flugelhorn solo and Mike contributing a relaxed, harmonically probing and passionate tenor solo. Though it's only four tracks long, *You Can't Live Without It* ranks high among all-time great Michael Brecker tenor saxophone performances.

As Wilkins recalled, "I met Mike and Randy early on. We played in a lot of different rehearsal bands together at Lynn Oliver's studio on the Upper West Side, which was a good place for jamming and working on reading stuff. Michael, of course, was a brilliant player. I always loved his playing, and we got along well. We played little gigs around town like at Sweet Basil, that little club on Seventh Avenue near Bleecker Street. I played there with both Randy and Michael, and I also played there separately a bunch of times with Randy, Eddie Gomez, and Jack DeJohnette. For *You Can't Live Without It*, we actually went into studio after the gig at Sweet Basil was over. It was Halloween night . . . it must've been about one o'clock in the morning. It was a very last-minute thing, like, 'Let's record this right now!' Hank O'Neal was the owner of the record company (Chiaroscuro), and he said, 'Come into the studio and record it.' And he got Fred Miller, who was the producer, over to the studio, and we did it. We just jammed. We didn't really have anything worked out. It was a jam session record, which turned out pretty nice, actually. And I think some of Michael's best playing is on that record."

Wilkins added, "Michael, frankly, didn't really know the tunes that well. I think he knew 'Invitation' OK, but he really didn't know 'What's New?' and 'What Is This Thing Called Love?' 'Freight Train' was just a blues, so he picked that right up. But you'd never know that he didn't know those tunes, because he had such great ears. And his playing on

'Invitation,' man . . . what can you say about that? It's brilliant. You can't get much better than that. You can get different, but not better. He obviously loved Trane, but he made his own statement, though. Absolutely. You could hear Trane had some influence there, but that's normal, that's natural. But when Michael played, he was his own man for sure. There's no doubt about that."

While Randy and Mike may not have been able to showcase this kind of uninhibited jazzy playing in the contest of The Brecker Brothers, especially when commercial considerations began putting the creative clamps on the band, they held nothing back in their jazzy encounters with Galper and Wilkins. Galper's quintet had a weekly Monday night residency through March and April 1977 at The Players Tavern. "We worked every club in New York City, including Boomer's and the Village Vanguard, the Other End, but Sweet Basil was our home base," he explained. "Basil gave us our first shot, and that's how the *Reach Out!* album came out, because Nils Winther of SteepleChase Records heard us there and offered us a recording session. After that album came out, there were lines around the block, and we were the official sub band. Whenever anybody canceled or couldn't make a gig, the guy at Sweet Basil would call us, and we would fill in at the last minute. So, we were really able to develop something there, and it was pretty hot. All the musicians would come in. The bar was filled with them."

"That band was great," Galper continued. "I was working on the pentatonic and modal playing during that period, and Mike was deep into his Trane bag on this gig. I believe the wags in town called us the Average White Trane. And I loved it! That band was kind of a cult phenomenon of its time. It was very influential in terms of younger players trying to duplicate that kind of modal playing. And Mike was a kind of focal point for that. He was really channeling some Coltrane energy on the bandstand back then."

The Galper quintet made one trip down to New Orleans, where they played at Rosy's jazz club (where the live album *Children of the Night* was recorded and released twenty years later, in 1997, on the Double-Time Records label). There was also a memorable gig in Mike and Randy's old stomping grounds of Bloomington, Indiana, where they had both gone to college. "We had been on the road for two weeks, so our chemistry was really tight at the time," Galper recalled. "Then we got stranded for three days in Bloomington because of an historic snowstorm. People were coming to the gigs in snowshoes. And money was going down the drain every day from other gigs we had to cancel because we couldn't get out of there."

In November 1977, the Galper Quintet, with Mike, Randy, Bob Moses on drums, and Wayne Dockery on bass, traveled to Europe to play the Berlin Jazz Festival. "That was an insane gig," Galper recalled. "We played a song that's never been recorded before called 'Hey Fool,' which is my tribute to Cannonball Adderley, whose band I played in during the mid-'70s. It's kind of a heavily gospel-flavored tune, and Mike plays a tremendous solo that just makes you want to jump out of your seat. That whole gig was just nuts. We were looking for the edge that wasn't there, as we used to say."

Michael delivers in intense, show-stopping fashion throughout the group's set at the Berlin Jazz Festival on November 4, 1977 (documented on a board tape that was retrieved forty years later from Galper's personal archives and finally released in 2021 on Origin Records as the two-CD set *Live at the Berlin Philharmonic 1977*). Along with his dynamic playing on "Hey Fool," Michael can be heard stretching heroically on Galper's runaway romp "This Is the Thing," on the modal burner "Now Hear This," and the up-tempo swinging jazz waltz "Triple Play." He also unleashes with cathartic abandon and rare authority on the marathon twenty-four-minute "Speak With A Single Voice," a tune that captures the sheer kinetic momentum and Trane Quartet-inspired heights that Galper's band aspired to on any given night in 1977.

Galper recalls that it was a double-edged sword trying to book gigs for his quintet with the now-famous Brecker Brothers in the band. "Mike and Randy weren't playing any jazz at the time, hardly at all, because they were so wrapped up in the studio stuff. So, we made an agreement that they would lend me their names, and I would create the band and do the work and get the gigs. And that worked fine up to a certain point until it became so obvious that promoters were just using me to get to Mike and Randy, to the point where at one gig that I booked was billed as The Mike & Randy Brecker Quintet featuring Hal Galper. One club had put it up on their marquee in plastic letters on their outdoor sign, and I was out there with a broom knocking them off. And because of the hype of The Brecker Brothers, everybody in the audience was expecting a rock 'n' roll band at my gigs. So invariably I had to get on the mic and say, 'If this isn't what you expected, the club mis-advertised it.' And a lot of people left the club after that announcement, and the club owner got really pissed at me."

He added, "After three years, this mendacious use of The Brecker Brothers name by some club owners kind of spoiled everything for both of us. It just made the whole agreement tainted. And we decided that we achieved what we tried to do and broke the band up."

At the same time that they were stretching with jazzy abandon and blowing off steam with Wilkins and Galper, Mike and Randy also kept one foot solidly in the pop world. The brothers were extraordinarily busy session players throughout 1977, racking up innumerable album credits including Wild Cherry's *Electrified Funk*, Average White Band's collaboration with Ben E. King on *Benny and Us*, Kiki Dee's self-titled debut, Phoebe Snow's *Never Letting Go*, J. Geils Band's *Monkey Island*, and Ringo Starr's *Ringo the 4th* while also putting their stamp on numerous lucrative jingles. Michael's signature tenor voice can be heard at the opening to Odyssey's 1977 anthemic disco hit single "Native New Yorker," which also includes a burning sax solo midway through. He also guested on several jazz recordings in 1977, including Joanne Brackeen's *Tring-A-Ling*, Chet Baker's *You Can't Go Home Again*, Don Cherry's *Hear & Now*, Charles Earland's *Revolution*, and Idris Muhammad's *Turn This Mutha Out*. A cursory look through Michael's appointment book for that year reveals just how active he was:

January 9—Norman Connors date—$140
January 12—Bette Midler, Atlantic Studio
January 14—Hank Crawford, A&R Studios
January 19—J. Geils Band, Record Plant
January 27—Toyota commercial, 1 p.m.
January 28—Noxema commercial, 10 a.m.
February 16—Chet Baker/Sebesky, Sound Idea Studios
February 23—Charles Earland, Soundworks Studio (three sessions)
March 20—TV bumpers
March 31—Average White Band, Atlantic Studios
April 20—Arif Mardin, Atlantic Studios, 9–12
April 26—Will Power, three songs
June 27—Wild Cherry, Suma Recording Studio
June 28—Beach Day
June 30—Bob James, A&R Studios

July 26—Rupert Holmes, Power Station
August 2—Toyota commercial
August 8—Phoebe Snow, A&R Studios
August 13—Phoebe Snow, Central Park, 6:30
August 16—Players Association (leaders fee—two sessions)
August 19—Patti Austin, Electric Lady (double scale)
August 31—Fred Wesley, United Sound Studios
September 1—Paul Simon, 7–10 p.m. (tenor)
September 2—Dan Weiss, Sigma Sound, 7–11 (bring lyricon)

By the end of 1977, Mike and Randy took out a ten-year lease on a downtown space that would become a popular haven for them and other like-minded musicians to put together new projects and experiment with impunity. Seventh Avenue South, as it was christened, would also become a notorious den of iniquity for those people who were interested in doing the wrong thing right. Coke fiends and fusion fans rubbed elbows at the downstairs bar and in the upstairs performance area, and the lines flowed like champagne. After all, it was the '70s.

# 5

# THOSE PERFECT EIGHTH NOTES

nderscoring all of the popularity, acclaim, and admiration from fellow saxophonists that Michael accrued during his first seven years in New York—with Dreams, Horace Silver, Billy Cobham, The Brecker Brothers, and as an in-demand, first-call session player—was a dark secret. As older brother Randy put it, "Mike had some personal problems with substance abuse. He had his things he had to do to feel OK."

Randy Sandke mentioned that Mike had been "anesthetizing" himself on alcohol going back to their time together at Indiana University, possibly in reaction to the horrible circumstances of the night in Chicago in 1968 when an acquaintance of the band, tripping on LSD, leaped to her death from their crash pad and rehearsal space in the heart of Old Town. Or perhaps it was to numb the lingering pain he felt from a childhood of constantly competing for his father's approval, as some intimates have suggested. Whatever the cause of his pain, Mike upped the ante on his self-medication by the time he settled into New York by switching from alcohol to heroin.

Part of the motivation for this decision may have come with the territory. From the bebop revolution of the '40s to the '60s loft jazz scene and into the '70s and '80s, jazz lore was inextricably woven with the thread of substance abuse. Iconic figures such as Charlie Parker, Bud Powell, Billie Holiday, Lester Young, Miles Davis, J. J. Johnson, Dexter Gordon, Lee Morgan, Jackie McLean, Sonny Stitt, Gene Ammons, Sonny Rollins, and the musician that Michael idolized most, John Coltrane, all struggled with heroin addiction at some point in their careers while also reaping its benefits.

It was the great drummer and bandleader Art Blakey who once suggested that heroin didn't make anyone play better, but it did make you *hear* better. The late tenor sax great Jimmy Heath put it this way in his autobiography, *I Walked With Giants* (Temple University Press): "Heroin doesn't affect your musical ability, as long as you can get it. I felt that mental concentration was better with heroin than with any other stimulant. Alcohol throws your talent out; your technique gets sloppy. Marijuana makes you get plenty of ideas, but then your mind moves too fast. You move off one idea to another. Heroin was a concentration drug . . . With heroin, you could zoom in on something and block everything else out. If you can concentrate better, you can work on things very meticulously. Coltrane used to get high and practice all day. He would practice endlessly. Heroin enhanced your practice. I don't know if I would have practiced as intensely if I hadn't been on heroin. That's a question mark. I'm not endorsing heroin by any stretch of the imagination, because it has too many things that are bad about it. That's the only thing that was good about it, its effect on your concentration level. Everything else was a drag—your social life, your health, your reputation, all of that was a drag."

Just as Stan Getz and many fellow musicians of his generation followed in Bird's wake by dabbling in heroin themselves, so, too, did many saxophonists of the '70s follow in the wake of their hero Trane by shooting up. Michael was among a number of tenor saxophonists from the late '60s loft jazz scene who began using. "When I met Mike, we were both doing heroin," recalled tenor saxophonist Bob Mintzer. "And that was part of our connection; that was the scene. Our heroes were junkies, you know."

Mintzer addressed another motive for getting high. "I know that in my case, whatever uncomfortability I had as far as my own self-esteem or my playing ability or what other people might think of me . . . that all went away as soon as I got high on heroin," he said. "I didn't give a fuck anymore. And it just sort of turned down all self-doubt to zero, so all of a sudden you just don't care. And in fact, I don't think I would have made it in the music scene were it not for heroin, because I was too scared, and I didn't feel worthy."

He added this other telling anecdote: "I went down to the Vanguard on this Sunday night, and I sat in with Art Blakey because I had heard that Sunday was the night where you could actually sit in with the band. I was high on heroin, so I didn't care; I had no doubts about it whatsoever. I just walked in with my chest out, went up to Art, and said, 'Can I play on the last set?' He said, 'Yeah.' So, I played, and immediately afterward he asked me to join the band. But I never would have done that if I wasn't using heroin. If you have fear, you're not gonna be relaxed. And if you're not relaxed, your playing will reflect that, and it will lack everything—connectivity, projection, all of it. And heroin eliminated the fear."

Said saxophonist Dave Liebman, "Everybody knew from the beboppers that heroin was a thing. And I must admit, it does help you get to that zone of just hearing so well. That's why guys did it. And when you played, especially when you practiced, you really could zone in. Nothing else mattered. It was like a one-way path. There were no distractions, there was no stopping off and saying hello. It was just, 'I'm practicing; I'm gonna keep doing it until I feel tired. Then I'm gonna get up and start again.' That was your job. And Michael was very dedicated to that ethos."

Bassist Will Lee, who had come up from the University of Miami to join Dreams in 1971 and became a charter member of The Brecker Brothers in 1975, recalled a scene that illustrated Michael's allegiance to the drug: "Mike used to say 'perfect eighth notes' about smack. He'd mime injecting his arm and say that, like he was telling himself, 'I'm doing this because I was trying to achieve those perfect eighth notes,' you know? And I was like, 'Wow! Now I see the attraction for him. But no thanks for me. I'm OK with my coke over here."

Randy said that while he only dabbled in heroin, he did see the benefits of the drug. "I did heroin, yeah, but not with needles. I was what they would call a 'weekend junkie.' I'd snort a little on a weekend, and then I'd spend two days just feeling shitty. But I never did it continually, and I never used needles, so it wasn't that hard to eventually just stop everything. Unfortunately, I can vouch for the fact that music and heroin really fit like a glove. It's terrible to say, and I don't recommend it, but I'm not gonna bullshit you. It just makes you want to play. I don't want my kid using, and we're all better off not doing it. And I'm not saying you play better on heroin; it just *feels* better. You just wanna play and play and play."

He recounted one story of a Hal Galper session for *Reach Out!* where Mike's indulgence was obvious to one and all in attendance. "This was during one of Mike's worst phases as far as his drug habit. We were playing the tune 'Children of the Night,' and we were all kind of in a circle in the studio. Wayne Dockery's playing a bass solo before we're all supposed to come back in. And I look over, and Mike's perfectly perched on the stool with his horn, but he's nodded out . . . asleep. So, I kick the stool, and he wakes up, and we manage to come in on time. Later on, we got the test pressing of that session, and we put it on to listen back, and during that bass solo you can hear Mike snoring. Eventually they airbrushed it out on a later version, but you can still hear it. It sounds like Wayne breathing during his solo, but it's actually Mike snoring, nodded out on his stool."

Randy confessed that he wasn't privy to all of Mike's personal indiscretions and wasn't even sure when his younger brother may have picked up his heroin habit. "People might think since I was the older brother that I introduced him to things I shouldn't have, but it was indeed the reverse," he said. "Mike was doing all the things that I had never done, so I sort of said, 'OK, I'll try this, I'll try that.' But I always could put a break on it, and I never used needles. Basically, I was scared of that. But he got really deep into it, as did a lot of tenor players. I don't know if they were trying to emulate Bird or early Trane and Miles or whatever, but it really took a toll on Mike, although he could always function at a high level. You know, I never saw him out of control. It wasn't like some guys who are in the gutter with it."

While Michael continued indulging in heroin, cocaine was the recreational drug of choice for most of the denizens of Seventh Avenue South, the split-level jazz room located at the corner of Seventh Avenue and Leroy Street that the Breckers ran with their partner, Kate Greenfield. With seating for eighty upstairs, initially at the modest cover charge of $3 or $4, and a downstairs bar equipped with speakers projecting the music from upstairs, sans cover, the club soon became a magnet for studio musicians, cutting-edge contemporary jazz players, straight-ahead and avant-garde jazz icons, and the rare pop star. It was a wild Manhattan melting pot, and everyone was lit every night. "There was so much excitement and electricity in the air some nights," said vibraphonist Mike Mainieri, a colleague of Michael's going back to their White Elephant days together. "You just didn't get that at other clubs."

Downstairs the excitement was palpable to wide-eyed fans as they gawked at their favorite musicians mingling at the long bar, exchanging pleasantries, engaging in witty critiques of each other's work, or just dealing in the dozens in loose, good-natured, uninhibited fashion. On any given night at Seventh Avenue South, you might see the unlikeliest combination of people congregating downstairs or seated together at the same upstairs table—Miles Davis and Chaka Khan; Joni Mitchell and her partner, Don Alias; Average White Band drummer Steve Ferrone chatting with Max Roach; avant-garde pioneer Cecil Taylor rapping with fusion guitarist Hiram Bullock; Nile Rodgers talking with Paul Shaffer (pre-*David Letterman Show*); John Scofield catching up with Chet Baker; Jaco Pastorius laughing with CBS correspondent and fellow Philly native Ed Bradley. Some were fixated on the table top Pac Man and Missile Command video games in the downstairs bar area while others were openly hitting on the waitresses. Add to that potent party mix the presence of John Belushi, who lived just down the road and drifted in and out of the club, often with some of his fellow *Saturday Night Live* cast members in tow, and you had the makings of an urbane *Animal House*.

"It was just this crazy '70s jazz scene that was somehow mixed in with the whole pop-rock scene and studio scene of New York," said guitarist Scofield, who had played with Mike and Randy briefly in Billy Cobham's band and later became a regular at Seventh Avenue South, where he co-led a band with Dave Liebman and also led a trio with bassist Steve Swallow and drummer Adam Nussbaum. "Essentially, everybody was very fucked up in those times, but it was all done with this kind of hippie frame of mind, like 'everything's good and in moderation' or whatever. Which actually wasn't working at all. So, I went from being this hippie kid smoking pot and drinking beer to really snorting a lot of coke and being in the high life in New York. It was that '70s disco era coke thing, which was crazy."

Scofield described one scene that indicates just how prevalent cocaine was in the '70s: "I remember going to sign with Arista Records to make my first record for them [1979, *Who's Who*]. And at the signing, the guy who was running the jazz label offered me some coke right there in his office, like it was a completely uptown, legitimate thing. I mean, it was so everywhere." Pianist Richie Beirach, with whom Michael studied harmony during the loft days, concurred with Scofield about NYC in the '70s. "That was a whole other kind of a time, man. You'd go to the dentist, and he'd be doing blow . . . the dentist, the mailman, everybody was doing it!"

"Everybody was high in the '70s," added Liebman. "It was a period where everybody tried everything, with good intentions. We were all pretty out there at Seventh Avenue South, but nothing compared to what they were doing uptown at Studio 54. They were taking it *all* the way out there. I mean, pop compared to jazz . . . you can't even compare! Pop cats, they take it way out because they got the money."

Guitarist Barry Finnerty, who played with the Brecker Brothers from 1977 through 1980, confirmed that Seventh Avenue South was *the* place to be for hipsters, fusion fans, and music-industry insiders. "I used to leave my house at 1:30 or 2 in the morning every night and head for the club," he recalled. "All the guys in town would come down after their late gigs or recording sessions, and we would hang out and drink and play video games until 4, sometimes 5 or 6 in the morning. It was a great, fun time. Of course, the five-hundred-pound gorilla in the room during that whole time was drugs. Just about everybody on the scene was doing cocaine. Everybody was like, 'Hey, you want to go to the bathroom?' I was a hippie kid from San Francisco, I smoked weed, but a $25 quarter gram of coke would last me a week. Mike was a lot further down that road than I was."

Finnerty said he learned about Michael's heroin addiction after joining The Brecker Brothers band. "I was shocked, and I suggested he try just smoking pot instead. But he would say, 'No, because it leads to hard drugs, which is what I want.' He was pretty discreet about it, though. I never once saw him really noticeably fucked up in public. But I knew he was a lot unhappier and troubled than most people knew. And I was worried about him."

"When I first met Mike in 1977, I was strung out like a clothesline, and so was he," said guitarist Mike Stern, who would eventually join Brecker's first band as leader in 1987. "I was in Blood, Sweat & Tears at the time, and The Brecker Brothers were opening for us at this place in Chicago. We had two or three nights there, and at some point, I asked Mike if he knew where I could get some dope . . . some heroin, you know? And he said, 'Yeah, there's a guy,' so I ended up going to the guy's house. Mike helped me out that week by turning me on to this cat, and then I'd see him from time to time after that. One time he was in Boston when I was still living there, and he called up and asked me if I could return the favor and help him out, but I just didn't have anything that particular night, so I couldn't. There was another time when we were doing a bunch of blow together at a David Clayton-Thomas session in Toronto [for *Clayton* on the ABC label, 1978, featuring Mike,

Randy, and David Sanborn on four tracks—"Laying Down Rock And Roll," "Fooled Ya," "Sweet Sixteen," "Sugar Comes From Arkansas"]. We were always getting high together then. Our connection was the music, but it also definitely had to do with getting high, that's for sure. For me, music just had that correlation with getting high. From the time I picked up the guitar, it was always something in me where I would immediately relate the two—getting high and playing. And I think that was true for Mike as well."

After Stern joined Miles Davis's group and moved from Boston to New York, he would see Michael on the scene a lot, mostly at Seventh Avenue South. "I remember seeing him backstage at a Miles gig we did at the Savoy [July 18, 1981], and he was as high as hell. He really dug the band, and we were talking afterwards, and it was just so natural hanging out with him. He had a more of an edge in those days, when he was getting high. But he was still just a real sweet cat."

"He was always very complimentary back then," said alto saxophonist Steve Slagle, who remembers subbing for David Sanborn on an early Brecker Brothers rehearsal, "but also very kind of reticent. He seemed to be into something else . . . often would disappear at times. Later he told me why he was always so preoccupied in those days. He said, 'Man, there was a dealer on every corner, and I knew it.' He said, 'At one point my life I realized that in any neighborhood of New York City, I knew a dealer within five blocks.' And that was kind of on his mind all the time in those days."

Randy confirmed Slagle's dealer story. "Once, we had just copped from Burt, our regular guy on 15th and Sixth Avenue. Our nicknames were Huey and Dewey. We'd go to this place and say those names, and they'd let us in. Anyway, this one night we were standing in the street, and we were figuring out that we had drug connections east to west from Wall Street up through Harlem about every fifteen blocks. Wherever we were in Manhattan, we knew some nefarious character that we could cop from. That's how crazy it was in those days."

As keyboardist-producer Jason Miles recalled, "One night Mike came up to Wizard Studios in Briarcliff Manor to do a session with me. This was after he had gotten clean. Anyway, after the session I decided to drive him back home. And we get to his place on Grand Street and he says, 'Come on, I'll take you on a tour.' So, we're walking around his neighborhood, and he goes, 'See that corner over there? That was one of my copping spots. And if he wasn't over there, I knew to go over there. Then you see that building over there? Guy on the third floor, he would shoot me up. He had this fucking needle that would combine the heroin and the coke,' and I'm like, 'Come on, man.' And he says, 'It's all the truth.' And I said, 'Man, I'm so happy that you're done with all that and that you're here.'"

The Breckers and Kate Greenfield had initially signed a ten-year lease on Seventh Avenue South in 1977. The triumvirate then brought Bob Cooper on board as prospective manager and gave him a piece of the club. "He was the person that knew the business, who was going to guide us," said Greenfield. "Bob had managed Boomer's, a jazz club on Bleecker Street that I used to hang out at. And he actually put me together with Mike and Randy. We were all in our twenties—bright, talented, creative, but certainly not experienced in running a business like this. So, the way we set it up was, I was gonna be the working partner by investing some money and running the restaurant, Mike and Randy were going to play at the club and invest, and Bob Cooper would be the one who would manage the place and teach us stuff."

"Mike and I were big fans of Boomer's," added Randy. "We played there with Hal Galper a bunch, so we got friendly with Bob, and he always let us in for free. So, when Boomer's closed, that put a real dent on the jazz scene, because it was just a great second-rung place. I remember hearing Freddie Hubbard there and attending jam sessions there. Nobody hassled you to buy a drink. It was a great place to hang out. Several months after Boomer's closed, I got a call from Mike who had just heard from Cooper that he found a spot that he thought he could turn into a club, and he needed a modest investment. We were both working a lot in the studios then and were in the midst of Brecker Brothers activities. So, Mike loaned him four grand, and I kicked in another two grand. The three of us went over to Brooklyn to meet Kate, who was a schoolteacher then and had some money saved up that she wanted to invest. So now it was the four of us. We went over and looked at the space, it had two floors . . . looked like it'd be a nice thing. So, the four of us went all-in on it.

"Mike and I just wanted to be silent partners," Randy continued, "and eventually get paid back for the loan. But as it turned out, Cooper had trouble getting his name on the liquor license because he had seven hundred outstanding traffic violations. But we eventually smoothed it over with the guy at the liquor license place by giving him some blow . . . it was a sign of the times. But Bob got pissed off because his name couldn't go on the license, and he didn't want to be 'working for us,' so he split. So, there we were, the three of us—Kate had been a school-teacher and knew nothing about the business, and I don't have to talk about Mike and my business acumen, which was zero. But Kate really stepped up to the plate and organized the whole thing in the beginning stages. She was really a hard worker and worked twelve hours a day keeping the place open."

"We started out with a very ambitious menu," said Kate. "I ended up wooing away the cook from Ashley's in the Village to come work with us, so we had the kitchen covered. And we hired a guy named Steve Resnick, who had the All State Café uptown on 72nd and Broadway [where a young actor named Kevin Bacon waited on tables while waiting for roles] to work with me for a week, teaching me systems—how to order, how to count the register, stuff like that. And we just kept moving forward. To me, things that are meant to happen sort of take on a life of their own, and that's the way it was with Seventh Avenue South."

Rent on the two-level space at 21 Seventh Ave. S. was $1,000 a month. But as Kate pointed out, "There were other expenses before we could open the club, like passing a little packet under the table to the guy at the State Liquor Authority so we could serve drinks there. You know, the usual deal in Manhattan—pay off the liquor license guy, pay off the Mafia jukebox guy and the Mafia guy who takes the trash . . . whatever we had to do to keep the business moving forward."

Kate said that she realized early on that Michael was a functional drug addict. "One weekend he came and stayed at my apartment. I lived on Dean Street in downtown Brooklyn. He was so skinny and such a mess. And he said he wanted to clean up his act but couldn't. We both looked skinny and pale and not healthy, but somehow we kept it together to run the club."

While Kate managed the club, she was also getting high with all the musicians in the small walk-in dressing room in the back of the club or in her office. "There was a lot of coke going on there all the time," she said, "And I always foolishly thought that if I didn't do heroin, that meant I wasn't a drug addict. But I was."

Greenfield confessed that she, too, tried snorting heroin later into the club's existence. "I remember saying to Randy, really proudly, 'Oh, guess what? I did heroin, but I'm not going to be like you guys. I bought $50 worth, and I've had it for a week.' And he said, 'Yeah, everyone starts that way, Kate, but it's not going to last.' He said, 'Nobody wins with heroin.' And he was right. Heroin was the first drug that I couldn't control. Even with coke—and I did a lot of it—I was controlled. With heroin, I couldn't control it."

Although they managed to keep Seventh Avenue South open for eight years, it was never a profitable business. "It wasn't run very strictly," admitted Jerry Wortman, who was the booker toward the end of Seventh Avenue South's run and who would later become Michael's road manager and close friend. "It was more of a clubhouse, and Mike and Randy bought into it for that reason. They decided to get into it because they wanted a place to go hang out and play."

"We lost untold sums of money in that place," said Randy. "The only money Mike and I ever took out of it was about a month after the club opened, we each took $100 bill out of the cash register, and that was it for eight years."

At some point toward the end of the club's existence, Mike, Randy, and Kate turned to John "Cha Cha" Ciarcia (aka The Mayor of Little Italy) for help in financing a loan. A well-known restaurateur, boxing promoter, actor, Sirius Satellite radio host, and longtime owner of Little Italy's popular Cha Cha's In Bocca Al Lupo Café on Mulberry Street, a popular hangout over the years for such movie stars as Robert DeNiro, Martin Scorsese, Danny DeVito, and Vincent Pastore, Cha Cha was well connected and a jazz fan to boot. "He would come in to the club with his wife, who was a singer," said Randy. "And he helped us out. He was our connection to a lot of things there. Word has it that the movie *Get Shorty* was about him, because he had one foot in the movie business, too. He had managed Tony Danza when he was a prizefighter, and he appears in anything filmed during the '70s, '80s, and '90s involving Little Italy, including *The Sopranos*. He was an amazing guy."

All told, Seventh Avenue South ended up costing the Brecker brothers $30,000 in back taxes to state and city agencies. When their lease ended in 1987, the building was purchased by an Indian couple who promptly tripled the rent, effectively ending the reign of the club. "But we did keep it open for eight years, and it became quite the hangout during that time," said Randy in retrospect. "Bad business venture, but we had a lot of fun. It was a helluva run, but it didn't help my mental faculties any. And it got tough for a few years. That's when I first started to say, 'I gotta change my lifestyle a little.'"

During the early years of Seventh Avenue South, Michael got involved with one of the waitresses at the club named Jacqui Smith (now Perrine). As she recalled, "Michael really was one of the sweetest, kindest people, but he was also kind of lonely and didn't like being alone. There was one night where it was four in the morning at the club, and he invited me into the bathroom to do some coke with him. And then he asked me if I would stay at his house with him but no sex. He said, 'I just don't want to be by myself tonight.' So, I went to his house, I stayed, we slept, but then in the morning that 'no sex' thing changed. And from then on it became sort of an on-again, off-again thing between us. I always had my own apartment, but I stayed with him a lot when he lived on Grand Street. And when I was in his loft with him, he would be in the other room, practicing all the time. There's a reason he was as good as he was."

Through hanging with Michael, Jacqui got an intimate look at his habits. "I wasn't a heroin buddy of his, but I ended up many nights at Michael's dealer's apartment when he went there to score, just listening to their heroin talk. I don't know which was worse, coke talk or heroin talk. They would get high—Michael did shoot it a couple of times but his preferred method was snorting heroin and coke, speedballs. And sometimes Chaka Khan would be there with us. Or we'd all go over to Joni Mitchell's loft, which was right down the street across from Seventh Avenue South, and they'd be doing the same thing there. I'd end up playing pinball while everybody sat around snorting heroin. So even though I wasn't a participant, I was actively involved in the junkie life."

Throughout the duration of the club, the Breckers used Seventh Avenue South to promote their latest recordings. The launch party for their live 1978 release, *Heavy Metal Be-Bop*, took place in September 1978, some weeks after the club had begun booking music. Featuring a new lineup of bassist-vocalist Neil Jason, guitarist Barry Finnerty, keyboardist Mark Gray, and Terry Bozzio on drums, the album included their hit single "East River," the lone studio track which was cowritten by Jason and a mysterious figure known as Cash Monet. "To this day I don't know his real name," said Randy. "He was just Ralphy from Brooklyn as far as I knew. He and Neil were writing partners back then. They had a lot of tunes in their arsenal, and they picked that one to put on the record because Clive Davis, once again, said, 'OK, we'll put a live record out, but you need a single or I won't put it out.' So, we went into the studio and spent as much money on that one tune as we did on the rest of the record, which was recorded live at My Father's Place on Long Island. But I'm still a fan of that tune. Neil and Cash knew exactly what they wanted. They had the whole thing mapped out, and there were a million overdubs on it. So, it was pretty well done, and it ended up being a big hit for us."

Aside from that funky anthem, *Heavy Metal Be-Bop* contained some of the heaviest, funkiest grooves and most audacious soloing by Mike, Randy, and guitarist Barry Finnerty. "It was a fantastic band," Finnerty recalled, "and we had an incredible month of gigs, culminating in that show at My Father's Place in Roslyn. Bozzio was the most dynamic drummer around at that time, and he had gained all this notoriety from playing in Frank Zappa's band." Indeed, Zappa's extraordinarily difficult, through-composed solo opus for Bozzio, "The Black Page," is still regarded as a proving ground among drummers. Mike and Randy played their horns through Seamoon Funk Machine envelope filters to attain the automatic wah-wah effect that appears on the urgent shuffle blues "Inside Out" as well as on "Sponge," "Squids," and an exhilarating live rendition of Randy's chops-busting "Some Skunk Funk." And in concert they cranked up the volume on two massive Sunn amplifiers on stage.

"It was one of the highest energy bands I have ever been in," added Finnerty. "We had a ball every night, a real camaraderie. I was old friends with Bozzio, too, because he had played in my band when we were in high school together in the Bay Area. But, unfortunately, the record company had other priorities, finance-wise, and we weren't able to go out on the road again until 1980, despite having a surprise Top 40 hit in England with 'East River.'"

Reflecting on the drug factor during his time with The Brecker Brothers band, Finnerty said, "I knew they were doing tons of blow. Like when we started doing *Heavy Metal Be-Bop*, they needed a gram of blow each before we'd even start rehearsing. And I was a lightweight at that time. I could make a quarter of a gram last a week. So, I knew they were doing blow and drinking and stuff. But when Mike told me he had a heroin problem, I was like, 'Damn! Are you kidding?!' That was really heavy stuff for me. My father (actor Warren Finnerty) had been in a famous play called *The Connection* [which also featured the iconic alto saxophonist Jackie McLean in a supporting role] where he played the lead junkie and ended up overdosing and dying onstage every night. I saw that when I was nine, and it really affected me. I guess maybe just seeing my father die onstage scared me off of heroin, but I never tried it once. So, when Mike told me that, I was a little freaked out. Suffice it to say, Mike understood well the misery of just being strung out."

In spite of his constant drugging, 1978 turned out of to be one of Michael's most prolific years in the studio. Along with The Brecker Brothers' *Heavy Metal Be-Bop*, he recorded on several potent jazz albums, including Hal Galper's *Children of the Night* (a brilliant and uncompromising live set by Galper's quintet with Mike, Randy, bassist Wayne Dockery, and drummer Bob Moses, documenting their gig at Rosy's nightclub in New Orleans), Mike Nock's *In Out And Around* (an overlooked gem that has Mike swinging in ferocious fashion in the company of the New Zealand pianist and a killer rhythm tandem of bassist George Mraz and Al Foster), Charles Mingus's monumental *Me Myself an Eye* (Michael is heard wailing on "Three Worlds of Drums"

At Bill's Rehearsals in February 1978, preparing for a Steve Khan gig at Avery Fisher Hall (from l. to r.): Don Grolnick, Steve Khan, Steve Gadd, Will Lee, Michael Brecker *(Photo by Laura Friedman)*

and positively tearing it up on "Devil Woman" and "Wednesday Night Prayer Meeting"), Tony Williams's fusion outing *The Joy of Flying*, Al Foster's audacious electric Miles-inspired recording *Mixed Roots* (his solo on "Ya' Damn Right" is edgy and intense), and Quincy Jones's savvy bridge between disco and jazz, *Sounds . . . And Stuff Like That!!*

He also performed that summer at the Montreux Jazz Festival with an all-star fusion ensemble featuring Randy on trumpet along with vibraphonist Mike Mainieri, pianist Warren Bernhardt, guitarists Larry Coryell and Steve Khan, bassist Tony Levin and drummer Steve Jordan, which yielded the live albums *Blue Montreux I & II*, the latter featuring Michael's tune "Uptown Ed."

Michael's avalanche of pop studio work during that remarkably busy year included appearances on Carly Simon's *Boys in the Trees*, Tina Turner's *Love Explosion*, Chaka Khan's *Chaka*, Robert Palmer's *Double Fun*, Angela Bofill's *Angie*, Phoebe Snow's *Against the Grain*, Garland Jeffreys's *One-Eyed Jack*, Melanie's *Photogenic: Not Just Another Pretty Face*, Rupert Holmes's *Pursuit of Happiness*, The Brothers Johnson's *Blam!*, the Average White Band's *Warmer Communications* as well as the Quincy Jones-produced soundtrack to *The Wiz*.

Michael was also involved in a group of fellow studio musicians collectively known as The Players Association, which was essentially Vanguard Records' attempt at cashing in on the disco craze. With Mike and fellow jazzers such as saxophonists Joe Farrell, David Sanborn, and Bob Berg, trumpeters Jon Faddis, Tom Harrell, and Marvin Stamm, guitarist Steve Khan, and leader/drummer/arranger Chris Hills, all delivering slickly produced instrumental versions of hits by Donna Summer, Diana Ross, The Trammps, and The Village People, these Players Association albums were popular with club DJs. Their two 1978 releases, *Turn the Music Up!* and *Born To Dance*, were followed in quick succession by *We Got the Groove* (1979) and *Let Your Body Go* (1980). Somehow in the midst of that hurricane of activity, Mike also found time to travel to Japan in September with Jun Fukamachi & New York All-Stars, a kind of Brecker Brothers offshoot band featuring the three Brecker Brothers horns of Mike, Randy, and Sanborn, with guitarist Khan, vibraphonist Mike Mainieri, bassist Anthony Jackson, pianist Richard Tee, drummer Steve Gadd, and led by the popular Japanese fusion keyboardist-composer and synth specialist Fukamachi. Recordings of their performances at Tokyo's Korakuen Hall on September 17 and 18 and also at

Yubin Chokin Hall on September 19 later appeared on *Jun Fukamachi & New York All-Stars—Live* (on the Japanese Alfa label) and included sizzling renditions of Randy's Brecker Brothers staples "Rocks" (from *The Brecker Bros.*), "Inside Out" (from *Heavy Metal-Bebop*), and "Jacknife" (which would later appear on 1981's *Détente*).

In early 1979, a few months after the release of *Heavy Metal Be-Bop*, Michael met Jerry Wortman. Their connecting point, like a lot of other things for Mike around this time, was heroin. "Mike came over to my loft on 30th Street to cop," Wortman recalled. "He had heard from someone that maybe my roommate Gary Gold had something, and he was right."

"Jerry and I were best friends from Long Island," Gold explained. "We grew up together on Long Island in the Five Points area, Woodmere. We moved into the city together and got a place on Sullivan Street for a few years and then ended up in this loft at 251 30th St. on the sixteenth floor. It was 2,200 square feet, and it was $450 a month, and we split it three ways with another guy. Jerry and I were both drummers, and the fact that we had a place where we could play music twenty-four hours a day meant people could stop by at all hours. And it became kind of a hot spot for music hanging. Kenny Kirkland and I were in a band at the time with some guys at the Manhattan School of Music, and through that he wound up sort of living on our couch. But in that loft, it was all about playing. This space was formerly a furrier, and it had a walk-in safe that was a four-hundred-square-foot room. That was the music room, and it was just constantly music going all the time.

"And somehow Mike heard that I had drugs," Gold continued. "So, he came by the loft this particular night and knocked on the door, and Jerry answered, and I just looked over, and I was like, 'Holy shit, it's Mike Brecker!'"

Wortman continued the story: "He was coming from a session, and he had his sax case strung over one shoulder. He peeked into the loft and saw my drums set up and he said, 'Oh, you play?' I was kind of timid and embarrassed and said, 'Yeah, but . . .' I probably put myself down a little bit, but he was totally encouraging and said, 'Come on, let's play!' And I was thinking, 'Are you kidding me? This is Mike Brecker! What the fuck am I doing? There's a million guys that should be sitting here, not me.'"

Nevertheless, they played—Gold remembers them jamming on "Giant Steps" so long that they filled up one side of a C-90 Memorex cassette—and afterward Mike complimented Wortman on his feel. "I don't know why he befriended me like that or said those encouraging things about my playing," Jerry said. "I suffered from extremely low self-esteem at the time I met Mike. I was really in trouble then. I had no sense of who I was or what I was going to do. I had dreams, and I had fantasies, but I didn't know how to put the work in. I wasn't at the level of the people around me were at in terms of their artistry, but I wanted to become part of that. And I used to think and hope that it would just come to me, that if I listened to Elvin Jones enough, I would be able to play like Elvin. But I didn't really have that obsession/compulsion to practice. So, I felt accepted when Mike encouraged me. He just came over to cop, but he ended up lifting my spirits. It wasn't like some passing moment where somebody came by, was looking for some drugs, and then said, 'OK, I got what I want. I'm outta here.' The guy actually cared. And I just felt special when he told me that. I think there was always some good stuff inside of me, but I didn't know how to get to it. And Mike was so encouraging that he helped me find it."

The following day, after their introductory jam, Michael took Jerry record shopping at Soho Music Gallery on Broome Street. "I didn't have any money, and he bought me two records that he said I, as an aspiring drummer, had to have . . . and which I still have to this day—Larry Young's *Unity* with Elvin Jones on drums and *Free for All* by Art Blakey and the Jazz Messengers. And Mike was a great drummer himself. If you listen to 'Bessie's Blues' on John Coltrane's *Crescent*, that's the style that Mike emulated when he sat down at the kit. That's what he used to play all the time. He did all the kick drum shit the way that Elvin did it. He could do it verbatim. And he'd sit down and just slap the ride cymbal at a certain kind of hit and just do this Elvin thing that was always so totally cool that I was like, 'I wish I could do that, man.'"

Wortman well remembers first seeing Michael perform two years earlier with Mike Mainieri's sextet on the bill with Dave Liebman's Lookout Farm at The Bottom Line in 1977. "I went there with my parents, and we sat with Liebman's parents," he recalled. "My dad was a school principal in Bell Harbor, Far Rockaway, and Dave's mother, Fran Liebman, was his assistant principal for many years. So, we actually went there to see Lookout Farm. But Mainieri's group opened, and that was the first time I ever saw Michael play. He was very, very high that night. He had a big hat on, and you couldn't see his face at all, but he had a presence. He didn't just stand up there and play. I don't think it was so much for show biz reasons, but his personality drew you in when he was on stage. He was aware that he was a good-looking guy and that he connected with an audience. There are great players that the audience doesn't get into at all, but people connected with Mike. You watch a lot of Mike solos—he knows how to take a crowd the way Mike Stern does with his little bag of tricks. Mike knew how to do his thing and make it interesting for the audience."

Case in point: There's a YouTube clip where Mike is sitting in with the Average White Band at the Montreux Jazz Festival in 1977, playing "Pick Up the Pieces." He comes out with sunglasses on, and by the 1:40 mark he very deliberately removes them before bending notes and launching into some ferocious double-timing on his solo. It's a kind of old-school bit of theatricality in the tradition of James Brown's famous cape routine from back in the day; or for a more recent example, when Aretha Franklin dropped her fur coat at the peak of her performance of "(You Make Me Feel Like) A Natural Woman" at the 2015 Kennedy Center Honors. "Oh man, he was very aware of that stuff," said Wortman.

At the time he actually met Michael, in early 1979, Wortman had a day job at The Village Copier on 12th Street, but at night he continued to jam with Mike and others in the loft. "Mike was living on Grand Street then, and he'd call me up and say, 'Let's play.' He was always encouraging me that way. And I would be like, 'Really? You just finished two sessions with Steve Gadd. You want *me* to come over and play?' Of course, I was already a huge fan of Mike's. I loved all the Brecker Brothers records, especially *Heavy Metal Be-Bop*, which had just come out. I spent hours listening to that record. I also spent a lot of time listening to that Jack Wilkins record that Mike and Randy were on, *You Can't Live Without It*. We especially liked that record because it had a black cover, and we used to cut up blow on it. I still have it—has white stuff all over it. But in my head, whenever I'd play with Mike, I'd be like, 'This guy is on records! He's famous!' He was like Eric Clapton to me—a big rock star. I didn't understand that jazz wasn't really like that, and that jazz musicians were more like normal people. But Mike seemed so much in another world than I was ever capable of being in."

And yet, the friendship of this seeming odd couple deepened over time, as did their drug dependency. As Wortman noted, "I was barely getting through a day, financially. Meanwhile, Mike had money. He was way more high-end than me. And it always blew my mind when I would go along with him to the Musicians' Union above Roseland Ballroom to pick up his checks. There'd be a line of guys waiting around—checks would come in every thirteen weeks, and you'd pick them up at the union—and then some union guy would see Mike, go in the back and bring out this basket full of checks for him. He'd thumb through the stack of checks and pluck one out, smile, and start humming the theme from a popular Toyota national ad campaign that was running on TV at the time. Then we'd go cash it and cop."

And as Peter Erskine confirmed, "Mike told me once that back in the day, when jingles were a real good source of income, the most money he ever made from a studio session was him, Randy, Sanborn, and Ronnie Cuber playing four notes on the tag of a Toyota commercial: *You asked for it, you got it . . . Toyota.* And that got used as a tag on every Toyota commercial for years."

For ten days during the summer of 1979 (July 19–29) Michael was involved in intensive rehearsals in Hollywood for Joni Mitchell's *Shadows and Light* tour of the States, which kicked off in Oklahoma City on August 3 and culminated with a five-night run at L.A.'s Greek Theatre September 12–16. The all-star band for that *Shadows and Light* tour included Mike on tenor sax, Jaco Pastorius on electric bass, Don Alias (Joni's romantic partner at the time), keyboardist Lyle Mays, and guitarist Pat Metheny. This was not only a high-profile, high-paying gig for Michael, who was featured blowing his tenor with typical ferocity on Joni's "Free Man in Paris," Charles Mingus's "Goodbye Pork Pie Hat," and Joni's "The Dry Cleaner from Des Moines," it also marked a personal connection with Metheny, who would become an important collaborator and dear friend through the rest of Michael's career.

As Wortman recalled, "I went up to see them at Tanglewood [in Lenox, Massachusetts]. Gary Gold and I drove up in a Mercedes 280SZL that he borrowed for the occasion, and we brought some dope with us because Mike was sick. We got to go backstage after the gig, and I remember they were all rushing around. They left the stage and got right on a private jet. Mike had never done anything like that before, and he was so into it."

As Michael himself recalled in an interview with this author, "That tour was pretty much a drug blowout. There was a lot of partying going on. It was just a symptom of the times—everybody was doing cocaine then."

Wortman remembers being starstruck later on while attending a few hangs at Joni Mitchell's loft on Varrick Street, just down the road from Seventh Avenue South. "She and Don Alias, who I was already good friends with, were living together at the time. It was an office building, closed at night, but Don had a key to the elevator. Joni had the top floor, and she had the whole roof, so you could walk around outside there. I think she had a basketball hoop out there, and she had a telescope as well. I had never been in a place like this. All of her paintings were everywhere, and there were a bunch of pinball machines that they had out on the *Shadows and Light* tour. And there was a beautiful Kawai nine-foot piano and Don's congas and drums. She also had a full-blown kitchen, restaurant quality. And we used to go over there and just get fucked up, me and Kenny and Don. Joni was never there. She was out in L.A. recording at the time, so Alias had the run of this place. I was using [heroin] every day at that point, and Alias would say, if I had anything, 'Come on over.' So, we'd go and hang. And I remember one night when Alias was jamming with Jerry Gonzalez, Daniel Ponce, Milton Cardona, and all these conga players, they wanted me to play cowbell, but I was so fucked up I had no clue as to where one was. So, I let that alone."

On May 31, 1979, Mike Mainieri had assembled an acoustic jazz quintet to play at Seventh Avenue South that consisted of himself on vibes, Michael on tenor sax, and Don Grolnick on piano along with Bill Evans's former bassist, Eddie Gomez, and all-world drummer Steve Gadd. This same lineup of musicians, minus Gomez, had previously played on Mainieri's 1977 Arista/Novus album, *Love Play*, with Michael guesting on the title track. And although that album was geared to the smoother, more accessible side, this quintet that Mainieri had put together for two consecutive nights at Seventh Avenue South was a far more adventurous, bop-oriented affair that put a premium on stretching. Strictly through word of mouth, this exciting new group took off.

"After those initial two nights in May, we played four consecutive nights in October [Thursday through Sunday, October 4–7] at Seventh Avenue South, and each night was packed," said Mainieri. "It started developing a pretty ridiculous crowd. And by the time we came back for three nights early December, there were huge lines of people waiting to get into the club to see us."

Michael Brecker on stage at Seventh Avenue South with bassist Marcus Miller, unknown drummer, with Miles Davis looking on, 1981 *(Courtesy of Kate Leviton Greenfield)*

An ardent fan of the group was Japanese journalist and fusion advocate Kiki Miyake, who had served as production coordinator for the Jun Fukamachi & New York All-Stars project, recorded live in Tokyo the previous year. Kiki loved the band and Steve Gadd in particular. "Gadd was really popular in Japan at the time and had been over there two or three times with Stuff," said Mainieri. "So, Kiki arranged with Nippon Columbia for us to come over, do these two nights at the Pit Inn in Tokyo [December 15–16, 1979], which were all recorded live, and then do a separate studio album the following day [December 17, 1979]. I produced both albums, and we were working day and night there. And because I had just signed a contract with Tommy LiPuma and was under contract with Warner Brothers, I couldn't record for Nippon Columbia under my name. So, I had to come up with a band name. We ended up calling it Steps."

(In 1982, Mainieri learned that the name Steps had been trade-marked by a band in North Carolina, resulting in the name change to Steps Ahead.)

The two nights at the Pit Inn, located in the popular Roppongi section of Tokyo, yielded the double live album *Smokin' in the Pit*. Released in February 1980, it was awarded a gold record in Japan on the strength of thrilling performances of Mainieri's "Tee Bag" and "Sara's Touch," Grolnick's surging samba "Fawlty Towers," Michael's driving "Not Ethiopia" (featuring an explosive guest appearance from Japanese fusion guitar star Kazumi Watanabe) along with tender renditions of Mal Waldron's achingly beautiful ballad "Soul Eyes," the mournful torch song "Lover Man," and a scintillating take on Joe Zawinul's Weather Report anthem, "Young and Fine." The daytime studio sessions yielded *Step by Step.* Released in the summer of 1980, it featured Michael flying on Grolnick's swinging "Uncle Bob." He also demonstrates uncommon lyricism on Mainieri's poppish "Kyoto" and his beautiful waltz-time ballad "Belle." And for sheer saxophone heroics, Michael unleashes with tenor fervor on Mainieri's churning, Latin-tinged "Bullet Train."

"After the live album went gold, and the studio album came out that summer of 1980, it was like this explosion," said Mainieri. "When we went back to Tokyo, it was a mob scene. On one of our last Steps concerts with Gadd in Japan, thousands of people would show up outside the hotel room when we arrived. It was like we were a rock band. It was amazing. And even though that first album went gold, it wasn't released here. They didn't even know who we were in the States."

On that last Steps concert with Gadd in Tokyo, Mainieri remembers that the drummer didn't come out for the second set and that Michael Brecker took over on the kit. "And, man, he sounded good," he said.

Steps manager Christine Martin, who was at that concert, remembers the backstage incident involving Gadd that prevented him from going on stage for the second set. "I'm out there in the audience, and all of a sudden Steve stops playing and walks off the stage. And the Japanese promoter came up to me and said, 'What can we do?' They couldn't talk to him. They couldn't speak English. So, I went backstage, and Steve was sitting there, and he was almost on the verge of tears. And he was saying, 'I'm not good enough for these guys.' And I didn't know what to say, so I just hugged him and said, 'Hey, everything's gonna be OK. Sure, you are good enough! And you have to go back and play.' And eventually he did go back on stage and finished the set. But he was going through a lot of shit at that time and was just freaking out a little bit. Luckily, Michael played drums well enough until Steve got it together to go back on stage."

On February 1, 1980, The Brecker Brothers released their George Duke–produced album, *Détente*, to a less-than-stellar reception. As Jason Elias wrote in AllMusic.com, "Some tracks here come off as a little too radio-friendly. Not surprisingly, the best cuts have both the classic intelligent Brecker Brothers sound as well as George Duke's production prowess. Despite a few lukewarm tracks, *Détente* is well worth picking up."

Or as John Kelman wrote in All About Jazz, "If some considered *Heavy Metal Be-Bop* to be excessive—and to some extent it was, but in the best possible way—then *Détente* seemed like a step backward, to the more song-oriented approach of *Back to Back* and *Don't Stop the Music*. And with keyboardist George Duke producing, The Brecker Brothers finally had a producer who could successfully marry the group's instrumental proclivities with an interest in soul and R&B."

Mike would later comment on his extremely gaunt and emaciated junkie look on the cover of *Détente*, calling it his Auschwitz photo.

With the rhythm tandem of bassist Marcus Miller and drummer Steve Gadd on four tracks, and drummer Steve Jordan and bassist Neil Jason on the remaining five, *Détente* had Don Grolnick and newcomer Mark Gray sharing keyboard duties while guitar parts were handled by Hiram Bullock, Jeff Mironov, and David Spinozza. "You Ga (Ta Give It)" sounds like warmed-over Average White Band while Randy's Zappa-esque "Don't Get Funny With My Money," with a sly vocal turn by Randy himself, registers some ticks on the funkometer.

Randy's "Baffled" is glorified disco with some cool breaks. Michael provides some much-needed edge with his angular funk work out "I Don't Know Either," and the classic Brecker Bros. sound is rekindled on his "Tee'd Off," which has Mike digging deep into his King Curtis bag. Randy lets off some steam on his high-note trumpet showcase, "Squish," but the Earth, Wind & Fire-ish "Not Tonight," with soulful vocals by session singer Carl Carlwell, seems out of place here.

By May 1980, Pat Metheny would recruit Michael to play on his fourth ECM outing, *80/81*. Recorded May 26–29, 1980, at Talent Studio in Oslo, Norway, this freewheeling affair also featured jazz icons Charlie Haden on bass, Dewey Redman on tenor sax, and Jack DeJohnette on drums. Michael is featured prominently on the moving ballad "Every

Day (I Thank You)," a gorgeous Metheny composition hailed as one of Michael's most expressive ballad vehicles. His outré instincts also come to the fore on forcefully swinging versions of the title track and an Ornette Coleman classic, "Turnaround." And he delivers some of his most searing lines of the set on the aptly titled improv piece "Open."

Wortman remembers that *80/81* session in Oslo having bad repercussions for Mike. "He got very sick there because they were gone for a week, and Mike had no connections there. And he couldn't bring any shit over there. Just look at the band photo on the back cover of that album. He looks terrible. He was sick from withdrawal, and he was hurting. He couldn't wait to get back home. And I remember the minute he came back, I had some dope there for him. Because he just didn't feel good, and he needed it."

In an interview with the BBC's Jez Nelson for a tribute to Michael Brecker on his "Jazz on 3" show, which aired on January 19, 2007, Michael called *80/81* and subsequent tour with Metheny, Redman, Haden, and DeJohnette a pivotal point in his career: "The record was a lot of fun to make, but it was the ensuing touring that we did in Europe where I really was turned around. That was kind of an epiphany for me. I had never played that way. I had been playing a lot of jazz in New York, as well as other kinds of music, but I never had the opportunity to play with this kind of rhythm section, and it just swung open a whole bunch of doors at once. They had me. And I've never been the same since."

By the end of 1980, The Brecker Brothers had assembled a new band to record what ended up being their swan song, which carried the quintessential NYC title of *Straphangin'*. With Marcus Miller on bass, Barry Finnerty on guitar, Mark Gray on keyboards, Don Alias on percussion, and Richie Morales on drums, they recaptured some of that old Brecker Brothers swagger (and a touch of humor) on Michael's funky title track and also on his rampaging showcase "Not Ethiopia," which featured a very Jaco-esque bass solo by Miller. Randy's swinging "Jacknife" contains some bristling solos from both Michael and Randy while Michael's Latin-tinged "Bathsheba" and Randy's gospel flavored "Threesome" offer some sparkling moments. Michael's smooth ballad "Dream Theme" is another expressive tenor sax showcase.

One of the stops on the Brecker Brothers summer tour of 1980 was at the Hamburg club Onkel Pö's Carnegie Hall, which was documented and later issued in 2020 on Randy's wife Ada Rovatti's Piloo Records label as *Live and Unreleased*. Said Randy, "That was a helluva tour. The band was killing every night. We had been playing together for a while at that point, so it was really a tightly knit ensemble. We were all at the top of our game."

As drummer Morales recalled, "I met Randy and Mike in 1975 when I was in this progressive funk-rock group from Ann Arbor, Michigan, called Sky King, which was led by Chris Brubeck, the son of Dave Brubeck. We got a record deal with Columbia, and we put one record out [*Secret Sauce*, 1975, produced by Steve Cropper, who had produced Dreams' second Columbia Records release, *Imagine My Surprise*, 1972]. We were making a second record and we got Randy to produce it. He brought Mike in to play on a track, and there's actually a funk saxophone-drum duet that was part of this tune."

As Chris Brubeck recalled, "We had a song on that album [which inevitably got shelved due to record company politics] called 'Red Tape,' and it had this great funk break in it. And I remember Randy saying to me, 'Boy, I can really hear Mike playing on this.' And I said, 'Oh, man, I can, too!' I had been deeply into the group Dreams, so I was a big Mike fan. And the first Brecker Brothers record with "Some Skunk Funk" was out by then. At the time, I thought it was one of the best recorded, most musical, just wonderful top albums of all time. So, I convinced Bruce Lundvall to let Randy Brecker produce our second album, and Randy ended up bringing Michael in to play on that track. So, we're in the studio, and Mike showed up to overdub. We left a sixty-four-bar area open for him to improvise over. And Randy conspired with me. At some point he says to me, 'I'm going to tell Mike that the engineer is just trying to get some sound on this take, but don't say anything because we're really going to record it.'

"And, so, Mike is hearing this tune literally for the very first time, and Randy says to Michael, 'Hey, why don't you just play along so we can get some level?' So, we are hearing him playing along with it, and he is kicking unbelievable ass! And then when it's done, Randy's winking at me. And he says, 'Now you watch, he's going to do two or three takes, and we will go back and use the very first time he ever heard it. Because my brother is such a genius, I know his most creative playing will be him having no idea what's coming next and reacting to it. And that'll be the best performance because it's before he starts analyzing everything that he knows is coming and how he should react to it in advance.' And he was right. After doing three or four takes, which, of course, were all brilliant in their own way, Randy says, 'Hey Mike, let's listen to that first take again." And it was evident to us all that it was the best take. It had that magic spark because you're hearing that raw genius right there in real time reacting to everything."

Morales also recalls being a fan of both Breckers going back to the early days. "I had been listening to Dreams and the Billy Cobham band after that and then that first Brecker Brothers album," he said. "And I also used to also see them with Jack Wilkins at Sweet Basil whenever they were in the New York area. I was really in awe of them, but they were both very approachable. In fact, they would let me hang at their recording sessions, so I got to sit in and observe *Back To Back, Don't Stop the Music*, and *Détente*. I saw a lot of classic master takes go down. Watching Chris Parker, Steve Gadd, and Lenny White work in the studio on that stuff was a really great education."

When Sky King disbanded, Morales began freelancing around New York and eventually began hanging at Seventh Avenue South. Eventually Michael approached him with an offer. "I'm at the bar downstairs, and Mike comes up to me, and he says, 'You want to join the band?' I'm like, 'What?' Because I know the line is long, and there's a lot of guys in front of me. And he says, 'I'd like you to do the gig, but the bread's not very good.' And I go, 'Oh, you're going to *pay* me to do it?' The first gig I played with them was a week run at Seventh Avenue South leading up to New Year's Eve 1979. Grolnick was still with the band when I joined, but soon after that Mark Gray came in on keyboards. I already knew him and Barry Finnerty and had played with both of those guys at Seventh Avenue South. So, we all played together on that summer tour of Europe in 1980, then in the winter of that year I went in the studio with them, and we recorded *Straphangin'*, which was the last record of that deal that they had with Arista. And I feel like that record has aged really well."

In January and February 1981, Michael recorded on Chick Corea's *Three Quartets* alongside bassist Eddie Gomez and drummer Steve Gadd at Mad Hatter Studios in Los Angeles. One of the tracks on that superb outing, "Quartet No. 2 (Part II)," was dedicated to Michael's main inspiration, John Coltrane. Michael's performance on that Trane tribute is a staggering example of his heightened virtuosity. Said Corea, "Mike always seemed to have Trane as part of his gorgeous sound. But we were all students of Trane—Mike and I especially. I spent many memorable nights listening to Trane, McCoy, Jimmy, and Elvin at the Half Note. I used to turn down gigs to be able to spend the whole weekend listening to every set. Coltrane University!"

Later that year, Corea's Three Quartets supergroup would play a few select gigs in the States and in Japan. The Brecker Brothers would then reunite for a tour of Japan May 3–14, 1981, with guitarist Kazumi Watanabe as special guest with the group. Michael then did a brief two-week tour with Metheny's *80/81* band August 23–September 4, 1981.

Michael recounted his ear-opening experience of that Metheny tour in a 2000 interview with *Downbeat*'s Ted Panken: "During the tour with Pat, Charlie, and Jack I experienced freedom differently than in the early New York days. It was such an open environment; the way they interacted, the way the music was conceptualized made me feel a tremendous sense of freedom, like I could play anything. There was a type of communication in present time on stage that I hadn't experienced before. Something about it caused a directional shift in my approach to playing."

By the third Steps album, *Paradox,* recorded live at Seventh Avenue South, Weather Report drummer Peter Erskine had replaced Gadd in the Steps lineup. "The first time I got to meet Michael was actually in Los Angeles," recalled Erskine. "He had been flown out to overdub solos on a Michel Colombier album (the French keyboardist-composer-arranger's self-titled on the Chrysalis label, 1979). Jaco had already played me some of those tracks when I first flew out to L.A. to begin rehearsals with Weather Report after I joined the band. And then Columbia booked me to play on Colombier's album, so I was in the loop as well. And when I got wind that Michael Brecker was going to come out to L.A. for the session, I was so excited about that. I remember telling every friend I had, 'Wow, I'm on a record with Michael Brecker!' And the most exciting news for me wasn't, 'Hey, I'm the new drummer in Weather Report' but rather, 'Man, I'm on a track with Michael Brecker!' I just thought it was the coolest thing."

Erskine had been a fan of Michael's going back to the first Dreams album, which he listened to in high school. "I was just floored by it," he said. "What Mike and Billy Cobham we're doing, that was the Coltrane and Elvin for our generation. I was a huge fan of everything Trane and

Elvin did, but I never got to hear them live, so to suddenly hear this tenor player and a drummer kind of doing the same thing but with a funky thing going on . . . it was thrilling! It just set this kind of impossible bar that was fun to aim for. Plus, it was interesting to hear that in the context of what was essentially a pop record with vocals and lyrics and stuff. And here these cats were really stretching in that."

Actually, Erskine's appreciation of Michael and Randy Brecker went back even farther than that, as he recalled. "I remember when Randy's *Score* came out. I found a pair of bell bottoms that looked like what Randy was wearing on the cover, I got the same boots he was wearing, and I got the fringe leather jacket. I couldn't grow the beard, but I was like, 'Yeah! I kind of want to be like that when I grow up.' And, you know, Michael was always very skinny, so I had no chance of looking like that. I wasn't tall and skinny like Mike. But Randy was someone I could emulate at the time."

When Michel Colombier premiered his new music at The Bottom Line in April 1979, both Michael and Erskine were in the band, along with guitarist Lee Ritenour, synth specialist Michael Boddicker, and bassist Will Lee. "That was the first time that I got to work live with either Michael or Will," said Erskine. "After that, the Seventh Avenue South scene kind of became like home base for me."

Both Erskine and Brecker subsequently played on a 1980 album that Mike Mainieri produced for guitarist Kazumi Watanabe (*To Chi Ka*, recorded at Media Sound Studios in New York) as well as on Mainieri's Warner Bros. debut, *Wanderlust* (sessions on February 25 and 26, 1981). "That's when I met Don Grolnick and first got to work with Steve Khan in the studio," said Erskine of that *Wanderlust* session. "And again, this is a little bit like a dream come true," he continued. "I'm getting to work with all my heroes. On the first day of tracking for *Wanderlust*, we're at the Power Station, and Michael's late. And, so, this informal betting pool gets started: What's the first thing Michael's going say? What's his excuse going to be? One guy says, 'He's going to come in and say he didn't get any sleep last night.' Another guy says, 'No, the first thing he's going to say is, 'I'm fucked.' And then the third guy says, 'No, the first thing he's going to say is, 'I can't find a reed.' So, everyone puts down their five dollars and then all of a sudden, the studio door bursts open, and here comes a very haggard-looking Michael. And in one sentence he says, 'I'm fucked, I didn't get any sleep last night, and I can't find a reed.' We all just looked around and started laughing. And Michael was like, 'What? Did I say something funny?'"

Erskine was still living in Los Angeles at the time that Don Grolnick invited him to come to New York to play a gig at Seventh Avenue South. "It was Don's first gig as a leader, and it was a killer band with Bob Berg, Marcus Miller, and John Tropea. So, I came to New York and played that gig, and it went very well. The next thing I know I was invited to do a gig with Steps, then I got asked to join that band. And that's when I decided to leave L.A. and move to New York."

On that Erskine-driven Steps live recording, *Paradox* (recorded Thursday through Sunday, September 17–20, 1981, at Seventh Avenue South), Michael demonstrates some typically jaw-dropping displays of virtuosity. "With Michael, it really was always music first," said Erskine. "He was a valiant warrior when it came to music. He really didn't have much tolerance for mediocrity."

*Paradox* finds Michael breaking loose for a heroic tenor solo on Mainieri's avant-gardeish "The Aleph," spurred on by Erskine's powerhouse drumming and Gomez's insistent walking pulse, then exploring with impunity on the open-ended Mainieri piece "Patch of Blue." Michael also contributes the jaunty, angular blues, "Take a Walk," which finds him blowing forcefully in a boppish bag, with a couple of allusions to Joe Henderson thrown in for good measure.

That same Steps lineup—Michael Brecker, Mike Mainieri, Eddie Gomez, Don Grolnick—would appear on Erskine's self-titled Contemporary Records debut, released in 1982. Michael offers a beautiful unaccompanied intro to Erskine's "All's Well That Ends" before breaking loose for a passionate solo on that track. And he stretches on a crackling rendition of Wayne Shorter's "E.S.P." that also features an outstanding solo from pianist Kenny Kirkland, who would later play on Michael's first album as a leader in 1987.

Seemingly at the top of his game, Michael was nevertheless growing more conflicted by his heroin addiction. "He talked about it all the time," said Jacqui." It was that 'I don't want to do this, but I feel bad when I don't' kind of talk. He felt bad every time he got high, but he needed to do it to not get sick. It was like he felt guilty about it. It seemed like he was ashamed or upset about it. He was not a happy junkie. It was almost like he did it to stay normal, not to get high. From what I felt of

Michael, there was no real euphoric feeling connected to it. He was just doing it so that he wouldn't withdraw."

Michael ended up renting a beautiful house in Westport, Connecticut, that belonged to Eleana Steinberg (Jimmy Cobb's widow) in a halfhearted attempt at going cold turkey on heroin. "Jacqui, Mike, and I drove up there, and Jacqui tried to help Mike kick," recalled Wortman. "But Mike and I really weren't ready to get clean. We'd make these pacts with each other that we're not going to get high tomorrow. But we never stuck to it."

Added Mike Mainieri, "I knew he was sick, in terms of the drugs he was doing. I wouldn't go near that myself, and he didn't want me to lecture him. Because the few times I did, I'd say, 'Mike, you don't know what this is going to lead to.' And he'd say, 'I know, I got to clean up.' And it wasn't like he was just fucking around with coke. Gadd was inhaling piles of coke. Those moments in Seventh Avenue South in that little room in the back? You remember the dressing room? It was just crazy. So, there was a ton of coke at Seventh Avenue South, but Michael had deeper problems than just coke."

Michael eventually began to acknowledge, if not seriously address, those problems. "Mike was on a mission constantly," said Wortman. "It was like a daily mantra with him: 'This has got to end.' He was always saying, 'This is no good,' and I'd say, 'Well, it's working for me. Look, I'm getting to hang with you!' I never really wanted to admit that I had a problem because that was too scary for me. In my head, I was too afraid that I'd be left with . . . what? . . . if I didn't have drugs. That was my only identification as a person was that I was a good drug addict. And I hung with people because of drugs. So that became my personality. It was who I was."

Mike indicated that he may indeed resolve his problem by going into rehab, but that idea did not sit well with Wortman. "The institutionalization of it scared the shit out of me," he said. "Because fear is what the whole thing is based on. The reality was, I didn't think I could do it. You know, 'I'm a fuckup at everything; why am I trying to fool myself? There's no way that I'm going to be able to do this.' And I got so comfortable setting the bar so low, so basically if my only mission in the day was to get twenty bucks to get a bag of dope so I didn't get sick, then I had my day set out. The obsession/compulsion to use was strong for me. When your body is telling you that you're uncomfortable, you want to make it comfortable. And once your body is taking stuff from the outside, and suddenly you're not using it, it's tough to replace it."

Jacqui did make other attempts at getting Michael to clean up his act. "It was very hard trying to get him sober," she recalled. "We used to go on these vacations—'geographics' we called them—where there was no heroin, and he wouldn't know where to get it if there was. And so, the vacation would be spent on, sort of, Michael kicking. One time we went to Barbados with Don Grolnick, who was Michael's closest friend. Don was a stellar person, and he never did drugs. He read a book a day, he was quiet, thoughtful . . . a really sweet person. And Michael absolutely loved him, like a brother. So, we went on that vacation together, and, of course, when we got back home a week later, Michael was getting high again."

By the end of 1981, the constant need to cop, the eternal quest for those perfect eighth notes, and the guilt that followed after getting high all began to weigh heavily on Michael. As Wortman said, "With all the talent, with all the work, everything falling in his lap—he had great looks, never had trouble getting girls, any of that stuff . . . very sociably capable on a lot of levels and had a fascinating mind—he was still unhappy. He was miserable." [Michael himself confessed to students at a clinic at North Texas State University in 1984, after he had gotten clean, "I'm just not into killing myself anymore. I tried that route. It was not happy. I sometimes played well, but I was very miserable."]

As their health began to unravel due to their drug use, Wortman's bond with Michael strengthened. "Our relationship just went to another level," Jerry recalled. "It became about stopping, knowing that we had a problem. That became our new mission."

It may have been a letter from his dear friend Don Grolnick that finally pushed Michael to take action. As Jacqui recalled, "Don had written this really beautiful letter to Michael, telling him how much he cared for him and that basically he was concerned that he was going to die. And that letter precipitated Michael to actually go into rehab."

As Randy recalled, "Our parents, as you can imagine, were pretty mortified by the whole thing. They held kind of an intervention for Mike, which I wasn't quite ready for."

"In the family, there were issues with rehab for Mike's parents about how people perceived it," added Wortman. "So going to get help was kind of a drastic move. When Mike decided to do that, I thought he was going too far. It brought the reality in my face, and that's maybe what scared me about it. 'Oh, wow! You're going to check in? You're not going to do it the bullshit way we've been trying to do it? You know . . . 'Let's just stop!' But that wasn't working."

It came down to Michael finally admitting that he couldn't take the junkie life anymore. "He was seeing doctors and getting vitamin B1 shots, but he needed to do something more direct," said Wortman. "And one night he said to me, 'If I can't do this, if I can't get sober . . . I'm gonna quit playing music.' And I remember the words cut right through me. I could see that he was not fooling around. Mike had made a lot of efforts to get clean before, but this time he was serious about it."

With the help of his sister, Emily, who had researched numerous rehab facilities, Mike finally entered the Palm Beach Institute on December 2, 1981, the day after a wild blowout at Mr. Pip's in Fort Lauderdale with the Word of Mouth big band in celebration of Jaco Pastorius's thirtieth birthday. Recorded remotely by engineer Peter Yianilos on his twenty-four-track mobile truck and later released by Warner Bros. in 1995 as *The Birthday Concert*, it features Michael unleashing with pure cathartic abandon and manic energy on a ridiculously up-tempo version of Bronislau Kaper's "Invitation" that has him engaging in some ferocious exchanges with fellow tenorist Bob Mintzer. Michael also played with remarkably expressive lyricism on Jaco's beautiful ballad "Three Views of a Secret" (on which his tenor substitutes for Toots Thielemans' poignant harmonica playing from *Word of Mouth*). Elsewhere on this wild big band blowout at Mr. Pip's, Michael dips into his King Curtis funk bag for an urgent solo on Pee Wee Ellis's "The Chicken," then delivers toe-curling tenor performances on Jaco's "Liberty City," "Punk Jazz," and particularly on "Domingo," on which he demonstrates uncanny acceleration and an almost superhuman propulsive double-timing prowess.

And, then, at what seemed like the very height of his saxophone primacy, Michael Brecker disappeared from the scene for five weeks. "That was the beginning of my recovery period," he recalled in a 1992 interview with this author. "I was grappling with a powerful addiction at that point, so my memories of that gig are very, very hazy. But I do remember Jaco visiting me in the hospital a few days later. He brought me a basketball and three juggling balls—but he showed up drunk, so it kind of defeated the purpose of his visit. They were reluctant to let him in, but eventually he got to see me for about two minutes. Believe it or not, he snuck back in after they kicked him out. He climbed over a fence and somehow got back in. I thanked him for the gifts and told him I was trying to get sober and asked him to leave. That was pretty much the end of it for me and Jaco. I couldn't associate with him after that."

Jacqui recalled being with Michael shortly after he got out of rehab in January 1982. "He had to do a gig at the Beacon Theater with Rickie Lee Jones, and I remember he was very nervous about it because she was still getting high. I had never been around Michael when he did a gig where he felt kind of tense and nervous. I mean, he played great, and it went off well, but he was on edge because I think he lived in fear every moment that he may go down the rabbit hole again. But that would have been the first gig he was doing in a band where there was somebody still actively getting high.

"And I know from going to Al Anon meetings that the person trying to get sober has to disconnect from certain things in life that trigger you or remind you of those drug times," Jacqui continued. "And for Michael, that was me. Unfortunately, I represented a part of that life that he had to leave behind. It was just a matter of months before we broke up. It was a very intense relationship; I adored him. It was very hard that it didn't work out between us. Probably the biggest heartbreak of my life was losing Michael."

Now newly committed to a clean and sober lifestyle, Michael rededicated himself to the music, triumphantly returning to the scene with a spirit of renewal while also intent on helping others get on the good foot.

# 6

# WORKING THE PROGRAM

After his time at the Palm Beach Institute, Michael returned to New York healthy and ready to begin the gradual process of turning his life around. As brother Randy noted, "He spent five weeks in rehab, and that was it. He never touched anything after that. If anything, he became a beacon of light for people that had problems. And he got just scores and scores of people into the program."

Indeed, part of Michael's legacy, apart from his prodigious contributions as composer, bandleader, and tenor titan, was the vast number of people he helped to get clean and sober. And his method— gentle, nonjudgmental, never pushy or proselytizing—was typically Michael. "He did come to people's aid, but it's not like he put it in people's faces or anything," said Jerry Wortman. "For me, Gary Gold, Bob Berg, and a whole lot of other guys that were strung out, Mike was there to help. I think he liked to make sure that people knew that there was another life, and it was important for him to spread the message that you could get clean if you have a problem. So, recovery really added a big dimension to his life."

It's hard to explain how Michael became such an important factor in the recovery of others without mentioning how hard he himself had fallen. And because of all that he had gone through in the '70s, he spoke with rare authority about the benefits of being clean and sober. "I knew Mike from the height of his addiction," said alto saxophonist Steve Slagle, who subbed for David Sanborn on some Brecker Brothers band rehearsals in the mid-'70s. "And I really admire anybody that can come through that to the other side, because they know what they're talking about; they went through it. And so, to me, Mike was one of the best people you could ever imagine to talk to if you had some kind of problems like that yourself. Because he went through the worst of it and came out the other side as a better person."

"Michael had a real renaissance," said pianist-composer Richie Bei-rach. "You could tell he was really glad to be finished with the dope, because there's certain kinds of junkies that get clean, but they really miss it. Michael didn't miss it. And what did he replace it with? Helping every other motherfucker! What a great fucking legacy that is."

"I think we were all surprised and impressed when Michael came out of rehab," said drummer Peter Erskine. "And it just endeared him that much more to us from when we all learned about it. Because he kept that very quiet, of course. I met him before he had become sober, and this was during a time when musicians getting high was kind of normal. It was rare to run into someone who didn't get high back in those days. So, when Mike made the transition, it caused everyone, I think, to stop and look at what they were doing. He was looked up to by so many people that I think we all looked at ourselves and went, 'Hmmmm . . . maybe Michael's onto something here.' Because he was the head of the pack. Sobriety became such an important part of his life, and he helped so many others get sober."

"He started this movement," said Bob Mintzer. "I mean, he defi-nitely started a musical movement, but he also started a movement into sobriety for the musical community in New York. Everybody respected him, and the fact that he cleaned up his act really made everybody take pause and say, 'Well shit, maybe it's time.' In fact, much of the whole jazz community cleaned up kind of together. That was comforting, and it made me feel like I could do this."

"Just on that level, aside from the music, he was a heroic figure," said drummer Adam Nussbaum, who would later become a member of Michael's first band as a leader in 1987. "He had a very positive, caring concern for people. He was a sponsor for a lot of people to get it together. I was a fortunate guy in that I never really had any problems. I was able to have my fun along the way, hither and yon. But Mike went all the way in, and in the process of recovery he wanted to help others. I think we all want to try and make this world a better place, and music is one way you can do that. But if you can also help people help them-selves by giving them the support, that's very important. We have to try to pay it forward in this life. And that's what Michael did in his life."

"The light of revelation Mike got was the fact that other things in his life were more important than getting high," said David Sanborn. "And it's easy to say when you're a little removed from that, but when you're in the thick of it, that's not such an easy thing to grasp. But Mike was able to do it, and he did it in context of the times, where there weren't a lot of people getting sober like that. People were out there white-knuckling. But Mike did it the right way, and he stuck with it to the end of his life. And that was the power of example, to me. He was out there by quiet example and patient interaction with people, really saving lives.

"And honestly, if it hadn't been for Mike, I don't know if I would have gotten sober on my own," Sanborn continued. "But he certainly saved me a few years at the very least. And he didn't do anything other than say, 'Well, this is what I did.' He respected the fact that everyone needs to find their own path. He was there if you needed him. And I will always love and respect him for that."

Bassist Dave Holland, who had met Michael when he was a fresh-faced nineteen-year-old tenor player on the loft scene, believes that his time in rehab not only put him on a path to recovery, but also renewed his musical journey as well. "I think when you go through that kind of life challenge that he went through, if you come through it in one piece, it gives you a new perspective on things and maybe a new beginning, a sort of redemption," he said. "And it occurs to me that that was a sort of turning point for him, in many ways, in his life. And I think he decided at that point to make the most of it.

"You know, there's a very isolating aspect to drugs," Holland continued. "And sometimes it closes you off to a lot of things. And when Mike stopped using, he began a much more engaging approach to the music in terms of looking at lots of different other options besides the ones that he had been working on. He really embraced some beautiful artistic projects after that, and his writing expanded. I mean, there were a lot of very positive things in him after rehab, and he really wanted to share that experience with others. That's part of the healing process, isn't it? You use your experience to try and help other people, and that in turn is a help to you as well."

"Michael was kind of ahead of a lot of people at that point," said guitarist Mike Stern, who would also become part of Brecker's touring band in 1987. "A lot of musicians were bottoming out, but here was a well-known cat going straight, and he was actually pulling it off. And people could see that he was doing better. People were inspired by Mike. So basically everybody, one by one, started getting sober, myself included. I had been playing with Jaco, and I was really bottoming out. And at some point, I knew it was time to go into someplace—both me and Leni—to try to get sober. We were both completely out of our minds, living above 55 Grand Street with Jaco. Michael just took it to the extreme, too. He had been through so much crazy shit and suffering before getting sober, and then he just worked the program. Mike was a great candidate for something like that because he was so open anyway, but that really pushed him even more. So, he just worked it, and he really helped a fuck of a lot of people."

Drummer and longtime friend Gary Gold maintains that everybody's got a 'Mike saved my life' story.' Here's his: "Mike had always told me, 'Go to the musicians' union if you want to clean up, because they'll help you.' I remember it was the winter of 1984, and he was doing *Saturday Night Live*, and I went down to see the show. It was a Christmas show [December 15], and Robert Plant and the Honeydrippers with Brian Setzer were the musical guests. [Indeed, Michael unleashes in the spirit of King Curtis on the group's seasonal tribute, "Santa Claus Is Back in Town."] After the show, I remember Mike and I walking in the snow, and I was just feeling so desperate. We walked for an hour in the freezing cold, and finally he said to me, 'You gotta go down to the musicians' union. They'll get you to rehab.'

"So, I went down to the musicians' union a couple of weeks after that, because I wasn't ready to stop running, you know? At the musicians' union, there was an old guy named Teddy Gompers, a retired musician who had started this thing called the Musicians Assistance Program, which has since become a whole big thing. But back in the day, it was just this little old man in this little tiny office that they gave him, wanting to help musicians get clean. And, so, I walked in, and Teddy was like this sort of cartoon character. I mean, here's this guy in his eighties, and he's like, 'So, whattaya on, kid . . . H? Yeah, back in the '40s, we used to stick lettuce up our asses to try and get high. Yeah, back in the '40s, me and Bird used to cop on the corner of so-and-so . . .' It was crazy!

"So, Teddy took me to the person in charge of insurance for musicians, and she looked me up and, of course, my dues were not paid for months, so I was bumped from the union. Teddy told her, 'We'll backdate his membership to January first,' and she said, 'OK, we'll just need $400 in back dues.' But I was broke at the time and told Teddy so. Then he said, 'Who do you know that will give you the four hundred bucks?' I told him that Mike was the one who told me to come down here and maybe he could help. So, Teddy got Mike on the phone right away and said, 'This is Teddy Gompers. I'm over here at the musicians' union with your friend Gary. He needs $400, and he needs it right now. We gotta get him into a rehab.' Mike hung up the phone, jumped in a cab, and came over to the musicians' union and wrote a check for four hundred bucks. And they booked me on an airplane to the same rehab place in Florida that Mike had gone to, the Palm Beach Institute. So, Mike saved my life that day, and we became really, really close after that. For the next thirty years, we were best friends. We talked every single day."

Guitarist Mike Stern offered this testimony: "A year before I went into rehab, Mike took me to my first meeting. I lasted half of the meeting and split. Mike saw me leave halfway through, and I felt kind of guilty about that. The next night I saw him at 55 Grand St., where I was playing and hanging out. He thought the place was really great, with the exception of all the extracurricular activities. But just as a music club, he dug it. And, of course, he was sober then. And at some point, as we were talking, I just came out with, 'You know, meetings don't really do it for me.' And he said, 'That meeting was a little strange. You gotta try some more.' But I told him, 'Look, it's not gonna work for me. I've been to therapy. I've been through this and that. I'm just not gonna make it. I'm not going to live long, and I can't really get sober. It's not possible for me.' And I listed all these reasons why. Years later when I was straight and playing in his band, he said to me, 'Remember that conversation we had at 55 Grand? You almost had me convinced.'"

Stern did go into rehab, but it didn't take initially. "I'd been sober and out of rehab for not even three months when I had this big slip where I ended up face down on the sidewalk. The guy who took me back to the rehab was actually the same guy who was selling me coke. And the way it works is, you can put somebody in for seventy-two hours, and then they can sign themselves out. I wanted out after the first hour, but I had to be held there for seventy-two hours. At the end of the first twenty-four hours, I said to myself, 'What the fuck am I fighting for? This shit sucks.' So, I called Mike. That was the first cat I thought of. And I told him, 'Look, man, I've really had it with this shit! Something happened in me, and now I just feel really committed to really cooling this shit out.' And we started talking about it.

"Of course, I had never really played sober before," Stern continued. "Every time I picked up a guitar, pretty much since I was twelve years old, there was always something in me. So, I was worried that I couldn't play without it. And at that point, when I was still getting high, the guitar was always a trigger for me."

Michael could relate to Stern's angst. He had experienced those same feelings when he first got sober. As Stern recalled, "Mike told me, 'The most important thing is to stay sober. If you can't play for a while, just let it go. Don't do it if it pushes too many buttons.' And, so, I took his advice. I found a little place at 55 Christopher St. in the West Village that was out of the way and unknown. And that was a perfect little place for me to start playing again because it didn't seem like I had much pressure on me since nobody knew I was there. And Mike thought that was a good way to get back to playing in public again."

Meanwhile, Stern's former running buddy, Jaco Pastorius, tried recruiting the guitarist to go out on the road with him again. "Jaco started bugging me about it, and I called Mike and told him, 'Jaco's gonna really be upset because I kind of promised him before I went into rehab that we'd be playing and touring together when I got out.' And Mike was adamant. He said, 'You can't do that! You do what you want to do, but he's gonna get you more fucked up than before, and you know it. He's gonna drag you down with him, and it won't be his fault. Because he's still getting high, and you're still very vulnerable.' And he was totally right. I saw that, I could feel it. And I said to myself, 'I'll never last a fuckin' day with Jaco again.' So, I had to stop playing with him."

Stern mentioned that Michael continued to offer sage advice about staying clean and sober. "He emphasized that it's one day at a time, and you kind of work on it all the time. And he was also a big one for going to meetings. When I got in his band in '87, we went to meetings all over Europe and Japan. I remember one meeting in Oslo where everybody in the room was speaking a different language, but you didn't have to understand the words to get what was going on. You didn't need a translator. You could kind of infer exactly what people were talking about because it's from the heart. Michael went through that himself, and that's part of what AA is about, that you help other people get sober, and that strengthens your own sobriety. And he really took that to heart. I mean, he really worked the program. That became his main priority . . . as much as music, if not more."

Beirach had a similar story about Mike's persistence in helping out a friend in need. "He would call me up, because I had my own problems at that time, and he would say, 'Richie, I've been hearing bad things about you.' I'd say, 'I know, I know,' and he'd say, 'You want to come over, and we'll talk?' I was obviously fucked up at the time, and at some point, he said, 'You've got to fix this. You can't go through your life like this. This is terrible. It's not funny anymore, is it?' And then he said, 'I will be your sponsor; I will do whatever you want. I want to help you.' He was always reaching out like that and helping motherfuckers. After he got clean, he was helping everybody. And you could see it made him feel good. He was more than nice, he was magnanimous. He was fucking Albert Schweitzer, man!"

Meanwhile, several in Michael's inner circle noticed a big change in his post-rehab personality from his pre-rehab self. "Until he got clean, it was all about surviving for Mike," said Seventh Avenue South's Kate Greenfield. "It isn't that he wasn't nice and that he didn't try to be warm before, but it was always about finding and using and getting ways and means to get more with Mike. You know, it rules you. And, so, he was constantly distracted by it. After he got clean, he was very approachable and open to helping people and talking to people and listening to people. He just became more thoughtful. Because, you know, you're more present when you're not fucked up. You're not just constantly obsessed with: 'You got a hit? Is this person going to meet me to bring me some? Do I have to go get it? How am I gonna cop today?'

"Michael was such a wonderful power of example for me and for a lot of people to get clean and sober, because we watched him change," she continued. It's the power of what one addict can do for another that no doctor or therapist or social worker can do. And he was amazing because he didn't preach. He didn't tell you what you should do. So, Michael's greatness is not only his musical legacy; it's also how he helped so many people. And he definitely helped me. I feel like he gave me my life back. I feel like I am blessed that I had a friendship, a recovery relationship, and a business relationship with Mike."

"He just seemed happier in a lot of ways post-rehab," noted trumpeter Randy Sandke, Michael's Indiana University pal and bandmate. "He didn't seem to be so burdened by things as he had been. It definitely seemed like he came out on the other side. And, of course, he was just so inspiring that way."

"He was still the same guy with the same incredible musicality and ability," said former Brecker Brothers drummer Chris Parker. "It's just that after rehab, he was not distracted by the other shit. His focus intensified, and you could talk to him longer. And the conversations were not just about music but about family and health and things that were going on in life. Before he went into rehab, he was the same sweet guy with a beautiful heart, really smart, but you always felt there was a lot more going on behind what he was currently saying. You know, he was thinking about a lot of things all the time. And without drugs and alcohol fogging his brain, he was that much clearer and that much more focused. And I also think that really allowed him to blossom as a composer."

Saxophonist Slagle noticed a distinct change in Michael's demeanor post-rehab. "With drugs, people always typecast it as like one thing, but it's not really true. Everybody is different. For example, I got to know Dr. John, who is someone who used heroin and had a very gregarious personality when he was high, where he'd be like talkative and happy and sociable. Whereas, Mike definitely was a more introverted, shy personality to begin with, and the drugs made him even more reticent and self-involved. And as soon as he got rid of that, he became a much more sociable person. So, to me, the Mike after rehab was a completely different person from when I first met him in 1977. He was more connected, more in the moment, more reflective.

"And maybe he was making up for lost time by suddenly becoming an extremely good listener to what you were saying and actually caring what you were going through in your life," Slagle continued. "But he really became very caring toward others, and he was very helpful, whether it was offering advice or just empathy. Post-rehab Mike would talk about his kids all the time. I was becoming a new father, and he offered me all kinds of advice on the subject of fatherhood. Or we would talk about our common interest in Bulgarian music or electronic music and sequencers and stuff. So, I really miss the relationship we had for that five or six years toward the end because it meant a lot to me, and I think maybe it helped him in some ways, too."

Christine Martin, who had met Michael in 1969–1970 during the White Elephant phase and later managed Steps in the band's formative years, including their trip to Tokyo in 1979 that resulted in the live *Smokin' in the Pit* album, recalls being surprised by the revelation of his stint in rehab. "I never knew that he was a drug addict," she said. "I could never tell by talking to him; he was able to hide it, I guess. And the day he told me that he had gone to rehab and finally cleaned up, I was like, 'Oh? I didn't know you had a problem.' Because high or not, he still played like Michael Brecker. Always. Maybe inside he didn't feel that great, but on the outside, nobody would know what he was really feeling. So, nothing had changed in that regard."

Michael did, however, confide in Christine his worries about committing to a clean and sober life. "I remember I had a conversation with him once after he had gotten out of rehab, and he said that he had been afraid that he wouldn't be able to play after he got clean," she recalled. "You know, he expressed that inner fear of, 'Am I going to be the same person anymore?' But, of course, he played beautifully after he got out of rehab . . . maybe even on a deeper level in some ways."

"Mike never felt like he was playing great, and he was always overly self-critical about that," said close friend and confidant Jerry Wortman. "But after rehab, it eventually got to a place where he didn't have to suffer and beat himself up in that way. He had acquired the tools to deal with whatever it was that was inside of him that made him so depressed and self-critical. But it took him a long time to find that place."

Wortman added, "I remember him going to Japan with Steps for the first time after getting clean [January 1982]. He was very scared to go on the road, very nervous. And he was being very cautious. He prepared, he got the contacts for where to go to meetings over there ahead of time, he did everything right. His sobriety and recovery came before everything. Because, as we understand, without that, the other shit doesn't have any purpose. And he was really focused on that."

Following his five-week stay in rehab, Michael jumped right back into circulation by tackling Claus Ogerman's achingly beautiful Warner Bros. album *Cityscape*, which was billed as a concerto for saxophone and orchestra with jazz rhythm section. It was the first album that Michael recorded where he shared coequal billing on the cover, his name prominently displayed right alongside maestro Ogerman's. Mike had previously played on Ogerman's 1976 album *Gate of Dreams*, another marvelous classical-pop-jazz mix that was called "a reminder of finer things" by no less an authority than legendary pianist Bill Evans, who contributed the liner notes. Michael appeared on only one of the eight tracks from *Gate of Dreams*, blowing through myriad changes on the surging pop-jazz number "Caprice." His solo, which begins at the 2:40 mark, showcases his signature facility and exhilarating flights into the high register, a prime example of crafting a Trane-inspired "sheets of sound" aesthetic to a slickly produced pop-classical format.

Michael's playing on the brooding three-movement suite "In the Presence and Absence of Each Other" from *Cityscape* is an astounding showcase that ranks among the finest recorded moments of his career. "Pt. 1" opens with Ogerman's lush strings before Mike enters at the :54 mark, carrying the memorable melodic theme in a robust, vocal manner. No pyrotechnics here, just warm, relaxed, and breathtakingly beautiful. He continues with some glorious melodic improvisation until finally unleashing the first of many fusillades at the 4:40 mark, nonchalantly double-timing while following the harmonic contour of the piece before culminating in some high-register Breckerisms. And although he only appears on the last 52 seconds of "Pt. 2" and the final minute of "Pt. 3," Michael's passionate contributions on each are deeply impactful as he covers the full range of the horn with signature virtuosity.

His most direct nod to John Coltrane comes on the pensive title track, where his references to Trane's opening nine-note figure from "Pt. 1: Acknowledgement" from *A Love Supreme* can be readily heard at the 3:40 mark and again at the 4:48 mark of the piece. Michael turns in another toe-curling performance on the soothing, Gadd-paced groover, "Habanera." There's a little bit of funk and swagger on this one, and Mike digs in accordingly, summoning up some Grover Washington Jr., a touch of Sanborn, and bits of King Curtis along the way.

Some years after the recording, Ogerman himself said, "Every twenty-five years a musician like Michael comes along. He reminds me of Glenn Gould, because Glenn played everything very brisk but extremely clear. No wishy-washy statements with him. And this also applies to Michael. He has a pristine sense of execution where you can follow every note. No matter how fast Michael plays, you can follow him perfectly. Stan Getz once told me, 'Just put a piece of music in front of me, and I'll give you a masterpiece.' This also applies to Michael. I think he's pretty phenomenal in terms of sight-reading, his command over the instrument, his improvisational and interpretive abilities . . . everything, really."

David Demsey, who has a copy of Michael's score to *Cityscape* at the Michael Brecker Archives at William Paterson University, explained Michael's approach to Ogerman's imposing opus: "His sheet music is all marked up. He was very studious about it, very detailed about what scale to play here, and how he was going to attack that passage there. And he circled things to practice. It looks like how a classical soloist would mark up a concerto part. And a lot more is written out than you would think. He just made it sound like he was making it up. Mike had a way of making written-out parts sound like his own voice. I was surprised by looking at the score, and I know a number of other individuals have reacted the same way. They looked at it and said, 'Oh, that's Ogerman's line? I didn't realize that.' It sounds like Mike's improvising it, but Ogerman actually wrote all that out. That's an amazing statement, that you can't really tell what Mike's improvising and what the composer wrote. It all sounds the same. And that's part of Mike's gift."

Demsey added, "Looking at his practice notes pre-rehab and post-rehab, there's no difference. That's an important thing to know, too. It's just as detailed, just as studious, just as much notating. Like, for example, there's a note with three stars in parentheses: 'Learn this in all keys.' And the handwriting is super neat. His manuscript is unerringly neat."

In his four-star review of *Cityscape* for AllMusic.com, James Manheim wrote, "The key to Ogerman's success has been his ability to stay in the background behind the musician he's working with and yet create something distinctive. This 1982 collaboration with the jazz saxophonist Michael Brecker is one of his most successful works, not least because the overlap between the extended harmonies of jazz and the chromaticism of the late German Romantic polyphony in which Ogerman was trained is large enough to allow Brecker to operate comfortably—his improvisations seem to grow naturally out of the background, and the intersections between jazz band and orchestral strings come more easily here than on almost any other crossover between jazz and classical music. The mood is nocturnal and reflective. Brecker at this point had not yet made an album as a bandleader; he was primarily known to those who closely followed jazz and R&B session musicians. The album was originally billed as a release by Claus Ogerman with Michael Brecker. Yet, notice how skillfully Ogerman eases the fearsomely talented young saxophonist into the spotlight."

(Ogerman and Brecker would collaborate once again, on their 1991 GRP album, *Corfu*.)

Richie Beirach called Michael's performance on *Cityscape* "stunning and unbelievable." As he said, "It's so revealing, it's almost like you don't want to see it, you know? Coming out of rehab, all his nerve

Michael Brecker and Claus Ogerman during the *Cityscape* session in New York, 1982 *(Photo by Suzanne Nygeres)*

endings were exposed and vulnerable, but his technical command was so unconscious, so deeply imbedded in his DNA, that he never had to think about intonation, technique, time, chords. All that intellectual shit that we have to struggle with, it was all intuitive for him. So, all he had to do was keep it together on that session. And can you imagine how good he felt not being strung out and looking for the next fix? So, I'm hearing even a little bit more joy in his playing there than he usually has because that pressure has been lifted. To me, he sounds liberated on that record."

Steps compatriot Mike Mainieri said Michael expressed some trepidation before going into The Power Station to record *Cityscape*. "When Mike came out of rehab, he called me, and he said, 'I don't know if I can do this. What do you think it's going to be like?' He was asking about being in that orchestral scene, because I had done a lot of dates like that [most notably George Benson's 1979 album *Livin' Inside Your Love*]. And I said, 'Man, you're gonna fucking walk through it.' He was always worried about sight-reading. Randy was a great sight-reader, but he did a lot more sessions than Michael. Randy really was fearless and could just sight-read anything, including difficult big band stuff, which he had done with the Thad Jones-Mel Lewis Orchestra and with Clark Terry's big band and Duke Pearson's big band. The harder the charts, the better for Randy. Whereas Michael wasn't really doing big band stuff all that much, and he was just a little skittish about sight-reading. Because to be really sharp, it's something you have to do almost every day, not like once every three months. You gotta get with a rehearsal band or get on a session where the music is really hard, and that's how you learn. And because Michael hadn't done as much of that as Randy had, he always questioned his sight-reading chops. But he did spectacularly on that album."

(Ogerman's composition "In the Presence and Absence of Each Other, Parts 1, 2 & 3" from *Cityscape* lost out to John Williams's "Flying" (Theme from *E.T. the Extraterrestrial*) in the Best Instrumental Composition category at the 25th Annual Grammy Awards.)

Once he had conquered his fears about playing on Claus Ogerman's imposing orchestral project, Michael had to confront his fears about returning to the belly of the beast—Seventh Avenue South. Once a notorious nexus for cocaine, sex, and jazz, it now presented the ultimate challenge for post-rehab Michael in his quest to remain clean and sober. "It turned into a nightmare for him after he got clean," said Wortman, who got sober himself in September 1982 after Michael had sent him down to the same Palm Beach Institute rehab facility where he had gone the year before. "He just wanted to get out of that situation, and he couldn't because they owed money on the place. So, he was trying desperately to balance out the books and then get rid of it."

Meanwhile, The Brecker Brothers band had come to the end of the road, it seemed. *Straphangin'* had been released in March 1981, and their last gigs together as a group came in Tokyo in May 1981, six months before Michael entered rehab. With no Brecker Brothers gigs on the horizon, the band went on hiatus. "Mike didn't want to continue with The Brecker Brothers," explained Randy. "He wanted to, as he put it, 'spread his wings' because we had been doing The Brecker Brothers for so long. So, it was just nice to get out of it and do something else."

Steps continued touring Europe, the States, and Japan through 1982 before the group finally morphed into Steps Ahead in 1983. And Randy took over Michael's spot as featured soloist in Jaco's Word of Mouth big band. "It was a good move for me," said Randy. "I was happy to play with Jaco and do those U.S. and Japan tours. It was a thrill for me."

(Randy was on the 1982 Word of Mouth tour of Japan that produced the two-LP Japan-only release *Twins* and its scaled-down Stateside counterpart, *Invitation*; he also appeared on the DVD *Live and Outrageous*, from the 1982 Montreal Jazz Festival.)

"So, Mike went off with Steps Ahead, which became a really popular band," added Randy. "And his writing continued to develop in that band. He wrote some great tunes for them. I have to say, I was always a little jealous. But now I listen to Steps Ahead, and I really enjoy that stuff."

During The Brecker Brothers' long hiatus, Randy formed the Randy Brecker/Eliane Elias group with his pianist/wife. Together they released the 1985 Brazilian-flavored contemporary jazz album *Amanda*, named in celebration of their newborn daughter. Michael appeared on one track, "Pandamandium," adding his signature robust tenor voice to that rhythmically charged number, which also included contributions from former Brecker Brothers bandmates Will Lee and Barry Finnerty, along with drummer Dave Weckl and former Weather Report percussionist Manolo Badrena. Later in that decade, Randy led two superbly swinging straight-ahead sessions, *In the Idiom* (1987) and *Live at Sweet Basil* (1988), and a more commercial offering in *Toe to Toe* (1990), which featured a sax solo by Michael on the ultra-funky, Prince-inspired track "It Creeps Up On You."

"During that ten-year period from '82 through '92, we really didn't play together very much," said Randy. "We kept talking about it. It wasn't that we were having any problems together; it's just that the record contract for The Brecker Brothers had run out in '82, and we kind of went our separate ways."

Though Michael wasn't quite as active in the studios as he had been in his pre-rehab years, he did play on a few other recordings in 1982 besides *Cityscape*, including Steps Ahead's self-titled debut, Donald Fagen's *The Nightfly*, George Benson's *In Your Eyes*, Ron Carter's *El Noche Sol*, Luther Vandross's *Forever, For Always, For Love*, Bob James's *The Genie: Themes & Variations from the TV Series 'Taxi,'* Michael Franks's *Objects of Desire*, and Barry Finnerty's Japanese release, *New York City*.

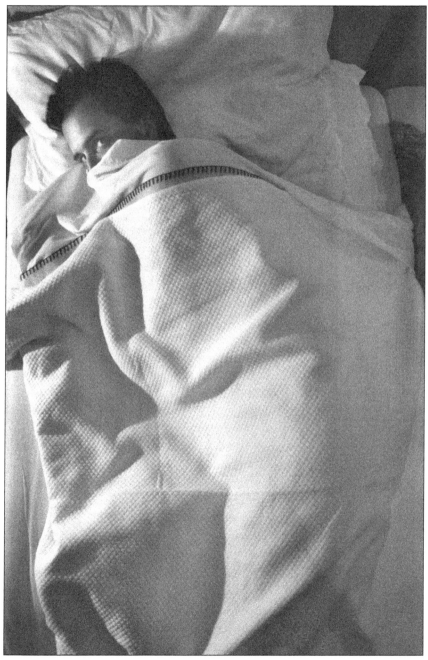

Michael at the Eden au Lac Hotel during the 1982 Montreux Jazz Festival
*(Photo by Darryl Pitt)*

Michael also played on Peter Erskine's self-titled debut for Contemporary Records, which showcased him in total "beast mode" on "All's Well That Ends." As Erskine recalled of that June 22, 1982, session at Eurosound Studios in New York, "I remember the night before we recorded the album, we had done a gig somewhere around Albany, and there was a bit of tension because I was using all the Steps Ahead guys [Mike Mainieri, Don Grolnick, Eddie Gomez, Michael Brecker] on the recording, and they hadn't done their first album yet for the Elektra Musician label. And I knew it would sound completely different, but now looking back I understand why [Steps Ahead manager] Christine Martin was not pleased by the fact that I had all the guys on my album as well. But I didn't know that many other players in New York, and they were just my favorite players. So, I wanted to make the record with them." Also appearing on Erskine's self-titled debut as a leader for John Koenig's Contemporary Records label were Randy Brecker, Bob Mintzer, Don Alias, and the gifted pianist Kenny Kirkland, who would later appear on Michael's own self-titled debut as a leader on the Impulse! label.

Although Michael curtailed his touring activity for 1982, preferring to stay closer to home during the initial phase of his recovery, he did appear frequently at Seventh Avenue South that year, playing in Grolnick's group Idiot Savant and also Bob Mintzer's big band as well as in bands led by guitarists Chuck Loeb and Finnerty and drummer Lenny White.

It was at a November 21, 1982, appearance at The Bottom Line by the newly reconstituted Steps Ahead that Brazilian pianist Eliane Elias (Randy Brecker's future wife) was introduced as the new replacement for original Steps pianist Grolnick. By that time, the group had finished its self-titled recording and North American debut on Bruce Lundvall's newly launched Elektra/Musician label, the jazz subsidiary of Elektra Records. Released the following summer, *Steps Ahead* (bearing the tagline "And introducing Eliane Elias") had Michael stretching in typically heroic fashion on Eddie Gomez's up-tempo romp "Loxodrome" as well as on Don Grolnick's brilliantly constructed set opener, "Pools," and on Mike Maineri's driving and catchy "Islands." Mike also showcases his inimitable chops on his lone compositional contribution, "Both Sides of the Coin." On the strength of this potent album, UK's *Jazzwise* magazine dubbed them "a perfectly poised jazz chamber group that can take your breath away" while *Downbeat* called them "a sophisticated sound striving for your attention."

In his August 1983 cover story for *Downbeat*, Howard Mandel proclaimed, "Steps Ahead could be a significant musical force in these mid-'80s: five veteran players, for all their experience still young, devising a repertoire that's fresh, accessible and tasteful for an audience that likes natural acoustics, polished concepts and intellectually honest emotions. There is balance and dimension in this quintet, as in the Modern Jazz Quartet or Codona—a composed balance rather than the balance of contrasting soloists over a dependable base. The players of Steps Ahead relate to each other as a team, or as Gomez suggests, 'a family. We're there for each other.' They relate in a way that their listeners can hear."

And yet, Mainieri confessed that Steps Ahead confused some critics and record buyers. "On the first album that we did for Elektra, which was all acoustic, we came in second in the Downbeat Readers Poll for electric ensemble and second as the best acoustic band. But we weren't an electric band then. That didn't happen until *Magnetic* [1986], where Mike was playing a lot of EWI, and I MIDI'ed up the vibes."

By 1983, Michael had taken to performing with a bandage around his neck as a means of alleviating discomfort he still felt from a botched herniated larynx surgery he had in 1973. As his Steps Ahead bandmate Peter Erskine recalled, "He was traveling and playing with an improvised brace—this kind of support band that he wore around his neck."

"It was like a Velcro band that was designed to keep his neck from inflating when he played," added Michael's friend and fellow saxophonist David Demsey, now curator of the Michael Brecker Archives at William Paterson University. "And I don't think it actually worked very well. He felt like he was getting strangled by it, so he stopped using it."

Michael's herniated larynx problem had initially manifested from severe overblowing during his loud rock band days with Mrs. Seaman's Sound Band at Indiana University and with Dreams, fueled by powerhouse drummer Billy Cobham and featuring the heavily effected overamplified guitar of John Abercrombie. Mike's partner in Mrs. Seaman's Sound Band, trumpeter Randy Sandke, had experienced the same herniated larynx problem a few years earlier and also spent some time playing with a gauze bandage wrapped around his ballooning neck. As Sandke recalled, "That very loud jazz-rock band that we had together at Indiana University was one of the leading causes, I think,

Steps Ahead performing at London's Capital Jazz Fest, 1983 (from l. to r. Eddie Gomez, Mike Mainieri, Peter Erskine, Michael Brecker (wearing protective bandage around his neck) (© *Stuart Nicholson*)

of us both getting this condition. We were playing with an amplified band—loud electric guitars and organs. We were using microphones, but the sound systems then were kind of primitive, so we were both really forcing to be heard."

That situation didn't change much at all for Michael in Dreams, which opened for other loud bands at rock emporiums such as the Fillmore East and Steve Paul's The Scene, or for that matter with Billy Cobham's powerhouse fusion band, which played at an extremely high decibel level.

Regarding Michael's botched surgery in 1973, Demsey said, "They cut right at the windpipe area. You could see the where the incision was, and they apparently cut the nerves that keep the neck in its shape. So, when Michael blew, his neck would inflate like Dizzy Gillespie's cheeks when he played the trumpet." Jerry Wortman said that Mike may have actually taken some bad advice in deciding to wrap his neck in a bandage for support during his early stint with Steps Ahead. "There was a period after he got clean where he was doing his own fixes for his problem. He started putting this neck thing on because he was told that it could pop and that he'd never play again. I used to think he was over-reacting to it, and I didn't like it when he wrapped it, because I could still see his neck bulging around it. And I remember asking him, 'Did somebody tell you to do that?' But he had this thing where he was so afraid, because he was told that if his neck happened to pop, he'd never be able to play again. That was frightening to him. And it certainly was affecting him mentally in terms of how he approached playing.

"That's also a primary reason for all the work he put in on the mouthpieces," added Wortman. "He was trying to find a way to play with more air flow that didn't put undue pressure on what was happening in his neck."

Dave Guardala eventually designed a mouthpiece for Michael that would play easily enough so that he could get the sound he wanted without it hurting him. As Demsey recalled, "His years of work with Dave Guardala was largely his continued attempts to get the right core in the sound—not too bright, nasal, or strident—but losing the back pressure and resistance that put too much strain on the throat. There were several instances when he'd ask to try my Otto Link [Michael's original brand of mouthpiece], and he'd say, 'Yes, that's it! I only wish I could still play on one of these, but it hurts too much.' But the Guardala mouthpiece reduced the pain enough that he could exist with it, so he kept playing the saxophone."

The introduction of the Electronic Wind Instrument (EWI), a Nyle Steiner invention which came along in the mid-'80s, was a godsend for Michael. It alleviated the problem with his neck somewhat because it required far less forceful blowing to activate notes, and it also offered him a rainbow of colors and timbres and textures to explore. "It was a sort of savior for him," said Demsey. "The original herniated problem stemmed from overblowing, and the EWI eliminated that stress. And Mike told me that one of the original motivations for experimenting with the EWI was because he feared that he would not be able to play saxophone for much longer, that there was too much pain. Of course, he then figured out the mouthpiece resistance thing so he could keep playing the tenor, and the EWI transformed into something much bigger and more musically important than a sub for his saxophone. But he put a scare into me with that mid-'80s conversation. I won't forget it."

Looking for some kind of grounding away from touring and the hectic scene at Seventh Avenue South, Michael took a job playing in the house band of *Saturday Night Live*. As Wortman, who was booking Seventh Avenue South at the time, said, "Michael was still worried about going on tour and slipping. He was still kind of new at being sober."

Michael appeared on two full seasons of *SNL* (Season 9, October 8, 1983–May 12, 1984; and Season 10, October 6, 1984–April 13, 1985). For that weekly gig, he could be seen on screen for just a few seconds at the opening of each show as the camera panned from the elevated catwalk high above the stage to the backstage door down below at stage level that each guest host walked through following Don Pardo's introduction. And Michael, of course, nonchalantly double-timed the lively *SNL* theme, invariably soaring up into the altissimo register to add an extra kick to that opening salvo each week.

Michael would make his first extended on-air appearance on the show in a swimming suit and bathrobe for Eddie Murphy's iconic "James Brown's Celebrity Hot Tub Party" skit that aired on November 5, 1983. As he told students at a University of North Texas State workshop a year later, "There's two things I don't like to do, and I always get embarrassed by them. One is go to the beach; the other is dance. I'm generally queasy about that. For the James Brown in a hot tub routine . . . what did I have to do but get dressed up in a bathing suit and dance."

Concurrent with his two-year stint on *SNL*, Michael racked up more impressive recording credits, including his memorable, emotionally charged playing on Mark Knopfler's powerfully optimistic theme song from his soundtrack to the 1983 film *Local Hero*, starring Burt Lancaster. He also made significant contributions to Kenny Wheeler's 1983 masterpiece on ECM Records, *Double, Double You* (with pianist John Taylor, bassist Dave Holland, and drummer Jack DeJohnette) and to guitarist John Abercrombie's brilliant 1984 ECM recording *Night* (with DeJohnette and keyboardist Jan Hammer). Michael also had a soulful turn on Ashford & Simpson's "Cherish Forever More" from their topselling 1984 R&B album *Solid*; and both he and brother Randy got an onrecord shout-out from Ol' Blue Eyes himself ("We got da Breckah Brothas . . .") on Frank Sinatra's version of "Mack the Knife" from his 1984 studio recording *L.A. Is My Lady*, which featured the siblings playing in Quincy Jones's all-star big band.

Steps Ahead's aptly titled 1984 release *Modern Times* was a radical departure from the group's acoustic-oriented self-titled debut from 1983. With an emphasis on high-tech, progressive, jazz-of-tomorrow sounds courtesy of Warren Bernhardt's throbbing synth-bass lines and sequencers, Erskine's DMX drum machine, Mainieri's synthi-vibes, and an overall hot DDD production, *Modern Times* was an early techno-jazz masterpiece. Michael played forceful tenor sax throughout, adding subtle splashes of EWI for coloring, a foreshadowing of things to come. As he said at the time in a 1984 clinic at NTSU, "Right now, I'm real excited by what's happening in the whole techno world. I know it freaks a lot of people out because they think that the machines are going to take over. For me, it's a state of mind. With Steps Ahead, we're working now with a lot of synthesized sounds and a sequencer and drum machine, and we're trying to work it into the music. And we've been really considerably successful, and I'm real pleased about it. All of a sudden, it's like I'm playing in technicolor instead of black and white."

Michael made use of soprano sax on two songs from *Modern Times*—his own brilliant and eminently catchy "Safari" and Peter Erskine's "Now You Know." Mainieri recalled struggling with Michael to get him to play soprano sax on his 1981 Warner Bros. album, *Wanderlust*. "There was a tune on that album called 'Flying Colors,' and I remember saying to him, 'Mike, I'd love you to play soprano on this one. I've never heard you play soprano, but I hear soprano on this tune.' But he says, 'No way.' And I say, 'Mike, just play the head. You don't have to play a solo.' He says, 'I can do it on tenor.' And I grabbed him by the legs—I was just goofing around—and I said, 'I'm not letting you leave until you bring your soprano tomorrow.' And he started laughing, and he said, 'All right, I'll play the head.' He comes in the next day with the soprano, and the fucking thing has dust on it. I don't even know if it works. But he played the head, and he sounded beautiful. We played that same tune on *Live at Montreux* with the New York All-Stars, but he played it on tenor. I couldn't con him into playing soprano on that one. But then when the EWI came in, and he was so fascinated by it because he could play as high as you wanted to go with it—eight octaves, I think—he didn't need to ever play soprano again."

Newly committed to a clean and sober path while investigating exciting musical possibilities with a new axe, Michael still had the albatross around his neck of Seventh Avenue South. But that same club that had been a den of iniquity for him would soon become the scene of a fortuitous meeting that would change his life forever.

# 7

# SUSAN AND A NEW LEASE ON LIFE

They met on the staircase of Seventh Avenue South, that spiral set of steps leading from the downstairs bar, where musicians and moochers hung out to avoid the cover charge, to the upstairs performance area, where paying customers sat at tables around an elevated stage. She stood 5 feet 4; he towered over her at 6 feet 4½. And although the petite psychotherapist and lanky saxophonist may have seemed an unlikely match to gawking onlookers, Susan Neustadt sensed an instant bond between them. "It really was just this immediate connection," she recalled. "In the old days they used to talk about 'love at first sight.' That's what Mike called it, and he always repeated this when he told the story of how we met . . . and it was true."

This perfect match had been set up by Kate Greenfield, Mike and Randy's partner in the club. "Mike had a lot of girlfriends," said Kate. "It was an endless string of 'monthers' as I called them—two months here, four months there, five months there, and a lot of one-night stands in between. Meanwhile Susan, who I got to know when I began doing volunteer work at Gracie Square Hospital after I get clean, had both feet on the ground and struck me as a solid citizen. And a lightbulb just went off in my head."

"Kate kept telling me, 'Oh, there's this guy . . . I think you'd be great with him,'" Susan recalled. "I sort of knew his name, but not really. I wasn't really a Brecker Brothers fan, I was actually more of a blues fan. Meanwhile, she'd give me little updates about Mike's situation. First it was, 'Well, he's seeing somebody.' And then it was, 'Well, he's not seeing anybody, but he's not ready.'"

Michael and Susan's fateful first meeting finally took place on the staircase at Seventh Avenue South on September 29, 1984—nearly three years after he had gotten out of PBI (Palm Beach Institute) and began turning his life around. He was playing at the club that night with Steps

Ahead, and Kate introduced them between sets. "When I first saw him, I thought he was really handsome and very striking," Susan noted.

Following some casual ice-breaking chit-chat on the staircase, an awkward pause in the conversation led Mike to sheepishly ask Susan, "What do I do now?" She responded matter-of-factly, "How about take my number?" Whether absentminded or lovestruck, Michael quickly jotted down Susan's phone number before going back upstairs to play another set while she split to her Upper East Side apartment. "And then he went on tour for ten days," Susan recalled. "And he called me every day."

Michael returned from touring with Steps Ahead in early October, just in time to start his second season as a member of the house band on *Saturday Night Live*. For Michael, that weekly high-profile job offered him some stability and routine after his stay in rehab. As Susan explained, "That was sort of his post-using, stay-at-home-and-get-his-shit-together gig."

Upon arriving back in New York from that Steps Ahead tour, Mike made plans to meet up with Susan for their actual "first date" following their initial encounter on the Seventh Avenue South staircase. "We were going to meet for coffee, and he kept having to delay it because the *Saturday Night Live* rehearsal was going on and on and on. Finally, at like nine o'clock at night he calls and says, 'Do you still want to meet?' I said yes, so we met at a little place on 74th Street and First Avenue, just one of those little places on the Upper East Side where you can eat. We had tea, and we talked, and it was very nice. When we left the place and started walking, I stopped him on the sidewalk and said, 'Aren't you forgetting something?' He said, 'What?' And I said, 'Your saxophone!' So, he quickly ran back into the restaurant and got it and was totally flustered when he came back out. I could tell he was completely smitten."

And it was clear that Susan was also smitten with Michael. "He was such a gentle spirit, and we just connected," she said. "And then for our second date, we went to see *Purple Rain* in Times Square, and we both flipped out . . . like, it changed our worlds! And we remained huge Prince fans after that. And I remember we walked from Times Square all the way up to my apartment on 76th and First Avenue, just talking the whole way. And that was it. I mean, we were together, kindred spirits. He was just like . . . *the* guy!"

"We were really lucky that we found each other," Susan continued. "Mike's composition teacher at the time, Edgar Grana, used to say that if Madison Square Garden was filled to capacity, we still would have found each other. It really just felt like we were meant to be together. And it changed both of our lives."

"I remember when he started dating her," said Michael's Steps Ahead bandmate Mike Mainieri. "Here was this slight, really charming, happy, up, tiny little woman, and there's this big Michael Brecker. And there was such joy there between the two of them. I mean, he was like the happiest guy on earth with Susan. He was kind of floating on air. And that was a turning point where he started realizing his potential, and he started believing in himself."

"I think he was missing a real partner," added keyboardist-producer and Michael collaborator Jason Miles. "And when he found Susan, that really centered him so much."

"Early on, I remember Mike with one beautiful girl after another, but he wasn't really happy," said Darryl Pitt, who would later become Michael's manager. "And then he came to realize what was important and what he really valued. And it spoke volumes to Mike's growth as a man that he chose Susan."

Although Susan worked in a rehab hospital and therefore was privy to the problems of addiction, Michael was already well on the road to recovery when they met. "He was going to therapy twice a week and meetings five times a week when we met," she recalled. "I never knew him when he was using, so I don't really know that part of his life."

Susan Neustadt had grown up in Newton, Massachusetts, and went to graduate school in Boston. "I wasn't that much of a jazz fan," she recalled. "I knew what I liked, though. I was introduced to Coltrane, Dolphy, and Mingus at age fifteen but listened more to rock, folk, and blues later on. Michael and I immediately connected with the blues. We both had the same Albert King records and listened to them together and also had blues tapes playing in the car when we'd drive around.

"I don't think my ears were that well trained, though," she continued. "When I first heard Michael play that night at Seventh Avenue South, I thought he was good, but I don't think I was as trained as I am now, certainly, to really appreciate what he was doing at the time. You know, as simple as I can put it, I don't think I really understood jazz as well as I do now."

What they also had in common, besides Albert King, was a shared sense of humor. As Susan said, "He was funny. I'm funny. And Mike was hysterical because he was silly. And I'm really silly, too. So, it was perfect for us because we could get really silly together, and always did, to the exclusion of the rest of the world.

"Laughter was important for us," she continued, "but we also enjoyed the repartee, the verbal bantering. And Mike wasn't a real talker. It was more through the humor and through our lifestyle together and what we shared. We communicated so well. He really trusted me, and I really trusted him. And we were both intellectually curious people. We both loved art, we both loved travel. And we got along really well because neither one of us were really dug into any sort of neurotic patterns, like you have to have your coffee just this way or you can't sleep like this. We were both really loose people, we didn't have a lot of rules, so it was really easy to get along. So, when I moved in with him, it didn't matter to him where I put anything. And he loved everything I did for him. He was always so grateful for everything."

Susan left her place on the Upper East Side and moved into Mike's loft at 247 Grand St. in February 1985. "We were engaged in June of '85 but told nobody," she said. "It was our secret all summer. Then in August we told our parents, and we got married the following January. So, it was fast-ish."

Mike and Susan were married on January 25, 1986, with a reception at the Four Seasons in Boston. "We didn't have to have the wedding," said Susan. "I did it for my mother. Michael and I didn't care about that; it wasn't important to us. I mean, we laughed our way through our wedding, literally laughing so hard we were crying. Years later, after we had been married for many years, he said, 'We should redo the wedding,' because neither one of us cared the first time around. We had already made the commitment to each other emotionally and spiritually, so we were together. The wedding was just something my mother needed to do."

Susan recalled one scene early on in their relationship together that underscored Michael's humility and humanity. "We were walking down Eighth Street, and there was a guy who was playing saxophone with an open case on the sidewalk, trying to collect donations from people passing by. And, so, we stopped to listen. Michael threw twenty bucks in the case, and as we walked away, he said, 'That guy was better than me.' I said, 'Really? Tell me about that.' And he said, 'Well, his fingering was quicker than mine.' And when I pointed out the actual facts, he said, 'Yeah but his ability to put the air through the horn . . . he could do that so much stronger than me.' And I'm like, 'Well, he really couldn't.' So, with each point he raised, I refuted it. And after about twenty minutes, we're still walking, and I said, 'So you see, Mike? Actually, he was not better than you.' And there was this five-second bit of silence, and he goes, 'Yeah, but he was so much braver than me to stand out on that curb.'

"This is who Michael was," she continued. "He's always going to find something good to say about everyone. I mean, he had an ego like we all do, but he really felt that he had something to learn from everybody. He'd go up to the guy who mowed our lawn and say, 'How do you do that?' And he meant it! He wasn't saying it in a pandering kind of way. He was genuinely curious about how stuff worked and how people did what they did."

Michael's curiosity about the art of composition had led him to study with the aforementioned Edgar Grana, a Juilliard-trained educator-composer. He was introduced to Grana through the instructor's brother Matthew, a jazz fan who belonged to the same recovery group as Mike. "I approached him kind of traditionally, conservatively, with the usual student-teacher relationship," recalled Grana of their early encounters. "But I soon discovered that Michael is almost impossible to teach because he's so intuitive. Everything is intuitive with Michael, and I'm an intuitive guy, too. We're very much alike in terms of how we approach music. And the other thing he liked about me is that I have an ability to explain music in kitchen English. I'm not a stuffy academic type. I'm a working composer who can teach, which is very valuable to some people.

"Michael had a very curious mind," he continued, "and he took very quickly to a series of exercises that I introduced to him that were extremely simple and had a huge impact on the way he thought. My teacher who passed it down to me at Juilliard, Stanley Woolf, billed it as 'five ways of harmonizing a melody.' Basically, it was a series of tension exercises using vertical structures in music. And Michael just took to it like a duck to water because it was grab-able right away for him. It was something he could put his arms around intuitively and get along with it and not battle with it. That was the big breakthrough."

As Michael explained to a roomful of students at a 1984 clinic at North Texas State University, "It's been kind of an expansive thing, studying with Edgar. I'll probably be there for a long time. Part of it is just a psychological approach. But he's given me some basic tools. Right now, he has me working on twelve-tone writing, getting the voicings from the matrices. It's a whole other way of thinking for me. I'm used to chords and notes and lines. It's another tool that I've been using, trying to voice lines using Edgar's system. And I've written a couple compositions based on his approach."

Grana explained that he was unaware of Michael's accomplishments with either Steps Ahead or The Brecker Brothers when they first met. "I think one of the things that Michael was struck by with me is that I didn't know how famous he was, and so there was a kind of professional naïveté with me. I wasn't starstruck. And I think that made a big impact on him. I had been living in an artistic cultural bubble for six years at Juilliard. I lost a lot of the culture in the first part of the '70s because I was so focused on my work. And, so, when Michael came to me, I didn't care who he was, in terms of what he represented on the scene. I just wanted to teach him. And we made great progress and ended up having such a wonderful personal relationship that went way beyond just music. I became something of his mentor to him. I was somebody he could go to. So, we had this unspoken respect for each other, a knowledge of each other. And I also respected Michael's restlessness, his curious mind."

Grana's method with his students was strictly hands-on and extremely intuitive. "They were always stunned at the way I work," he said. "I would look them in the eye, lean on my elbow, and say, 'Let's look at Bartok's 4th String Quartet.' And it would connect with them, because it's musicians being shown music. It's not an academic writing this out; this was a musician talking to other musicians with music that was designed directly to respond to their issues, not a syllabus or a third-party listening list. That's what really amazed them. I remember showing David Sanborn a Schoenberg transcription using a cello in the tenor register. David flipped when he saw it. Mike Stern saw it and said, 'This is the shit, dude!'"

And while Grana was able to trigger some significant breakthroughs with Michael regarding their twelve-tone studies, the teacher acknowledged and admired the obvious gifts of the pupil. "Michael is an outstanding musician, but he has a certain genius that very few have and very few exercise, coupled with generosity. And that was that Michael could interface with another talent like nobody in New York City could. No matter what, whether it was Steely Dan or Joni Mitchell or Paul Simon or James Taylor, he had an ability to just put clothes on you, like a tailor. He had an incredible genius that way. And I've often felt that that was who he really was. His solo world was Michael Brecker. But to me, it never talked like Michael *with* somebody."

During their time together, Michael confided in Grana some personal thoughts and feelings about his career. "He was never really happy in Steps Ahead, I can tell you that," he said. "Michael loved the musicians in the band, but he was still searching for a voice. What they were doing in Steps Ahead was a little too close to the fusion-y Brecker Brothers sound that he had already done, so it was kind of a cul-de-sac for him. He didn't feel like he could move forward with that band because he didn't know if it could go to another level. And so, part of my work with Michael was to help him stand on his own two feet."

After working with Michael, Grana would go on to teach composition to Lew Soloff, David Sanborn, Mike Stern, and many others in the jazz community. "Once the word got out that Michael Brecker was studying with me, the floodgates were opened," he said. "And I'm really grateful. It was something I grew up into. I had to work it out, grow up, believe in my niche, take care of myself. The very same reasons Michael came to me, to help him stand on his own two feet . . . well, he helped me stand on my two feet in an indirect way."

Grana likened his working with jazz musicians to being a ship's chandler outfitting sailboats before they went to sea. "You know what a chandler does? When all the famous captains and boats come into harbor to dock, the chandler gets to refurbish the whole ship—put on new sails and ropes, outfit the ship with galley supplies. I was like that for these jazz artists. They came back into New York and looked me up because they were sick of playing the same five things all over the world. Believe me, that haunted them. More than one of them would admit to me that they were recycling the same licks over and over. They're changing audiences, but they weren't moving it around too much. So, I'm the guy they go to. I'm the ship's chandler. I refit them, and off they'd go."

Bob Mintzer acknowledged that Michael's compositional prowess developed after spending time with Edgar Grana. "Mike had always been really self-effacing about his composing before then, but he really took these studies seriously and delved deeply into the art of composition during his time with Edgar. And he just blossomed as a composer from there. And in keeping with great jazz artists, he managed to meld his compositional style with his playing style into this distinctive sounding thing."

By April 1985, Michael had finished his nearly two-year stint on *Saturday Night Live*. He would subsequently put in a lot of studio time that year, guesting on numerous recordings, including the Bob Mintzer Big Band's *Incredible Journey*, Eddie Gomez's *Discovery*, and Don Grolnick's superb 1985 Windham Hill release *Hearts and Numbers*, which featured Michael's brawny tenor on the reggae flavored "Pointing at the Moon," a reworking of "Pools," and the achingly beautiful ballad "Regrets." Elsewhere on Grolnick's acclaimed debut as a leader, Mike is turned loose on the chops-busting up-tempo burner "Human Bites," powered by the drumming tandem of Peter Erskine and Steve Jordan.

Michael also blew with typical authority on Franco Ambrosetti's 1985 Enja outing, *Gin and Pentatonic*, and on three tunes from guitarist Joe Beck's 1985 release, *And Friends*—"Snow Scene," "There's Always Time," and the urgent "NYC"—all in the company of Beck and Grolnick with drummer Steve Gadd and bassist Jay Leonhart. He also made a special guest appearance that year on trumpeter Randy Sandke's debut album as a leader, *New York Stories*. "Mike was super reliable, super professional," recalled Sandke, who played alongside Mike in Mrs. Seaman's Sound Band back in their collegiate days at Indiana University. "He was great to hang out with and to talk to during the session, and he seemed very positive."

Michael's last album with Steps Ahead, *Magnetic* (1986), was a total tech dive into electric jazz. With former Weather Report electric bassist Victor Bailey replacing acoustic bassist Eddie Gomez, Hiram Bullock and Chuck Loeb sharing electric guitar duties, Mike Mainieri alternating between keyboards and synthi-vibes, and Peter Erskine holding down the fort on drums, Michael summons up unearthly sounds on his Oberheim Xpander-fueled EWI on "Trains" and "Beirut" while contributing the compositions "Sumo" and "Cajun." He also goes into full beast mode on Mainieri's "Magnetic Love," which features some soulful vocals by Dianne Reeves. But perhaps the most striking track on *Magnetic* is Michael's EWI showcase on Duke Ellington's tender ballad

"In a Sentimental Mood," highlighting the expressive powers of this new piece of technology, a territory that Michael would tap even deeper and more profoundly on subsequent projects.

"Mike was always intrigued by new technology," said Erskine. "He was the first guy I knew to have Logic on his computer, so he was a real cutting-edge guy early on. He had been messing around with the Condor box back in the Dreams days and then with wah-wah effects with The Brecker Brothers. So, Mike and Randy were both cutting edge way back when. He was always messing around with electronics, so the EWI was a natural for him. And with Steps Ahead, it made sense that it would evolve from this acoustic band into something else. They had already started to double Eddie Gomez's double bass with a synthesizer, so the writing was on the wall that things were about to go electric."

*Magnetic* was, indeed, a turning point for the band. "It was right after *Magnetic* came out that things really changed," said Mainieri. "By then, Peter had left the group. It had been just the three of us who were like partners—me, Mike, and Peter. But Peter hated the *Magnetic* album. He didn't like the more electric direction we were going in."

As Erskine said, "At one point I recall remarking, 'This is getting crazy!' You know, Mainieri's trying to sound like a guitar, the guitar is trying to sound like the vibes, and Mike's trying to sound like a piano with the EWI. And we were carrying around so much equipment, and this was in the pre-MIDI days. The band just had a lot more power."

Around this time, Joe Zawinul called Erskine to go out on the road with a reconstituted Weather Report. "So, Peter moved all his stuff out to the West Coast from New York, but then Zawinul ended up not using him," recalled Mainieri. "I remember getting a phone call from Peter saying, 'Man, I really got fucked here. Zawinul hired another drummer.' And he added, 'I need a change of scenery, so I'm gonna live out here.' And that's why we went looking for a drummer and got Steve Smith to do that *Magnetic* tour as well as the next album, *N.Y.C.* [1989]."

By the end of 1985, Michael had given up hope of continuing Seventh Avenue South. The final gig at the club on December 31, 1985, was a gala performance by the Seventh Avenue South All-Stars featuring Jaco Pastorius, Hiram Bullock, Mitch Forman, Kenwood Dennard, and special guest Michael Brecker. It was a wild night ending eight years of wild times and great music. Once party time central, the club had remained open well past the point that many of the regulars there, including Kate Greenfield, Jerry Wortman, Michael, and Randy, had turned their lives around and gotten clean and sober. "The last couple years of the existence of the club it became kind of an AA hangout, which wasn't such a great idea," said Randy. "We were trying to sell booze, and everybody's drinking Perrier. Not good for business."

"It was strictly a cash business," added Susan. "We had to be there every Friday and Saturday night. So, at the end of the night, we would take the cash home to the loft and count it out. I mean, it was really a drag. It was not a great business model; it was more like a clubhouse, a hang for them. They wanted a place to play. It was his own little scene, and everybody played there."

With Kate now out of the picture and Randy pulling back on his involvement with the club, the day-to-day duties fell to Michael. "I got involved to try and help him figure it out," said Susan. "And we realized we had to be onsite on the weekends because the staff was ripping us off. And it became so frustrating. For me, it was just a drain, and it started to run our lives. It wasn't good business, and it wasn't run by business people, so it was never going to be a success. Finally, I just said, 'Why are we keeping this club open? It's killing us.' And I was the one who had to be there for the Con Ed guy to shut it off and empty it. As a business, it was impossible. But the best thing about the club is that I met Mike there."

"Seventh Avenue South ran for eight years," Michael told Leigh Kamman in a 1987 radio interview. "We tried to rescue it . . . the responsibility fell on us. We tried to bail it out by the end of it, but it became too difficult. I miss the club just in terms of the music that was played there. It was great. A lot of groups had their start there, including Steps Ahead. So, it had its place, and its absence left kind of a void in New York for certain kinds of music."

But with the ending of the club came a new beginning in the tenor titan's career.

# 8

# GOING SOLO
## The "Pitt" Bull and the EWI

By early 1986, Michael began formulating plans for his long-overdue solo debut. He was thirty-seven, a universally respected figure and acknowledged "monster" player admired by fellow musicians from the pop, rock, and jazz worlds. He had ridden to fame through the '70s with The Brecker Brothers and blossomed into an accomplished composer in the '80s with Steps Ahead, the preeminent fusion band of its time. Now at the peak of his game, four years clean and sober, it seemed like the right time to make his move. And, yet, he had some apprehension.

As his wife, Susan, recalled, "He was doing *Magnetic* with Steps Ahead, and there was some trepidation about going out on his own. Of course, Mike had already made the leap away from Randy to do Steps Ahead. And that was sort of a big step . . . no pun intended. But I think he was more concerned whether he could do it all. Could he write all the music? Could he be a bandleader? But he never expressed any apprehension outwardly, so it wasn't like he was going to bed saying, 'Oh, I'm so worried that I'm not going to . . .' Mike wasn't like that. Mike was the kind of person where it was always an inside job for him; he did it all inside his head. You didn't see him nervous, and he wasn't all that forthcoming about it anyway.

"So, he was concerned, but he wasn't apprehensive to the point that it would stop him," she continued. "On the contrary, he was really excited about his first record. And as far as the music, he was very entrenched and embedded and loved it so much that it was constantly going on in his head. Constantly. So, it was an exciting time for him."

Michael was also being urged to branch out and go solo by Darryl Pitt, who had become his manager in late 1985 and had also acted as a conduit between Elektra Records' Bob Krasnow and Steps Ahead on the *Magnetic* project. "They didn't have a manager at that moment, so the responsibility kind of fell in my lap," he recalled of that interim phase. "Things at that time were kind of loosey-goosey with the group, so I tried to help bring some order to it."

Pitt also floated the idea of marketing Steps Ahead in a new way that went against the grain of established jazz protocol. As he recalled, "What I wanted to do with the group was, 'Let's make it more showbiz. Let's have lights and cue up some music before they take the stage and that sort of thing.' I wanted to make it a more fun experience for everyone."

"I remember getting very angry with Darryl," said Jerry Wortman, who worked as Steps Ahead's road manager at the time and later became Michael's road manager. "He started this idea of T-shirts and merch tables [tables selling merchandise at gigs], and my attitude was, 'These guys don't need this stuff. These are the greatest jazz musicians in the world.' I didn't understand show biz at that time, but I learned a lot from being around Darryl and began realizing that if an artist has a name and is able to make some money, you should do whatever you can to promote that artist, without being ridiculous."

Beyond the show biz aspects of the group, Steps Ahead also had business issues that needed to be addressed. Part of that involved getting Michael to be the deciding vote on band decisions between Mike Mainieri, Peter Erskine, and him. "The issue with Mike was that he was such a sweet, sweet man, and he would just go with whatever direction the winds would blow at that moment and basically agree with people," said Pitt. "And if people had differing opinions, he would agree with both of them, which became a burden for me as a manager. Peter Erskine had a point of view, Mike Mainieri had a point of view, and Mike Brecker was in the middle with the deciding vote, but he would invariably agree with both of them. And it became a problem because things weren't getting resolved.

"Finally, I had to say, 'Mike, you have to break the tie. It's wonderful to have three people calling the shots, so there's a majority decision that's being made, but that's not happening here. Break the tie.' Well, I broke the tie, and it was in favor of the Mainieri camp. And that was the catalyst, I believe, to Peter leaving the band."

Shortly after *Magnetic* was released, Pitt began urging Michael to compose more. "Mike had two songs on *Magnetic* and collaborated on a third," said Mainieri. "And, finally, Darryl really put his foot down and said, 'OK, Mike. It's time to write some stuff.' Then when Elektra dropped us in 1986, Darryl said to me, 'I'm going to get you guys a deal at GRP. I'm gonna get Steps Ahead a deal, and I'm going to get Michael a solo deal.' We had a meeting with Larry Rosen at GRP, and it turned out he wasn't interested in Steps Ahead. He said something to the effect of, 'I have too many bands, but if you're going to start another band with another label, Michael can't do it because I really want to present him.'"

Though Michael was initially hesitant to leave Steps Ahead and go out on his own, Mainieri encouraged him. "I said, 'Mike, it's time that you present your solo work. You need to go out.' We were at the end of whatever it was anyway. Peter had left the band. And now Steve Smith was in the band with Mike Stern on guitar and Darryl Jones on bass. We had just done that one little tour with that lineup, and I was feeling like I needed a break. I had a chance to build a recording studio, so I just told the other guys, 'I don't want to be on the road for a while.'"

That opened the door for Michael to commit wholeheartedly to a solo career. "He was really coming alive on so many levels," said Mainieri. "He started writing more, and that really took root. I had always been on Mike about writing more. I knew it was there in him; it was just a matter of prompting him. He was that exotic flower that a botanist finds in the woods. It's one of a kind, so you just have to be patient and let it grow slowly."

Going solo would also mean a distinct change of mind-set on Michael's part. As Wortman said, "Mike really started getting frustrated being a hired gun for studio sessions. He felt like he had crossed into this zone where it was kind of like whoring out a little bit. He didn't quite put it like that, but it was a sense that he just wasn't inspired by that kind of work anymore, and he felt like it was time to step up. He had other things in his head he wanted to do."

As Michael's manager, Pitt was key in helping Michael make that transition. A former editorial photographer who had done innumerable magazine and album covers, Pitt had freelanced for *Rolling Stone* and was a staff photographer at the Montreux Jazz Festival in Switzerland when Swiss electro-acoustic harpist Andreas Vollenweider made his debut there on July 11, 1981. Pitt met and befriended Vollenweider, and as their friendship developed, Darryl would pay regular visits to Andreas's home in Zurich whenever he was on a photo assignment in Europe. "I'd make a point to fly into Zurich and spend time with my new friend Andreas and his crazy, wonderful Hungarian wife, and then go on my way to wherever it was that I was going to shoot. And on one of these visits, he asked me if I could please try to help find a manager for him. So, I spoke to all of these agents and managers and business guys that I got to know, and I'd put headphones on these people so they could listen to this tape of Andreas's harp playing. And they all had the same response: 'That's really interesting, but he'll never be successful.'

"Finally, one day I flew into Switzerland and had lunch with Andreas's mom, and she said, 'Will you be my son's manager?,' and I was like, 'What?!' Andreas had said to me at one point, 'I'm too embarrassed to ask you to involve yourself so much in my life.' And I had no idea what was really involved in being a manager at that point anyway, so I naively said, 'Sure. I'll do that.' It happened pretty fast, actually."

While Pitt embarked on his new career of managing the Swiss harpist, he continued juggling work as a freelance photographer. "The pivotal moment for me, in terms of my own career trajectory, came when I started turning down calls to do freelance photography work because the Andreas thing was beginning to take off," he recalled. "I had an editor at Time-Life named Rose Keyser, and I was turning down her calls. And she said something to me for which I'm so grateful. She said, 'Look, you need to know, you're making my life more complicated. I want to make one phone call, get one person to do the one gig that I want them to do, and move on to something else.' And she goes, 'I don't know what the fuck you're doing on the side, but you better be successful at it because people are going to stop calling you, including me. So, you just better make sure it's successful.'"

Bruce Lundvall at Blue Note Records was also helpful in Pitt setting his priorities. "I did a photo shoot of Bruce for *Forbes* magazine, and I had already started becoming a manager at that point. And Bruce said to me, 'You're going to have to make a choice or use a pseudonym, because you're not going to do yourself any favors as a photographer.' I had already done work for Bruce—a couple of album covers for Columbia Records when he was there—so I knew him. And he helped me realize that I needed to focus my attention on Andreas because he was so original and so different. And I became convinced that all we had to do was work really, really hard, trying to get the music to be heard, and that it would resonate with the world. I really deeply believed that. And that's what happened." (Pitt came up with the pseudonym Odasan Macovich for all subsequent photo work that he did. The name was a tribute to his father, the popular Detroit-based orchestra leader Mack Pitt; "Macovich" is Russian for "son of Mack" and "Odasan" means "other son." As Pitt explained, "He had his son the doctor, which was my brother Steven, and then there was the other son, me.")

Vollenweider's breakthrough album, *Caverna Magica*, recorded in '82 and released Stateside on the CBS/Sony label in January of '83, put the harpist on the "space music/New Age" map. Pitt would establish his Depth of Field Management later that year with Vollenweider as his sole client. Vollenweider's follow-up album, *White Winds* (1984), sold in six figures. The Swiss harpist premiered his swirling, gently pastoral music in New York at the Beacon Theatre on October 20, 1984, which Stephen Holden covered for the *New York Times*. Pitt had clearly become a successful manager right out of the gate, and several people in the industry took notice, including Michael Brecker.

Darryl recalled first seeing Michael perform in person when he was a student photographer at the University of Michigan and was shooting a Bob James concert on campus (February 2, 1979). "Bob James was an alum at the University of Michigan and came to play at Hill Auditorium with a super-band consisting of Mike and Randy Brecker, Steve Gadd, and David Sanborn. I didn't know anything about anything then. The show was promoted by Roger Cramer of Eclipse Jazz [student-run concert promotion company operating under the auspices of the University of Michigan's Office of Major Events]. Roger Cramer went on to become a notable attorney in our business as well as the manager of Living Colour. Anyway, he knew that I was a photographer, and he said to me, 'Why don't you come and photograph our concerts?'"

After shooting the Bob James show out front of the proscenium stage in Hill Auditorium, Pitt was invited to go backstage to do individual portraits of the artists. And he was particularly struck by Michael Brecker. "He had on a hat and sunglasses indoors, and I was like, 'This guy is so cool!' And he had to have been extremely high at the time, which I wasn't aware of then. I had no idea that maybe there was a degree of pain or whatever else he may have been experiencing at the time. All I knew was he was just very nice to me. He let me do the photo shoot backstage, and he sort of got a kick out of it."

After college, the microbiology major and former wedding photographer in the Detroit area landed a job as the official photographer of the Montreux Jazz Festival, a prestigious position previously held for ten years by his idol, Giuseppe Pino, who later revolutionized theatrical photography and became a great fashion photographer. "I would run into Mike there each summer," he recalled. "And not only did I tremendously admire his great talent, there was something that I genuinely liked about him. Also, he went out of his way to be nice to me, so we got to know one another a bit in Montreux."

Back home, Pitt brought his father, a former lead alto sax player in Artie Shaw's big band, to see Michael play live. "On this occasion, Mike was a sideman in someone else's band. And I'll never forget my dad saying to me. 'This guy . . . oh, my goodness! You just introduced me to a genius.' And that really resonated with me."

Pitt's affection for Michael took an unorthodox turn the following summer at the Montreux Jazz Festival. As he explained, "Maybe it was his likability, or maybe I was looking for an older brother figure or something, or maybe it was because of what my Dad said about Mike resonated with me, in addition to my love of what it was that Mike was doing on the saxophone, but I had a yearning of wanting something more in my relationship with him."

The watershed moment in their relationship took place on a hill outside of the Montreux Casino, on the side facing Lake Geneva. As Pitt recalled, "There were stairs alongside the hill that you could take to get into the casino, but walking up the grassy knoll was a shortcut. However, it was a little bit slippery because it had rained in Montreux earlier that day. So, I spotted Mike walking up that grassy knoll to go inside the casino. He was wearing a clean, freshly pressed suit, and the only thing I could think of doing, as a way of expressing myself, was tackling him. So, we're both going up this slippery hill, and I'm thinking, 'If I just cut him underneath the legs and see him land on his back, he'll slide down the hill.' And that's what I did. Of course, I could have been fired right on the spot for doing that, but somehow Mike found it really funny, even though he was now wet and grass-stained. And he intuited what it was that I was yearning for that I couldn't find words to express.

And it came through in this crazy gesture. And that's kind of when our relationship changed a bit."

Fast-forward to October 5, 1985: Steps Ahead is playing New York's premier showcase venue, The Bottom Line. Pitt comes down to the gig to reconnect with his old pals. "By this time, Mike had heard about my involvement with Andreas," Darryl recalled, "and so he rhetorically asked me, 'What are you doing?' I responded, 'I guess I've become a manager.' And almost instantly he said, 'Would you be my manager?' I literally had tears in my eyes when he said that because, although he didn't know it, he was this kind of big brother figure to me. And there was this strange point of intersection for me—my love of Mike, my love of his music, my dad's respect for him, my respect for him. And I said something to the effect of, 'Mike, I would love nothing more than to be your manager. But for me to be able to provide any expected boost, you will need to embark on your solo career—make your own records, not just continue as a coleader of different bands.' He had always leaned on Randy or somebody else like Mike Mainieri. There was always somebody else that narrowed Mike's ability to feeling strong enough to be a leader. And he thought for a moment and said, 'I'm ready.' And so it began."

Taking the reins of Michael's solo career was personally satisfying for Pitt, but it also represented some challenges. "My work for Andreas was creative advocacy for what was the beginning of a career that was exploding. My work with Mike was different. It was learning to acclimate to how people would be upset with me. Among my first tasks was to disabuse about a half dozen record labels that Mike would be making his first record for them," he recalled. "In what was classic 'nice-guy Mike' style, he assured every major label head that inquired—and they all did—that he would make his first record with them. Mike had promised CBS. Mike had promised Bruce Lundvall at Blue Note. Mike promised Warner Brothers. Mike promised ECM. Mike promised everyone that he would make his first record with them. So, I had some cleaning up to do. I was the guy who had to say 'no' to all of those labels.

"My work as Mike's manager started with that," Pitt continued. "And that became the template for our lives together, where I was the bad cop, and instantly people hated me as a result of my having to be the bad cop. But I loved being Mike's bad cop. I loved it!"

Pitt would become an unrelenting pit bull on his new client's behalf, negotiating tough deals while always keeping an eye toward the big picture of Michael's career. With an unapologetically dogged style that could be described as "effectively tenacious," Pitt was reviled by some with whom he had business dealings. As one record executive wrote in a letter upon learning that Brecker would be leaving the label, "Mike, I want you to know I am so sorry. I love you. I'm so sorry we're going to be losing you. But the one thing I'm really glad about is that we'll never have to see Darryl Pitt again."

There is no denying that Pitt's methods were brusque, but they also greatly benefited his client, who over time would also become a dear friend. As Jerry Wortman noted of Darryl and Michael, "They had a completely special, unique relationship that went deeper than just the business. But business always got taken care of."

In 1986, Pitt secured a record deal for Michael with MCA's Ricky Schultz, who had directed the label's reentry into the jazz market via the newly relaunched Impulse! Records imprint—the same hallowed label for which John Coltrane had made some of his most potent recordings. "The notion of getting Mike a record deal was incredibly easy, and the reason why was because everyone wanted Mike to be able to record for him," said Pitt.

Michael's best friend, keyboardist-composer Don Grolnick, was enlisted to produce the saxophonist's self-titled debut, which featured an all-world band of guitarist Pat Metheny, bassist Charlie Haden, drummer Jack DeJohnette (reprising their role together from Metheny's *80/81*), and pianist Kenny Kirkland, who had previously played alongside Michael on Kazumi Watanabe's 1982 album *To Chi Ka*, Peter Erskine's self-titled 1982 debut, Franco Ambrosetti's 1983 album *Wings*, and his 1985 follow-up, *Gin and Pentatonic*, as well as on Steps Ahead's 1986 album, *Magnetic*. Grolnick also contributed three superb compositions in "The Cost of Living," "Nothing Personal," and "Original Rays." As Michael said, "I had the luxury of having Don Grolnick as a producer. He was my closest friend and my musical cohort. He had a keen eye for detail, and he had the ability to see the big picture as well."

Added Susan, "Mike really trusted Don. He trusted him not only as a friend, but as a steward of the music. Because Don was such a great composer and was so thoughtful and so thorough that Mike felt very

Michael Brecker jamming with guitarist Henry Johnson and drummer Roy Haynes at MCA/Impulse party on June 23, 1986 at Sweet Basil in Greenwich Village *(Photo by Rick Laird)*

safe with him, not only to explore different types of music and different arrangements, but that it would come out OK. Because Don really held himself and others to a very high degree of excellence. And Michael appreciated that, because he was the same way. Don was more stringent about the rules, but Mike held himself to that same very high degree."

Grolnick's relationship with Brecker went back to their days together in Dreams during the early '70s and through a five-year run with The Brecker Brothers. "They were both a little quirky in the same way," said Susan, "and they talked for hours at a time on the phone. They were just really good friends, and they were both so funny. I mean, Don was clearly, hands down, one of the funniest people I've ever met. And Mike was a close second. I mean, Mike could make me laugh till I'd cry. Both were very dry, very witty. All Don had to do was lean over and say something completely deadpan, and I'd be in tears laughing. I actually had to stop eating food with Don, any dinners, because once he made me laugh so hard on the Upper West Side that I threw up in the restaurant. He was such a funny man."

Engineer James Farber, who had worked on 1983's *Steps Ahead* and the group's 1984 follow-up, *Magnetic*, was brought in to work on *Michael Brecker*, which was recorded at the Power Station Studio A in December of 1986. Farber recalls getting the word about the project via phone message from Mike. "I was in Chicago visiting a friend when I checked my phone machine, and Mike had left a message: 'I'm going to make a jazz record!' And I was like, 'Wow, this is so great. It's really about time.' And, of course, he got this super band. And the album became a classic."

Farber offered some insights about the working dynamic in the studio between Michael and producer Grolnick on that first Brecker album. "They were brothers. Don was Mr. Instinctive, and he always made Mike feel so relaxed. Mike would sort of get a little nervous about things, which you wouldn't expect. But the fact that he went all those years with The Brecker Brothers and Steps Ahead and never made his own record until the age of thirty-eight . . . the expectations alone would naturally add some stress to the situation.

"But Don was kind of a guru," Farber continued. "And his sense of humor was so disarming. Don was the voice of reason, of not over-thinking and not overdoing and not getting too technical or getting too obsessed with fixing things. Don was the earthy guy, and he kept certain of Mike's instincts in check. For instance, Mike might get a little tunnel visioned about some little technical thing or something, and Don would always give it some perspective. That's something that he always offered."

In terms of content, Michael was clear from the outset what direction his solo debut would take. Said Wortman, "In the past, Mike had always been so torn between what he was going to do for his first album—a fusiony Brecker Brothers-type record or a jazz record. He was always toying with that notion. Then, after he finally made that first record for Impulse!, I distinctly remember him calling me and saying, kind of mischievously, 'Guess what? I made a jazz record.' And it was such an amazing record. Kenny Kirkland, who was my roommate at the time, told me that it was one of the greatest honors of his career to play on that record."

Dreams debut on Columbia Records, 1970

Michael Brecker in Dreams, 1971
*(Photo courtesy Randy Brecker)*

Father Bobby Brecker flanked by sons Randy and Michael, 1972
*(Photo courtesy Randy Brecker)*

Inner sleeve from Mike Mainieri & Friends' *White Elephant*, circa 1972
*(Photos by Lee Marshall)*

Back cover of the Brecker Brothers' 1977 album, *Don't Stop the Music*
*(Photo courtesy David Arky)*

Spot the celebrities in the crowd from this 1979 New Year's Eve party at Seventh Avenue South *(Photo courtesy Kate Leviton Greenfield)*

Sibling rivalry re-enacted backstage at the 1980 Aurex Jazz Festival in Japan *(Courtesy of Peter Erskine)*

Susan Neustadt and Mike take their first vacation together in early 1985 *(Courtesy of Susan Brecker)*

Album cover for Michael Brecker's second album as a leader, *Don't Try This at Home*, 1988

Susan, Sam, Jessica and Mike at home in Hastings-on-Hudson in 1995 *(Courtesy of Susan Brecker)*

Michael performing on the Electronic Wind Instrument (EWI) with The Brecker Brothers in 1994 in Maastricht, Holland *(Photo by Louis Gerrits)*

Mike and Elvin Jones between
takes at the *Time Is of the Essence*
session at Right Track Studios, 1999
*(Photo by Odasan Macovich)*

Directions in Music: Michael Brecker,
Herbie Hancock, and Roy Hargrove, 2002
*(Photo courtesy Hans Neleman)*

Saxophone Summit holding forth at Birdland, 2003
*(Photo courtesy Robert Hoffman)*

Mike Mainieri and Michael Brecker pose for a publicity photo to promote the 2003 Steps Ahead reunion tour. *(Photo by Peter Freed)*

Steps Ahead in concert at the Mt. Fuji festival, 2004 (from l. to r.): Mike Stern, Michael Brecker, Steve Gadd, Darryl Jones (not pictured: Mike Mainieri, Adam Holzman) *(Photo by Jun Sato)*

Brecker family on vacation, 2006 *(Courtesy of Susan Brecker)*

A light moment at the *Pilgrimage* session, 2006 (from l. to r.: Jack DeJohnette, Michael Brecker, Gil Goldstein, Herbie Hancock; not pictured: Pat Metheny, Brad Mehldau, John Patitucci) *(Photo by Osadan Macovich)*

Susan, flanked by Jessica and Sam Brecker, accepting posthumous Grammies for Mike's 2007 swan song, *Pilgrimage* *(Photo by Vince Bucci)*

Michael Brecker posing in the photo studio with his sax and a Weimaraner, 1986
(Courtesy of John Sann Estate)

"That first record was a big record for him," Susan conceded. "That really set the tone for the rest of his career." From the glorious, gospel-tinged shouts from Michael's horn on the album's opener, "Sea Glass," to the all-out burn of "Syzygy" (featuring a Trane-Elvin–inspired, whirlwind sax-drums breakdown with Jack DeJohnette for the first two and a half minutes of the track) to Don Grolnick's "Nothing Personal" and the exhilarating EWI showcase, "Original Rays," *Michael Brecker* surges with energy and ideas. And for exquisite nuance and grace, there's Grolnick's melancholic ballad "Cost of Living," featuring a remarkable bass solo by Haden that Michael proclaimed as "one of the high points of the album, for me." Michael's powerfully expressive, keening tenor solo on that moody Grolnick requiem, along with his extended solo tenor intro for the first two and a half minutes to "My One and Only Love," stand as other high-water marks of his impressive debut as a leader.

In an interview I did with Michael for the June 1987 issue of *Downbeat* (a cover story titled "New Axe, New Attitude"), he expounded on his self-titled debut, the significance of recording on Impulse!, and his current fascination with the EWI:

"This year I felt ready to make a record under my own name, probably for the first time in my life. I had always shied away from it previously, or had worked in collaborative-type efforts, either with my brother, Randy, or with Mike Mainieri and Peter Erskine. I guess I never really felt that I merited doing an album. I felt afraid to do it, really. But the feeling that I wanted to do something took hold this year, followed by various feelers from different record companies. So, I was approached by Ricky Shultz at Impulse! Initially, it scared me, just the aura of Impulse! Well, not scared me—I was awed by it, considering the rich history of the label—Trane, Sonny Rollins, and everybody.

"And we talked about doing a jazz record, which is really what I wanted to do," he continued. "So, I started batting around in my mind certain rhythm sections—people that I wanted to play with, who I felt would really create the right musical environment. I had an association with Pat, Charlie, and Jack from years back, beginning with Pat's record *80/81*. We subsequently did a tour, which opened up a door for me. And it's remained open. I just hadn't really had a chance to pursue that type of playing since then. I guess I hadn't taken it quite as far as I wanted. I wanted an opportunity to take it further, particularly with those guys—and with Kenny Kirkland, whose playing I admire very much. It's a way of playing where there's a lot of space, where it's open, and it just seems like the harmonic and rhythmic possibilities are infinite. And there's a warmth that the four of them are able to generate that's very appealing to me. Really, all four of them almost transcend their instruments. They play with such musicality and originality that they transcend the difficulty or the limitations of their instruments."

Regarding his fascination with the EWI, Michael added, "It's an instrument unto itself—very different from taking a sax and electrifying it and expecting it to sound good. The fingering positions are basically identical to a saxophone, the main difference being it's touch sensitive. So, there's no moving keys, which is hard to adjust to at first because saxophone players are taught to rest their fingers on the keys. But on this, it would activate a sound if you did that. So, you have to be very careful what you touch. It requires a lot of accuracy both in fingering and tonguing. The horn is attached to a suitcase-type container with all the electronics, and there's a set of eight rollers on the back of the instrument for making octave leaps. Whatever roller I'm touching determines the octave I'm playing in. So, by rolling your thumb, you can make incredibly quick octave leaps. And the unique thing is the warmth of the sounds you can get. You can make some gorgeous acoustic-like sounds—alto flute, violin, shakuhachi, a harmonica that sounds like Stevie Wonder. They're organic sounds instead of cold, brittle synthesizer sounds. It's really a fascinating instrument."

Michael's approach to programming sounds for the EWI revealed his scientific acumen, an intrinsic quality going back to youthful days with his chemistry set in his parents' Cheltenham Township basement: "For me, the instrument is wide open. The only limit is your imagination. It's opened up new vistas for me, yet I'm not putting my sax on the shelf. If anything, I've been playing the saxophone more than I ever did. Having the EWI has kind of freed me up, and yet, somehow for me, one can't exist without the other. I enjoy synthesizing and making sounds, blending sounds, dealing with wave forms and experimenting with timbres. And after playing around with that stuff, I get a craving to get back to playing an acoustic instrument like the tenor. But I play the EWI because I enjoy it. It's fun. I've always, on some level, been fascinated by electronics. I went through a period about five years ago where I seriously got into video games. So, I just took that energy and applied it to this. I guess I got tired of wasting quarters."

In discussing the very expressive nature of his playing throughout *Michael Brecker*, he also touched on the spiritual aspects of making music: "It's something that I've always felt able to summon, particularly more so in the last five years than ever before. That's also probably because I've been in touch with myself emotionally to a much greater degree in the past year or so, but it really takes being with the right musicians to bring it out in a musical way. It's not something that I've developed intentionally, but I think I've become more comfortable with it lately—more in touch with my own feelings. That has had a huge effect on my playing.

"But the emotional part, really, has a life of its own," he continued. "It's almost like the feelings get in touch with me rather than me getting in touch with them. And it just comes out in the music. It sounds kind of pseudo-spiritual, but I feel when I'm really at my best that I'm not really playing at all. It's almost like it takes on a life of its own. And those moments seem to be coming more often now than they used to. It's a very exhilarating feeling, but it seems to be something that, at this point, I have no control over. So, I just try to move forward—keep up with technique, keep listening, trying to expand and learn, play as much as possible, and just try to have a good attitude. And the rest is really—I don't know . . . it almost feels like I'm being played by some other force."

Following its release in April 1987, *Michael Brecker* hit number one on the *Billboard* traditional jazz chart on June 20 and remained there for ten weeks. "That record came out, and we could do a week at New Morning in Paris and have lines around the block for six nights, sold out," recalled road manager Wortman. "I mean, nobody does that anymore. Nobody plays more than one night anywhere anymore. We played Fat Tuesday's in New York, played the Bottom Line . . . all sell-outs. There was definitely a lot of momentum going for Mike at that time."

And though Michael was unable to take the stellar lineup that appeared on his Impulse! debut out on the road, he assembled a potent touring band featuring Kirkland on piano, Mike Stern on guitar, Jeff Andrews on electric bass, and Adam Nussbaum on drums. "Mike came by the 55 Bar, and he hired the trio I was playing with, which was me and Jeff and Adam," recalled Stern. "We had a regular weekly gig there, and Mike just came down one night and said, 'I want you to be in my band and go on the road.' So, we started shedding with him, practicing the tunes, and figuring out what to play and when. And Michael had this thing of being so vulnerable and so honest about stuff in a way that you'd just come to expect from him. At one point he said to me, 'You know, I can't play anything. I'm so nervous about all this.' Meanwhile, he was killing! But I understood the feeling of insecurity that he had."

Stern and Brecker had crossed paths several times before, first ten years earlier when the guitarist was in Blood, Sweat & Tears and the tenor titan was touring with The Brecker Brothers. Both were in a bad way then regarding their drug use. They met several times at Seventh Avenue South in its heyday and once backstage in 1981 at a Miles Davis concert when Stern was in the band and both were still dealing with their addictions. In 1985, both now on the path to sobriety, they had an unexpected but significant bonding. "I saw Mike at an AA meeting, and he just gave me a hug, and we talked about it for a while," Stern recalled. "And then the gig with Steps Ahead opened up in the summer of '86, so I got to play with Mike Mainieri and Mike Brecker together. What an amazing experience that was playing with both those cats."

The first official gig for the new Michael Brecker Band was at Hunt's Tavern in Montpelier, Vermont, on March 26, 1987. The following day, they appeared at the University of Maine in a gig booked by Michael's old tenor sax comrade David Demsey. "I had gotten a job teaching at University of Maine in Augusta and was living up there," Demsey recalled. "I had already booked Steps Ahead for some gigs on campus the year before, and I kept poking Mike in the ribs, going, 'Why haven't you made a solo album? I don't understand.' And he would say, 'Well, I don't feel ready.' And I'd said, 'Well, we're ready! The world is ready.'"

Michael would eventually call his friend Demsey to green-light a gig on the Maine campus. "I remember him saying, 'Well, I've finally done it! Do you have a venue? I need a place to get the kinks out with this new band in a place where I'm not going to get a *New York Times* review.' And I told him, 'Well, here in Augusta, I can guarantee that you're not going to get any kind of a review.' So, they came up and spent three days and rehearsed and played this titanic concert where they basically played everything twice, just to get the kinks out."

Four days later, on March 31, 1987, the Michael Brecker Band made its NYC debut at Fat Tuesday's, the subterranean club on Third Avenue between 17th and 18th Streets run by Stan Getz's son Steve. Their week-long engagement, from Tuesday through Sunday, drew packed houses of Brecker Brothers and Steps Ahead fans who had lined up to see the scintillating chemistry between Michael, Stern, Kirkland, Andrews, and Nussbaum. This dynamic and eminently swinging ensemble had the makings of a small group juggernaut. But then, with the prospect of a highly anticipated European summer tour lying just ahead of them, an unexpected bit of bad news threatened to derail their momentum.

On the eve of a May 5 gig at Mississippi Nights in St. Louis, road manager Wortman received a call from Kirkland, explaining that he had to leave the band. "We had just finished up a gig at the Vic Theater in Chicago, and Kenny calls me and says very quietly, 'Sting called. I gotta go.' And I'm like, 'What do you mean you gotta go?!' I was relatively new to this whole road managing thing at this point. I had a little experience working with David Sanborn's band and Billy Cobham's band before this, and also with the PDB trio of Jaco Pastorius, Kenwood Dennard, and Hiram Bullock, but those gigs were not at this level I was at now with Michael's band. We have a truck out, and we have a tour booked, and it's Mike's first tour. We're about to travel to Europe in July. Meanwhile, Kenny Kirkland is the only one who ever played the music from that record. No other piano player had ever played it before."

While Kirkland offered to send a sub to the Michael Brecker Band's next gig, Stern felt uncomfortable doing the rest of the tour with an unknown quantity on keyboards. "He was freaking out about having a piano player that he didn't know and that might affect his thing. And I remember him saying, 'Call somebody we know. Call Mitch Forman.' [Forman had played on Stern's 1986 Atlantic Records release, *Upside Downside*, and Michael had played on the keyboardist's 1985 release, *Train of Thought*.] But then I talked to Michael about the situation and he said, 'What about that kid I played with at the clinic? I think he might be OK. He's very young, but he's got that thing . . . he's got the vibe."

The kid was Joey Calderazzo, a twenty-year-old keyboard phenom from New Rochelle who had sat in with Michael several months earlier in a clinic at Long Island University hosted by veteran alto saxophonist-educator Pete Yellin. Wortman remembered the events leading up to that pivotal encounter. "Michael was living on Grand Street then, and he didn't have a car, so I came by in my old Saab and picked him up, packed his EWI and all his gear into the car, and drove him to Brooklyn for the clinic. In general, Mike steered clear of clinics because he said, 'Half the kids can't play, and it's really a struggle, and I gotta pretend.' But he agreed to do this one."

After arriving at Long Island University, Wortman began setting up Michael's equipment. A student trio was on hand to provide backing for Michael during the clinic. "It was a French kid on piano [Laurent de Wilde], a bass player, and a drummer, who turned out to be Joey's brother [Gene Calderazzo]," Wortman recalled. Although Gene was still a student at LIU, Joey had already dropped out by this time, but he came by the clinic anyway because he had heard that Michael Brecker was playing, and he hoped to somehow insinuate himself onto the scene. Calderazzo's boldness paid off, as he ended up jamming with Michael on John Coltrane's "Impressions," making a strong impression on the tenor titan. As Wortman recalled, "Afterward, as we were driving back to Mike's place on Grand Street, I said to him, 'Am I crazy? You were telling me these kids can't play.' And he said, 'No, that was something I never experienced before.'"

At that time, Joey held down a regular Friday night gig at La Reserve, a hotel in White Plains, near where he grew up. It was a trio led by bassist Rich Syracuse and including Joey's brother Gene on drums. Special guests such as saxophonist Dave Liebman had already sat in with the trio, and Calderazzo got up the nerve to invite Michael to come up as a featured guest on a Friday night. "It was a funny scene," Wortman recalled. "It's a restaurant in Westchester, people are eating dinner, and these guys are just burning out in the corner. And Mike went up there and played with them."

As Calderazzo recalled of that engagement at La Reserve, "I paid Mike two hundred bucks to come do the gig. It was a Friday night, the place is tiny, and it's completely packed. And at some point, the manager of the place came up to me and said, 'You know, this guy's good. Can we get him every week?'"

Some months later, when Michael called about Joey filling in for Kenny Kirkland on the Michael Brecker Band tour of the States and Europe, the young pianist explained that he couldn't make the first two dates due to a prior commitment. "I was playing in a group at the time that was in the Hennessy Jazz Search, where bands from all around the country were competing for the grand prize [$2,000 and an appearance at the Playboy Jazz Festival]. I was just a sideman in the band, and we made it to the finals, which were held at the Hollywood Bowl. Hennessy was going to fly us out to Los Angeles and put us up in a hotel for two days. So, I inquired about pulling out of the gig in order to go out with Mike, but it turned out that if I didn't make it out to the finals, the band would be disqualified. So, I had to tell Mike, 'Sorry, I can't do it.'" Calderazzo flew to Los Angeles with the band, and they did indeed play the Hollywood Bowl, but they ended up losing to tenor saxophonist Rick Margitza's band in the finals.

Michael had gotten pianist Phil Markowitz [who had played along-side Mike and Randy on *You Can't Live Without It*, Jack Wilkins's 1977 album] as a last-minute sub for Kirkland on the Mississippi Nights gig in St. Louis. Calderazzo met the band in Pittsburgh for a May 7 gig at Graffiti, which turned out to be a memorable initiation into the group for the young keyboard phenom. As Wortman recalled, "I go pick Joey up at the Pittsburgh airport, and he's got a DX7 keyboard on his lap, no case. I don't know how he got on the plane with it. We drive to Graffiti, and I notice the marquee out front of the club says 'Kenny Kirkland.' And right before the set starts, I ask Joey, 'What do you want in the monitor?' And he said, 'I don't know, man. Let's just play!' And I realize he's probably never played with a monitor before. So, the set starts, and people think it's Kenny Kirkland on keyboards. They don't know who Joey Calderazzo is."

The band opened their set, as usual, with "Nothing Personal," the up-tempo Grolnick minor blues from *Michael Brecker*. "Joey soloed first, and he just tore the place apart!" said Wortman. "Mike couldn't even play after that solo. The place went nuts. It was classic!"

Just before hooking up on that Michael Brecker Band tour, Calder-azzo was living in his mother's house in New Rochelle and also spending time at his girlfriend's place nine miles away in Mamaroneck. And since he had lost his father at age seventeen, Michael soon became a kind of surrogate father figure to him on the road. "That's what my relationship with Mike was, and it kind of stayed that way," said the keyboardist.

"Joey was this little kid," Susan remembered. "I mean, we always considered Joey our son, you know? When Joey got the call to join the band, and he came to the loft on Grand Street to get the charts for his first European tour with the band, he was like a baby, just twenty-one. And I remember him coming up the stairs to the loft, singing one of Mike's tunes. It was really cute."

But a troubling side to this gifted kid was soon revealed on the road. "I was touring with Michael Brecker, and I felt like a rock star," Calder-azzo said, recalling his virgin tour with the band. "I was drinking a lot then, and they were all concerned for me because I was so wild. And it got to where I started keeping things from Mike because I didn't want him to be disappointed in me. I was wild in those years, man. And I didn't want him to know."

Because Michael had gone through the same scenario himself earlier in his career, he not only could empathize, he could easily read all the signs that Joey was putting out. "Mike used to do this thing whenever he noticed that I was getting out of control, where he'd say, 'Check!' and then make like he was making a mark in a ledger he was keeping on me," Joey recalled. "And then it got to the point where he'd just have to mime the check mark. Because I was fucking up so much."

"Joey was a wild man," said Wortman. "We were all married guys and older. Mike was thirty-eight on that tour. Joey was young, single, and horny all the time, which is how he got the nickname 'Chubby' (an inside reference to the fact that he was forever 'popping a chubby' on the bandstand)." Joey confirmed, "I was fucking everything in sight at that time."

"It was unbelievable," said Jerry. "And there were some scary moments, too, where he was picking up people that maybe seemed dangerous. He was pretty wild, but he was around a lot of really good, solid people."

"Joey was a little terror at that time," added Stern. "We were all looking out for him, but you can't lecture anybody, and he wasn't ready anyway. You know, he still wanted to party. His attitude was, 'All you guys did it for all those years. Why can't I have my slice?' When you have that propensity to go in that direction, you can't be talked out of it by anybody. You really have to make your own mistakes. And, so, we were kind of there as examples for him. Mike was, of course, a very powerful example. And I was sober, too. All that kind of helped Joey eventually, even though it got really bad for him."

Pitt recalled a humorous story about Calderazzo's naïveté regarding his onstage demeanor. "We were playing a concert, and the first set had finished, and the band leaves the stage. It's intermission, and suddenly Joey walks back out on stage and goes out to the edge of the proscenium stage, and he sits down. I'm standing by the sound booth, and I see this happening—and by now people are coming up to him and chatting with him. So, I walk up to the edge of the stage, and I tell him, 'Joey, what are you doing? You can't do this now. After the gig, if you want to meet people . . . fine. But not during intermission. Go backstage!' It turned out he was trying to meet girls."

Generally, after concerts, Michael and Darryl would routinely chat about how the gig went. But on this night, Pitt raised the issue of Joey's behavior. "I said, 'Look, Mike, I gotta tell you something that was just really odd tonight. During intermission, Joey just came out on stage and sat down on the edge of the stage and was just hanging out there talking to people. I told him how he needs to comport himself a bit differently moving forward, and I think he heard me; he got it.' And Mike goes, 'Oh, my God, it's my fault!' And I didn't expect to hear that from Mike, so I said, 'What do you mean, it's your fault?' And he goes, 'I told him that if he wanted to meet girls, he should just sort of stroll around on the stage and busy himself with some little stuff and just hang out there, and the people would come up to him and introduce themselves, and that would be a great way for him to get to meet girls. But I forgot to tell him not to do it during intermission.'"

Wortman offered this classic Joey Calderazzo road story: "We're playing Salt Lake Arts Festival in Utah. It's three stages at this huge fairgrounds, and we're just one component of this big arts festival with many different kinds of things going on. It's not just a jazz festival or even a musical festival. And I see off in the distance a big explosion, and suddenly all the power goes off. We're supposed to be the closing act on the big stage, which is now dark. But the promoter says to me, 'Please, we have another stage, and there's power there. Can you at least give the people something? And Mike says, 'Of course.' So, we pack up all the gear, and we drive around the festival grounds to the other stage. And Joey walks out on stage to check the piano and he's going, 'Hey man, where's the piano at?' Then somebody yells, 'Hey! Get out of here!' Joey had walked on stage in the middle of this Mummenschanz-type dance performance going on. They're all on stage in the dark in various positions, and Joey's walking around out there looking for the piano while ten thousand people are watching, wondering what the hell is going on."

Those minor mishaps aside, the Michael Brecker Band was cooking on all burners every night in every city they traveled to. And with Calderazzo bringing his forcefully swinging, McCoy Tyner–inspired "piano pounding" and heightened harmonic extrapolations to the proceedings, it only brought out the Trane aspect in Michael's playing to an even higher degree. Add to that volatile mix guitarist Stern, with his envelope-pushing, distortion-laced scorched-earth approach to soloing, and you had the makings of one of the most electrifying acts on the jazz circuit in 1987–88.

"That band had a lot of fire," said drummer Adam Nussbaum. "It was always exciting, because everybody in that band could throw down. I mean, it was dazzling every night! Joey could burn. Stern could burn. Mike could burn. So, it was a lot of fun, and also just being able to play every night with the same people . . . there's no substitute for that."

"It was a band of lunatics," added Calderazzo. "I mean, I listen to some of those tapes now, and it was just . . . BOOM! We'd go from zero to one hundred right out of the gate. And generally, Mike Stern would take things up a notch, like his solo at the end of 'Nothing Personal' would go to 110, then I'd have to follow him! And as that first tour continued, we were pushing it to a 150 some nights."

Meanwhile, Wortman's jazz purist attitude persisted when he became road manager for the Michael Brecker Band. "We had a show, our first one at The Bottom Line [October 10, 1987], and I didn't want to deal with all that merch and showbiz shit," he recalled. "But Darryl had the vision that Pat Metheny also had, which I learned many years later after working with Pat—that presentation and lighting and show business mattered. My attitude was always, 'Who needs that? You're hearing the greatest saxophone player in the world with a great drummer and a great band. What do you need lighting for?' Now that I'm much further down the road, I see that it's kind of narrow-minded to think that way. I see now that there's an audience, and the show is much more enhanced, and it gives a sense of being something else—an event. And Darryl is the guy who showed me the aesthetic value of having it more show-business oriented, even in a jazz context."

Calderazzo remembers Michael's preshow ritual on the road in that first year as being extraordinarily focused and intense. "He'd be backstage practicing and really psyching himself up to go on stage, almost like he was a heavyweight champion boxer coming out already warmed-up in a full sweat, ready to go into the ring. I mean, it was deep. And I learned not to fuck with him during that ritual, because I used to come in and bother Mike when he was in that psyching up mode, and he'd point to the door and yell, 'Out!' It was amazing how intense he'd get before a show."

On the lighter side, Calderazzo recalled one funny experience involving Michael. "We were embarking on a three-week tour of the States that began at the Iron Horse in Northampton, Massachusetts. And we were going up there to start a day of rehearsals before the gig.

I drove up with Mike, and we get to the Iron Horse, which is like four hours from Manhattan. And Mike realizes he left his tenor at home. So, he had to pay a neighbor to drive the tenor up there for him. It was a typical Mike story, and he just laughed it off."

Michael would dive deeper into his new EWI on his second release as a leader on Impulse!, *Don't Try This at Home* (1988). Tunes such as the Celtic-flavored romp "Itsbynne Reel" had him running intricate unisons on EWI with guest fiddler Mark O'Connor. And on the frantically swinging title track, featuring Herbie Hancock on piano, Michael expertly doubled EWI and tenor sax lines on the theme. Several people contributed compositions to *Don't Try This at Home*—Grolnick's "Chime This" and "Talking to Myself," Stern's slinky, swinging "Suspone," Vince Mendoza's emotionally charged "Scriabin" (featuring Hancock), Jim Beard's "The Gentleman & Hizcaine." Michael contributed two compositions, the aforementioned turbo-charged "Itsbynne Reel" and his haunting ballad with the extended solo tenor sax intro, "Everything Happens When You're Gone," which also featured a remarkably mature and gently lyrical piano solo by Calderazzo, underscored by Charlie Haden's bass and Adam Nussbaum's drums.

Peter Erskine, who appeared on one track to *Don't Try This at Home*, recalled swapping studio time in order to get Michael to play on his own record, *Motion Poet*. "That was Mike's kind of peak years as a solo artist," he said. "And Don was producing *Motion Poet*, so we had a another connection there. And somehow all of the sides got talking, and we worked out a deal. I had a lockout on Master Sound Astoria Studio, and I said, 'Michael, I'll trade you studio time, and I'll play on one tune on your album if you'll play one solo on my album.' And he agreed. So, I played on the Don Grolnick tune 'Talking to Myself' on Mike's album, and then Mike overdubbed a solo on a Vince Mendoza tune with really difficult chord changes, 'Hero with a Thousand Faces,' on my album. Mike was amazing on that."

Wortman was present when Mark Seliger took the striking cover photo for *Don't Try This at Home*—a shot of Michael precariously balancing his Selmer Mark IV on the index finger of his right hand with a sly smirk on his face. Wortman also revealed a long-kept secret of that album—that Mike had actually played a different tenor sax on "Suspone" than his trusty Selmer. As he explained, "Mike was always searching for the next horn because he was convinced at some point

Don Grolnick and Michael Brecker in the studio for Peter Erskine's *Motion Poet* session, 1988 *(Courtesy of Peter Erskine)*

that his horn was not going to have the right sound. He was always worried about buzzing. He explained to me that the metal becomes porous, brass changes over time, and when the sound is not centered, it starts spreading and gets this buzzy sound. You really have to be an audiophile to hear it, but that's just classic Mike. And if the horn got knocked or put down heavy, he'd say, 'I gotta take it to the shop now.'

"I had to learn how to handle his horn for him because he was very sensitive to any kind of leak or anything," Wortman continued. "He could still play it, and nobody would know that there was anything wrong, but he knew. So, in his mind, there always had to be something else to search for. So, we got this horn from Ishimori, the famous saxophone store in Japan that had all these certain Selmer horns of a particular serial number that everybody was lusting after. We had been at his shop in Tokyo. There was this basement at Ishimori's with a fireplace where they'd serve drinks, and they'd have pillows. I'd sit down there with Mike, and Mr. Ishimori would come and present Mike with a horn to blow, and Mike would look at it and go, 'Where'd you get this horn? I know this horn. This is Lew Tabackin's horn. How'd you get this? What'd you pay for it?' And I remember Ishimori saying, 'I lend you for life.' And we looked at each other kind of quizzically. Mike wasn't sure if he was giving him the horn or lending it to him. Anyway, we took it home—a beautiful Selmer Mark VI, untouched, everything was lacquered like it had just been bought brand-new. It was in a beautiful case that had never been used, right in the zone of serial numbers that Mike was looking for. And during part of the session for *Don't Try This at Home*, something was wrong with Mike's regular horn. It was being overhauled at the shop—all the springs and pads were adjusted just to make sure there was no leaking. So, for that one tune, 'Suspone,' Mike played that other Selmer he had gotten from Ishimori."

One song from *Don't Try This at Home* still stands out for both Calderazzo and Nussbaum. "'Itsbynne Reel' is where Mike sort of found Mike, in my opinion," said Joey. "I think that was a pinnacle thing in Mike's career because nobody did anything remotely like that before, and it was just pure Mike. What he plays on that tune is all fueled by years of playing 'Impressions' and studying 'Giant Steps' and all the Coltrane shit he was into. It all came out on that song. And it's got the EWI at its most organic sounding. Then mid-song, it's the biggest breath of fresh air when he comes in with that tenor. And it's just killing!"

Nussbaum recalled how in the early days on tour, Michael wrapped colorful headbands around the mouthpiece of the EWI to keep the electronic circuitry dry. "He'd be drooling all the time. In fact, I used to call him Droolius Seizure. But it was fascinating to watch Mike develop that thing. The EWI was a whole new sonic world for him, and it was something that also gave him the ability to project and have the power to cut through like an electric guitar, which he loved."

"The EWI was a way for him to go up into Mike Stern playing guitar," added Wortman. "He wanted to be able to do that. He always felt with all these loud electric bands he played in, the saxophone didn't have a place. He had been experimenting with electronics his whole career, going back to the days of Dreams, when he and Randy were playing through Condor boxes (Hammond's Innovex Condor SSM Multi Effects

Unit) and later with The Brecker Brothers when they were going through wah-wah pedals, harmonizers, and envelope filters (the Seamoon Funk Machine). Mike needed a vehicle to express himself in a way that he couldn't do on just the saxophone. He couldn't compete with the guitar player on the saxophone. That's why he developed that whole guitar sample thing on the EWI to push back against the loud electric guitar. He was always coming from that place of wanting to push it."

With his EWI eventually going through an Oberheim Xpander to get chord voicings and to a Yamaha TX7 and Akai S900 digital sampler to trigger all kinds of otherworldly effects, Mike could now go toe-to-toe with Stern in concert on slamming numbers such as "Original Rays" or Stern's own "Upside Downside" (title track of the guitarist's 1986 Atlantic album), where he would unleash cool turntable scratching effects or emulate screaming electric guitar and scorching Mini-Moog licks on the EWI. As Michael said of the EWI in a backstage interview before a performance at the Newport Jazz Festival on August, 16, 1987, "I've had a lot of fun with it, and I hope to do more. It's opened up a whole new panorama for me. It's given me another avenue." He later told Lorne Frohman in a March 10, 2004, interview, "It's an electronic instrument that can play a whole orchestra . . . from Venus. I took to it pretty much immediately and learned about it and loved every minute of it."

Another upside to Mike's use of EWI is that it required far less blowing power than his trusty Selmer Mark VI saxophone. As his tenor buddy David Demsey noted, "I remember Mike saying to me that one of the reasons that he was working so feverishly with the EWI was because he didn't know how much longer he could play saxophone, because it hurt so bad."

And so, Michael embarked on a deep dive into the EWI, as deeply as he had gone with the tenor saxophone in the late '60s and early '70s. "He was always searching on that thing," said Wortman. "And what he came up with was just amazing."

"I was there when Mike got his original Steinerphone delivered to his loft on Grand Street," recalled keyboardist-producer Jason Miles, who worked frequently with Michael on his own projects and also did synth programming for Miles Davis's albums *Tutu* (1986) and *Amandla* (1989). "The original Steinerphone, or EWI, didn't do all that much on its own. It kind of sounded like a lyricon. But it was meant to go into MIDI and all this other stuff. Mike had a setup in his house—a Yamaha

DX7 with a couple of modules and a Roland sequencer. He was basically just messing around with it, and the big deal was when he was able to incorporate breath into it. Another big thing that happened was when Akai took over and actually developed the instrument further. And Mike jumped into that immediately. It was another outlet that he wanted. Mike wanted to grow into all forms of music. But that's what genius brings you. Genius brings you into a whole other space."

Miles added, "Mike was like the ground zero for EWI. And the way he developed that instrument is incredible. I still hear people playing the EWI now, and I've gone on YouTube and seen clips of people playing it. Trust me, nobody's doing what Mike was doing on that thing. Nobody! Michael was tuning the thing in fifths; he was creating ensembles inside of things by taking different voices in the Oberheim and tuning all of them different. He used that instrument the way that it should have been used. Because 90 percent of the people that were using synthesizers back then had no idea what they were doing."

Said Steps Ahead's Mike Mainieri, "The EWI really took up a lot of Mike's time. He was developing it and making it a better instrument. And he would come up with these things that were just symphonic. It was astounding what Mike was doing on that instrument. He was really on the forefront of developing that thing."

Added fellow saxophonist Tim Ries, "Mike was like a kid in the laboratory, and he was making sounds like nobody had ever done before on that instrument. He was discovering a new language there."

Bob Mintzer, who had played alongside Michael in Jaco Pastorius's Word of Mouth big band and also in his own big band at Seventh Avenue South, remembered getting a personal tour of the EWI and accompanying gear at Michael's Grand Street loft. "This was around the time that sequencers hit the scene, and Mike got fascinated by them. He had programmed this demo on a sequencer, and he pushed the start button, and it was this overwhelmingly evolved, developed, deep composition that this machine was playing. And my reaction was just, 'Holy shit! This guy does everything!'

"Later on, he experimented with the EWI like he did everything else—to the fullest," Mintzer continued. "He really went way deep into it and did some stunning things, particularly some of those solo pieces where he'd use a looper to build a composition spontaneously. He was one of the first guys to do that. Of course, Jaco used a primitive looper on 'Slang,' that solo thing he'd do with Weather Report and also on the Joni Mitchell *Shadows and Light* tour. But Mike took it to a whole other level with the programming of different sounds. I mean, he had it sounding like a symphony orchestra at times. So, he really got way into that instrument, more so than anybody else did. By using all of the external modules, Michael got into some advanced sound design with the EWI, which is way beyond where most people, including myself, have gone with that instrument."

"Looking back on it now, I don't know how he had time to develop the EWI, practice the saxophone a couple hours a day, and still be doing whatever he was doing to make a living," said Michael's road manager and EWI tech Wortman.

Wortman recalled one trip that he made with Michael to the Akai factory in Japan. "Mike had been playing Nyle Steiner's handmade Steinerphone, which had all these weird tubes and everything. But being a musician himself [Steiner was a trumpeter], Nyle really understood what musicians needed in an instrument as far as feel and execution. And while the Japanese at the Akai factory were brilliant engineers, they weren't musicians. So, there was a bit of a disconnect there. So, we're at the Akai factory, and they ask Mike why he wasn't playing the new Akai EWI, and he says, 'It doesn't feel right. It doesn't have the glitch that I'm used to.' So, we leave the factory. Two days later, they call and say, 'Michael-san, what is gritch?'"

Although fellow musicians stood in awe of Michael's progress with this new piece of technology, manager Pitt felt it was a detriment to some degree, at least in the eyes of some influential critics. "It upset me that Mike wasn't getting what I felt was the full due to which he was entitled, and that was because of the EWI," he said. "In my opinion, he wasn't being considered seriously enough by the jazz police because he wanted to explore the possibilities of the EWI. And there were some serious conversations Mike and I had about whether or not, despite his profound affection for the instrument and devoting endless hours sometimes in the basement at home, he should continue playing it. But he was so dedicated to creating new sounds—actual performance pieces—that it soon became a moot point."

In the summer of 1988, Michael was invited by Herbie Hancock to tour as a member of Headhunters II, an updating of his pioneering funk-fusion group from 1973. Pitt not only secured featured billing for his client for that tour, but he also negotiated a solo spot in the show for Michael to display his burgeoning techno-chops on the EWI to awed concertgoers. "He had been developing the EWI on tour since 1987," recalled Wortman, who served as Michael's EWI tech and Charley Drayton's drum tech on that thirty-night Benson & Hedges-sponsored tour on a split bill with Headhunters II and Chick Corea's Elektric Band. "I built these two massive racks of gear for the EWI for that tour with Herbie. I called them the Twin Towers."

Every night on this Headhunters II tour, Michael had a stunning solo EWI spot, where the band left the stage, and he would create an atmospheric ambiance with sampled rainforest sounds and Pygmy chants before breaking into full orchestral mode on that high-tech gadget. It was a jaw-dropping performance, complete with dramatic lighting, and served as a strong manifesto on the potential of the EWI (as well as a foreshadowing of what he would get into two and a half years later on tour with Paul Simon).

"He was perfecting it, and he was having fun with it," Wortman continued. "He was doing call-and-response scratching things with D.ST [turntablist Derek Showard, whose stage name GrandMixer D.ST was derived from an abbreviation of Delancey Street in Lower Manhattan]. And he was doing a bit of a Jaco thing—that kind of looping and then playing over it that Jaco did in his solo spot on Joni Mitchell's *Shadows and Light* tour. Mike learned a lot from Jaco's showmanship."

Wortman added, "Herbie's thing was great but was technically a mess. He'd put the keytar around his neck to do 'Rock-It,' and it would never work. He'd hit a key, and nothing would happen. The band is grooving and . . . no sound from Herbie. Meanwhile, Chick Corea's thing was always precise, everything was so perfectly done, not a hair out of place. And we were just the opposite. At one point, Herbie lost a hard drive with all the keyboard sounds on it. He had left it in a cab. So, stuff would happen from time to time on this tour."

Pitt added, "There was one time where on half the gig Herbie was busy with a screwdriver onstage during the course of the show, trying to fix his Kurzweil synth, oblivious that there's actually a show going on in which he's participating. So, it got messy at times."

Following his brief tour with Headhunters II in June, Michael headed to Europe in July 1988 to perform several acoustic jazz concerts with the Herbie Hancock Quartet, featuring bassist Buster Williams and drummer Al Foster. On a few of those dates, they were joined by the vocalist Bobby McFerrin, who would engage in some freewheeling and at times humorous call-and-response with Michael on Sonny Rollins's "Oleo" (in Munich on July 15) and also perform a captivating voice-sax duet on Brecker's ever-popular Steps Ahead tune "Safari" (at Jazz Vitoria Gasteiz in Spain on July 14). Michael sounds particularly deep into a Joe Henderson bag on this acoustic quartet tour with Hancock, which would later raise the ire of the elder saxophonist.

After spending most of the summer with Headhunters II and also Hancock's acoustic quartet, Michael resumed touring with his own band. For an appearance on September 4, 1988, in Rio de Janeiro at the Free Jazz Festival in Brazil, drummer Dennis Chambers subbed for Adam Nussbaum, who had remained in New York to witness the birth of his first child. Chambers, who would later emerge as the drummer for a newly reconstituted Brecker Brothers band, recalled a scene with Michael at their hotel that revealed just how humble the tenor titan was:

"A whole bunch of guys we knew were there for the festival, and we were all staying at the same hotel," he recalled. "At some point before the concert, I'm in Mike's room, and we're talking, and over in the next room we can hear Ernie Watts practicing, just running scales on his tenor. Suddenly, Mike sneaks over and puts a glass to the wall to listen intently, and he's freaking out because it's Ernie Watts, who he obviously dug. And, so, we're standing there, with Mike's glass to the wall, and if somebody happened to walk in the room at that moment and make a lot of noise, Mike would be like, 'Be quiet! Be quiet! Ernie's next door! He's warming up!' And we'd be like, 'Who cares? You're Michael Brecker!' And he said, 'Yeah, I'm Michael Brecker. But that's Ernie Watts!'"

(Nearly a year later, Watts and Brecker would join fellow saxophonists Bill Evans and Stanley Turrentine along with drummer Nussbaum, pianist Don Grolnick, and bassist Yoshio Suzuki for a special Select Live Under the Sky Sax Workshop in Tokyo on July 29, 1989.)

Michael would close out 1988 with a series of Stateside concerts with his regular Michael Brecker Band lineup of Stern, Calderazzo, Andrews, and Nussbaum. The following year kicked off in grand fashion with a live performance in Tokyo on January 21, 1989, of Claus Ogerman's majestic music from *Cityscape*, with guitarist Pat Metheny, bassist Charlie Haden, drummer Nussbaum, pianist Fumio Karashima, and Kazuhiro Izumi conducting the Shin-nihon Philharmonic. This was the pinnacle event of the fifth annual Tokyo Music Joy Festival, produced by renowned Japanese composer Toru Takemitsu and Toshinari Koinuma, the latter having been Keith Jarrett's exclusive promoter in Japan since 1974. As Wortman recalled, "Adam had such a difficult time trying to mesh with the conductor because the guy didn't get how Adam was swinging. And the other hilarious moment at that concert was when Charlie did a bass solo, and all the bassists in the symphony—all these young girls—they had never seen anybody rock back and forth with the bass like that before. And they all just started giggling, but they also realized how phenomenal it was. And the sight of Charlie playing with these airline baggage handler headphones on was an incredible scene. It was a really funny night."

"That was a memorable concert," added Nussbaum. "And for me, it was especially fun getting to hang out with Charlie Haden, a true legend. It was just another of so many amazing experiences that I got to have because of Michael."

On the evening of February 22, 1989, Michael won his first Grammy Award in the Best Instrumental Jazz Soloist category for *Don't Try This at Home*. But he was not in attendance at Shrine Auditorium in Los Angeles to receive his award. Instead, he was at the hospital in New York with Susan, who was in labor. Their daughter, Jessica, was born the following day, February 23.

Michael continued touring with his regular working quintet of Stern, Calderazzo, Andrews, and Nussbaum through the summer of 1989, with numerous stops throughout Europe and the States. They made a return trip to Japan on July 31 for the Live Under the Sky festival in Tokyo. Following a gig on September 7, 1989, in Fort Worth, Texas, Stern and Andrews left the band.

The following month, Michael premiered his new quartet (sans guitar) featuring Calderazzo on piano, Nussbaum on drums, and Jay Anderson on bass at the Jazz Jamboree in Warsaw, Poland, on October 28. As Anderson recalled, "The first tour we did was a State Department-sponsored tour of Eastern Europe for a few weeks. And Mike had asked me to bring an electric bass on that tour as well as my upright bass. The problem was, I had quit playing electric bass at this point. I had sold my electric bass to Kip Reed, so I actually didn't have one to bring out on tour. But Michael was pretty insistent that I play electric bass on a couple of tunes during each set, so I rented back my old bass from Kip and ended up paying him more in rental than he bought it for."

During that Eastern European tour, Michael was in deep composer mode. "I remember Mike was writing stuff for his third album when we were on the road," Anderson recalled. "He traveled with a big anvil case on wheels that was the size of a medium-size refrigerator. Nowadays guys travel with a tiny keyboard and their laptop, but he would take this anvil case into his room every night, and he played his EWI and his keyboard with headphones on all night. And he wrote a lot of the music for *Now You See It . . . (Now You Don't)* on that tour."

"We were over in Eastern Europe when the Berlin wall came down [November 9, 1989]," added Nussbaum. "That was pretty heavy. I even got pieces of the wall as a souvenir. Then we played in Czechoslovakia when Shirley Temple was the U.S. ambassador. We met her after that gig. It was like meeting somebody you've known your whole life. She was the perfect person to be a diplomat and an ambassador for America. Everybody loved her around the world, right? I remember on the gig Joey throwing in a quote from 'On the Good Ship Lollipop' in the middle of one of his solos, then afterwards at the reception she came up to him and goes, 'I heard you!' She was so hip, man!"

Nussbaum recalled another time on that State Department tour when the band played in Krakow, Poland, and the following afternoon drove to Auschwitz to tour the memorial and museum there. "That was a pretty heavy experience," he said. "We had so many rich experiences together on the road, and I'm very grateful for that time I had with Mike. He was just very good people, and he had a great sense of humor, which definitely comes in handy on the road. He once said to me, 'You know, I got a weak back?' And I go, 'Oh, really, Mike? When did you get it?' He goes, 'About a week back.' It was that kind of humor on the whole tour—very dry, very witty, a lot of puns. We had a good time together."

Jay Anderson ended up playing acoustic bass on one track from *Now You See It . . . (Now You Don't)*—a soulful reading of Bobby Troup's "The Meaning of the Blues." Released on August 17, 1990, the Grolnick-produced album on GRP Records featured former Weather Report bassist and Mike's Steps Ahead bandmate Victor Bailey playing electric bass on the seven remaining tracks, including Michael's intricate, up-tempo burner "Peep" and his polyrhythmic "Escher Sketch (A Tale of

Two Rhythms)," which seamlessly meshed three against four in a kind of magical way; the sonic equivalent of the mathematically inspired, jigsaw puzzle artwork (a 1938 M. C. Escher op art woodcut print titled "Sky and Water I") that appeared on the cover of *Now You See It . . . (Now You Don't)*. Bailey also played on Jim Beard's atmospheric Weather Report-ish "Quiet City." Other highlights on Michael's third release as a leader included two Grolnick compositions—the African-flavored "Dogs in the Wine Shop" and his moody "Minsk."

Later that year, Michael played EWI on five tracks for Paul Simon's *The Rhythm of the Saints*, which was released by Warner Bros. on October 16, 1990. Simon premiered some of his new music from that album a month later in a November 17 appearance on *Saturday Night Live*. With Michael playing EWI in the band, that *SNL* performance served as a dry run for Simon's upcoming Born at the Right Time Tour of 1991, a mammoth undertaking that would involve a huge commitment of time from everyone participating, from sound and tech guys to musicians and road crew alike.

"Paul Simon was going to go on the road with the *The Rhythm of the Saints* band, and Mike opted to do that for a couple of years," recalled Anderson. "The bread was amazing, and he really liked the idea of playing that kind of music. So that was the end of the quartet. But at least I got to be in it for a couple of years."

# 9

# PAUL SIMON AND A BROTHERLY REUNION

As Michael was busy breaking new ground with his EWI, critics, colleagues, and industry icons took notice. One such icon was Paul Simon, who became captivated with the strangely organic universe of sound that Michael was generating in concert and on record with this new piece of technology. And he was determined to have that sound on his next album, *The Rhythm of the Saints*. A follow-up to the South African-tinged *Graceland* (1986), the new album's prominent percussive undercurrent (courtesy of Grupo Cultural Olodum) was recorded in Brazil while several guests were invited to the Hit Factory to add melodic and lyrical flavoring along with unique sonic textures, atmospheres, and "spirit voices" on top. Mike and Randy were among several guests at the sessions, along with zydeco accordionist C. J. Chenier, Talking Heads/King Crimson/Frank Zappa "stunt guitarist" Adrian Belew, roots rock guitarist J. J. Cale, jazz trombonist Clifton Anderson, and Fabulous Thunderbirds harmonica ace Kim Wilson. The album also marked Simon's first collaboration with Cameroonian guitarist Vincent Nguini, who would later become a key Michael colleague and confidant.

"I remember setting up the EWI at the Hit Factory for that session," said Jerry Wortman. "And afterwards, Mike was so enthusiastic about Paul's new music. He said to me, 'You will not believe these tracks. They're incredible.'

Of course, Michael had already played on Simon's *Still Crazy After All These Years* back in 1975, but that was primarily set up by high-powered producer Phil Ramone, who was a big Mike fan. But this time out, he was handpicked by Paul, who was producing *The Rhythm of the Saints* himself. And through his curiosity about the EWI, he and Mike bonded during the extensive studio sessions. "Paul is one of those guys who knows what he doesn't like but doesn't always know what he wants," said Wortman. "So, he and Mike would sit there together for hours and find whatever they were looking for. Mike loved the fact that Paul was interested in the EWI and understood that it was a breath-controlled synthesizer, so the expressiveness of it was like nothing else. The depth of what Mike could do on the EWI was only limited by his imagination. And Paul wanted that on his new album."

*The Rhythm of the Saints* was released on Warner Bros. on October 16, with "Obvious Child," picked as the lead single of the album, being one of five tunes that Michael played EWI on. A month later, Simon performed material from *The Rhythm of the Saints* on *Saturday Night Live*, with Michael playing EWI in the band.

By then, he had already signed on for Simon's worldwide Born at the Right Time Tour, which promised to take up the latter part of 1990, consume all of 1991, and take a big bite out of 1992 as well. As he told friends before embarking on that marathon engagement, "OK, see you in two years!"

To back up to the summer of 1990, Michael was still on the fence about joining Simon's tour. His new album, *Now You See It . . . (Now You Don't)*, was coming out, and he had been looking forward to touring with his own band in support of his third release as a leader. "His band was working a lot then," recalled Wortman. "Mike Stern had left, and so we were doing some gigs with Wayne Krantz on guitar, which was great. And though electric bassist Jeff Andrews had left, I liked it even more with Jay Anderson on acoustic bass. It was suddenly infusing the electronic and acoustic in a brilliant and tasteful way. It wasn't quite Weather Report or Steps Ahead, but it was like a new era being developed there."

Guitarist Steve Khan, a former Brecker Brothers bandmate and longtime friend of Michael's, recalled having a phone conversation with Mike about going out with Simon. "At that point, Mike had finally cracked through, and he could go out and play as Michael Brecker at any jazz festival in the world. Whatever he wanted to do, he could do it. Being able to make a record and tour as yourself with your own band and play clubs, concerts, whatever it is, and the seats will be filled, and people will come to hear you . . . it's something we'd all dreamed about doing. I mean, it's the dream of a fucking lifetime for anybody who wanted to play.

"And, so, Mike says to me, 'I've got this offer from Paul Simon to go on tour with him for two years. If I do it, my house will be paid for, I'll have money put away, my kids can go to college. On the other hand, I've worked my whole life to find myself, and now I can go out and play as me. And what's gonna happen if I put that on the back burner and go do this Paul Simon gig for a couple years?' My position, which is easy for me to say, was the same as it was when we were in The Brecker Brothers band together, which is: 'Don't do it! You've worked your whole life for this. Go play with your own band.' In the end, I suppose he made the right decision. But he lost a couple years of his life in the process."

While Michael remained hesitant to pull the plug on his own momentum by going away for two years with Simon, Wortman and the band members were also understandably concerned about their own livelihoods should Mike decide to commit to the marathon Simon tour. "We were all worried," said Jerry. "We had just come back from a very successful summer tour of Europe, and now he was looking at potentially a two-year commitment to this thing. So, Adam, myself, Joey, and Jay . . . we're all kind of freaked, thinking, 'There's no way he'll do it.' But nobody knew for sure."

Meanwhile, Michael assured Wortman that the tour would not materialize. He was planning to make Simon an offer that he absolutely *could* refuse. As Jerry recalled, "Mike kept saying, 'Don't worry about it, it's never going to happen. We're going to ask for some ridiculous amount of money, they'll never give it to us.' And BOOM . . . they gave it to him! Then he said, 'I have this record coming out, so I'm going to ask for some advertising support. But don't worry, they'll never give it.' And BOOM! There's a full-page ad for Mike's new album with a picture of Mike in the slick program in every town on that gigantic American Express-sponsored tour worldwide. Everything he asked for, Paul had given it to him."

Credit Darryl Pitt's steadfast negotiations with the Simon camp for getting all of Michael's demands met. "On top of that, Paul gives Mike special guest billing, and then he decides that he needed a break during the show, so he gives Mike his own extended solo spot," said Wortman. "Basically, their attitude toward Mike was, 'Give him anything he wants.' Because every time he asked for something, he got it."

Michael also asked that Wortman be allowed to come along on the Born at the Right Time Tour as his EWI tech, and they granted that request as well. "Somebody had to set the thing up," said Jerry, "and I knew how to get it up and running for him so he could concentrate on doing a read or other stuff. Mike couldn't do it without me at that point, so if the EWI was there, I was there." But Jerry confessed, "They actually had keyboard techs who could've taken care of Mike's gear once they learned how to do it. It didn't take a rocket scientist to do any of this stuff. But they got me on the gig because they wanted to keep Mike happy."

Rehearsals for the Born at the Right Time Tour began in Riverhead, Long Island. As Jerry explained, "Paul had done the *Graceland* tour in 1987 where he had Miriam Makeba and Hugh Masakela as special guests. But this tour was on an even bigger scale. He had sixteen musicians—Brazilian and African musicians along with Americans Steve Gadd, Richard Tee, Chris Botti, and Mike Brecker. They rented these gorgeous homes in the Hamptons—one for the back-line guys, one for the sound guys, one for the African musicians, one for the Brazilian musicians. Everybody had a house; everybody had their own bedrooms. Mike, Richard Tee, and Steve Gadd wanted nothing to do with it, so they insisted on hotels. They ended up staying at a Best Western in Riverhead."

The rehearsals took place in a police academy in Riverhead. And as Wortman recalled, "When I arrived, a couple of days after rehearsals had begun, I distinctly remember Mike saying to me, 'Get me out of here!' He was having second thoughts about the whole deal. He said, 'How am I going to do this for two years? I'm going to go out of my mind.' On the summer tour we did with Mike's band before Paul's rehearsals began, we kept screwing with Mike by singing that catchy riff from Paul's 'You Can Call Me Al' [Simon's hit single from *Graceland*] and then telling him, 'Get used to it, pal. You'll be playing that riff every night for the next two years.'

"I mean, here's this guy going from improvising every night in jazz clubs, playing his ass off at the highest level possible, working as a bandleader and earning his reputation as a hard-core jazz improviser on the road for the past four years—and making good money doing it—to suddenly having to play this simple repeating riff from 'You Can Call Me Al' over and over every night. It must've freaked him out a bit."

But the Simon tour was an incredibly lucrative gig for Michael. He stood to make enough money on that Born at the Right Time Tour to assure a comfortable future for himself and his family. "It was life-changing money," confirmed Susan Brecker. "And even though Mike was gone for a long, long time, it afforded us to buy our house in Hastings. And I'll always be grateful to Paul for that. Michael was paid really well, and he got to see parts of the world he hadn't seen and do things he had never done before, like going to South Africa and meeting Nelson Mandela. Of course, his old pal Steve Gadd was on that tour, and he got very close with [trumpeter] Chris Botti and [Cameroonian guitarist] Vincent Nguini. And it was fun to be on private planes and that kind of thing. So, it was really, really fun for him. And it was on that tour that Mike and Paul really started to develop a relationship."

Michael and Paul would eventually bond on that marathon Born at the Right Time Tour tour over their mutual love of African music. "We talked about music often," said Simon. "Mostly jazz and African rhythms, but we also talked about songwriting and record making. And I was always interested to hear his thoughts on the potential of the EWI. He was such a beautiful, visionary guy and a great, great musician."

Regarding their budding bromance on tour, Susan said, "Paul is a tough person to reach emotionally. I would imagine with a life full of that much fame and notoriety that you'd have to be a little weird. I mean, look at Dylan. So, he's just not that accessible. But he's a really good guy, and he really loved Mike, and he's been very deeply supportive. At the first 'The Nearness of You' benefit concert that I put on [in 2015], he was the first person I called. And when I told him, 'I'm doing a concert to honor Mike,' he said, 'Just tell me when and where.' I mean, he's a mensch. And I trust him."

Prior to their marathon 1991 tour together, Michael had recorded with Simon on and off in the studio over the years. But as pop icon and studio session guy, they inhabited two very different existences. As Susan put it, "Paul was a pop guy, and he didn't really understand the whole jazz world," said Susan. "The first thing he said to Mike at the first rehearsal was, 'What's the whole big deal about Coltrane anyway?' Can you imagine? And Mike didn't really understand Paul's music. When Mike went out to Riverhead for rehearsals on the first day, he called me up, and he goes, 'Honey, sing me the bridge to 'The Boxer.' And I started to laugh. Now, everybody knows 'The Boxer,' right? It's iconic. And I'm like, 'What do you mean?' He goes, 'Just sing it to me!' So, I sang it to him over the phone, and he says, very abruptly, 'Great. Bye.' He had to play it at rehearsals, and he didn't know the tune."

As Cameroonian bassist Armand Sabal-Lecco recalled, "Before the tour rehearsals, I had worked on *The Rhythm of the Saints* and a couple of benefit shows with Paul, so I had a glimpse of the intensity of that environment. Mike joined the actual tour rehearsals when we already were a couple of weeks in, so he had to hit the ground running. And it probably was more intense for him. But I was surprised to see how such a musical giant like that could quickly bend and twist, become completely organic and malleable, welcoming any idea. It was a lesson in humility and professionalism."

Though it was a top-tier band, most of the members of Simon's aggregation had never heard that type of West African music he had become enamored with and that manifested on *The Rhythm of the Saints*. "So suddenly you had Paul, who's inspired by the new band, trying new things, rearranging older songs, exploring new ideas with these West African rhythms," said Sabal-Lecco. "It was so intense, we candidly called it The Paul Simon Rehearsal Tour!"

Following intensive rehearsals on Long Island, Wortman and the entire crew moved the whole production to the massive Teaneck Armory in New Jersey, which was close enough for Michael to commute from home for rehearsals. As Jerry recalled, "The whole rehearsal process was at least three months before Tacoma, Washington, where we again set up for production rehearsals in preparation for the first show at the Tacoma Dome on January 2, 1991."

The 135-city Born at The Right Time Tour swept through the States in 1991 from January 2 to April 17 on the first leg of the tour, then swung through Europe from May 3 to July 23 on the second leg, returned for another swing through the States on the third leg—commencing with a free show in Central Park on August 15 that drew more than a hundred thousand people and concluding with a September 29 performance at the Shoreline Amphitheater in Mountain View, California. The sprawling Paul Simon enterprise went global on the fourth leg of the tour with trips to China, Japan, Australia, Brazil, Argentina, and Mexico. The culmination of the Born at the Right Time Tour came in January 1982 with five triumphant concerts in South Africa, from Cape Town to Johannesburg to Port Elizabeth. And every concert in every city along the way was totally packed. "Mike and I used to kid," said Wortman, reflecting on that mega-successful international tour. "He'd point to one tiny little corner of the arena on any given night and say, 'You see that section right there? That's a sold-out house for me.'

"But it was an exciting tour to be on," he continued. "Everything was first class. We were traveling separately, which was sometimes hard for us as friends. I wasn't used to it. But I learned so much on that tour. It made me what I am today. That tour showed me a world that I never was ever gonna get to see from the ground up. And I volunteered for everything on that tour. I learned from the accountant; I would go up with the riggers. I didn't know how they hung lights or put sound up or built a stage every day, so I made a point of learning that. The whole thing was so foreign to me, and I was excited to learn everything. I was used to doing jazz gigs where I'd drive the car and get dinner, do the sound, count heads at the club, and yell at the promoter. But this was a whole other world. We were like a moving city with cases and a production office and assistants and people. I didn't know this kind of stuff was out there, but I learned the ropes fast."

Wortman added that Mike revealed himself to be a real mensch on that tour. "After the first leg of that tour, the first six months, I discovered that I wasn't making what all the other back-line guys on the crew were making, and I was definitely working as hard as them. So that was a drag. And Mike paid me out of his pocket an extra couple hundred bucks a week to make up the difference. I mean, who would do that?"

Remunerations aside, Michael did gain some invaluable insights into Senegalese music and West African music on that Simon tour, just from hanging out with Cameroonians Nguini and Sabal-Lecco. "Mike was curious and hungry for specific exploration," said Sabal-Lecco. "A lot of what he was familiar with at the time was Afro-Latin music, which must have come through Barry Rogers. But the kind of music that Vincent and I were messing with is a totally different thing and sometimes even unknown in our own country. And I said this to Michael from the beginning: 'African music is a culture, not something you can teach in an hour with tricks and easy buttons. It needs to be approached with respect like royalty or inspiration. You let it speak to you first, then you answer.'

"The reason is, each question the music asks is like a key to your DNA; and as your answers become more accurate, you start to play from the inside instead of phoning it in like a tourist with a dashiki," Armand continued. "And as far as the West African rhythms, Michael started to really play them from inside on that tour. I waited to hear a classic Mike Brecker lick from jazz records I loved, but he never ever slipped. He always was in context, and that quietly impressed and taught me."

Sabal-Lecco, who would later appear on *Return of The Brecker Brothers* (1992) and *Out of the Loop* (1994), had high praise for the tenor titan: "He played great and with enthusiasm every night. Michael brought the heat of a volcano with the dial of an angel."

He added that he and Michael spent a lot of time together off the bandstand during and after that Simon tour. "On days off in any country, the two of us would go find food at the local restaurants and go shopping for traditional music CDs. We spent about 85 percent of our traveling and days off listening to eclectic mixes I would make for him to show him different things. Later, I spent time at his home in Westchester with the family and noted that they also started to get on the African wave because Mike was so into it. You could see that in the decorations around the house."

He remembered Mike as "a gentle, generous, curious, creative, and humble soul," adding, "I have also watched him be that to many people

The Brecker Brothers performing in London, 1992 *(© Stuart Nicholson)*

he did not know nor needed anything from. He chose to be positive and could laugh about anything, including himself. For someone of that ilk to trust me early on with his music tremendously improved my own music and humanity. And I'm grateful."

Wortman said that Mike was invigorated by hanging with Nguini and Sabal-Lecco on that marathon tour. "He saw what these African guys were doing, and he started to see something of interest there for himself. Unlike Richard Tee or Steve Gadd, who just came in and did their thing and went back to the hotel, Mike said, 'Oh, wait a minute, there's something going on here.' And he became a student of theirs, in a way. So, he kept himself interested on that whole tour by studying their music. And that influence would show up later in his own music."

As Michael told Ted Panken in a 2000 *Downbeat* interview about hanging with the Cameroonians on that Paul Simon tour, "Having the opportunity to be around them was like a door swinging open, because they were a direct source I could ask questions to. If we were listening to something, I'd first ask where one was, then I'd ask what the words meant. I'd ask about the structure, the meaning of the rhythm, whether they were hearing it in 6 or in 12 or in 3 or in 4 or in 9. Armand would tap the rhythm on my arm as he heard it, which often was very different from where I was hearing it."

And as Michael told Jimmy Magahern of the *Phoenix New Times,* "Aside from the pleasure of just being around Paul and getting to kind of absorb what he does when he's making music, the opportunity to be around musicians from these other cultures is just an amazing treat. I know I'll be using the things I'm learning on this tour in all my future work, and I'm just scratching the surface right now."

Along with being immersed in African and Brazilian rhythms on a nightly basis on that 135-city tour, Michael was also given a significant showcase during each concert where he would introduce the uniniti-ated to the wondrous range and expressive powers of the EWI. As Jerry explained, "I made a pedalboard with seven pedals, so not only did Mike have to play and improvise, he also had to figure out a very intri-cate choreography with his feet on these pedals. And he incorporated all that almost like it was nothing."

Wortman continued, "We were carrying Mac computers. I had a MacPlus in an anvil case and was storing backups in case everything dumped. Meanwhile, Mike wanted to be able to control his own mix and his own reverb, which is unusual for a horn player. But it was very important for Mike to have his own level control somehow. So, I worked with Mike, and we had little boxes and little controllers to be able to do certain things to give him his comfort level."

Wortman added that Michael's solo spot on each Simon concert evolved over the course of the tour. "The piece started off as Don Grolnick's tune 'Dogs in the Wine Shop,' which was on *Now You See It . . . (Now You Don't)*. And it wasn't something that really fit into the overall show right away. And once Vincent Nguini got his hands on it and turned it into this completely African-oriented thing, it became this great, captivating piece of music. And that's also where Mike learned how to move across the stage with the wireless and get the audience involved in his performance. And this is something he learned from Paul, who explained to Mike that there was a big difference between playing in a jazz club and playing concerts in front of thirty thousand people each night. So, he learned to work the audience and bring them into everything he did with the EWI during those solo segments while Paul was taking his break. There was no intermission at those shows. Mike carried that part of it himself, and he was freakin' killing it on the EWI."

Opening his solo segment with the pastoral sound of a simple pan pipe sample, via the EWI, Michael would then trigger some lush chord swells with Simon's full percussion section percolating underneath. From there he would wail on his EWI with a distortion-laced electric guitar sample before triggering Pygmy chanting and rain forest sounds. Finally, he'd pick up his Selmer Mark VI and cue "Dogs in the Wine Shop," with the West African rhythm still churning away underneath. In this new, buoyant, Nguini-ized arrangement of Grolnick's piece, Michael's solo showcase suddenly fit in perfectly with Simon's West African–flavored show.

"The EWI gave him that ability to stretch and do this other thing that the tenor saxophone could not do," said Wortman. "And the next thing you know, The Brecker Brothers are back, and they're doing stuff with Maz & Kilgore (programmers and remix maestros Maz Kessler and Robbie Kilgore) that is totally futuristic involving the EWI. Essentially, they're doing house/acid jazz before anybody even knew what that was. I go back and listen to some of those tracks now, and they hold up as well now as any of the Snarky Puppy stuff you're hearing now.

Young kids today think they invented this stuff, but Mike and Randy were doing all that twenty years ago."

By 1992, the time was right for a Brecker Brothers redux. It had been ten years since Mike and Randy had played together as The Brecker Brothers; and given the innovations in technology and shifts in musical tastes, to reenter the fray with a new sound and the same old chemistry seemed like a good idea. Actually, the brothers did have a reunion some years earlier in an "under-the-radar" appearance with Steve Ferrone, Will Lee, Barry Finnerty, and Mark Gray at Seventh Avenue South in 1984, about a year before the closing of the Breckers' fabled Manhattan nightclub. But Act II of The Brecker Brothers was informed by musical sources that didn't exist in their earlier incarnation or they simply weren't aware of back in the days of *Don't Stop the Music*, *Detente*, and *Straphangin'*—specifically, hip-hop and Afro-pop.

Mike and Randy began recording *Return of The Brecker Brothers* on forty-eight-track digital at the end of April 1992 and delivered the final masters to GRP at the beginning of August of that year. And Michael's involvement in the Paul Simon tour, in particular, had a huge impact on the direction of this '90s incarnation of the band. "I had always been interested in African music going way back," Michael told me in an interview for the October 1992 issue of *Downbeat*. "But being on the Paul Simon tour gave me a chance to live and play with African musicians. So, I asked a lot of questions, and I really learned a lot. And these musicians were very gracious in sharing their knowledge, particularly Armand Sabal-Lecco. I spent a lot of time with him, and he showed me a lot of stuff that ended up greatly affecting my writing."

During their travels together on the Simon tour, Sabal-Lecco helped Michael get a grasp on both the subtle and obvious differences between the rich musical traditions of the African diaspora. "When I went into the Paul Simon project, I really didn't know the difference between West African and South African music," Michael admitted. "And I really didn't know the difference between music from Northern and Eastern Cameroon, or the difference between music from Senegal, Ghana, and Nigeria. But now I've got a pretty good handle on it. I still have a lot to learn because there's a tremendous amount of musical information coming out of those countries. But I started getting a grasp on it, and Armand was a big help."

Randy saw a continuum in all of The Brecker Brothers projects from the '70s and early '80s right up to *Return of The Brecker Brothers* (1992) on GRP. "A couple of things I wrote for the new record continued from where we had left off," he said, "but we tried to take it a few steps further in the process. So, there is definitely a common thread, but there is also a planned departure. And I think that shows up greatly in Mike's writing. Mike's writing now is more refined and more harmonically sophisticated than the old stuff, but still I don't think my writing has changed over the years as much as Mike's has."

Michael's time on the Paul Simon tour was reflected in his captivating composition "Wakaria" on *Return of The Brecker Brothers*. A joyous 12/8 groove based on bikoutsi, a style of music that comes out of Yaunde, the capital city of Cameroon, it features Michael alternately soaring on soprano sax (a rare moment for him) and blowing bold tenor lines over layers of intricate polyrhythms, hand claps, chants, and sampled wood flutes. As Michael explained of that dense and triumphant track, "In Ewondo, the language that Armand and Vincent Nguni speak, the title is the equivalent of 'hello' or 'what's happenin'?' There are a couple of other tunes on *The Rhythm of the Saints* that are coming out of this tradition, and I sort of got mesmerized by it during the tour. I started collecting records that had different examples of bikoutsi. There's a great new African band called Les Tetes Brûlées that plays a kind of punk-pop version of bikoutsi. And our version is another kind of weird adaptation of this traditional music."

Randy's "Roppongi" was a bit of classic Brecker Brothers pocket funk with earthy slapped bass lines, courtesy of James Genus, and slamming backbeats from Dennis Chambers while Mike and Randy team on the trumpet–tenor front line in the jaunty NYC fashion the brothers were so noted for. The attitude here is coming out of something like Randy's "Sponge" from the Breckers' 1975 debut album, but this new piece explores some new directions, such as the salsa-flavored middle section sparked by Don Alias's churning conga playing.

"King of the Lobby" is more pocket funk, this time from Michael. A '90s take on something from their own past, like Randy's 1977 tune "Squids," it is propelled by synth bass lines and drum tracks programmed by Max Risenhoover. David Sanborn joins the brothers on alto sax here to re-create the special chemistry they had as a horn section on The Brecker Brothers' first two albums. "We wanted to recapture the old section sound that we got together," said Randy. "The original band was three horns, and when David started his solo career, we played on his first album, *Taking Off* [from 1975]." Sanborn and the Breckers had also rekindled that same tight-horn chemistry a few years earlier on Hiram Bullock's Atlantic debut, *From All Sides* (1986).

Elsewhere on *Return of The Brecker Brothers*, they hit on a bit of high-tech hip-hop-flavored funk, courtesy of Maz & Kilgore, on "Big Idea" (catch the cleverly interwoven quotes from two earlier Brecker Brothers classics, "Skunk Funk" and "Squids"). Randy's "Good Gracious" is a rock-tinged backbeat number, and he gets all *irie* on his playful reggae-flavored vocal number "That's All There Is to It" (reprising his eccentric, talk-sing role from "Imagine My Surprise," the title track to Dreams' second album in 1971, and also "Don't Get Funny With My Money" from The Brecker Brothers' 1977 album, *Don't Stop the Music*, and "It Creeps Up On You" from the trumpeter's 1990 solo album, *Toe To Toe*).

Randy also contributes the frantic, chops-busting "Above & Below," which sounds like a page out of the Return to Forever playbook (courtesy of George Whitty's runaway Mini-Moog solo). Michael, of course, wails over the top of this churning number while Dennis Chambers erupts for a ferocious drum solo to take things up a notch. Michael tips his hat to the rhythmic eccentricities of Thelonious Monk on his quirky but killing funk-swing number, "Spherical," and Randy emotes on his tender flugelhorn feature, "Sozinho" (Portuguese for "Alone"). The big production number here is another Maz & Kilgore extravaganza, "On the Backside," reflecting the burgeoning new field of hip-hop jazz, which Miles Davis had entered around the same time with *Doo-Bop* (recorded in January 1991 and released posthumously on June 30, 1992, two months before the release of *Return of the Brecker Brothers*). Max & Kilgore also produced a twelve-inch remix of "On the Backside" that was strictly for club play.

Easily the strongest and most enduring tune from *Return of The Brecker Brothers* is the album's opener, Michael's "Song for Barry," which also served as a dynamic set closer in concert, where guitarist Mike Stern is turned loose for one of his patented "take-no-prisoners" solos. The piece was Michael's tribute to his former mentor and Dreams' trombonist Barry Rogers, who died on April 18, 1991. At Rogers's funeral, he had given a moving eulogy to the honorary Brecker Brother while also injecting a bit of levity intended to disarm the mourners. As Rogers's trumpet playing son Chris recalled, "At Barry's memorial service, Michael's famous opening line was 'Barry was the first Jew I knew who could fix a car.'"

A catchy, African-influenced number, "Song for Barry" employed a line that Rogers used to play every night with Dreams and he reprised on the Eddie Palmieri song "Condiciones Que Existen" from the salsa maestro's 1973 album, *Sentido*. As Michael explained in a 1992 *Downbeat* interview, "I built a melody around that line, which was a favorite of Barry's. And I also transcribed his solo on 'Un Dia Bonita' from Eddie Palmieri's *Sun of Latin Music* [from 1974]. It's probably my favorite Barry Rogers solo on record."

Added Michael of his late comrade and mentor, "He was like a father to me when I first came to New York. I was eighteen, fresh on the scene, and he sort of took me under his wing. Barry was the elder statesman of the group at thirty-six. He had this enormous record collection, and he really exposed me to a lot of music I had never heard before. I used to go up to his house in the Bronx, and he'd play me some African music, salsa music, Cajun music . . . and he'd get very excited about all of this stuff. It was inspiring to be around him when his creative juices were flowing."

The Brecker Brothers followed that recording with a summer tour of Europe, then made a swing through Japan before commencing a tour of the United States in the fall. Bassist Sabal-Lecco, who had played alongside Michael on the Paul Simon tour and made contributions throughout *Return of The Brecker Brothers* (1992), said he was extremely grateful to be involved in the brothers' return. "They came back, took chances, and set the bar very high for everyone," he said. "And although it was after the Simon tour, my bond with Michael was intact and ongoing."

Sabal-Lecco felt that the Breckers hit on some new musical terrain with *Return of The Brecker Brothers*, but they really pushed the envelope on their 1994 follow-up, *Out of the Loop*. "That is a fantastic, outside-the-box album," he said. "Living on different coasts, we would exchange DATs of arrangements and ideas by mail or on regular endless phone calls. I later came to New York City to rehearse and record Michael's tune 'African Skies.' That song is based on 12/8 bikutsi music from South Cameroon, where my mother is from. Mike had fallen in love with that style and a band called Les Têtes Brulées. After tracking my regular bass with the band, I layered vocals and electric piccolo basses to complete the picture. The band was killer on that track, including guitarist Dean Brown and keyboardist George Whitty, who was very instrumental in that whole CD."

Whitty, who had also been involved in synth playing and programming on *Return of The Brecker Brothers*, recalled his initial meeting with Michael: "It was in January or February of 1992. Previously, I had been playing keyboards with Eliane Elias's touring band, and she had some records with a lot of production on them, and she wanted somebody to handle all the synth sounds and strings and atmospheres on it so she could focus on the piano. So that became my job. And when the idea arose to do a reboot of The Brecker Brothers band, Eliane recommended me to Randy because she knew that I was a very early adopter of sequencer technology. Randy gave me these real rough cassette demos with a chart, and I kind of whacked those up into really nice-sounding pieces of music. And, so, they hired me on to be involved with that first Brecker Brothers comeback record. And that meant driving up to Hastings to meet Mike.

"I didn't know what to expect and was slightly intimidated," he continued. "I was twenty-nine at the time and didn't know much about Michael Brecker the person, even though he was like this unbelievable titan in my world. I had been aware of The Brecker Brothers' music since high school, when I was growing up in Coos Bay, a little town in Oregon about two hundred miles from Portland. I think the first Brecker Brothers record I got was *Back to Back*. And the intensity of that record was a part of my musical upbringing. I later transcribed their music when I went to the Berklee College of Music from '80 to '82. And it appealed to me in the same way that Chick Corea's music appealed to me, in that they're burning through these lines, but the unexpected turns and the weird twists and the little angles that they'd throw in there just made me laugh.

"I was also a big fan of that Pat Metheny record *80/81*, which Mike plays on," Whitty continued. "I used to stick my stereo speakers out the windows of my room and just blast that to the whole neighborhood until everyone got irritated with it. I wore that one out. Michael's playing was so intense on that record and just about everything else he had played on up to that point. So, I sort of assumed that he had to be a pretty intense person, too."

Whitty would find out differently when he arrived at Michael's home in Hastings for their first meeting. "It was funny because he was going up and down his stairs on his butt," he recalled. "He had messed up his back somehow and was doing this thing on the stairs and smiling this kind of silly grin at me. So that was a very odd first meeting. But we started talking about the record and figuring out what the process might be. Mike had a couple of tunes, so I started working with those. I had never expected back in my days in Coos Bay that I would end up working with Michael Brecker, but here I was doing it."

As far as their working process together, Whitty said that Mike and Randy always wanted something with "a weird wrinkle in it." "I've always told people that Mike and Randy both had the Thelonious Monk gene," he said. "I'd be sitting there working on a track for Randy, for instance, and he'd come over and listen, and he'd be like, 'This just isn't interesting enough. There's not that weird wrinkle to it.' So, I'd start transposing it around, and we'd end up with the clarinet part in a really weird key, and I'd look back and Randy would be beaming, and he'd say, 'Yeah, that's it!' Mike was the same way. They were both always like that—not satisfied to do the normal thing."

Whitty added, "One thing that Mike told me that I thought was really interesting . . . and I think Randy feels the same way . . . is that he wrote his tunes for an audience of one. And that one was Randy. Mike really wanted Randy to dig the tune. So, if it was too ordinary or too simple, it wasn't making it. It had to have those wrinkles in it. But it was always easy to work with Mike on his compositions. They were just good pieces of music with a lot of inspiration in them."

The band for *Return of The Brecker Brothers* tour of 1992 consisted of Mike and Randy, Mike Stern on guitar, James Genus on bass, George Whitty on keyboards, and Dennis Chambers on drums. In 1993, GRP released a VHS video capturing their dynamic performance together at The Palau de la Musica in Barcelona on November 5, 1992. Each show on that triumphant '92 tour ended the same way, with an expansive and utterly captivating version of Michael's "Song for Barry." Opening with an epic EWI solo by Michael that incorporated atmospheric elements inspired by a 1952 field recording, *Africa: Music of the Malinke and Baoule*, which Barry Rogers had turned Mike onto when he was a wide-eyed youth, the West African-flavored piece builds to a rockish crescendo, culminating with a pulse-quickening "chops of doom" solo by Stern that invariably had audiences leaping to their feet with excitement.

That same potent unit continued to tour through 1992 (with former Brecker Brothers guitarist Barry Finnerty subbing for Stern on a tour of Japan that included appearances at the Mt. Fuji Festival on August 23, 1992, and subsequent Blue Note gigs in Osaka, Fukuoa, and Tokyo). The Stern-Chambers unit remained together through the spring of '93 with tours of Europe and Japan, concluding with a performance at The Bottom Line in Nagoya on April 1, 1993.

Throughout their time on the road together, Chambers engaged in some "creative pranksterism" with Michael to pass the time. "That was a fun tour," he said. "I actually had met Mike and Randy years before that Brecker Brothers tour, back when I was playing with P-Funk in 1977–78 during the Seventh Avenue South days. And I found them both to be very interesting guys back then because that was another part of their life that they were dealing with that kind of fit in with P-Funk's lifestyle. So, we got along. And then I had subbed for Adam Nussbaum in Mike's band at the Free Jazz Festival in Rio a few years earlier [September 4, 1988]. So, we knew each other, and we definitely got along."

Chambers remembered the first day of rehearsals for that initial '92 Brecker Brothers tour almost starting off on the wrong foot. "Oh, man! I got off the elevator at the rehearsal place, and I hear some drums coming from our room, and I'm going like, 'Wow, that was quick. I guess I'm fired already.' I stood there at the door and listened, and I'm like, 'Who is that?! This guy's killing!' So finally, I open the door to walk in, thinking I was going to gather my cymbals and go home . . . and there's Mike sitting behind my kit! And I couldn't believe it! And I'm smiling, he's smiling, I'm looking at him while he's playing. And I just walked up on the stage and just stood behind him, just checking out his technique and everything. Finally, I snatched the drumsticks out of his hand and said, 'Man, get out of here. I never wanna see you behind my kit again, all right?'"

That confrontation kicked off a friendly but competitive game of one-upmanship between the two on the road that may have been taken a little too far at some point. "I would do all kinds of crazy stuff to him, and he would do all kinds of crazy stuff to me," Chambers recalled. "And it was all cool, as long as we respected the instruments. I would never touch his horn; he would never do anything to the drums. But he did something to my drum stool once where I was sitting there playing, and I notice in the middle of a solo the drums are getting bigger. What Mike did was, he had loosened up my all my stands. So, I'm taking a solo, and the drum stool is getting lower and lower to the ground. And I'm going, 'What the hell's going on here?' And I look over at Mike, and he's got this smirk on his face, like, 'Let's see you solo through this.' And I was like, 'That's all right. I'll get you back.'"

At that point, the Brecker-Chambers war of pranks was on.

"One night after a show somewhere in the south of France, Mike called me up to his hotel room to run some things by me," said Chambers. "So, I'm there talking to him, and I notice that he left the shades open. It's dark outside, he had the lights on, but the windows were closed. Finally, he says he has to go to the bathroom, and while he's in there he's still talking to me. Now I look over at the window, and it is filled with mosquitos. And right then a light went off in my head, like, 'Should I do this or should I not?' And, you know, I would've felt bad later on had I not done it, because it was the opportune time to do this prank.

"So, he's talking through the closed bathroom door, and I say, 'Hey Mike, I'll be right back. I forgot something in my room.' And before I left, I opened that window, and the whole room filled up with mosquitos. And as I'm walking down the hallway back to my room, I can hear him yelling like Mr. Wilson on *Dennis the Menace* . . . 'DENNIS!!!!'"

Michael didn't wait long to respond to Chambers's prank. "One day he got me good," Dennis recalled. "On the road with Mike, I had this routine where I would knock on his door and, when he opened it, I would give a running start and dive on his bed. One day I was about to go through that routine—and I don't know how or why, but he's got a big piece of board between the bed and the mattress—and man, I went to dive on that bed, and it was like I hit a wall of cement. In fact, I saw a flash of light when I came down on it. I almost knocked myself out. I'm like seriously hurt, laying on this bed. And he's over there laughing. But that's the kind of stuff we used to do to each other on the road."

The degree of difficulty with the pranks would escalate as the tour unfolded. "We're in Paris, and we're checking into the hotel," Chambers recalled. "The rooms weren't ready, and it was raining outside, and it was a day off. So, Stern had this thing he would do in cases like that where he would cause a ruckus in the lobby in order for us to get these rooms right away. So, Stern goes around the corner, and he gets this big ol' piece of chicken, and he comes back in the lobby of the hotel, and he's sitting there right across from the desk, and he's got chicken juice going down his arms, and his hair's all wet, and he's got this strange look on his face. You know, he looked like a crazy guy! Meanwhile, people are checking in, all dressed up with suits and ties, and they're looking at Stern like, 'Oh, my god! Who let this homeless person in?' And they immediately found us our rooms.

"So, Mike got his key, and he says to me, 'Dennis, you want to get some food later?' And I'm like, 'Yeah, let me know when you want to go.' And I knew something was up, but I couldn't put my finger on it. I had brought this suitcase that had these special panel locks, and you have to know where they are to unlock them. So, finally I got my key, and I'm getting ready to wheel this suitcase to the elevator, and Mike is standing there waiting for me. And as I take two steps from the desk, the suitcase opens up, and everything falls out of it onto the floor. And Michael says, 'Oh, well, I guess I'll see you when I see you.' And as the elevator door closes, I notice this grin on his face. And I am thinking, 'I am going to kill him!'"

Perhaps the peak of their creative pranksterism came when The Brecker Brothers tour landed in Aruba later that year. As Chambers recalled, "It was a day off when we got there, and Mike had the bottom floor, where he could walk out, and he's right on the beach. So, I'm up on the second floor looking down at the beach, and I'm like, 'Look at him. He's out on that lounge chair, reading a book. I've got to find a way to do something to him today. But I don't know what.' Suddenly, the phone rings to Mike's room, he goes in to answer the phone, and he comes back out to finish his call on the beach. So, this was an opportune time. I thought, 'I'll just go down there and get in his room somehow and mess it up in some way.' So, I go downstairs, and I'm sneaking through the bushes so he can't see me, and I creep into his room. And man, when I got in there, I tore that room apart. I took all the lightbulbs out of every socket. I took the phone apart, opened all the dressers, took his clothes and just threw them all on the floor. I took the bed, turned it over. Everything I could touch, except for the horn, I just tore it apart. Finally, I see Mike coming back into the room so I run into the bathroom and hide in his shower and close the shower door. Mike comes in, and he laughs. He knew what happened. So, he puts his phone together and calls up Jerry Wortman, and he goes, 'Jerry, Dennis has been in my room. He tore my room apart. You should see this. Come down, take a look.' Jerry was doing some paperwork; he didn't have time.

"So, Mike puts the room back together again—puts all the lightbulbs back in, folds his clothes nicely and puts them back in the drawer, turns the bed back over, puts the bedspread on it . . . the whole nine. Then he goes back out on the beach. He never came to the bathroom to see if I was there. So, as soon as he goes back out to the beach, I counted to like twenty, and I come out of that bathroom, and I look outside and see him sitting in that chair out there. And I tore his room apart again. And now he comes back into the room, and I go hide in the shower again. And I hear him say, 'Oh, no! Oh, man!' And I'm sitting there biting a hole in my lip so I don't laugh out loud.

"Now he's a little irritated. But he puts everything back, then he goes back on the beach again. I tore the room apart again. He comes back, and now he's mad. He's pissed off! He puts the room together again, and he calls Jerry: 'Dennis came down and tossed my room again. Tell him it's not funny anymore.' And this time he goes to the door, he makes sure the door was locked, and I couldn't get in. And then he goes outside. And I tore the room apart again before sneaking out the front door. But I could hear him in there cussing, swearing a little bit. And the next day he come up to me and goes, 'OK, man, you're the king of all pranks.'"

Chambers also recalled indulging in an on-stage prank whereby he would count off Randy's "Some Skunk Funk" at a superhuman tempo on some nights, just to see if the brothers could keep up. "I knew Mike had to play the initial line and then he had to solo right after that, and somewhere in there he's gotta breathe, right? So, I was trying to make it so fast that he couldn't breathe. And he'd look over at me and say, 'Hey, man, I don't care what tempo you play that in, I'll be there. I'll play it!' And I'm like, 'OK, let's see what you can do.' So, I count it off super-fast, and he turns around and looks at me like, 'You motherfucker!' He made it through, but at the end of that song, he was looking at me, shaking his head like, 'Goddamn it! I knew I shouldn't have let you count it off.' Later he told me, 'You're just back there swinging your arms. Meanwhile, I'm the one who's gotta play these lines. I gotta breathe, already. We don't want to be up here almost passing out.' Meanwhile, Randy did the smart thing. He just wouldn't play it. He'd just sit there tugging his fingers if I counted it off too fast.'"

Jerry Wortman also remembered Mike coming down with an annoying case of tinnitus during this run with The Brecker Brothers. "We did Yoshi's in San Francisco, and Dennis was playing drums," he recalled. "Yoshi's is a very tight spot, and the band was loud. And the cymbal was right next to Mike's stool. And I remember him telling me, 'This whistling won't go away.' He called it a teapot. And he struggled for years after that . . . seeing doctors, trying to have things made to filter out certain frequencies. The problem became as big a thing as his neck problem was in the '70s."

In the midst of rekindling The Brecker Brothers magic on the road, Mike suffered a personal setback from an unfortunate controversy that flared up in jazz circles in the fall of 1992. The issue centered around unflattering comments about Michael made in print by one of his own role models, tenor sax great Joe Henderson. Naturally, Michael was wounded by this accusation, which became a major brouhaha in the jazz community.

A Henderson cover story had appeared a few months earlier in the March 1992 issue of *Downbeat*. The writer of that piece, Michael Bourne, had intentionally disguised the subject of Joe's rant by referring to him only as "a popular saxophonist." As Bourne explained, "The backdrop of it is, I'd been assigned a feature about Joe Henderson, and my intention was to portray him as one of the unsung heroes of jazz. The editor wanted a combined interview—Joe with McCoy Tyner, since they had a new album out together at the time [*New York Reunion*, 1991, on the Chesky label], or Joe with Joe Lovano, the hook being two generations of tenor sax. I argued for doing a story on Joe alone, but the editor said Joe on the cover would not sell magazines. But he agreed to do the Joe story alone if I could also get quotes from Lovano, Brecker, and John Scofield, all of whom often mentioned Joe as a major influence. I got those sidebars, plus comments from Stephen Scott and Renee Rosnes, to print alongside a Joe Hen Q&A. And in the course of the interview, Joe indeed trashed Mike Brecker, insisting Mike 'stole his shit' and telling me he could prove it with recordings of Mike playing 'his' music. I'd pitched this story so much by then as a means to exalt Joe as one of the masters, and I believed that if I had included Joe trashing Mike, the story would no longer be about Joe's greatness, it'd be about Joe's anger at Mike. So, I left all that shit out of my piece."

Henderson is quoted in that issue of *Downbeat* as saying, after calling out the offending "popular saxist" for copping his licks: "When guys like this do an interview, they don't acknowledge me. I'm not about to be bitter about this, but I've always felt good about acknowledging people who've had something to do with what I'm about. I've played the ideas of other people—Lester Young, Charlie Parker, John Coltrane, Sonny Rollins, Lee Konitz, Stan Getz—and I mention these guys whenever I do an interview. But there are players who are putting stuff out as if it's their music and they didn't create it. I did."

Three months later, Henderson's vitriol was directed with full force at Michael in a competing publication. As Bourne put it, "Joe 'went there' in that other story and never forgave me for not printing him hammering Mike in *Downbeat*. And that became the scandal of the moment in the jazz world."

As Jerry Wortman recalled, "After Joe called him out, Mike had that stuck in his head. So, then, every time he recorded, he would stop a take midway through a solo and say, 'Too many Joe-isms,' and he would edit them out. He told Joe he never denied how much of an influence he had been on him, but Joe felt that Mike never gave him enough credit."

Added Wortman, "Later on, I went on the road with Joe, and he was telling me the same shit about Coltrane, how Trane stole all his shit. And I couldn't believe it! And I was like, 'Oh really? I didn't realize that, Joe.' So, when you hear that, you gotta take Joe's comments about Mike with a grain of salt."

Guitarist Mike Stern, who gigged with Joe Henderson's quartet in 1993 and 1995, recalled Michael being upset by the public dissing. "Mike comes back off the road with Paul Simon, and Joe says, 'You're ripping me off, blah blah blah.' Mike called me and said, 'What should I do? I almost threw up when I heard this. Joe's one of my heroes.' Joe was just bitter until all of a sudden he got recognized after he started doing those tribute records for Verve [*Lush Life: The Music of Billy Strayhorn*, 1991; *So Near, So Far (Musings for Miles)*, 1993; *Double Rainbow: The Music of Antonio Carlos Jobim*, 1995]. Because at that point, he won every poll and was on every magazine cover. Right before that, though, he wasn't doing shit, and then all of a sudden everybody gave him everything. He got more bread, and the gigs were rolling in, and then all of a sudden, he didn't care about Mike anymore. He didn't even bring it up. By the time I played with Joe, he had forgotten all about it. But he was just bitter at the time he made those comments in the magazine about Mike. Somebody had stirred it up with Joe, I think . . . maybe put the idea in his head. And it was horseshit!"

As Susan remembered it, "Joe said something to the effect that Mike was ripping him off, that he doesn't give the proper respect to him and doesn't mention him in interviews. And Mike was upset for weeks about it. He was an obsessive kind of person with this stuff anyway. He would think about it, ponder it for three days, and then say, 'You know what I should have said to him?' Very obsessive. That was just his personality. But he was so upset because he felt like he didn't do anything wrong. He didn't feel like he was ripping Joe off. First, he went through the thing of, 'Well, I am ripping him off. He's right.' And then he was like, 'But why did he say it?' He went through all these different scenarios: 'Should I call him? What should I say to him?' I don't remember him calling Joe, but he was tortured about it for some time."

At the peak of his self-reflection about the Joe Henderson incident, Michael would listen to his own records over and over and analyze his playing, searching for any possible references to Joe Henderson that might've slipped through. "He'd listen constantly, and then he'd conclude, 'Yeah, he's right. I am ripping him off,'" said Susan. "He was a little obsessed with it there for a moment. He was so upset about it. And there wasn't one interview after that where he didn't mention Joe Henderson. Not one. Because he felt like Joe was right. But what hurt him was that it was done so publicly and disparagingly to Mike. And whether Joe was wrong or right, or did it to everybody else, didn't matter. How Mike absorbed it was, 'Joe's right. I don't pay him the homage he deserves.'"

When asked if Michael ever found peace within himself about the Joe Henderson controversy, Susan said, "I would say probably not, though he forgot about it. He wasn't talking about it after months and months of talking about it. And that was the way I think he healed himself, is that he just constantly mentioned Joe after that happened. When people would say, 'Who were your influences?' he'd always mention Joe. You can go back and look at all the interviews Mike did or his thank-yous in liner notes . . . he mentions Joe in every one. That was the way he sort of dealt with it. That would've been his intellectual process. But emotionally, it still would've hurt him."

Following the Henderson incident, several people, including Jerry Wortman, mentioned that Mike was overly careful to steer clear of any

"Joe-isms" in his playing. "That obviously had a big impact on Mike," said bassist John Patitucci. "And I think it hurt Mike deeply because he loved Joe's playing so much."

Gary Gold concurred with Patitucci's sentiment. "Aside from the fact of having one of your idols dog you, emotionally that's gotta hurt, but it's also gotta hurt on the level that Michael was striving so hard to have his own voice," he said. "And the funny thing was, he already did. I mean, from Dreams on, his sound was clearly recognizable, and his playing was clearly his own. But he still was always searching for more original shit that nobody had touched on."

Added guitarist John Scofield, "I just remember Mike saying sort of, 'What the fuck?' at the time. He felt really bad because he was a real Joe Henderson fanatic, and he was aware of that influence creeping up in his playing after that incident. When I first met Mike and Randy, I was learning how to play sort of from a different perspective. And I always kind of thought, 'Well, learning solos . . . it's not right to do that. You should learn how to just do your own thing more.' My attitude was, 'Listen to music all the time and learn from it, but don't learn solos.' And then I met Mike, and he had this book of licks that he had taken off records. It was incredible. And it really showed me that that is a great way to learn music, too. Not that you copy it verbatim. You have to disguise it with your stuff, but it does teach you how music is constructed. And, so, I started to do the same thing. And I really learned a lot from the way Mike did that.

"But Mike was really hurt by what Joe Henderson had said about him," Scofield continued. "And you gotta remember, at the time Mike was huge and getting lots of attention and acclaim. He was really like a pop star almost. And Joe Henderson probably was jealous of that and felt bad because his thing wasn't happening on that level. And that was just before Joe's comeback with Verve Records. So, things did get much better for Joe in terms of attention and acclaim later on. He was winning polls and everything. But Mike loved Joe Henderson and listened to him all the time. I remember he had all of Joe's records. And when I first met Mike, he had this little cassette player that had speakers in it that he brought around with him. He would bring it on the road, and he'd play along with this Joe Henderson thing for like the first minute, and he could play it exactly. So, yeah, he loved Joe."

Anders Chan-Tideman, who began booking Joe Henderson in Copenhagen and promoting his tours around Europe in 1989, said he confronted Henderson about what he felt were unfair comments directed at Michael. "I felt his comment was very uncharacteristic of Joe. Usually, he was very eloquent in his responses. So, when I read his comments about Mike, I was absolutely appalled at what he said, because I felt like this was only going to reflect badly on Joe, and that there's absolutely nothing that stands to be gained from it."

The net result of the Joe Henderson controversy is that it drove Mike further into his ongoing EWI exploration to avoid any "Joe-isms" in his playing. As Stern recalled, "After this Joe thing came out, that kind of had Mike saying he wanted to get away from straight-ahead jazz for a while and do this thing again with Randy. He felt uncomfortable going in a more straight-ahead direction, so that led to The Brecker Brothers reunion. But the main reason was, he really wanted to play with Randy again. He loved playing with Randy. They were so deep together, and they were so cute together when they played. George Whitty would laugh whenever they were kind of doing these little arguments backstage or in the hotel . . . probably the same kind of 'Brecker Brothers bickering' they did growing up together. George would say, 'I can just see the bunk beds now,' and I could never get that image out of my head."

Moving forward from the Joe Henderson controversy, Michael immersed himself in The Brecker Brothers reunion with newfound enthusiasm as they barnstormed through Europe, Japan, and the States. For the summer tour of 1993, guitarist Dean Brown, who had played on *Return of The Brecker Brothers* in the studio, replaced Stern in the lineup (though Stern did return for a one-off appearance at the Newport Jazz Festival on July 30, 1993). And former Return to Forever drummer Lenny White replaced Chambers in the lineup. "It was a really busy time for me," says Brown. "I was very fortunate. I was playing with Marcus Miller's band and with David Sanborn's band and with The Brecker Brothers all at the same time, which for me was like surreal. But anyway, it worked out."

Michael would return home from that summer tour in time for the birth of his son, Sam, on August 1, 1993. Then it was back in the studio to work on *Out of the Loop*, which had the programming team of Maz & Kilgore returning and Whitty coproducing. And this time around, drumming duties were split between Rodney Holmes and Steve Jordan, who had last played with the Breckers on *Détente* (1980).

Trumpeter Chris Botti, who played alongside Michael on the Paul Simon tour, was recruited for one track, providing bass, drum, and keyboard programming on the mellow and atmospheric "Evocations," which he had cowritten with Michael. For the slyly funky "Scrunch," Maz & Kilgore sampled the groove from The Headhunters' 1975 track "God Made Me Funky" and grafted on a piece of Funkadelic's 1970 track "Good Old Music." Randy's Whitty-produced "Harpoon," fueled by Jordan's backbeat, was a challenging stop-time number with typically tight unisons over the top by the brothers, each of whom solos with unbridled conviction as the piece develops. They returned to slamming funk on Michael's multilayered "Slang," which is somewhat reminiscent of Miles Davis's album *Amandla* (1989). Michael delivers some urgent King Curtis licks on this organ-fueled, Whitty-produced throw down and also on the Maz & Kilgore pocket funk number, "When It Was."

Elsewhere on the acclaimed 1994 Brecker Brothers release, Randy reveals his soul on his tender ballad "And Then She Wept" and on the alluring, Brazilian flavored "Secret Heart," a flugelhorn feature that showcases Michael in a rare performance on soprano sax and also features background vocals and a piano solo from guest Eliane Elias, who also cowrote the song with her ex-husband Randy (they separated in 1990).

Maybe the most captivating and triumphant-sounding number on *Out of the Loop* is Michael's entrancing 12/8 "African Skies," which later earned him a Grammy Award for Best Instrumental Composition to go along with The Brecker Brothers winning Best Contemporary Jazz Performance for *Out of the Loop*. The piece is distinguished by another rare soprano sax performance by Michael that has him soaring as the piece builds to an ecstatic crescendo on the back of Holmes's whirlwind drumming.

Beginning with the spring '94 tour of Europe, drummer Holmes would replace White and remain in the group through the end of 1994 on tours of the States and Europe. Mike and Randy took a break from their extensive Brecker Brothers activities in late January 1995 to join Don Grolnick's octet (with trombonist Robin Eubanks, alto saxophonist and bass clarinetist Marty Ehrlich, bassist Peter Washington, drummer

Peter Erskine, and percussionist Don Alias) for an eight-city swing through the United Kingdom January 26–February 2, 1995, with stops in Southampton, Cambridge, Manchester, Birmingham, and Leeds. Their performance at Queen Elizabeth Hall in London was recorded and later released in 2000 as the live album *The London Concert*.

The Brecker Brothers, with the Dean Brown/Rodney Holmes lineup, were back on the road in spring '95 with tours of Europe and Japan, the latter leg culminating in a gala March 13, 1995, performance at Gotanda U-Port Hall in Tokyo. This same lineup would remain together through The Brecker Brothers' Summer '95 tour of the United States, including an appearance on June 18 at the Hollywood Bowl for the Playboy Jazz Festival hosted by Bill Cosby. Their last handful of gigs together in this incarnation of The Brecker Brothers came at Den Haag in the Netherlands, Berlin, and other European cities in July, followed by a stop at the Detroit Jazz Festival on August 31, 1995.

Brown recalled indulging in some road hijinks himself with Michael on those '94 and '95 Brecker Brothers tours to rival the creative prank-sterism of Dennis Chambers on the '93 tour. "People think of Mike as such a serious guy, but he's just a complete knucklehead when it comes to being on the road and touring and stuff. There was this ongoing thing that we had—this is back before the euro—where we'd come back from every tour loaded up with pounds of the local coins. We used to call it shrapnel, which was just coins from every country that you hit. And Mike would take a bunch of the coins, a lot of them, and hide them somewhere, like in your suitcase or in your guitar case or something like that. And, so, then your job was to try to secretly gather up all the coins and then put them back into his gear somehow. And this had been escalating over time until finally one day he got me really good. I opened my suitcase in a hotel lobby somewhere, and all these coins came crashing out on the floor, and Mike was in hysterics. But then I got him back good. We were doing a sound check somewhere, and Mike had left his horn on stage after the sound check to go do an interview. So, when he was gone, I poured all the coins into the bell of his horn, which in retrospect is really not cool. But it was so goddamn funny at the time. He picked up his horn, and he felt that it was heavy. And he was laughing so hard."

Brown recalled some other hijinks on the road. "There was another time in Japan where we were walking around in one of those convenience stores, and I'm carrying a basket. We had just arrived in Tokyo, so we wanted to get some supplies like water, snacks, and various stuff for the room before we turned in. So, Mike is talking with me, and for some reason during this conversation I notice he's got this stupid grin on his face, and I don't know what it's about. So, I get up to the counter, and I start taking the items out of my basket. Meanwhile, Mike had slipped all these really weird things into my basket like dried octopus and all these strange items that I hadn't seen before. As the person started to ring me up, Mike is back in another aisle, doubled over laughing."

Some of the hijinks happened on stage, but not intentionally. "We were playing in Malta at the jazz festival there, and back then, as you can imagine, their back-line system was a little challenged. There's no way to bring your own gear to Malta; it's just logistically not favorable. So, we're using gear du jour, and things are like falling apart on stage during our set. And something happened when we were playing 'Some Skunk Funk' that got us all screwed up in the middle of that song. Now, you have to understand that there's no chance that anyone that's ever played with The Brecker Brothers would ever screw up 'Some Skunk Funk,' because it's their hit. It's a goddamn anthem! But something happened that was gear related, and it distracted everybody to where we kind of lost the beat and came back in at the wrong place. We were trying to salvage it, and you could see Mike was laughing so hard but trying to play at the same time. And we're all just melting down . . . we can hardly play because we're laughing so hard, because it was just so absurd. I mean, you look around, and here were some of the greatest musicians in the world just unable to play two notes in a row that sounded right because we were all in such hysterics. The road can be hysterical sometimes."

Although Michael reveled in his time on the road again with The Brecker Brothers, that phase in his career eventually ran its course. Mike and Randy would go their separate ways again, musically—Randy heading into the studio in December '95 to begin work on *Into the Sun* for Concord Records (which he dedicated to his father, Bobby Brecker, who passed away on May 3, 1996) and Michael going into the studio to record his fourth album as a leader, *Tales from the Hudson*, released by Impulse! January 16, 1996. In the same auspicious year, Michael would also have some dream encounters with a few jazz legends that would prove richly rewarding.

# 10

# TIME FOR TYNER . . .
# AND HERBIE AND ELVIN

Following the release of The Brecker Brothers' *Out of the Loop* in 1994, Michael resumed his ubiquitous studio presence with a slew of wildly disparate sessions that year. Along with guest appearances on recordings by Aerosmith (delivering a King Curtis-styled solo on the raunchy rocker "Same Old Song and Dance" from *Box of Fire*), Bob James (*Restless*), and Jan Hammer (*Drive*), he reconnected with former Brecker Brother bandmate Steve Khan on the guitarist's *Crossings* and further explored his love of West African music with former Paul Simon tour running buddy Vincent Nguini on the Cameroonian guitarist's *Symphony-Bantu*. Michael also rekindled his chemistry with Mike Stern on the guitarist's seventh album as a leader, *Is What It Is* (particularly on the slamming Dennis Chambers-fueled "Swunk" and the lyrical, uplifting anthem, "A Little Luck") and he duetted with David Friesen on Sonny Rollins's "Airegin" and on the angular, hip-boppish "Signs & Wonders" from the bassist's *Two for the Show*. There was also a reunion with his old Indiana University classmate and Mrs. Seaman's Sound Band partner Randy Sandke on the trumpeter's *The Chase*, on which he delivered typically heroic performances on an up-tempo "Lullaby of Broadway," a surging "Booker" (an homage to one of Sandke's trumpet heroes, Booker Little), and a blazing 6/8 "Hyde Park" (named for the Chicago neighborhood where Sandke grew up).

Perhaps most significant of all of Michael's special guest appearances that year was his historic encounter with legendary pianist McCoy Tyner, a member of that very same John Coltrane Quartet he had worshipped most of his adult life. It happened in January 1994, when the two titans met for the first time on a gig at Yoshi's, the famous jazz club on Claremont Avenue in Oakland. Jason Olaine, who was booking Yoshi's at the time, gives the backstory:

"I had started at Yoshi's as an intern in 1993, and when Todd Barkan [previous booker at Yoshi's and previously proprietor of the famed 1970s San Francisco club, The Keystone Korner] left the premises, they had no one to take over. And that's how I started booking Yoshi's. Chuck LaPaglia, who was Todd's partner, had already booked McCoy for two weeks in January of '94 to start off the year. We were really struggling financially then, and Kaz [Yoshi's owner Kaz Kajimura] was going to pull the plug on the place. In fact, I had already gotten my pink slip in early December '93, saying basically, 'Hey, it's been a good run, but we're out of money. We've already sold the building.' Meanwhile, I went back over our profit-loss statements of all the times that McCoy had played Yoshi's before and discovered that he had only come through for week-long engagements in the past, and none of those broke even. So, naturally, I was worried about how he would do over two weeks' time. So, we had a meeting in September or October and decided we needed to shake up this McCoy run by having special guests each week, because otherwise we were going to take a bath on this thing."

Olaine's idea was to recruit some guest star for a straight-ahead residency the first week of the run and then present some kind of Afro-Cuban spectacular the second week. "That was basically off the top of my head," he recalled. "I was just riffing, not knowing that McCoy already had a relationship with Afro-Cuban music and had collaborated with Mongo Santamaria and recorded a Latin flavored album [*La Leyenda de la Hora* on Columbia Records, 1981]. I didn't know any of that at the time I made that suggestion."

After finally recruiting Mongo Santamaria, Paquito D'Rivera, Steve Turre, Claudio Roditi, and Orestes Vilató for an all-star Afro-Cuban blowout for the second week of Tyner's run at Yoshi's, Olaine then cast about for a special guest for the first week. "I had been on the phone a lot with McCoy's managers, Abby and Paul Hoffer, throwing ideas at them of who McCoy could work with that first week," said Olaine. "Finally, they told me, 'Look, why don't you just talk directly to McCoy' and gave me his number. So, McCoy and I began talking about who we could bring in to the club to play with him, but it was already so late in the game that I was getting really nervous. I mean, we're talking in October, and these dates are in January. So, I called Joshua Redman and Branford

Marsalis and Wayne Shorter, just going down the list of who we could get for that first week. But I kept striking out. And then from some kind of inspiration . . . I don't know why . . . I thought of Michael Brecker. And I'm like, 'Why didn't I think of Michael earlier? He's perfect!'"

Luckily, Michael was available for the week in question, so Olaine called Tyner to deliver the good news. "I'm so excited, and I say, 'Hey, McCoy, I think we got the right person for the first week. Michael Brecker is available, and I'm sure he'd love to do it.' And McCoy's like, 'Hmmm, I'm not familiar with him.' And I explain that he's really popular, and I start listing off all of Michael's accomplishments—who he's played with, and the whole Brecker Brothers story, and how he's carrying the tradition forward and all this stuff. And there's this long pause on the phone, and finally McCoy says, 'You know what? I just don't feel comfortable doing that. So, I'm afraid we're not going to be able to make it happen.' And I couldn't believe it! I was sitting at my desk with my hand on my head thinking, 'This can't be possible!' And then I kind of casually mentioned, 'You know, McCoy . . . he's from Philly.' And he went, 'He's from Philly? Well, in that case, it should be OK then.' And that's how the gig happened."

Olaine remembers being at the afternoon sound check before opening night of the week-long engagement of McCoy Tyner's trio with special guest Michael Brecker. "I had never really met Michael before that day," he recalled. "I was a publicist when he came through in '93. I think I said hi to him then, but we didn't have a relationship. So, Michael and McCoy meet for the first time in the club on that Tuesday afternoon. Mike comes in as he is in general—just this really humble, genuine cat— and he says, 'Mr. Tyner, it's such an honor and pleasure to meet you.' And McCoy's like, 'Yeah, great.' And they start the sound check. Mike's sitting on a stool up there in the middle of the small stage, and I'm the only one in the club. I don't even think our sound guys were there yet. And just before the music started, I remember Mike looking straight ahead at me with this kind of animated expression of amazement with his mouth open, shaking his head, like, 'I, I, I . . . have nothing to say.' It's clear that he can't believe he's up there about to play with one of his heroes. And then right away they started sound checking on 'Impressions.' And I'm sure that blew Mike's mind."

That evening, Yoshi's was packed. In fact, the club had sold out the entire week for this first-ever meeting of Tyner and Brecker. Olaine remembers one brief exchange he had with Michael that opening night. "They're playing the first set, and Mike comes off stage during McCoy's solo break, and he's not there with anybody—no road manager, no tour manager, his wife Susan's not there. So, it's just me and him hanging backstage by the mixing board during McCoy's solo. And at some point, Mike leans over and says to me, 'How do I sound?' and I'm like, 'Dude, you sound incredible!' And he's like, 'No, I feel like I'm totally *Hend-ing* out.' And I look up and I'm like, 'Hending out?' I had never heard that before. And he says, 'You know, playing like Joe Henderson.' I actually thought he was sounding more like Trane, myself. But in his mind, he was sounding like Joe Henderson, which I thought was fascinating."

It had been a year and a half since the Joe Henderson controversy had erupted, but clearly it still weighed on Michael's mind. Nevertheless, he seemed genuinely thrilled by his time with Tyner at Yoshi's that week in Oakland. "They were hanging out with each other upstairs in the dressing room every night, and Mike was asking McCoy all kinds of questions," Olaine recalled. "They really hit it off. And the club did such incredible business that week and the following week with the Afro-Cuban All-Stars that it kept Yoshi's going. We stayed open and never looked back. And when I found out later that Michael and McCoy made a record together for Impulse!, I was just totally psyched that something had come from that first encounter they had together at the club.

"The record is definitely different than what I remembered from their Yoshi's gig," Olaine continued. "They kind of smoothed out the edges on the record, and they didn't play as much of the Coltrane catalog as they did at that very first meeting. But the record was great, and they did a lot of touring together behind that for the next couple of years. So that became a really fruitful relationship for both of them. And I'm just really happy that it had its genesis in Oakland . . . out of sheer desperation."

Tyner's *Infinity* was recorded April 12–15, 1995, at Rudy Van Gelder's, the same studio in Englewood Cliffs, New Jersey, where John Coltrane's "Classic Quartet" had recorded several Impulse! albums. Released on the newly revived Impulse! label September 13, 1995, *Infinity* was not only a highly acclaimed outing; it is also that rare date in Michael's recorded output at the time where he plays on more than one or two tracks as a guest on somebody else's album, which had been the standing edict laid down by manager Darryl Pitt. But an exception was made for Michael's boyhood idol, the great McCoy.

Michael rose to the occasion on *Infinity* in the company of Tyner and his working rhythm tandem of bassist Avery Sharpe and drummer Aaron Scott. He holds nothing back on scintillating performances of Thelonious Monk's swaggering blues "I Mean You" (featuring some fiery exchanges with drummer Scott) and Tyner originals such as the modal "Flying High," the energized, stop-time swinger "Changes" (which had Mike alternately conjuring up King Curtis's grit and channeling Trane's sheets of sound), and the lilting 12/8 Afro-gospel number "Happy Days," inspired by the pianist's recent trip to Senegal, West Africa. *Infinity* would win a Grammy Award for Best Instrumental Jazz Performance, Group, and earn Michael a Grammy in the Best Jazz Instrumental Performance, Soloist, category for his absolutely incendiary playing on a rendition of John Coltrane's "Impressions," the first tune he had ever played with Tyner during their sound check at Yoshi's the year before and one that had become deeply ingrained in Mike's DNA after thirty years of playing it.

For the January 1996 issue of *Downbeat*, Michael and McCoy posed together for the cover photo with the accompanying headline: "Monsters Meet." In the story, Mike explained his reaction to being approached by Tyner about doing *Infinity*: "It was something I dreamt about for a long time. It's hard to explain. For me, it's more than the fact that I'm influenced by McCoy and John Coltrane. I think the quartet was the reason I became a musician. So, when the chance came, of course, I jumped at it. And the only way to characterize it is that it's the most comfortable I've ever felt in any context."

When asked by writer Martin Johnson if he was fearful of inviting the ghost of Coltrane, Michael replied, "It just so happens that I'm very strongly influenced by John Coltrane. Very much so, too, by Joe Henderson and Sonny Rollins. Those are the three, as far as saxophone players go, dominant forces, the roots of my playing. Then there is other stuff that has grown out of that. But when I get up and play with McCoy, I just play. I don't think 'I don't want to sound like this.' Harmonically, it has worked out wonderfully. I don't have to think about it."

In his *Jazz Times* review of *Infinity* in the April 1996 issue, Owen Cordle wrote, "The tour de force of the album is Coltrane's 'Impressions,' in which Tyner unleashes some of the stabbing lines and chordal intensity of the old days and Brecker blows a furious, Herculean solo from the Coltrane (and his own) book of saxophone technique. This reminds us that Brecker has done more to bring the Coltrane sound and style into the contemporary vocabulary than any other saxophonist."

Shortly after recording *Infinity* with Tyner, Michael went into the Manhattan Center in the spring of 1995 to record with another legend, Herbie Hancock, on *The New Standard*, an ambitious reimagining of contemporary pop classics by the likes of Stevie Wonder, the Beatles, Prince, Steely Dan, and others. Released February 19, 1996, *The New Standard*, which boasted an all-star cast of guitarist John Scofield, bassist Dave Holland, drummer Jack DeJohnette, and percussionist Don Alias, was acclaimed for its inventive, freewheeling spirit on beguiling interpretations of Peter Gabriel's "Mercy Street" and the Beatles "Norwegian Wood" (both featuring Michael in rare soprano sax performances), Sade's "Love Is Stronger Than Pride," and Kurt Cobain's "All Apologies," along with an earthy soul-jazz spin on Prince's "Thieves in the Temple" (a stunning showcase for Mike's King Curtis-meets-Trane sensibilities on tenor sax) and an urgently swinging take on Don Henley's "New York Minute." Allmusic.com's Scott Yanow wrote, "On first glance this record would not seem to have much promise from a jazz standpoint. However by adding vamps, reharmonizing the chord structures, sometimes quickly discarding the melodies and utilizing an all-star band, Hancock was able to transform the potentially unrewarding music into creative jazz. Hancock has successfully created a memorable set of 'new' music well worth investigating."

By the end of February 1996, Michael was reunited in the studio with another legend, his former mentor Horace Silver. Recorded at New York's Power Station February 29–March 1, the Messengers styled Impulse! release, *The Hardbop Grandpop*, had Michael soloing in signature virtuosic fashion on new Silver compositions such as "The Lady from Johannesburg," "I Want You," the flag-waving jump-blues tribute to Coleman Hawkins, "Hawkin'," and the earthy shuffle-swing number "I Got the Blues in Santa Cruz."

In March of '96, Michael headed to Europe for a month-long tour with Herbie Hancock's The New Standard band. Upon returning to the States, tragedy struck on June 1, 1996, with the passing of Don Grolnick from non-Hodgkin's lymphoma at age forty-seven. A lifelong friend and colleague of both Mike and Randy, Grolnick was a former member of Dreams and The Brecker Brothers as well as Steps and Steps Ahead. He had also attended Stan Kenton music camp with Randy and David Sanborn when they were all fifteen.

Grolnick's death was a crushing blow to Michael, who loved Grolnick like a brother and shared a sort of wry sense of humor with him that also came in handy on the road or in the studio. The year before, on May 19, 1995, Michael and fellow Steps/Steps Ahead member Mike Mainieri had both played on what turned out to be Grolnick's last recording. A beautifully inspired, Latin-tinged project, *Medianoche* also featured Andy and Jerry Gonzalez of the Fort Apache Band along with flutist Dave Valentin, drummer Steve Berrios, and percussionists Don Alias and Milton Cardona. Released posthumously August 13, 1996, it was nominated for a Best Latin Jazz Performance at the 39th annual Grammy Awards in 1997.

At Grolnick's funeral, Michael delivered a moving and memorable eulogy with some much-needed levity injected into the somber proceedings. "Mike was so tortured about what to write," recalled Susan. "And what he did was he talked about Don as a person. And then he made a list of all of the funny names that people called Don instead of Grolnick, all the mispronunciations of his name. So, it was like 'Don Groinlick' and a bunch of others. He went through thirty different mispronunciations of Grolnick, and we were crying, it was so funny. It was a perfect tribute to Don."

Former Brecker Brothers guitarist Steve Khan recalled this humorous anecdote regarding Grolnick: "When we were traveling with The Brecker Brothers during the mid-'70s, one thing that would consistently happen, no matter where we might have been, was that someone was always either mispronouncing or misspelling Don's last name. This, of course, drove him completely crazy and caused great laughter throughout the band. We would all gleefully await the keys and room lists to be passed out when we arrived at a new hotel or motel to see just what would happen this time with Don's name. The best misspelling ever, and it could have been in Japan, was when Don Grolnick became Don Grp;mocl. Of course, this sent shock waves of laughter throughout the band for days, weeks, even years. We would pronounce that 'Don Grip-mockle.'

"Decades later, after Don had passed away in 1996, Mike was trying to formulate what he was going to say during his eulogy for his closest friend at Don's memorial service. And so, Mike called me to run some ideas by me," Khan continued. "Of course, one wants to be respectful and loving during such a moment, but because Don had such a great and very intelligent sense of humor, you could not escape wanting to provide some warm laughter for all those gathered who loved Don so much. And so, I suggested that Mike and I should make a list of all the incredible mispronunciations and misspellings of Don's last name. And as we were assembling this list and laughing all the way through it with each name we had remembered, we finally came to the classic: Don Grp;mocl. It was at that moment that Mike said to me, 'Steve, you know, I finally figured out just how that kind of wild error could have happened. I was in the shower one day, and it came to me that if you just type Don's last name, and you were not looking at the keyboard, and your right hand was one key off to the right, the result would be Don Grp;mocl. Try it, you'll see!' Of course, he was right. And I was amazed that Mike had actually given this so much thought and had completely and totally figured it out. It's a silly story, but it shows what a brilliant mind he had."

Added Susan, "Boy, did Mike miss Don! Missed him every day. I miss Don every day. We spent a lot of time together with the records and stuff. And he would call up and leave these hilarious deadpan messages on our answering machine. Because I would never answer the phone during dinner, so we'd be eating, and this would be his message: 'Hello? It's Don. Don Grolnick. Yep. I'm here alone. Just me and my furniture. All alone. Old Donnie.' And he would never say good-bye. It would just go click. He'd call like every night at the same time: 'Must be nice sitting around a dinner table with your family. I'm alone. Just sitting alone.' He was such a good guy, and so funny. He and Mike: they were a real pair."

A couple of weeks after Grolnick's funeral, Michael's fourth album as a leader, *Tales from the Hudson*, was released on June 17, 1996. Helmed by Pat Metheny, this superb release featured a core group of Metheny on guitar (in subdued but brilliant Jim Hall mode), Dave Holland on upright bass, Joey Calderazzo on piano, and Jack DeJohnette on drums along with special guests McCoy Tyner and percussionist Don Alias. "That was a real treat for me," said Holland, "because it was the first time I had an opportunity to play with McCoy. I had opportunities subsequently, but that might have been the first time. And so that was a thrill for me. And, of course, Mike brought together a really strong group of musicians and provided us with some really interesting and fun compositions to play and explore."

*Tales from the Hudson* included such potent Brecker compositions as "Slings and Arrows," "Beau Rivage," "Naked Soul," and "Cabin Fever." Tyner soloed magnificently on Metheny's anthemic "Song for Bilbao" and also on a reimagining of Michael's "African Skies," which had received a more high-tech, big production number treatment on The Brecker Brothers' 1994 album, *Out of the Loop*. This acclaimed outing earned Michael two more Grammy wins for Best Jazz Instrument Album and Best Improvised Jazz Solo for his blistering tenor work on the up-tempo burner "Cabin Fever."

The summer of 1996 found Michael touring Europe extensively as special guest with the McCoy Tyner Trio. From Prague to Rome to Warsaw, Glasgow, Paris, Hamburg, Copenhagen, Montreux, Nice, Pori, then finally coming back to the States for an appearance at the Newport Jazz Festival, they collectively stretched on John Coltrane's "Impressions" and Tyner's gentle 12/8 Afro-gospel number "Happy Days," among other Tyner originals, throughout their energized sets.

McCoy Tyner and Michael Brecker teaming up for a tour of Europe in 1999 *(Photo by Luca A. d'Agostino/Phocus Agency)*

Following a two-week engagement in Japan with Hancock's all-star The New Standard band during the first part of August, Michael joined Randy in Israel on August 26, 1996, to rekindle The Brecker Brothers magic one more time at the Red Sea Jazz Festival. Guitarist Adam Rogers, who was subbing for Dean Brown, joined The Brecker Brothers for this special one-off gig in Eilat, Israel, while Scoota Warner subbed for Dennis Chambers. For Rogers, who had never played with Michael before and had never seen him play EWI live, the experience was eye opening. "His fluency and creativity on EWI was just amazing," said Rogers. "Of course, I had heard it on record, but he played an extended EWI intro to one of the tunes, and it was un-fucking believable! It was like an acid trip. He made it sound like a klezmer clarinet, and then he'd trigger like a West African drum group, and then heavy-metal guitar, orchestral stuff. It was like this encyclopedia of musical instruments, but done really creatively and really spontaneously. He was so fluent on this instrument, and his understanding of the technology necessary to be fluent on it ran so deep that he played it like it was the freest thing in the world. And it was just mind blowing."

By late fall of 1996, Michael would recruit acclaimed drummer Jeff "Tain" Watts for his working quartet, which also featured pianist Joey Calderazzo and bassist James Genus. Watts had made a name for himself on the scene during the mid-'80s with Wynton Marsalis's group and early '90s with brother Branford's group. Watts's time with Brecker coincided with a period when Branford Marsalis was focusing on his funk/hip-hop project Buckshot LeFonque, which incorporated the heavy-duty backbeat drumming of Rocky Bryant into the mix as opposed to Tain's more agile and eminently swinging approach to the kit.

Watts recounted his entry into Michael's quartet: "I returned from doing the *Tonight Show* out in Hollywood in 1995, and I had been around New York for like a year or more when Joey Calderazzo told me one night, 'Michael wants to check you out.' I think right before that I had gone to see Michael's *Tales from the Hudson* band in Boston in early '97. I was playing at Sculler's in Boston with Danilo Perez, and they were over at the Regatta Bar, so we finished our set, then went over there and hung with them. So, I ran into Mike that night at the Regatta, and then I remember running into him again at the North Sea Festival. And it did seem like Mike really wanted me to play with him. Don Alias was

Recording *Tales from the Hudson* in 1996 (from l. to r.): Joey Calderazzo, Michael Brecker, Jack DeJohnette, Dave Holland, Pat Metheny *(Photo by Odasan Macovich)*

already in his band, and he had an idea about getting us together to capture whatever me and Alias could get together.

"Mike called me to come up and play at his house in Hastings," Tain continued. "James Genus picked me up, and we drove there and rehearsed. It was kind of like an audition. We played 'Slings and Arrows,' and I heard clave on it and did something different to it that he thought was really cool. So, immediately, I kind of had the gig."

During that initial encounter in Michael's Hastings basement studio, Watts remembered being somewhat uncomfortable during his lunch break with the Brecker family, due to his unruly hairstyle. As he explained, "Susan had gone to a deli and picked up some soup and sandwiches for a spread there. The kids were really small then, and they sat down with us for lunch. And at this point I had been around Mike, but I'm still kind of getting to know him.

"I should explain that at the time I had a really, really big Afro," Watts continued, "but I had on a really tight hat all day, including while we were playing. So, at some point before lunch, when I went to wash

243

my hands, I took off my hat in the bathroom and looked in the mirror and noticed that my Afro was really fucked up. Usually, I would carry a pick with me, but I forgot to bring one, and I was like, 'Aw, man, what do I do now? Should I go to the table with a fucked-up 'fro? I can't wear a hat to this man's table. I'm not going to insult him in his house by wearing a hat to the table.' Finally, I just said, 'Fuck it,' and walked to the table and sat down with his little kids with my hair looking like half a slave Afro or something. I mean, it was really fucked up. But nobody batted an eye. And I immediately thought, 'These are very comfortable and cool people.' Michael and his family were really gracious and very sweet to me in that first meeting."

A highly respected rhythm master, Watts's irrepressible poly-rhythmic flow—a force of nature on any bandstand—brought a new vitality to Michael's quartet. It was the beginning of a musical hookup that would continue for three years and have a significant impact on Mike's music. As the tenor titan told me for a June 1998 *Jazz Times* story, "Tain's swing is really deep. He sits right up on the drums. He gets that hunkered thing, and he grooves with the music. There's nothing like it. He's one of those great old-time drummers. The unique thing about Tain is he has that conversational ability within his playing which doesn't interfere with the swing. He gets in there and mixes it up and is constantly feeding you things and echoing things. It's not so much even echoing; it's a language that goes on at the same time. It's in the present. He comes up with such great ideas . . . backwards kind of rhythms and things. And it makes for very interesting journeys during solos. He always surprises me."

By January of 1997, Michael hit the road for the first time with his *Tales of the Hudson* super-band (Metheny, Calderazzo, Holland, DeJohnette). They would play the Iron Horse in Northampton, Mas-sachusetts, on January 30, 1997, followed by a six-night engagement at Birdland in New York February 4–9, two nights in Philadelphia, and one night in Washington, D.C., before flying to Japan for a fifteen-day tour through February and into early March, with stops in Fukuoka, Tokyo, and Osaka. They finished that whirlwind *Tales from the Hudson* tour with five nights in Brazil in April 1997 at the Heineken Festival in São Paulo. "It was just a great tour to be involved with," recalled bassist Holland. "The level of musicianship was so high. And Mike, as he would always do, played it very low key. He was just a member of the band, happy to be the saxophone player and enjoy the group approach. Of course, it was all initiated by his music and his project. But he certainly never did the thing like, 'Hey, this is my band and my gig.' It was more like, 'OK, we're out here together, and this is a band,' which is why it was such a great experience. We were all able to stretch our wings and play in a way we all felt comfortable playing on that tour."

Back in the States, Michael reconnected with Horace Silver in New York City for another encounter in the studio (on May 29 and 30) with the hard-bop pioneer and prolific composer. *Prescription for the Blues* featured Michael playing alongside his brother, Randy, on trumpet, Ron Carter on bass, and veteran drummer Louis Hayes, a member of Silver's great quintet from 1956–1959 that also featured Blue Mitchell, Junior Cook, and Gene Taylor. Both Mike and Randy shine on the funky title track and on "Yodel Lady Blues," both of which have Michael dipping deeply into his King Curtis/Junior Walker bag, as well as on the boogaloo "You Gotta Shake That Thing" and the earthy, waltz-time number "When Lester Plays the Blues." Elsewhere on *Prescription for the Blues*, Michael unleashes some heroic tenor solos on the Latin-tinged "Dr. Jazz" and also on the two most modernist tracks on the album, "Free at Last" and "Walk On."

Michael spent most of the summer of 1997 touring extensively with Hancock's The New Standard band, beginning with a gala performance on June 27 at the Montreal Jazz Festival, then traveling to Europe for a twenty-city tour at all the major jazz festivals from Paris to Perugia to Pori, Montreux, Madrid, Molde, London, Vienne, Hamburg, and Copenhagen. From there Michael traveled to Japan to take part in a Live by the Sea concert in NK Hall on Tokyo Bay on August 23 and 24 with his Tales of the Hudson super-band. Also on the bill at this Tokyo concert was "A Tenor Supreme," a tribute to John Coltrane featuring Michael and three fellow tenor saxophonists—Dave Liebman, George Garzone, and Joshua Redman—accompanied by pianist Jeff Keezer, bassists Holland and Christian McBride, and drummers DeJohnette and Brian Blade. Their expansive and scintillating twenty-six-minute interpretation of Trane's "Impressions" would pave the way for Brecker's future excursions with the Saxophone Summit featuring Liebman and Joe Lovano.

Rather than returning to the States after that gala Trane tribute, Michael headed directly to Switzerland on August 30, 1997, to appear at the Willisau Jazz Festival as special guest with the Harald Haerter

Group, featuring Haerter and Philipp Schaufelberger on guitars, Benz Oester on bass, and Marcel Papaux on drums. That musical hookup would ultimately prove to be an important one for both Harald and Michael. "My connection with Michael came through [concert and nightclub promoter] Todd Barkan," recalled Haerter. "I had given Todd the record we had out with Dewey Redman [*Mostly Live* on Enja, 1996], and he offered to show it to Michael, which seemed like a great idea because we occasionally needed subs for Dewey, whose health was not totally stable at the time. So, we had this concept of getting Joe Lovano and Michael Becker alternating as subs for Dewey, whenever their schedules permitted. So, Todd gave the CD to Michael to listen to, and he loved it and seemed to be extremely interested in the band. And he told Todd, 'If at any time they have the need of a saxophone player, they should call me.'"

Michael had some availability in August 1997, so he agreed to embark on a brief tour of Switzerland with Haerter and his freewheeling musical cohorts. "Michael explained to me that he had been searching for a long time for a situation where he could play differently than he played in all the other projects where he was leader or appeared as special guest," Haerter recalled. "Because none of them had the musical conception that we had, which was about that fine line between playing changes and playing free. He explained that he had this urge to get rid of his typical Brecker patterns, this typical chromatic approach and very fixed language he had. Mike perfected that, but also mentioned that he felt sort of encaged by that kind of pattern playing he was into. He was basically always playing over a piano player or guitar player who played exactly the chords that evoked in his flow of ideas these same patterns, and he had gotten tired of it at that stage in his career, which is why he loved to play with us. He was searching for a new element, and at one point on tour, he said to me, 'I'm here to learn. I want to learn harmolodics, how Ornette and Dewey do it.' He was interested at that point in very strong melodically rhythmically based music that was not into the typical functionality of a ii-v progression or Coltrane-esque semi-modal stuff or even structured stuff. And he said he finally found guys, meaning us, that are in between that and can change wherever it changes on the bandstand, freely as the moment comes."

A key to this more liberated, in-the-moment approach was Haerter's bass player, Benz Oester, whose minimalist, open-ended style recalled

Charlie Haden's playing with Ornette Coleman or Pat Metheny's *80/81* band. As Haerter explained, "Benz invented chord changes in the moment, which was not free playing but rather providing shifting harmonic centers. And Michael really seemed attracted to this kind of playing, which was seemingly free but also had an inner logic to it. And that's why he always wanted to tour with us. He once mentioned to me, 'With you guys I can hear what I want to play, and sometimes I play it.' And he'd sometimes apologize and say, 'Oh, I'm playing too much Brecker shit now. I hate that!' And he'd often say, 'The American bands have these other more functional harmonic structures so deeply ingrained that I always resort to my same old language I've been using for forty years. And I want to feel open to get into a more stream-of-consciousness kind of playing.' So, we shifted between quite rigid concepts to totally free, but always interconnected. It's not like a typical free avant-garde thing, where you just begin and play. It's always very near to the free parts, but also like the ii-v structures. And the changing between these two worlds is exactly what fascinated him.

"So, Michael and the band had a huge experience together in finding these in-between styles between hard bop and avant-garde. It was a beautiful band we had, so open eared. And by playing with us, Michael tried to enhance and develop further beyond his typical lines, patterns, melodies, and rhythms he used for many, many years. That was the aim for him. He wanted to develop a new language."

Michael's time with the Harald Haerter Quintet is documented on the album *Cosmic*, which included loose renditions of Thelonious Monk's "Misterioso," Ornette Coleman's "When Will the Blues Leave," and Dewey Redman's "Mushi Mushi." They take things even further out on *Catscan* and *Catscan II*, the latter featuring the tenor titan stretching in cathartic fashion alongside Haerter's caustic Sonny Sharrockisms on the freewheeling skronk vehicle "You Could Be Gone by Tomorrow (GBT)," the audacious set-closer on their 1997 concert at the Willisau Jazz Festival. "As this piece develops, it gets more and more crazy with the comping of two guitars that are getting anarchic and harmolodic—two guitars, twelve notes, putting sounds and chords together that no piano player could match," Haerter explained. "And Michael is carried away more and more on this tune into total crazy free stuff until by the end of the piece it was just a real noise-exploding supernova, an incredible cacophony where he's screaming like Coltrane in his last years, or

Albert Ayler where he comes into this ecstatic state. I love music that has this very strong ecstatic development, where it gets hot, hot, and even hotter at the end until it's like a total orgasm . . . where we're just playing sounds and not notes anymore, and there's no brain involved anymore. It's just the body that trembles and shakes in ecstasy. And Michael was so happy to have that experience onstage with us. He was totally emphatic and loved the fact that suddenly the music went somewhere where it never went before and that he was a part of it."

Back in the States, Michael tempered things considerably from his avant excursions with the Harald Haerter Group by appearing as special guest with the Danilo Perez Trio, featuring bassist Avishai Cohen and drummer Jeff Ballard, at the Village Vanguard on September 24, 1997.

By the fall of '97, he was reunited with his reliably swinging quartet with Watts, Calderazzo, and Genus fueling the heated proceedings. Tain recalled it being a particularly busy time for him. "I was at an impasse because I was in everybody's band at the same time," he explained. "I was doing Kenny Garrett's band, Branford's trio started playing, and then I started playing in Mike's band. At a certain point, I had to choose between Kenny's band and Michael's band, so I went to Mike's band, which turned out to be just really, really fun. He encouraged me to be myself, and there was not a lot of instruction. It almost felt like the band was put together around me. In retrospect, I would have maybe taken more advantage of the breadth of Michael's musicianship and just tried to follow him in more of the places that his musicianship would lead him to. But at the time, I was just mostly consumed with the assignment of trying to listen and digest and get something personal happening. So, in general, I wish I had more time with Mike, and my head was in another space so I could take in more of it."

Watts described Michael's quartet as an odd juxtaposition of characters. "On the road we were a humongous party band while Mike was the straightest guy in the world. James and Joey and myself were just closing down bars all over the world, and the next day Mike would be like, 'Tell me what happened last night.' And I'd be like, 'Well, we were in a bar, and there's a guy who wanted to fight, and Joey almost hit him . . . but then we left.' And Mike just wanted to hear these stories, the filthier the better. And he was like, 'Oh, man! I would have been all over that back in the day.' And we'd be drinking or having beers at like ten in the morning, and he'd say, 'Just let me smell it.' And he'd sniff the drink and say, jokingly, 'Ah, those were the days. That's a good one! I would've enjoyed that.'"

As busy as Michael was—gigging with his own band, doing studio sessions, and planning new albums—he still sought out fresh, new blood for jamming scenarios, just to keep an ear to the ground and maintain an open mind. One of those was guitarist David Fiuczynski, who led a renegade group called The Screaming Headless Torsos. Mike had heard the unorthodox six-stringer and was intrigued by what he was putting down. "I was on the road with Meshell Ndegeocello in the mid-'90s, and there were a couple of different occasions where I bumped into Mike at festivals," Fuze recalled. "And Mike was like, 'Hey, man, we should play!' And, you know, I was kind of like shaking in my boots and just said, 'Yeah, sure.' We had another encounter at a festival in Paris, and Mike says the same thing to me, and I'm like, 'OK, give me your number.' Shortly after that, Mike came down to my rehearsal studio on Rivington Street on the Lower East Side. You know, THE Michael Brecker—a real '70s legend, one of the leading tenor players on the planet—in my total piece of shit place on the funky Lower East Side. So, there's Mike playing with me and Matt Garrison on bass and Gene Lake on drums, and we also had this cat rapping. It was a wild scene! I think he really came down because he was just a curious guy. In the end, I think he really dug it and wanted to do something together, but I think he was also really trying to push his career, and I was just too 'out there' for him. But it was a great experience. When somebody is that talented and that magnanimous at the same time, it leaves a lasting impression."

Bassist Scott Colley had a similar encounter with Michael around the same time. "I had met him previously, but the first time I remember playing with him was around maybe 1996 or so. I had a sublet apartment on 72nd and Riverside with three bedrooms, a piano in one room, and we had a drum set up. And a bunch of friends—Chris Potter, Dave Binney, Donny McCaslin, Jeff Hirshfield, and Kenny Wollesen—would get together there and just play all the time. That's actually where I workshopped stuff for my first record [*Portable Universe* on the Free-lance label, 1998] with these guys. And I remember getting a call one day from Mike. He was living up in Hastings, and he just called out of the blue and says, 'Man, I hear you're playing a lot there at your pad. Do you mind if I come by and play?' I had just moved to New York then, and it kind of blew me away that Michael Brecker just wanted to play for the sake of playing.

"So, we'd get together," Colley continued. "There were three or four sessions that we did with Mike. We'd play standards and maybe some original stuff, just to play. And what I remember about those sessions is that they were just super-relaxed, and he would just hang out and play. It was a great experience."

The following year, 1998, saw the release of Michael's fifth album as a leader, *Two Blocks from the Edge*, named for a deadpan quip often uttered by his late pal Don Grolnick ("I like living on the edge . . . well, not on the edge, exactly. Maybe two blocks from the edge"). As engineer James Farber, who worked on seven Michael Brecker recordings, recalled, "That album title was a classic Grolnickism. Don had a knack for taking everything to its logical extreme and then backing off just a little. For instance, instead of saying, 'When hell freezes over,' he'd say, 'You know, in hell . . . when you're just starting to need a little sweater.' That was Grolnick. He'd take some concept and make you think about it in a way that you never did before."

Coproduced by Michael and Joey Calderazzo, *Two Blocks from the Edge* included four superb Brecker originals in the earthy mid-tempo swinger "Madame Toulouse," the beautiful "How Long 'Til the Sun," the funky second-line vehicle "Delta City Blues" (which featured the tenor titan's astounding, note-bending solo intro), and the blazing title track. Michael's crackling quartet of Calderazzo, bassist James Genus, and drummer Jeff "Tain" Watts would play these tunes, along with Calderazzo's mood-shifting "El Niño" and his beautiful ballad "Cat's Cradle" and Watts's blazing "The Impaler," on their late spring and summer tours of 1999.

While the music on that tour was consistently smoking, Michael was disturbed to see that Joey's indulgence with alcohol had picked up considerably. "I was drinking around the clock," Calderazzo confessed. "If I woke up at 7 a.m., I was drinking a beer at 7:01. And then I couldn't hold beer down, so then it was vodka. It got deep. If I drank too much, I would do blow. I never did heroin. In hindsight, I probably would have been addicted to pills like Percodan or some shit, but that wasn't something that was in front of me, so I stuck with alcohol instead."

With fatherly concern and gentle instincts, Michael finally got Calderazzo to take stock of himself. As Watts recalled, Michael would sometimes use Calderazzo's nickname as a way of getting him to toe the line. "He'd pull out the 'Chubby' when he was trying to persuade Joey. He say, 'Hey, Joey, can you do this?' And Joey would say, 'No, Mike, I'm not . . .' And then Mike would look over the top of his glasses and he'd go, 'Chubby?!' You know, he put the Chubby on him."

Calderazzo said he hit bottom right before the band embarked on a three-week tour of Japan. "Prior to going to Japan, we did a gig in Nashville, and I hadn't had anything to drink for like two days," he recalled. "I was also taking some kind of pill for withdrawal that made me feel awful, so I stopped taking it. And right before the Nashville show, I went to some fancy French restaurant across the street from the gig and chugged two beers, just standing right there at the waitress station in this fine restaurant. I had two Heinekens—Boom! Boom! And they were looking at me like, 'Who the hell is this guy?' And then I went back across the street and played the gig."

On their flight to Japan the following day, Michael made a request of his pianist. "I'm sitting on the plane next to Mike, and I'm driving him nuts," Calderazzo recalled. "And at some point, he says, 'Joey, do me a favor. Drink! Just drink. You've been doing it your whole life. Drink. When we get home, we'll find a place for you. I'll work it out. We'll send you to a thirty-day house.' And I told him, 'No, Mike. No way.' I don't know why, but the idea of going into a rehab facility scared the shit out of me. So, I didn't drink the whole flight over to Japan. Finally, we get to Tokyo, and I go out to dinner with Tain. I was planning on having just two or three drinks. Then, seventeen drinks later, I was shit-faced. We hadn't even played our first gig yet. I ended up throwing up in the street, right in front of our hotel. And that was my last drink, on that first night in Tokyo."

The next day, Calderazzo accompanied Brecker to an AA meeting. "I had been to a bunch of meetings by this point, but I still remember this one meeting, twenty-something years later. There was an American guy there that Mike knew from going to meetings in Japan all these years, and he ended up becoming like my surrogate sponsor. And that was it. I never drank again after that meeting."

For the duration of that Japan tour and subsequent trip back home to the States, Calderazzo was experiencing some serious withdrawal symptoms. "I was a wreck, man," he recalled. "I had a gout attack from withdrawing from alcohol, so I had to go to the emergency room because my foot was swelled up and so painful, I couldn't walk. I was actually in a wheelchair. So here I am newly sober, I'm playing every night, and I'm on crutches. I mean, it was totally fucked up. And then flying home I got severe jet lag. Meanwhile, I'm not drinking, I'm not sleeping, and I'm praying to God I don't resort to drinking to help me sleep."

Upon arriving in the States, Michael brought Joey to the rehab facility. As Calderazzo recalled, "Mike just delivered me there and walked away. That's so fucking profound. Because here's a guy who's been like my dad for ten years and cared to death about me, and just like that he dropped me off and, 'You're gonna be fine,' and walked away. It was just an amazing thing. He walked me in and walked away. He didn't coach. He didn't lecture. He was just really cool."

In the fall of '98, drummer Ralph Peterson Jr. subbed for Watts on a swing through Europe. A powerhouse drummer in his own right and a protégé of Art Blakey, Peterson brought something wholly unique to the Brecker band. As bassist James Genus recalled, "Ralph came on board, and he was a monster, too, but he wasn't in there trying to play like Tain. He carried on that same intensity, but he had his own voice in the process. And at some point, he said, 'Hey Mike, I can play trumpet for a couple of tunes, and you can come in and sit in on drums.' And that was perfect." Indeed, that incarnation of the Michael Brecker Quartet ended each set with Peterson playing pocket trumpet, which he had previously recorded with and also featured in his own Fo' Tet performances, and Michael switching to drums, which allowed him to showcase his adeptness on the kit while revealing his obvious love of Elvin Jones.

Michael's sixth studio recording, *Time Is of the Essence* (1999), was his first-ever organ group project, harkening back to his own memories of going to see Hammond B-3 champ Jimmy Smith in Philadelphia as a teenager with his jazz-loving, piano-playing father, Bobby Brecker, who also kept a B-3 in the family's living room at home in Cheltenham Township. A key component for this project was organist Larry Goldings, whose droll sense of humor and somewhat dark demeanor reminded Michael of his late pal Don Grolnick. "I have a very distinct memory of Mike introducing himself to me at the old Iridium when it was near Lincoln Center uptown," recalled Goldings. "I was playing there with Peter Bernstein and Bill Stewart, and after we finished our first set, I remember getting off stage, and there he was, unmistakably Michael Brecker. He came up to me and introduced himself, and he said, 'Did you write that last tune?' I remember it was a song of mine called 'The Grinning Song,' which we hadn't played in years. And then he did that thing where he sort of laughs and nods his head in disbelief and said, 'I wish I had written that one.' And it was one of those things, whether he realized it or not, that just made my day by him saying something like that to me. And we briefly spoke. Then, later on, he called me about this project that he was going to do with three drummers, and I was all-in on that."

As Michael told Ted Panken in a *Downbeat* interview from 2000, "I just knew that I wanted to record with Larry Goldings. His sensibility reminds me of Larry Young. I love everything about Larry's playing—his sound and sense of time. He's funky as hell and has a comprehensive harmonic palette that's unusual for an organist—possibly because he's also a superb pianist. I thought it would be fabulous to couple him with Pat, which turned out to be a natural. Pat plays compositionally, melodically, intensely; he has his own sound, which blends with mine in a way that pleases my ear. I love Pat's thinking process, quick and very decisive. My last three records have all been jazz, where you have only a few days to resolve problems, unlike more produced records with electronics where the mixes are more convoluted and complex. When I'm sitting on the fence, Pat will express very firm opinions and force me to make a decision."

Produced by George Whitty, *Time Is of the Essence* was the third Michael recording to feature the warm-toned, legato flow of guitarist Metheny. Whitty noted the indelible chemistry that existed in the studio on that session between the two musical forces. "Pat and Mike have always had this ability to just start from nothing and play a really beautiful piece of music, just completely pulling it out of thin air. Both of them are harmonically quite adventurous, but they had this weird sixth sense thing where it's like you almost never hear a wrong note. They were so simpatico and just such good musicians that it was almost like you couldn't have written it any better."

Drumming duties on that outstanding organ project were split up among three extraordinary players—Jeff "Tain" Watts, Bill Stewart, and the legendary Elvin Jones. Just as he had such a deep affinity for McCoy Tyner's playing from so much exposure to classic John Coltrane Quartet recordings while growing up, Michael's connection to the legendary drummer went even deeper. As an accomplished drummer himself going back to the loft days of the late '60s, early '70s, Mike had emulated Elvin's style of drumming, particularly at mid-tempos, to such a convincing degree that even other drummers envied his skill on the kit. "Michael Brecker can actually sit down at the drums and play more of what Elvin Jones played than I can," noted Watts. And as Michael himself confessed to Ted Panken in a 2000 *Downbeat* interview, "Every day as a teenager after school I played drums along with Larry Young's *Unity*, which Elvin is on."

Consequently, getting Jones on *Time Is of the Essence* was a major coup for Mike. "I was thrilled to have him on this record because he's one of my idols and such a consummate artist in every way," he told Panken. "And his beat even felt wider than I expected, like an open field. It feels like utter freedom playing with him."

Jones appears on three tracks on *Time Is of the Essence*—Michael's "Arc of the Pendulum," which has him flowing loosely over the bar line in classic Elvin mid-tempo fashion; Metheny's earthy stroll, "Timeline," which contains some of the guitarist's bluesiest playing on record; and Michael's surging "Outrance." That ten-minute heightened romp opens with a quintessential Elvin drum solo and later features the drumming great squaring off in a titanic tenor sax-drum breakdown for a full two minutes, no doubt triggering memories for Michael of all the kinetic Trane-Elvin duets he absorbed from the classic John Coltrane Quartet recordings he heard growing up. (Michael would later return the favor by appearing as a special guest with Jones's Jazz Machine at the Blue Note in New York September 11 and 12, 1999, which was later documented on the 2004 Half Note recording *The Truth: Heard Live at the Blue Note*, featuring Brecker's titanic tenor work on the modal, Trane-inspired Keiko Jones composition, "A Lullaby of Itsugo Village," and on a restrained reading of "Body and Soul" underscored by Elvin's alluring brushwork.)

Elsewhere on *Time Is of the Essence*, Watts's killer instincts on the kit fuel Goldings's up-tempo swinger "Sound-Off," featuring outstanding solos from Michael and Larry; and Brecker's loosely swinging "Dr. Slate," where Tain's jaunty pulse on the kit brings out some playful abandon in Metheny's solo. Watts also provides some supple brushwork on Michael's evocatively named "The Morning of This Night." Stewart lays down a sly second line groove on Michael's misterioso number "Half Past Late," then paces Whitty's soul-jazz salute to Eddie Harris, "Renaissance Man," a tune that has Michael fairly walking the bar with extroverted tenor fervor.

Following the official release of *Time Is of the Essence* November 2, 1999, on the Verve label, Michael toured Europe and the States with his potent quartet of organist Goldings, guitarist Adam Rogers, and drummer Idris Muhammad through November and December. Rogers, who had played with The Brecker Brothers at the Red Sea Jazz Festival that one time in Israel three years earlier (August 26, 1996) recalled that fall '99 tour as being an enriching experience, both on and off the bandstand. "There aren't that many people who loomed large in the way that Mike did for me, as a New York musician," he explained. "I grew up in the city knowing about Mike and Randy and their careers in the studio, and I used to go to Seventh Avenue South a lot. I was one of those people who just looked up to Mike so much and respected his playing and his sound. So, there was this sort of high level of excitement just being on the bandstand with him, in addition to the musical excitement that happened every night.

"I mean, Mike completely slayed every set in a way that you could analyze from fifteen different vantage points—musically, rhythmically, sonically, harmonically," Rogers continued. "But ultimately, it was this energy that he would generate on his solos that would really blow you away. He could generate this incredible power, like a fuckin' freight train of energy. And following that, you might naturally want to turn on a distortion box to just keep that force going, but that was an easy answer, and it wasn't appropriate for this gig anyway. That was more of a Brecker Brothers thing. You hear that energy coming out of Mike's horn, and then you're supposed to create something as an improviser that is not in competition with that but rather inspired by that. So, I had to learn how to generate energy on my jazz box with notes and rhythms, not some freak-out noise solo."

Rogers also maintained that Idris Muhammad brought out something special in Mike's playing on their tour together in '99. "Idris didn't play anywhere near as much as the drummers that Mike typically worked with, like Tain or Jack DeJohnette. But his swing was so deep, and it was so exciting to hear Mike dealing with that. The chemistry they had together was just incredibly thrilling. Mike, of course, had his own powerful voice on tenor, but when you add Idris's swing factor to that, it just made for this high level of excitement on the bandstand every night. I remember this one night looking over at Idris, and he was playing quarter notes on the cymbal and playing 2 and 4 on the hi hat and nothing else. And it felt like I was on a train that was like a mile wide going down the tracks. The amount of force and energy he was generating just from going bing-bing-bing-bing was like nothing else I had felt from a drummer before. Afterwards, I came up to him and just stood there staring at him, and I said, 'Idris, man. What you just did is so amazing to me.' And he was like, 'What? I was just playing the way I've been playing since I was a kid.'"

While on that particularly hectic fall tour of '99, Rogers was privy to the tenor titan's pre-gig practice rituals. He remembers one brief but particularly revealing encounter backstage before a concert. "There was literally no time to practice on that tour," he recalled. "You'd get to a sound check, you'd warm up a little bit, or maybe you had already warmed up back at the hotel. You'd eat, and then you'd do the gig and go to sleep and wake up and run around some more the next day. But one time I was practicing in some small Italian city in some strange tile dressing room where the sound reverberated so much that you could hear everything everywhere. And I was practicing this Stevie Ray Vaughan pattern lick that I had transcribed . . . one of those great things where you bend strings. And Mike came in and he goes, 'What is that? You gotta show that to me!' So, I showed it to him, and within seconds he nailed it on the saxophone. Now, those patterns are very idiomatic for the guitar but not so much for saxophone. And when I asked him how he was able to come up with something like that so fast, he said, 'What do you think I was listening to all these years? I used to listen to and transcribe all kinds of rock and blues guitarists.' So, some of those things that are very unique to Mike were at least to some extent influenced by guitar. That classic blues lick, where you bend one string up to a unison with the next string . . . Mike had that down, which you really hear on a tune like 'Delta City Blues.' That's Mike playing guitar licks through his horn."

Rogers remembers that his very first gig with the Michael Brecker Quartet, in July of '99 at Toni Bishop's Restaurant and Jazz Club in Fort Lauderdale, Florida, was marred by a confrontation with a pushy waiter that almost led to fisticuffs. "Mike thought this was the most hysterical thing," he explained. "What happened was, I was standing in this area backstage in this club with Goldings, and as it turned out, we were sort of in the way of the waiters, which we didn't know at the time. And as opposed to asking me if I wouldn't mind stepping out of the way, this waiter grabbed my guitar neck and pushed me and the guitar back against the wall. So, this kind of stuff doesn't work with me. I mean, within a second, I had the guitar down and was so far in this guy's face. I mean, I was about to get into a fight with him. Goldings couldn't believe it! Idris loved it. Idris was like, 'Don't take any shit off anybody.' Then somebody kind of broke it up, but the timing wasn't great because it was right before going on the stage for my first gig with Michael Brecker. And Mike was upstairs somewhere when this happened, so he didn't see it.

"So, we played the gig, which was a blast," Rogers continued. "And afterwards we're in the van going back to the hotel, and Goldings goes, 'Mike, Adam almost got into a fight tonight with the waiter.' And Mike says to me, 'What? Are you serious?!' And Idris was like, 'The guy fucking deserved it.' And Mike was like, 'How did this happen? Who did this?' And he paused for a minute, and then he was like, 'That's fantastic! I never get into fights with people. You got into a fight! I love it! You're my hero!' He was certainly not condoning it, but at the same time he thought it was hysterical."

The band drove to Clearwater, Florida, to play their next gig, then flew back to New York, where Rogers started feeling exhausted and strange. On the day before he was supposed to leave for a European tour with Michael's quartet, Adam went to the doctor and was diagnosed with pneumonia. "I told the doctor, 'Tomorrow I'm supposed to start a European tour,' and he said, 'Well, I wouldn't advise it.' And I was like, 'You gotta be fucking kidding me! It's my first time touring with Mike in Europe, and I have to miss it?'" So, the doctor finally said, 'Listen, if you can stay in bed for three days, get right on the medication I'm going to prescribe, you'll be fine. But if you keep running yourself down and don't take these antibiotics, you could be in trouble."

Rogers remained behind while Michael's band flew to Italy the next day to kick off the tour in Pescara. "I stayed home and chilled out for four days, immediately got on the medication and whatever physical symptoms I had vanished pretty quickly," said Rogers. "I was feeling fine, so I flew to Ireland a few days later and met them at the alcohol-soaked bacchanal that is the Cork Jazz Festival."

A few days into the tour, Rogers got into another brouhaha at the Blue Note in Milan. As he explained, "We were playing in the club that night, and before our set started, I asked somebody who worked there if I could smoke a cigarette in the club, and he said, 'Yeah, go ahead.' So, I lit up and was smoking the cigarette, and this fucking waiter-bartender dude runs up to me, and he grabbed me and starts yelling at me in Italian. And mind you, I'm not some guy who just walked in off the street; I'm playing in the band. But this guy just starts screaming at me! And then as I'm trying to walk outside to put it out, he fucking gets in my face about it. So, we got into it. Afterwards we go upstairs, and Goldings goes, 'Mike, Mike, Adam got into a fight with the bouncer.' And Mike goes, 'Adam, what are you doing?!' And I'm like, 'Eh, the fucking guy was in my face!' And Goldings goes, 'Mike, he deserved it. Adam was in the right.' And Mike says to me, 'You know what, man? I think you should go downstairs and apologize to that guy.' And I was like, 'What???! I'm not going to go apologize to that asshole. He was in the fucking wrong!' And Mike says to me very calmly, 'It doesn't matter who was right.' And then he says, 'I never get into these situations. How is it that you keep getting into these situations with people?' And I was like, 'Come on, Mike! The fucking guy grabbed me!' And Mike says, 'It doesn't matter. Something is going on where you keep getting into these situations. What are you doing? How did you get into this? You could avoid a situation like that.'

"Mike was never, ever judgmental," Rogers continued. "I think he had seen far too much to be like that. But he said it again: 'I think you should go apologize to the guy.' And I'm still like, 'I don't want to go apologize to this fuck!' Finally, Mike said, 'It's not about the guy. It's not about the situation. I just think it would be good for you to do, for yourself.' And though I didn't go apologize to the guy, I thought about it a lot. And I still thought it was warranted, that the guy provoked it, but what Mike said really made me think. And by virtue of him saying this, I thought about some other things differently, too. And that's one of the things I really loved about Mike is that he would never offer up advice readily or gratuitously. But he did with me on this night, and I took his advice to heart."

Michael would continue touring with his potent quartet of Goldings, Rogers, and Muhammad in Europe and the States through November and December before closing out the millennium by unveiling an adventurous new group that brought him full circle back to his early NYC loft days.

# 11

# EXPANDING HORIZONS

By the end of 1999, Michael joined David Liebman and Joe Lovano for the New York premiere of their Saxophone Summit during a three-night engagement (December 16–18) at Birdland. This adventurous triumvirate inspired by latter-day Trane marked Michael's coming back full circle to the original source of inspiration that fueled his experimentations during the loft days of 1969–1971, when he explored with impunity alongside such like-minded and eternally searching souls as Liebman, Steve Grossman, Bob Mintzer, Bob Moses, Clint Houston, and others. Accompanied by Rufus Reid on bass, Phil Markowitz on piano, and Billy Hart on drums, the three saxophonists blew with abandon and searing intensity over six incredibly powerful sets at Birdland. As Michael told interviewer Bret Primack (YouTube's Jazz Video Guy) backstage between sets at the Sax Summit's December 17 performance at Birdland, "The thing that makes this a really interesting combination is that we all play really differently. We're coming from very different places, and that makes for an interesting juxtaposition of sounds, colors, and rhythmic approaches. And it's fascinating for a listener as well as for us. I met Dave when I first moved to New York when I was nineteen years old. We had adjacent apartments. And I've learned from him over the years. He's been somewhat of a teacher to me, was always ahead of me, and I'm still learning. He's such an amazing thinker with a clear, decisive, organized, incredible mind. And his improvisations are outrageous."

Liebman explained that the Saxophone Summit had actually come together two years earlier at the invitation of the Red Sea Jazz Festival in Eilat, Israel. "I don't remember what the premise was, maybe a Coltrane tribute. But I remember after the performance, back at the hotel, saying to Michael, 'The shit that we used to do . . . none of us do it now. What we learned from late Trane, it's not on the map anymore. It's like that period has been forgotten, like Mozart being forgotten. And I think it's our responsibility to bring this to the table. And if we did, it would be a little bit of a shock.' And Michael said, 'The critics will kill us!' And I said, 'Good! That's exactly what we need. Because nobody plays this stuff the way we used to play it the way we were doing in our twenties—a lot of group ensemble playing, screeching, playing free. And now we're in our fifties, and we've all taken a vacation from it. So, in a certain way, we've gone backwards.' And, finally, Mike said, 'I'm with you.' And then we decided to ask Joe Lovano to join us, and that's how that band came together."

"I think the fact that Mike heard Trane live at that Temple concert in '66 made a big impact on him," said Lovano. "He was a pretty young cat then, and he was able to hear that very explosive, amazing music that captured everybody, and that spirit was all coming out in the Saxophone Summit. Liebman was kind of a spearhead in wanting to do something that gave respect to the influence from the later period of Coltrane, from albums like *Meditations, Expression, Kulu Se Mama, Ascension* . . . those important recordings that we all lived with, and still do. Dave was really strong about wanting to do that. Of course, Mike and Dave had a long relationship from playing a lot of sessions together during the late '60s and early '70s, where the focus was definitely on the later-period Coltrane. They executed this certain attitude and approach that later really crystallized when we put Saxophone Summit together. That was the foundation of the group."

While latter-day Coltrane was the mantra for the Saxophone Summit from its inception, it didn't represent the full scope of this innovative sax ensemble. As Liebman explained, "We played tunes like Trane's 'India' and 'Impressions,' but then mixed it in with maybe a couple of standards, a ballad feature like 'Body and Soul' and a blues like Miles's 'All Blues.' We didn't play any original material early on, not until we made the record in 2003."

For their initial Birdland gig, things happened pretty spontaneously on the bandstand. "We just went in and called tunes," recalled Lovano, "and it came together because we all had the same kind of approach about how to play within the sextet—the collectiveness, the way we played the heads together and everything. We had a complete ensemble sound right from the beginning."

Saxophone Summit: Joe Lovano, Dave Liebman, Michael Brecker, 1999
*(Photo by Jimmy Katz)*

That Michael and Liebman were able to navigate through their respective careers over the course of thirty years and come full circle back to the source of this liberating, deeply spiritual music from their youthful, freewheeling loft days without missing a beat is a testament to the enduring power of Coltrane's message. "Well, you don't forget when you see the light," said Liebman. "It's just a matter of how much you want to do it, committing your heart and soul to it."

The Saxophone Summit had not only rekindled Michael's deep connection to the message of John Coltrane, but it also triggered a desire to expand his horizons. As the new millennium kicked off, Michael dedicated himself to pushing the envelope while maintaining his saxophone primacy. And his natural sense of curiosity would lead him to some fascinating discoveries in the coming years. "Generally, each project that I take on now is something that I haven't done before," he told Lorne Frohman on Canada's *Distinguished Artists* TV show. "It's something that's new for me, that I can learn from but also bring my own musical experiences to. I'm at the point where I kind of surround myself with musicians who push me in ways that I need to be pushed. That, combined with choosing tunes that can steer me in a direction that I haven't been in, helps as well."

Michael's first leap into the new in 2000 was a project headed up by his longtime friend, drummer-percussionist Don Alias (they had played together with Pat Metheny, Jaco Pastorius, and Lyle in 1979 on Joni Mitchell's *Shadows and Light* tour). Billed as "Don Alias & Friends," this Afro-Cuban ensemble, featuring his brother Randy on trumpet, former Weather Reporter Alex Acuna on drums, Steve Berrios, Giovanni Hidalgo, and Alias on percussion, Gil Goldstein on keyboards, Mitch Stein on guitar, and Spain's Carles Benavent on bass, embarked on a seven-city tour of the United Kingdom on January 17, 2000, with stops in London, Leeds, Bristol, and Birmingham. This Arts Council of England–sponsored tour would pave the way for Michael to lead his own large ensemble tour of the United Kingdom a couple of years later, which in turn planted the seeds for what would become his acclaimed Quindectet.

Following that one-off Don Alias project in the United Kingdom, Michael led his working quartet of organist Larry Goldings, guitarist Adam Rogers, and drummer Idris Muhammad on a swing through the States as well as a stop in Cancun. As writer David Adler reported in *All About Jazz* on their February 3, 2000, appearance in New York: "A hook-and-ladder company is probably still working to put out the fire that Michael Brecker's quartet ignited last week at the Blue Note. For this six-night run the tenor titan stuck to the organ-driven format heard on his latest record, *Time is of the Essence*. But of the musicians that appeared on that CD, only organist Larry Goldings was on hand. Taking over on guitar for Pat Metheny was Adam Rogers, and behind the drum kit was Idris Muhammad, who rocked the house. And not only did Adam Rogers outdo Pat Metheny by a considerable measure, he also blew his esteemed boss, Mr. Brecker, clear off the stage. Brecker came out kicking up dust on the opener, 'Madame Toulouse,' yanking double-time lines out of the horn that defied imagination. But when Rogers took his turn, he easily matched Brecker's velocity, then surpassed him in terms of rhythmic invention and melodic content. And every time Rogers took the spotlight, Idris Muhammad's pleasure was palpable. In fact, the inspired interplay between Rogers and Muhammad was what drove the show over the top, especially on the monster funk vehicle, 'Renaissance

Man.' When that tune ended, the band members looked around at one another, dazed, as if to say, 'How did that happen?'"

Michael spent most of June and July abroad, touring Europe with the Brecker-Metheny Special Quartet, featuring Larry Goldings on organ and Bill Stewart on drums, then in August he traveled to Bologna, Italy, to premiere a concerto for tenor saxophone, drum kit, and orchestra by New Zealand contemporary classical composer John Psathas. The ambitious sixteen-minute "Omnifenix," featuring the Orchestra Sinfonica Dell'Emilia Romagna "Arturo Toscanini" conducted by Marcello Rota, was a commissioned work geared specifically for Michael and was performed at an outdoor concert before an audience of eight thousand in Bologna. According to a reviewer who was present for the world premiere on August 2, 2000, "The work was written for the particular skills of legendary tenor player Michael Brecker. It achieves a compelling synthesis of the jazz and art music streams, and allows plenty of space for the individuality of the saxophone soloist to shine."

(The piece was later recorded by tenor saxophonist Joshua Redman and the New Zealand Symphony Orchestra and released in 2006 on CD and DVD as *View from Olympus* on Rattle Records.)

The Brecker-Metheny Special Quartet resumed its tour in the fall of 2000 with a swing through the States, then Michael headed to Seoul, Korea, and Tokyo to guest with the Kenny Barron Trio, featuring Ray Drummond on bass and Sylvia Cuenca on drums, in a series of straight-ahead acoustic jazz performances. He closed out the year on a smoldering, romantic note with *Nearness of You: The Ballad Book*.

Recorded December 18–20 at Right Track Recording studio in New York City, Michael's eighth album as a leader was coproduced by Pat Metheny and bassist Steve Rodby. It was a collection of sublime standards such as Irving Berlin's "Always," Kurt Weill's hauntingly beautiful "My Ship" (a Gil Goldstein reduction of a Gil Evans's arrangement of the tune from Miles Davis's classic *Miles Ahead*, 1957), and Hoagy Carmichael's beguiling title track (sung by James Taylor) mixed with tasty originals by Metheny ("Sometimes I See," "Seven Days") and Michael himself ("I Can See Your Dreams," "Incandescence"). *Nearness of You: The Ballad Book* registered with listeners across the board in much the same way that John Coltrane's *Ballads* did in 1963.

As Michael noted in a promotional interview for Verve accompanying the release of *Nearness of You: The Ballad Book*, "I used the John

Coltrane *Ballads* record as sort of a subconscious template for this record. That was always one of my favorite Coltrane albums for its sheer beauty, and Coltrane's simple approach to playing the melodies and making simple statements . . . the fact that the album had so much incredible information on it musically, but you could also listen to it and just dream with it. It's listenable on so many different levels, and I wanted to try and capture that same thing with this record. We were trying to create music you could dream with but also music that is really challenging to listen to. There's a lot of information there in each tune. We played in a way that we were burning, except in slow motion . . . a very relaxed slow burn."

One other particularly effective track on *Nearness of You: The Ballad Book* was the gentle Joe Zawinul composition "Midnight Moon," which Metheny had suggested, having fond memories of the Wes Montgomery version from the guitar great's Verve album, *Tequila* (1996, produced by Creed Taylor with lush string arrangements by Claus Ogerman).

With an all-star cast of Michael on tenor sax, Metheny on guitar, Charlie Haden on bass, and Jack DeJohnette on drums, the core of *Nearness of You: The Ballad Book* not only resembled Metheny's *80/81* lineup, but Michael's self-titled Impulse! debut in 1987 as well. Adding Herbie Hancock to the mix made for even more interconnectedness among the musicians during the sessions. Said Michael, "It's particularly fun to play with Herbie because you never know what he's going to do. We have a kind of running conversation throughout the record and also when we play live. I love his sense of orchestration and where he puts things. It's a very unique and special thing that Herbie does on the piano. And the combination of him and Charlie Haden was striking, as I expected it would be. And if you add Jack DeJohnette to the equation . . . Jack is such an all-around spectacular musician, his musicality really transcends the drums. And his take on ballads is really unique. He comes up with a different way to color a ballad that I've never heard any other drummer do. He doesn't just keep time; he's there playing with you in a conversation. And, of course, Pat is one of the great ballad players and ballad composers. And there's a special sense of sonority that happens when we combine our sounds."

Michael added that Metheny was a natural choice to produce the record. "First of all, we know each other so well and have a good rapport, and we had talked about it quite a bit previous even to my asking him to produce it," he said. "And there are certain characteristics about Pat that are phenomenal. He has a tremendous ability to focus, has a great attention to detail without losing the big picture and is willing to spend time on small things that other people would traditionally move past. And that works really well for me. Add to that his amazing ability with sound, being able to find ways to make instruments blend in an interesting way, and it all made him an obvious choice. And it turns out he was an amazing producer. Having him running the show, I could just completely focus on playing the saxophone and listening to the other musicians. And that was a luxury for me."

Along with contributing vocals to the mellow title track, Michael's friend and collaborator of thirty years, James Taylor, also reprised his classic ballad "I Don't Want to Be Lonely Tonight," which Michael had so famously soloed on back in 1972. "The idea of using vocals on this ballads project kind of reflected the *John Coltrane and Johnny Hartman* record, which I also loved," he explained. "Relatively early in the process, I thought of James Taylor, and the prospect of putting James with Herbie, Pat, Jack, and Charlie just excited me. It was an intriguing and exciting idea, and there was never any question in my mind that it wouldn't be amazing. I could hear it. And it turns out that James is really a kind of closet jazz singer. We did a few takes of every song, and he sang differently on each take of the song. You know, he was improvising."

Goldstein remembers Michael calling him to do an arrangement for James Taylor's vocal feature on the title track, Hoagy Carmichael's tender ballad "The Nearness of You." "I said, 'Mike, you're not going to believe this, but for the last two years, that's the only song I've had in my head!' And he goes, 'You're messing with me.' I said, 'Seriously, Mike.' And it was true. I love that song. I mean, could this be more of a gift? So, I sit down at the piano, and I think, 'I need an intro that's going to set up the song so we don't feel like we've already heard it a thousand times before.' So, I came up with that figure at the beginning, which is not rocket science. But to me, that was the send-off that we needed. And then we worked on it together. Mike, Pat, and I played through the song, and Pat had the very good idea to say, 'Hey, how about if we start on F and then we modulate to another key?' James originally wanted to sing it in F, then Mike soloed in G, and then we ended it on E flat. And the way James sang it, I was like, 'OK, I could get hit by a bus now, and

I'm fine. James just sang my arrangement.' And before James left the studio, I was talking to him, and he goes, 'That's the best band I've ever recorded with.' Yeah, that was a good band!"

Michael picked up his eighth Grammy (Best Jazz Instrumental Solo) for his super-relaxed and highly emotive playing on Herbie Hancock's willowy "Chan's Song," which had originally appeared on the soundtrack to *Round Midnight*, the 1986 Bernard Tavernier film starring Dexter Gordon. As John Murph noted in his *Jazz Times* review, "Brecker's tentativeness on ballads oftentimes creates striking effects as on Hancock's 'Chan's Song,' which moves at such a stately pace it almost threatens to fall apart. But the ultra-slow tempo allows you to focus on Brecker's beautiful tone and emotional persuasiveness when he zeroes in on the melody."

The process of recording *Nearness of You: The Ballad Book* would have a significant effect on Michael's whole approach moving forward, as he mentioned in the Verve promotional interview CD: "There has been a shift that I've noticed as I've been playing live since we made this record. I think it's enabled me to simplify even more. What I would've said previously with more notes, I seem to be more willing to say it with less. And some of that is an emotional process, but it's more of a process of giving the notes weight by playing fewer of them. So, it's more about where the notes are put now."

He added, "It's good to be able to grow from these projects. For me, it's important that each project that I get involved in or that I do breaks new ground for me—not necessarily in the grand scheme of music, I'm not so concerned with that. But I'd like to continue to pursue avenues that I haven't done before, to try and go into areas that I haven't been in, just for my own edification. For instance, I used a rubber mouthpiece for this session, which I'm not so accustomed to. But I felt the morning of the date, I started recording and realized I wanted a fatter sound. So, I put it on and ended up using it for most of the session. And I think it affected the way I interpreted the tunes. It actually forced me to play less. And I was more focused on the sound as a result and shaping the sound . . . playing in a more horizontal way than a vertical way, which I'm more accustomed to doing. And I'm happy with the result."

In that same Verve promotional interview for *Nearness of You: The Ballad Book*, which was released on June 21, 2001, Mike also revealed how he prepped for the recording: "Generally, my approach with this recording as well as all the other records I've made is that I show up to the studio very prepared. We know what we're going to play, I know the tunes we're going to record, the arrangements are set, the forms are set, and what that allows me to do, and the other musicians too, is to be completely free and play. I'm not weighted down with making big decisions. My main intention when I make a jazz record is to be able to improvise and not think about anything but playing and listening to the other musicians. And the way I seem to accomplish that is by being prepared and showing up with a definite agenda each day. That's the approach that works for me and allows me to improvise freely within these structures. And they might be very open structures; nevertheless, they are there. And we play freely within those confines. And it works for me that way."

In a rare reunion to kick off 2001, Michael and Randy got together on January 12 at the International Association of Jazz Educators (IAJE) convention to perform expanded big band versions of popular Brecker Brothers tunes such as "Sponge," "Night Flight," and "Song for Barry" with the Netherlands' Metropole Orkest. It was a foreshadowing of things to come in 2003 when they would revisit some Brecker Brothers tunes with the WDR Big Band Köln, featuring Will Lee on bass and Peter Erskine on drums, at Germany's Leverkusener Jazzfestival (documented on the Telarc live recording *Some Skunk Funk*, 2005).

During the first week of July 2001, Michael was the featured guest at the Montreal Jazz Festival's annual Invitation Series, which found him performing in solo, duo, and trio settings with bassist Charlie Haden and pianist Danilo Perez. For the remainder of that summer, Mike and Randy toured Europe with an acoustic incarnation of The Brecker Brothers that featured Dave Kikoski on piano (he had played on Randy's two straight-ahead albums—*In the Idiom*, 1987, and *Live at Sweet Basil*, 1988) and with the solidly swinging rhythm tandem of veterans Peter Washington on bass and Carl Allen on drums. Together they performed Jazz Messengers styled renditions of Randy's "Tokyo Freddie" (from *34th & Lex*, 2003) and Michael's "Dr. Slate" (from *Time Is of the Essence*, 1999) along with the obligatory set closer, Randy's chops-busting "Some Skunk Funk."

Kicking off the Acoustic Brecker Brothers tour at the Montreal Jazz Festival on July 2, they then traveled to Europe with stops at major jazz festivals in Glasgow, Lugano, Lisbon, Den Haag, Munich, Pori,

Stockholm, San Sebastian, Paris, and Marciac on an extensive run that took them through August. Stateside fans, unfortunately, did not get a chance to see this incendiary straight-ahead quintet in action, nor was any official recording of the group ever released.

Back home by the beginning of September, Michael was scheduled to open a week-long engagement at New York's Iridium near Times Square on Tuesday night, September 11, 2001. That gig, of course, was canceled, along with just about everything else in town, due to the terrible national tragedy that had happened at the World Trade Center earlier in the day. As Dave Demsey recalled, "That night and the next couple at Iridium were canceled. But then on Friday, Mike told the club he wanted to play, and he donated all of the proceeds from that gig to the Red Cross. I was there that night. It was his quartet with Jeff Watts, Joey Calderazzo, and James Genus, and I remember he played just terrific. The audience was really light—basically Susan and the kids and a couple of people from Mike's management office . . . maybe ten people were there. And I remember at some point before the show standing outside the club on the yellow line of Broadway, and the street was completely empty. No traffic, nobody on the sidewalk. It was just eerie. And you could still smell the jet fuel in the air. Then right before the first set started, Mike addressed the whole situation on mic. He said, 'This is New York! We play jazz music here! They can kill as many people as they want, but if we shut this down, they win. So, we have to keep playing this music.' And that, I think, really speaks to his humanity and his ability to step up in a big situation."

A week later, Michael embarked on a month-long Directions in Music tour of the United States and Canada with Herbie Hancock, trumpeter Roy Hargrove, bassist John Patitucci, and drummer Brian Blade. In addition to taking liberties with Miles Davis's "So What" and John Coltrane's "Impressions," performing them as a dreamy sloweddown medley, they also played Coltrane's surging "Transition," Hancock's "The Sorcerer," Hargrove's "The Poet," and Brecker's scorching Coltrane tribute, "D Trane," the latter showcasing some particularly cathartic blowing from the tenor titan. Michael also had a solo spot in the show where the band left the stage and he performed a nakedly revealing, unaccompanied version of Coltrane's tranquil ballad "Naima" that showcased his unparalleled virtuosity and forceful presence on the tenor sax. This emotionally charged set piece had Michael alternately blowing so passionately and with such remarkable nuance and control that it raised goosebumps and dropped jaws. In displaying his mastery of multiphonics while executing precision arpeggios, daring intervallic leaps and altissimo screeching, all done with impeccable time and perfect intonation, Michael conducted a veritable master class of saxophone playing each night he hit the stage on that thirty-city tour, which began in Santa Cruz, California, on September 19 and concluded in Naples, Florida, on October 29.

"So many nights of that tour were mind blowing to me," Patitucci recalled. "Just listening to what Mike and Herbie were getting into was really something. Herbie's comping was very provocative, and we would just marvel at what he would come up with each night. I mean, you'd be playing a tune with a chord sequence, and he would hollow out each chord. The roots would be the same, but he would reharmonize his own tune on his solo, playing all this amazing stuff. And you're like, 'Wow, you can't do this unless you play piano. And you really can't do this unless you're Herbie Hancock.' He was finding all these deep and broad sounds. And Mike, of course, would eat it up. It was really inspiring and challenging, too, to be on the bandstand with both of those guys."

It was during that Directions in Music tour that Michael began showing the ill effects from a long-standing health problem. "I remember he mentioned that he was dealing with hepatitis C, which is pretty bad," recalled Hancock. "And Roy was on dialysis, so we had some trials and tribulations on that tour."

Susan Brecker confirmed that Mike was indeed being treated for hep C when he went out on that Directions in Music tour. "He really wasn't feeling that great. And I said to Herbie, 'You've got to take care of him.' And he promised me, 'I will.' And Michael felt that. He responded to people like Herbie, who's got the biggest heart. The genius of Herbie, Michael was in awe of. But as a person, he just felt like there was just something really special about Herbie."

Their subsequent Verve release, *Directions in Music: Live at Massey Hall*, 2002, documenting an October 25, 2001, gig in Toronto, Ontario, would win a Grammy Award for Best Jazz Instrumental Album, beating out Wayne Shorter's *Footprints Live!* and McCoy Tyner's *Plays John Coltrane: Live at the Village Vanguard* at the 45th Grammy Awards show. Hancock's solo on Kurt Weill's lush "My Ship" would beat out

Michael's remarkable solo showcase on "Naima" from that same album for Best Jazz Instrumental Solo. "Officially, that record was supposed to be honoring Miles and honoring Trane," said Hancock. "Honoring Trane was Michael's idea, and honoring Miles was my idea. So, we kind of combined the two of them to make that record. I knew that Michael had a great appreciation for Trane. And unlike a lot of people who tried to copy Trane, he didn't try to copy him. He was just influenced by him. But it never came out as Trane's stuff; it came out as Michael's stuff."

Hancock also recalled that both he and Hargrove would chant *nam-myoho-renge-kyo* backstage each night before the show on that first Directions in Music tour. "I had already introduced Roy to the Nichiren Buddhist practice before then," he explained, "and he actually received his gohonzon, so he was officially a member of Soka Gakkai International [SGI], the Nichiren Buddhist organization. And, so, during that tour Roy would ask me, 'Are you chanting tonight? May I join you?' And I do remember trying to introduce Michael to the practice. I asked him, 'Hey, Michael, why don't you come and chant with me and Roy sometime?' And he said, 'I will one day.' But he didn't do it. And I would ask him a few times, 'You gonna chant with us today?' And he'd say, 'No, but I will do it before the tour is over.'

"So, one of the times near the end of the tour, Michael came in and chanted with us. That was the first time he chanted. And we did what's called gongyo, which is a reading of part of the Lotus sutra. So, we did a slow gongyo because he was doing it for the first time, and he was cool about it. So that was the only time he actually chanted with us. I don't remember exactly the path of his progression, but I do remember that at some point he agreed to receive his gohonzon and that he would practice. He liked the way it felt, and he thought it was a good thing. And maybe he knew something about his other health issues during that time, but he wasn't talking about it."

Michael continued his adventurous solo sax explorations, which had grown out of his unaccompanied performances of "Naima" on the Directions in Music tour, with daring solo recitals on November 7 in Basel, Switzerland, and November 9 in London inside the extremely resonant Union Chapel Hall. Building on that single solo showcase of "Naima," Michael would also present striking solo versions of his "Delta City Blues" and "African Skies" along with Thelonious Monk's "Monk's Mood" and "'Round Midnight" in those rare solo performances. (Actually, Michael had first stuck his toe in the solo sax waters three years earlier with a July 3, 1998, performance at Ronda Di Vael in the Dolomites in northeastern Italy.)

Drummer Jeff "Tain" Watts, who had been balancing duties with both Michael's band and Branford Marsalis's group, brought the two tenor players together for a kind of cutting contest in the studio on December 5, 2001, for his Columbia album, *Bar Talk*. As he explained, "I was blessed to be in Bran's and Michael's groups at the same time and was able to put my tune 'Mr. JJ,' named for a chow dog loaned to myself and Kenny Kirkland by a Korean family we were renting from during the *Tonight Show* days in L.A., in rotation on both their gigs. It was fun to play and had a classic air. So, both cats were familiar with the tune, and when it came time to record it, I got the idea to have them both play on it. Branford graciously allowed me to piggyback my *Bar Talk* session onto the end of his *Footsteps of our Fathers* session at Bearsville Studios adjacent to Woodstock. So, we did Branford's quartet session for two and a half days, with my recording beginning halfway through the third day. I tracked Mike and Bran's stuff then, as my band started to arrive. Ravi Coltrane was in my band at the time, and he was happy to kick it with his tenor brethren. There were lovely vibes all around.

"We did a quick rehearsal for entrances, and after a short, aborted first take, we did the take that's on the recording. Calderazzo gave an epic setup, and then the cats went for it. I'm sure they both could have gone longer but opted to be gentlemen and played perfectly for a studio recording. There was no need to listen afterwards, as they had played the shit out of my tune. The contrast worked well for me—two different approaches and a great workout."

As far as the two bandleaders' individual approaches to leading their respective groups, Watts confided, "Michael is probably a little bit more specific in the information he's conveying. Michael probably prepares himself a lot deeper than most people. And that's how he achieves his freedom. Branford's not as bogged down with the minutia. And he really trusts his ears to hear melody over songs. Somebody once asked me for an analogy between Wynton and Branford. There should be some parallels there. For example, if Wynton wants to play 'Stars

Fell on Alabama,' then he's gonna go and sit at the piano and learn the original changes from the score, and he's going to know the verse, and he's gonna listen to maybe four or five versions of it. Branford will just say, 'Let's play 'Stars Fell on Alabama' tonight,' and we'll just do it. The melody might not even be all the way there, but for him, the journey is the most important thing. Like, 'What expression am I gonna get to in all this?' The specifics of the information, he'll gradually accumulate them. So, in that sense, Michael is probably closer to Wynton in his approach than to Branford."

Continuing to tackle challenging music, his mantra for 2001, Michael closed out the year in grand fashion with a reunion of Chick Corea's Three Quartets Band with Steve Gadd and Eddie Gomez at New York's Blue Note on December 22 and 23 in celebration of the pianist-composer's sixtieth birthday. Said Corea, "I conceived of the writing of *Three Quartets* as a chamber piece, but instead of writing for classic string quartet, I conceived of it as writing for a jazz quartet. And Mike's playing on that material twenty years later at my Blue Note gig was very strong. He was all into it—passionate!"

Corea tapped deeply into Mike's Coltrane influence on the four pieces of that exhilarating and demanding suite. And while "Quartet No. 2, Part 1" revealed Mike's more lyrical side, the surging, up-tempo swinger "Quartet No. 2, Part 2," which Corea had dedicated to John Coltrane, found him bearing down in full-blown beast mode, unleashing with unparalleled passion and facility on his tenor sax.

Following a series of Saxophone Summit concerts in January 2002, Michael embarked on his own Arts Council of England–sponsored tour of the United Kingdom in February, with stops in London, Durham, and Birmingham. For that series of concerts, he enlisted Gil Goldstein to adapt several of his previously recorded compositions for an eleven-piece ensemble including Scott Colley on bass and Clarence Penn on drums. As Michael later explained in a Quindectet promotional video shot by filmmaker Peter Freed, "Our tour of England consisted of eight British musicians and a rhythm section from America. We did ten concerts of old tunes of mine completely arranged by Gil Goldstein. And the tour was successful, but beyond that I really enjoyed hearing the textures and colors of the large ensemble. I enjoyed it so much, in fact, that I was going to rerecord those tunes and make an album. That was a thought, anyway. And then we went home after the tour, and I started writing, and just a lot of music came out, and I started writing for large ensemble. And that grew into the Quindectet record."

Added Goldstein, "For that Arts Council of England tour, I arranged Mike's songs like 'Arc of the Pendulum,' 'Itsbynne Reel,' 'Syzygy,' 'D Trane,' 'Never Alone,' and 'Delta City Blues' for a larger ensemble of three strings (cello, viola, and violin) and three woodwinds (flute, a double reed, and bass clarinet) and two brass (trumpet and trombone). And it sounded really good. So, after the tour, Mike called me and said, 'You know what? I want to do a record like that, and I want to maybe write some new songs, thinking that it's gonna have that orchestration.' So that was the perfect outcome for what I wanted it to be."

Following that large ensemble tour of the United Kingdom, Michael resumed touring with his quartet before going into Signet Soundelux studio in Los Angeles May 14–17, 2002, to record as a special guest on Charlie Haden's grandiose *American Dreams*, featuring pianist Brad Mehldau, drummer Brian Blade, and a thirty-four-piece orchestra arranged by Alan Broadbent. Like his approach on his own *Nearness of You: The Ballad Book*, Mike took the approach here of being a "singer of songs," as Gil Evans had once cast Miles Davis on their collaborations together on *Miles Ahead*, *Porgy & Bess*, and *Sketches of Spain*.

Michael makes his presence felt on top of the majestic sweep of strings on the relaxed, heartlandish Lyle Mays/Pat Metheny tune "Travels," and on Keith Jarrett's "No Lonely Nights," which has him launching into some signature Breckerisms on the improvisation section midway through. Michael also unleashes in heroic fashion on Jarrett's "Prism," then goes for the unadulterated swoon on Don Sebesky's "Bittersweet." Elsewhere, he turns in gorgeous readings of Haden's relaxed ballad "Nightfall" and Mehldau's beguiling "Ron's Place." And his interpretation of the Albert Hague/Arnold Horwitt tune "Young and Foolish" finds him emulating John Coltrane's sublime work on "Too Young to Go Steady" from his classic *Ballads* album. The one tune that seems out of place on this otherwise reflective, mellow album is Ornette Coleman's "Bird Food," a swinging, stretching, harmolodic vehicle for the quartet that harkens back to Michael and Charlie's work together on Pat Metheny's *80/81*.

Recorded just eight months after 9/11, *American Dreams* includes a straightforward reading of "America the Beautiful" that has Michael singing through his horn in genuine, unashamedly non-ironic fashion.

As stated in a Barnes & Noble review of the album, "Charlie Haden's feelings for his country run deep. And even when there are no words involved, as on this all-instrumental album, the bassist's heart-on-his-sleeve pride in his homeland comes shining through. If only one song is explicitly a nationalistic ode ('America the Beautiful'), each of the other tracks is permeated by a glowing musical radiance that communicates heartfelt emotions. Each member of the all-star unit seems to have been touched by this same elation: tenor saxophonist Michael Brecker, pianist Brad Mehldau, and drummer Brian Blade all play with elegance and invention. It's fitting that Haden expresses his love of country through his obvious love of American music."

Haden himself had called *American Dreams* "a kind of quiet protest, that shows what America should be and what it could be." (He had posed similar quiet protests on his 1969 album *Liberation Music Orchestra* and would later push the protest envelope ever further on 2005's Liberation Music Orchestra outing, *Not in Our Name*.)

For the second leg of the Directions in Music tour, which stopped at every major jazz festival in Europe through June and July of 2002, veteran bassist George Mraz replaced Patitucci in the lineup, and drummer Willie Jones III filled in for Blade. Michael reunited with Elvin Jones on September 14, 2002, for a performance at the Blue Note with Elvin's Jazz Machine, featuring bassist Gerald Cannon, trombonist Delfeayo Marsalis, and the two tenor saxes of Mark Shim and Pat LaBarbera. It was part of a two-week celebration of the legendary drummer's seventy-fifth birthday and a tribute to Elvin's musical soulmate, John Coltrane. Michael was more than happy to participate in paying tribute to both giants. His love for Elvin was obvious, both on the bandstand and off. As drummer Peter Erskine noted, "I learned more about Elvin's style from watching Michael play the drums. He showed me one Elvin thing in particular that was like a really fast thing, and I just had no idea how Elvin did it. And I said to him, 'I see you doing this one Elvin thing. Do you know how he used to stick that?' And Mike showed me, and it was a real total eye opener. Like, 'Ah! So that's how he does it!' So, it would be true to say that every time I play, I am thinking of Michael, because sooner or later that Elvin thing pops up in my head when I'm playing. And I always remember Michael showing it to me."

There followed another daring solo sax concert on October 26, 2002, in Frankfurt, Germany. Then on December 4, Michael appeared in a rare live performance of Haden's *American Dreams* with the Berklee String Chamber Orchestra at the Berklee Performance Center in Boston.

The extraordinarily busy year of 2003 found Michael juggling engagements with his quartet and quintet, the Brecker-Metheny Special Quartet, the Saxophone Summit, and his dynamic fifteen-piece Quindectet as well as a nostalgic Mike-Randy reunion in Germany with the WDR Big Band, a stirring solo saxophone recital in England, and more performances of Haden's *American Dreams* at jazz festivals in the States and Europe.

Michael kicked off 2003 in grand fashion by going into Bennett Studios in Englewood Cliffs, New Jersey (owned and operated by singer Tony Bennett's son Dae) January 22–24 to record his magnum opus, *Wide Angles*, for Verve Records. In the first week of April 2003, he toured Mexico with a new quintet featuring Adam Rogers on guitar, Chris Minh Doky on bass, and Clarence Penn on drums.

It was on that brief tour of Mexico that Michael indulged himself in another favorite pastime—making humorous little "road movies" using only his handheld Canon video camera and then editing the raw footage on his Mac laptop using Final Cut Pro. "Mike's attention to detail on these things was amazing," said road manager Jerry Wortman. "He got so into it. And this was before iPhones, so he was doing it all on his still camera that took short video clips, and then he would edit them on his computer, put music to it and titles and effects. He had such an amazing talent for that stuff."

For these silly filmed pieces, Michael enlisted his bandmates as "actors." Jeff "Tain" Watts, Chris Minh Doky, Joey Calderazzo, and Randy Brecker had appeared on an earlier production from a November 2002 Brecker Brothers tour of Japan titled "Attack of the iPods," a pun-riddled bit of Monty Python–esque absurdity featuring a cameo appearance by "Osama Bin Poden." And in true auteur fashion, Michael credited himself as director under the tongue-in-cheek alias 'Stanley Kubrecker.' The plot line of *The Death of William Stewart*, an absurd murder mystery, had Bill Stewart playing a falsetto opera star who is mysteriously murdered, and the culprit turns out to be his grieving accompanist, played by Adam Rogers with a hilarious faux German accent to rival Sid Caesar's.

As Rogers recalled, "The inception of that really silly movie was at a gig we did (on March 29, 2003) at The Barns at Wolf Trap in Vienna,

Virginia, just outside of Washington, D.C. What happened was, Bill Stewart and I were goofing around, and Bill was pretending he was like a contralto, and he was holding the book of Mike's music and singing like faux Schoenbergian while I accompanied him on piano, playing my improvised version of twelve-tone music. Mike filmed this, and he was hysterical over it. Mike had an incredible sense of humor and loved to laugh, and I'm a really incredibly silly person, so it was the perfect match. So, we would go nuts with silly stuff on tour, and Mike would film it all on his Canon camcorder. Bill only did a couple of gigs with us in 2003, and Mike had this footage of him from that day at Wolf Trap. And since Bill wasn't around anymore, we came up with the narrative that he had been mysteriously killed. And I, as his longtime accompanist, Herr Damenbinden, which is 'sanitary napkin' in German, was under suspicion. At first, I was mourning his loss, and then it turns out I had murdered him out of jealousy.

"And Mike was totally into this filmmaking enterprise," Rogers continued. "He was always saying, 'We gotta get some more footage for the movie.' And I'd be like, 'So Mike, what tunes do you want to play tonight?' And he'd say, 'Fuck that! Let's go finish this movie!' So, we played an outdoor concert (on April 5, 2003) at the Zócalo, the main square in Mexico City. And Mike was filming these guys doing some sort of Aztec ritual that he ended up putting in the film, depicting it as a ritual to raise the dead. And then we went into the church where there was a service going on, and he filmed me fake crying there, like it was a service for the loss of this internationally renowned opera singer, William Stewart. And then he got footage in the dressing room, where he put water underneath my eyes, and I'm talking about how sad I am about his passing, with this fake German accent. Then, after it's discovered that I murdered William Stewart, he filmed Jerry Wortman and Clarence Penn as federal agents perp-walking me through the airport. This went on and on. Mike was constantly filming everything and creating all these scenarios for the film he had in his head. Then he'd edit everything together on his laptop, and it was really, really funny. It was total silliness, but he got so into it. Anything he'd get into, he just went in full bore. Whether it was the EWI, Bulgarian music, or these silly movies, Mike was utterly committed to anything he was doing."

Back in the States, Michael's quartet appeared on a triple bill with Dave Holland's quintet and trumpeter Wynton Marsalis's group at Avery Fisher Hall on April 25, 2003. Wynton ended up sitting in with Mike's band on "Madame Toulouse," and then Michael joined Wynton and Joe Lovano on a jam with Dave Holland's group to bring that gala event to a rousing conclusion.

The following week, on May 3, Michael performed another solo sax recital, this time at the Cheltenham Jazz Festival in the United Kingdom (his solo sax explorations continued later that summer with a daring recital on August 14 at the Middelheim Jazz Festival in Belgium). Then on June 25, he performed Charlie Haden's *American Dreams Suite* with guest pianist Kenny Barron and the Berklee String Chamber Orchestra at Carnegie Hall as part of the 2003 JVC Jazz Festival in New York.

Later that summer of 2003, while touring Europe with his quartet of guitarist Rogers, bassist Doky, and drummer Penn, Michael was a surprise guest at Norway's Molde Jazz Festival on July 17 with Farmers Market, a Norwegian band that presented a scintillating Norwegian/Bulgarian hybrid in concert and on record. Together they played a lilting, almost reggae-flavored version of Don Grolnick's "Nothing Personal." Drummer Jeff "Tain" Watts, it turns out, is the one who turned Michael onto this very eccentric band from Trondheim. "Somebody gave me a CD of that band, Farmers Market, which has a little Indian element and a little Gypsy element, but they're a Norwegian band," Tain recalled. "There's some really great saxophone and some great clarinet work on their recordings, and they play kind of interesting, warped examples of everything from Dixieland to fusion and things like that, but with a very personal perspective. So, we were riding somewhere, and I played some of this Farmers Market CD in the car, and Mike was like, 'Wow! What is that?' And after we listened to it for a while he was like, 'Let me borrow it.' He wanted to learn their music so bad that he just set up a gig and then went and played with them."

Mike and Randy got back together on August 23, 2003, for one brief hit as The Brecker Brothers at the Mt. Fuji Jazz Festival. The lineup consisted of Dave Kikoski on keyboards, Mitch Stein on guitar, Chris Minh Doky on electric bass, and Rodney Holmes on drums. After closing their set with a rousing "Some Skunk Funk," they encored with Randy's up-tempo shuffle blues number from *Heavy Metal Be-Bop,*

"Inside Out," replete with audacious guitar-emulating note bending on the tenor sax by Michael.

With the September 9, 2003, release of *Wide Angles*, it became widely acknowledged that Michael's compositional skills had blossomed considerably from his early Brecker Brothers days. As Jerry Wortman noted, "If you go back and do your homework, you'll see how Mike's writing was very mechanical and line based early on. Tunes like 'Escher Sketch' and 'Night Flight' were very technical. He'd play a line, and then he would work a tune around it. He hadn't tapped into the emotional side yet, but he became an incredible ballad writer. And his compositions on *Wide Angles* are just amazingly deep."

A seventy-minute suite spotlighting Michael's technically prodigious saxophone skills in the company of a fifteen-piece chamber ensemble, *Wide Angles* covers a wide range of musical territory and moods, with his electrifying tenor voice resounding in dramatic fashion on ten pieces. In some ways reminiscent of his work on *Cityscape*, his 1982 orchestral collaboration with Claus Ogerman, *Wide Angles* represents an incremental leap in both Mike's composing and soloing abilities. As he told Mike Flynn in a 2004 interview following a performance in the United Kingdom with the Quindectet, "I don't want to relax. I want to keep testing new waters. And as far as my soloing, I think it's because I'm playing with really good people, and it forces me . . . I can't help but try and stretch further."

Jason Olaine, who had previously been the talent booker at Yoshi's and met Michael during his 1994 appearance at the club with the McCoy Tyner Trio, is listed as executive producer on *Wide Angles* and acted as liaison between Verve Records and Mike on this pivotal project. "I was essentially a sounding board for Mike," he explained. "He called me up at one point when he was tracking to say, 'Oh, man, I need you here. You need to come to the studio.' I was supposed to have an important meeting at Verve and couldn't make it, but he wanted me to come out to Bennett Studios. So, I was like, 'When does Michael Brecker say he needs you? How am I not gonna say yes to him?' And when I got there, he was just so gracious and generous. When he saw me walk into the control room, he comes over and gives me a big hug and says, 'Thanks so much for being here.' I think I was maybe like some sort of security blanket or something for him. Because, in all honesty, what can I truly add to Mike Brecker? I mean, I was just grateful to be in the room with him. He was just asking me my opinion about this and that, and I'd be honest with my feelings. But to have him want me there was like a real solid boost for my own confidence. It really did more for me than I probably knew at the time."

From the driving complexity of "Broadband," full of interwoven countermelodies from the strings and horns, to the scorching intensity of "Cool Day In Hell," which has Michael unleashing Trane-esque flurries on his tenor, to the reflective and profoundly moving "Angle of Repose" and the rhythmically charged 12/8 vehicle "Timbuktu," chock-full of multiphonics and ecstatic overblowing, Michael pulls focus with his resonant tenor voice, like Pavarotti majestically soaring over Puccini's "Nessun Dorma." The swaggering pocket funk of "Night Jessamine" is named for his daughter, Jess, while the frenetic funk of "Modus Operandy," a sonic equivalent of a rush-hour romp through NYC traffic, is a nod to brother Randy's compositional style. As Michael told Lorne Frohman in a 2004 interview, "I really consider him one of the great writers of the last few decades. Randy came up with a way of writing and arranging that had a big impact on me as well as a lot of people in my generation."

The elegiac "Scylla," named for the six-headed sea goddess from Homer's *Odyssey* and cowritten with George Whitty, builds over a gradual swell of strings to a huge crescendo culminating in some ferocious blowing by Mike that finds him dipping deep into his latter-day Trane bag. "Brexterity" (the title is a play on words of Charlie Parker's "Dexterity") opens with a turbulent drums-tenor duet by Michael and Antonio Sánchez before segueing to a theme of staggering complexity and swirling counterpoint among brass, oboe, bass clarinet, alto flute, French horn, and strings, led by violinist and concertmaster Mark Feldman. Michael's exhilarating solo section comes in a pared-down quartet setting featuring John Patitucci's bass, Adam Rogers's pianistic guitar comping, and Sánchez's swing pulse on the kit. The one previously recorded Brecker composition here is a gorgeous adaptation of "Never Alone," the affecting ballad from the 1990 album *Now You See It . . . (Now You Don't)*. With swirling strings and subtle inner voicings, courtesy of arranger Gil Goldstein, this version stands as a masterpiece of form and feeling.

The lone piece here that Michael did not compose himself is Don Grolnick's elegiac "Evening Faces," a harmonically rich piece that opens in stately, chamber-like fashion with just the horns before strings and rhythm section enter swinging lightly, underscored by Sánchez's deft brushwork. As the piece develops, it gradually builds to the kind of loping mid-tempo swing feel that Elvin Jones was so noted for and Michael emulated so strongly. His commanding, highly expressive and eminently swinging tenor solo here, full of easy double-timing and daredevil runs, is one of the highlights of the entire album.

*Wide Angles* won a Grammy Award for Best Large Jazz Ensemble Album. As Susan Brecker recalled, "He loved that album. He loved the richness of the sound; he loved all the different musicians and all the different instruments. Yeah, he was really satisfied with that project."

A key figure in the success of *Wide Angles* was pianist-accordionist-arranger-conductor Goldstein, who won a Grammy for Best Instrumental Arrangement on the tune "Timbuktu." He had first met Michael when he moved to New York from Boston back in 1976 and later produced Mike Stern's 1992 album, *Standards (and Other Songs)*, which Michael played on. A former member of the Gil Evans Monday Night Orchestra in the early '80s, Goldstein earned his rep in the '90s through his string and horn arrangements on albums by trumpeters Chris Botti, Roy Hargrove, and Wallace Roney, alto sax star David Sanborn, singers Kevin Mahogany, Lea DeLaria, and the New York Voices, Brazilian guitar-singer Toninho Horta, and tenor sax elder James Moody. For *Wide Angles*, he took on the challenge of bringing a much wider palette and a whole array of new colors to brilliant Brecker compositions such as "Angle of Repose," "Scylla," "Evening Faces," "Never Alone," and the aforementioned Grammy-winning "Timbuktu."

As Susan Brecker explained, "Michael really liked working collaboratively. And he and Gil really had a great simpatico. He liked being able to call him up and say, 'Gil, listen to this. What do you think of this? I'm sending you this.' He loved that. It's exactly how he used to work with Don Grolnick. You know, musicians spend so much time alone practicing and writing and stuff. I think the joy of working with somebody was really satisfying for him, and he liked it. And, so, Gil was the new Don for him."

Goldstein, who had also played a significant (though strangely uncredited) role on *Nearness of You: The Ballad Book*, described his modus operandi on *Wide Angles*: "One of the things that always made me a little sad about Mike's records in the past was that he'd have an amazing head but, to me, the solos wouldn't have a challenging enough playing structure underneath. It would go into sixteen bars of G minor and D minor, and that's it. So, I said, 'I really want the chords to come out of the song and to be very challenging for Mike, to where he'd be like running the hurdles . . . just a lot of changes to navigate through. I wanted to hear Mike in more settings like that, like the stuff that he did on Claus Ogerman's *Cityscape*, where it's got a lot of changing chords and textures. And on the song 'Broadband,' where it's got like a million chords, Mike said to me, 'You know, Gil, I think it's like way too many chords there.' But I just took the chords pretty much from the song, and I wanted it to be that way."

The first piece that Goldstein arranged for *Wide Angles* was Grolnick's "Evening Faces." As he explained, "It was easier for me than any of the other songs because all I had to work with was just a recording of Don playing the song on piano. I wrote out the melody and the chords as I heard him, just trying to reflect what Don played, which is the arranger's job. And it went pretty quickly. For all the other songs, Mike would give me his very detailed demos, which had a lot of information in terms of voicings that he worked out in Logic on his computer. They usually had a piano part that was kind of the guts of the chords, and a bass line that was pretty specific, and a drum part that Mike played himself to indicate the precise groove of each tune. And they had all the complex contrapuntal stuff going on. Then, funnily enough, Mike would usually play the melody on soprano rather than tenor on all the demos, which was tricky because I knew that he was eventually going to be playing the melody on tenor.

"But, usually the demo was a minute and a half," Gil continued. "It didn't have an introduction, it didn't have a form to solo on, so I had leeway in my arrangements in terms of what other things I could add in. And like Gil Evans, who is really my inspiration, I didn't change that much. Gil said to me once when he arranged 'Concerto de Arango' for Miles Davis, 'I didn't change that much.' And I thought, 'Is he kidding me?' But he really didn't. He really tried to keep the actual sound of the original. There's also an Ahmad Jamal tune that Gil arranged on *Miles Ahead* ['New Rhumba'], and I checked the original Ahmad Jamal Trio recording of it. It's identical in the sound of it, but Gil orchestrated it. And where he could add, it grew out of knowing that information until it all becomes a bigger and clearer picture of the original idea. So, in my arrangements for *Wide Angles*, I really tried to get it to sound like Mike's original demos."

"Then maybe a couple of weeks before the recording session for *Wide Angles*, Mike said to Adam Rogers, 'Have you been practicing the changes on 'Evening Faces'? And Adam goes, 'Oh, yeah, I put them in my sequencer, and I've been practicing along with them for like two months now.' And Mike goes, 'Oh, I screwed up! I haven't practiced any of the changes.' But he really didn't need to practice. He tiptoed through all the changes. Mike's such a perfect player that you can't stump him. But I wanted to challenge him, and I was happy that he accepted the challenge."

Goldstein's adeptness with arranging strings on several previous projects came in handy throughout *Wide Angles*. "Sometimes, like on 'Timbuktu,' there were no real string parts on the demo, so I had to imagine, 'What would strings do on here?'" he explained. "'Scylla' is a tune that Mike had tried to record three times on different records. The working title was 'Chicky Thing' because it had a Chick Corea vibe with a Mini-Moog kind of sound on the demo. But instead, I said, 'No, this is a dark kind of Coltrane-Gil Evans kind of thing.' And I went for that. Mike actually had chord changes for that one that I completely overlooked. We just stayed in A minor on that one."

For his arrangement of "Scylla," Goldstein adopted a technique that his mentor Gil Evans had applied in his work with Miles Davis. "Gil liked the musicians to contribute. And he wanted them to add stuff in without it getting chaotic. For example, he wrote the song 'Stuff' on *Miles in the Sky*, and he gave a perfect chart that Herbie and Ron and Wayne could refer to, but then he opened the door for them to take liberties because he trusted them. Likewise, at the end of 'Scylla,' I had it written very specifically, and then I wrote, 'At this point, you can go off the page.' And Mark Feldman, who was in the string section, said, 'OK, I know how to keep going with this.' And we just let the strings have it. And Mike listened and went right along with it. So, they all contributed lightly through there. That was just the first time through, and as I was listening to it in the studio, I said, 'This is it! This is exactly what it's supposed to be.' So, at that point, I was happy that I could bring some of Gil Evans's spirit into Mike's thing."

He added that his arrangement of Grolnick's "Never Alone" was "pretty much one of those Gil Evans things, where I had his basic lead sheet on it, and I just tried to orchestrate it as clearly and instinctively as I could."

"My main thing was I just didn't want to mess up," Goldstein said of his superb work on *Wide Angles*. "I wanted to live up to what working with Mike should be, which was hitting a home run like he did every time he played. I remember one day when I was conducting the sessions, and I was standing on a milk crate so people could see me, and Mike says to me, 'So Gil, you're going to cue the orchestra here, and then they're gonna come in?' And I say, 'Yeah, yeah, I'll cue them.' And then he goes, 'And if you don't cue them, what's gonna happen?' And I say, 'Well, then it's going to screw up.' And he goes, 'And then I'll *scowl* at you.' And I say, 'Yeah, you could do that if you want.' But he said it as a total joke, and I was relaxed by it. From then on, things really went OK."

On the heels of the official release of *Wide Angles* (September 9, 2003), Michael went back on the road with his new quintet featuring pianist Joey Calderazzo, guitarist Adam Rogers, bassist Chris Minh Doky, and drummer Clarence Penn for a series of six consecutive one-nighters on the West Coast, October 1–6. Michael next joined Liebman and Lovano for a thirteen-city Saxophone Summit tour of Europe beginning on October 13 with stops in Warsaw, Budapest, Vienna, Palermo, Lisbon, Rome, and other destinations. It was at an instrument shop in Istanbul on that tour that Mike, Dave, and Joe picked up some new exotic horns and flutes that they would later incorporate into the act on pieces such as John Coltrane's "India" and "Peace on Earth." As Lovano recalled, "Mike and Dave and I went down to Taksim Square where there's all these shops and restaurants and tourist attractions. We went into this store, and we each bought all kinds of different flutes and reed instruments and percussion things. And then during that tour, I went into Mike's hotel room one night and heard him laying down some tracks on his computer that were just amazing. He had looped some percussion and was accompanying himself on duduk, a real low-pitched kind of big double-reed instrument that's down in the bassoon range. So, he laid that down, and then he started building up other things on top of it until he had this finished piece of music that was just amazing, just working with those instruments he had gotten at that shop in Istanbul that day. On the road we're always working on things in our own way. I do a lot of writing and composition, figuring out things inspired from the night's music that we just had played. But Mike would lay these incredible tracks on his computer and make amazing pieces of music out of them. He was a master at that technology thing as well as a master of his horn."

Two weeks after that Saxophone Summit tour of Europe, Mike and Randy had another brief reunion on November 11 at the Leverkusener Jazztage in Germany. Performing "The Music of Randy Brecker" with Will Lee on bass, Peter Erskine on drums, Jim Beard on keyboards, and Vince Mendoza conducting the WDR Big Band Köln, the concert was documented for a live recording that would eventually be released in 2005 on the Telarc label as *Some Skunk Funk*. It won a Grammy Award for Best Jazz Large Ensemble Album and earned Michael his twelfth Grammy (Best Jazz Instrumental Solo) for his searing performance on the title track. Said Erskine, "I had the bittersweet honor of being one of several musicians who went up on stage to accept his Grammy for the best solo. And when I got on the microphone to talk about Mike, I said, 'You know, to be honest, every solo I heard Mike Brecker play was worthy of a Grammy.' And it was. I never heard him play a bad solo. He's one of the few musicians that you can say that about. Everything the guy played was great."

A week after that gala concert at the Leverkusener Jazztage, Michael's Quindectet had its official premiere at New York's Iridium on November 18, 2003. At the end of their week-long engagement there, Michael commented that in retrospect he regretted not touring the Quindectet first before recording *Wide Angles*, as the music had developed during the run at Iridium, which ended on November 23, just four days before Thanksgiving. Michael would then close out 2003 with a series of quintet gigs in St. Louis and Seattle with the new lineup of Rogers, Doky, Calderazzo, and Penn. Doky had one fond memory from one of those year-end gigs. "Michael cracked me up one night," recalled the Copenhagen-born bassist. "We did 'Cost of Living,' which I would open with a bass solo. And right before we started that tune, and he came up behind me and whispered in my ear, 'OK, Minhgish, play that Danish shit!'"

The new year commenced with Michael, Liebman, and Lovano going into Avatar Studios on January 12 and 13, 2004, to finally document their harmonious blend as the Saxophone Summit, which had been touring successfully since the end of 1999. Accompanied by pianist Phil Markowitz, bassist Cecil McBee, and drummer Billy Hart, they dug deeply into a latter-day John Coltrane aesthetic on probing pieces such as Lovano's "Alexander the Great" (a hip reworking of "Bye Bye Blackbird" that alludes to the Four Brothers at the outset before taking off to outer realms) and Liebman's expansive eighteen-minute "Tricycle" (a deep exploration featuring all three horns dealing in full-out multiphonics mode). Markowitz's 7/4 Trane-inspired modal number, "The 12th Man," showcased Michael's remarkably rapid runs, culminating in some bursts of Trane/Albert Ayler intensity on his tenor. Michael contributed the title track, which finds all three skronking mightily at the intro before settling into a peaceful hymn-like melody. Elsewhere on the aptly named *Gathering of Spirits*, The Three Tenors explored with cathartic abandon on a freewheeling rendition of Coltrane's "India" before chilling on a reverential take on Trane's devotional "Peace on Earth."

Said Lovano of the Saxophone Summit's extraordinary chemistry in the studio, "We all knew each other, and we all had of an idea of how we wanted to play together. So, we would construct an orchestration of a piece without speaking about it and then let the magic happen. Like, how do you rehearse the unexpected? It's like—you know something, you feel something, you hear something, you enter the piece, and you execute within. And that was really happening, man."

The day after that Saxophone Summit encounter in the studio, The Three Tenors convened for three nights at Birdland in Manhattan, January 14–17, 2004, before Michael embarked on a two-week Quindectet tour of Japan, January 29–February 14, with appearances at the Blue Note clubs in Nagoya, Tokyo, Fukuoa, and Osaka. Drummer Antonio Sánchez, a marvel of creativity on the kit whose skill, power, and sensitivity had propelled the *Wide Angles* sessions at Avatar Studios just a few weeks earlier, was a driving force behind the fifteen-piece band on all of those Tokyo Quindectet gigs, with the exception of one near-disastrous night at the Blue Note.

As the Mexico City native and longtime New York City resident recalled, "I started feeling weird that morning, like I was going to get sick. But I figured it would probably go away as soon as I started playing. So, I left the hotel and went to the club, but before the first set began, I started getting chills. And then as we started playing, I began feeling really hot, then hotter and hotter and hotter as the set continued. At one point, I must've looked really bad because Mike's manager, Darryl Pitt, came over, and he asked me, 'Are you OK? Do you want a doctor?' while I was still on the bandstand. And I remember saying, 'No, no, I'm fine.' Finally, he just looked at me and said, 'OK, I'm going to get you a doctor right now!'"

As Michael and the Quindectet continued playing their set, Sánchez's temperature continued to rise. "I got such a fever that my ears completely went out, so I started hearing all this cacophony and couldn't understand anything that was going on," he continued. "I remember we were playing one of the tunes, and it all sounded so weird to me that I thought we were at the end of the tune, on the last note, so I just started bashing. And I remember Adam Rogers turned around and looked at me, and I just kind of smiled at him like, 'Yeah, this is great!' But all of a sudden, I heard another melody come in, and I realized we were just in the middle of the tune. It was like a completely out of body experience!

"When the set was over, I got off the drums and I went over to Mike to apologize because I realized that it had been a disaster. And as soon as I started apologizing, my voice completely disappeared! And he just hugged me and said, 'Don't worry about it. It's all good, it's all good.' Then I went into the bathroom of the Blue Note dressing room, and I started sobbing like a child for I don't know how long. It was really strange. Finally, the doctor came and gave me a shot to bring down my temperature. And he told me, 'You need to rest. You cannot play the second set.' So, they sent me to the hotel."

With his drummer out of action and one more set to play, Michael took over the kit himself. "Michael could definitely play," said Sánchez. "I had heard him play drums on sound check many times, and I tell you he could imitate Elvin Jones way better than I could ever imitate Elvin. So, he started the second set playing drums, and then Adam Rogers, who is also a good drummer, played a little drums, and the percussionist Danny Sadownick also played some drums. So that night, anybody that could play a little drums sat in on drums. And the next day, the three guys who subbed for me on drums said to me, 'You know, it's a lot harder than we thought.' And I was like, 'Yes! Of course, it's a lot harder. Mike's music is hard to play.'"

Sánchez's sickness turned out to be a twenty-four-hour virus, and he was back on the drums the next night. "It was such an amazing tour, in spite of that one disastrous night," he recalled. "And one of the things that I remember the most was playing duo with Mike each night. A lot of times he would start a tune by himself, and then I would join in, and we would play duo for a while before he would cue the band in. And the Trane-Elvin thing that happens with those two instruments really came out on the bandstand between me and Mike. And to me, playing duo with Mike was one of the best musical experiences ever, because his time was perfect, and his ideas were so clear. And I remember him telling me that he enjoyed playing duo with me the most of any other drummer that he had played with because he felt like I was in his head. Those were his words. And that was a huge compliment to me."

By the summer of 2004, Michael would make an extensive tour through Europe, alternating between the full fifteen-piece Quindectet on some select gigs and a scaled-down sextet featuring guitarist Adam Rogers, trumpeter Alex Sipiagin, bassist Boris Kozlov, pianist-accordionist Gil Goldstein, and drummer Antonio Sánchez on others. The sextet performed older Michael originals such as "Arc of the Pendulum" and "African Skies" along with the beautiful ballad "Nascente" (which he had recorded on *Nearness of You: The Ballad Book*) and Don Grolnick's "The Cost of Living," while the full-blown Quindectet stuck strictly to the new material from *Wide Angle*s. As guitarist Adam Rogers recalled, "We brought over a core sextet of Clarence Penn, Boris Kozlov, Alex Sipiagan, Mike, and myself, and we did some gigs with just that group. But for the Quindectet gigs we played there, we contracted different players—bass clarinet, strings, an additional saxophone doubling on flute—in each location. So, we had an additional group of Spanish musicians, a group of Dutch musicians, and a group of German musicians, and so on."

The Quindectet appeared at major jazz festivals from France to Spain, Germany, Denmark, the Netherlands, and the United Kingdom on that summer of '04 tour, with drummer Sánchez driving the proceedings from behind the kit. By then, Sánchez was a full-fledged, invaluable member of the Quindectet, but he remembered being slightly intimidated by the leader during the recording session for *Wide Angles* back in

January of 2003. "I started playing with Pat Metheny in 2001, and then we recorded *Speaking of Now*. And, of course, Pat and Mike were very tight. So, when Pat recommended me for *Wide Angles*, I knew I was more or less in, even though I hadn't spoken directly to Mike about it. Finally, his management called and told me I was on the gig. We had only one or two rehearsals for the Quindectet before recording. On the first day, I remember, I was already sitting there at the drums ready to go when Mike walked into the studio, and I was still starstruck by him. He was such an important figure in my life, musically. I remember listening to *Now You See It . . . (Now You Don't)* over and over again growing up in Mexico City. That was a big one for me, as was The Brecker Brothers' DVD *Live from Barcelona*. I consumed that thing, because I was also really into Dennis Chambers. So, when we recorded *Wide Angles*, I was starstruck through the whole session. Mike was in a booth right next to mine, and I remember when we started recording, and I heard my drums and his sax in the mix together for the first time . . . I couldn't believe it! You know, it was one of those kind of surreal experiences."

During the *Wide Angles* session, Sánchez was able to rise above being starstruck by Michael enough to make a suggestion that would salvage one of the songs the ensemble had been struggling with. As he recalled, "The music on this particular song was very difficult, and the rehearsals took a long time to get the orchestral parts really pristine. So, we as a rhythm section—me, John Patitucci, and Adam Rogers— had to kind of sit there waiting for the orchestra to get it together. There were a lot of intonation problems and, of course, under the magnifying glass of the studio, everything was very obvious. So, I could see that Mike started getting really stressed out, and Gil was also getting very stressed out. We tried a bunch of different takes, but it was just not working. And I had just been recording quite a bit with Pat using a click track, so I told Mike, 'What if you recorded with a click? That way you can pick and choose whatever parts of the orchestra you want, mix and match, and editing will be possible because everything will be the same tempo.' And I remember him saying, 'Yeah, but this is jazz. How are we gonna play jazz with a click?' And I told him, 'I've been doing it a lot lately. Nobody has to hear it. Only Patitucci and myself, and everybody else just can just play along with us.' So, we tried using the click, and it definitely helped. And we ended up doing the whole album like that.

"Then I remember running into Mike a couple of months later, and he told me, 'If it wasn't for that idea about the click, we wouldn't have a record. Because that was the only way we were able to finish it.' So, you know, he was always really nice and gracious to me about that."

In the summer of 2004, Michael and the Saxophone Summit would embark on a tour of Europe June 29–July 9, followed by two nights on Spain's Canary Islands, July 16 and 17. In the midst of that European tour, Mike reunited with his Farmers Market cohorts on July 9 at the Northsea Jazz Festival at The Hague in the Netherlands, where he played his fluid "sheets of sound" tenor sax on top of their eccentric, extremely intricate, and nearly unprecedented multidisciplinary jump-cut originals. As writer John Kelman said of Farmers Market's *Slav to the Rhythm* in his *All About Jazz* review: "Who else, after all, would use the music of classical composer György Ligeti as the foundation for a tune that rocks this hard, or combine searing electric guitars with the Bulgarian bowed gadulka, pedal steel guitar, ocarina, kaval (Bulgarian chromatic flute), clavinet and music box? There are also trace elements of surf music, Middle Eastern tonalities, Macedonian traditionalism (thanks to clarinetist Filip Simeonov, who appears on nearly half the record), traces of progressive rock and much, much more across the album's 53 minutes, and no shortage of beauty either, as on the gadulka / harp intro to 'It's Not Always True.' But it's the core of Farmers Market that drives and defines *Slav to the Rhythm*, in particular [Finn] Guttormsen (who is turning into a serious threat on electric bass) and [Jarle] Vespestad, a drummer who may barely breathe on his skins when performing with Zen pianist Tord Gustavsen, but is as muscular and downright thundering as he needs to be throughout this record."

Blending a quirky Raymond Scott Quintette aesthetic with the complex time signatures and impossible tempos of Ivo Papasov's Bulgarian Wedding Band, Farmers Market appealed to Michael's ever-curious mind. As Gil Goldstein recalled, "Mike had been fascinated with Farmer's Market. He would take things they recorded, and he'd slow them down on this transcribing program he had, and he would practice it at 35 percent, 50 percent, 60 percent, 70 percent, just gradually ramping it up until he really knew it. And from there, he'd incorporate some of that stuff into his own music."

Added Rogers, "The guitarist in Farmers Market played all that shit in 17/40 really, really well, and then he would solo and sing along with it like George Benson. And on top of that, when he sang a ballad, he sounded like Luther Vandross. So, this guy was a classic triple threat, and the whole band was amazing. And Mike would sit in with them, which, even for somebody with the level of ability on the saxophone that Mike had, is very, very difficult. The phrasing of that stuff is so unbelievably different, and technically on the saxophone the tonguing was something else. And, so, it was perfect for him because it was like this incredible challenge, which he loved."

Michael's ongoing fascination with juxtaposing lines and odd time signatures could be traced back to his own complex tune "Escher Sketch (A Tale of Two Rhythms)" from his 1990 album *Now You See It . . . (Now You Don't)*. And whether or not it was his encounter with Farmers Market that triggered his newfound fascination with Balkan music, Michael did undertake a deep dive into Bulgarian music, going so far as taking lessons with two Bulgarian master musicians living in Queens at the time—violinist Entcho Todorov and accordionist Ivan Milev.

As he told Lorne Frohman in a March 10, 2004, interview for Canada's *Distinguished Artists* TV show, "Right now I've been studying Bulgarian wedding music, strangely enough. I've totally fallen in love with that music, and I'm taking lessons now with a Bulgarian violinist in New York. And sometimes I think I'm insane, but I'm really having fun with it. And I sit around for hours trying to learn these melodies, which are really hard for me to learn. And as I'm getting older, it's harder for me to memorize stuff. But hopefully this new information that I'm just learning . . . I see my psyche and brain partially as a computer. I'm just putting information in right now, and I'm hoping that subconsciously it's going to mutate into some kind of composition . . . it actually already has. I'm hoping to write some things based on this language, but I'm trying to learn the language first before I really commit things to paper and pencil and computer."

Alto saxophonist Steve Slagle recalled Michael's newfound fascination with Bulgarian music. "I remember him telling me in the early 2000s, 'I'm writing this music that's Bulgarian influenced.' And to me, that was like far out, because even though I'm married to a Bulgarian woman, I hadn't really ever studied that music before. I listen to it a lot because she had a bunch of Bulgarian records around the house, and so I started to share some of these records with Mike. There was one cat named Petar Ralchev [virtuoso accordionist, formerly with Ivo

Papasov's Bulgarian Wedding Band] who had a band called the Zig Zag Trio. That was something that Mike and I were both listening to a lot and talking about. And I know that Mike started demoing some new tunes at his place in Hastings—his take on Bulgarian music.

"And I can tell you, man, that's another language," Slagle continued. "That's like somebody wanting to learn to write and speak Arabic. It's a totally other world, you know? Bulgarian music is not written down, and so you have to kind of learn it from another Bulgarian person or listen incessantly to the records. But the music's even a little bit too complicated to learn off of records. I think we both kind of agreed to that. There's some jazz music where you can listen to the records and kind of learn a lot by transcribing it. But Bulgarian music is even more far out than that, in a sense. So, the best way that it's passed down is from musician to musician, which is actually how jazz originally was passed down but isn't anymore. Jazz music has been more codified and is in schools now. But there's no schools of Bulgarian music anywhere that I know of or my wife, Theodora, knows of. It's more of an under-ground kind of folk music that isn't even that popular in Bulgaria any-more. It's considered far out. They like Queen in Bulgaria, not this stuff. But Mike really took the time and made the commitment to learning this very difficult and seriously deep music. It's like the commitment he made to absorbing and learning later-period Coltrane music. And I believe he was intending to put this stuff out one day. That was the last project that he spoke to me about doing."

Following his summer tour of Europe, Michael returned to the States to participate in a gala John Coltrane Tribute at the Newport Jazz Festival on August 10 with piano legend and former Trane bandmate McCoy Tyner, bassist Christian McBride, legendary drummer Roy Haynes, and fellow tenor saxophonist and son of Trane, Ravi Coltrane. Together they soared through an expansive rendition of Coltrane's "Moments Notice" (from his lone Blue Note recording, *Blue Train*, 1958) and built to a staggering crescendo on Coltrane's "The Promise" (from the Impulse! classic *Live at Birdland*, 1964). Michael responded on that gig as if he were trying to repay a debt he knew he could never repay. "If there was no Coltrane, there's no me," he said in a backstage inter-view. "His music really captured my imagination years ago when I was learning how to play the saxophone. It affected me on so many levels— on an emotional level, on a spiritual level, on an intellectual level, on a technical level . . . and just bowled me over. And it was really as a result of hearing Coltrane that I decided on music as a life's endeavor."

Ravi recalled the perfect synchronicity of that special tribute to his father at George Wein's annual clambake. "A giant storm was coming, and they were trying to get everyone into place quickly, and they wanted us to play fast," he said. "And we finished just before the monsoon came. But it was a treat playing with McCoy and Michael and Roy and Christian. And Michael was such a kind dude, just a very considerate person on and off the stage, musically and personally. In all kinds of ways, he was a very, very giving person."

Two weeks later, Saxophone Summit's *Gathering of the Spirits* was released to wide acclaim on August 24, 2004, with several critics weighing in on its connectedness to the Coltrane legacy. John Kelman wrote in his *All About Jazz* review: "What becomes increasingly apparent over the course of the program is exactly how influential Coltrane has been on all three players. And yet, that being said, each player has taken that influence and developed something distinctly personal and unique. There is absolutely no mistaking each player, regardless of where they are positioned in the mix. Brecker, Liebman and Lovano have crafted an album that easily stands amongst the best recordings of their collective careers, and makes one hope this isn't just a one-time affair."

The Quindectet reconvened in California on August 25 (the day after the official release of the Saxophone Summit's *A Gathering of Spirits*) for a concert at the Hollywood Bowl on a split bill with the Dave Holland Big Band. And it was backstage before their set that Michael began exhibiting some troubling symptoms. "There was something wrong with him, and we were all aware," said Adam Rogers. "He had some kind of pain in his chest and back, and I told him he should go get a lung X-ray to make sure it wasn't pneumonia. He wasn't incapacitated by it, but I think the following week when he went to Japan to play with Steps Ahead, it got really bad."

Added Susan Brecker, "He experienced severe back pain at the Hollywood Bowl concert. He called me from there and told me, and I suggested he go to the ER, but he never did."

The Steps Ahead gig on August 29 at the Mt. Fuji Jazz Festival was a triumph that ended in great concern on the part of Michael and all his bandmates. It had been eighteen years since Michael and Mike Mainieri had played together in that band, and for this gala reunion concert on Lake Yamanaka they were accompanied by Mike Stern on guitar, Darryl Jones on electric bass, Steve Gadd on drums, and Adam Holzman on keyboards. "Essentially, it was the 1986 Steps Ahead band, but with Gadd instead of Steve Smith," said Mainieri. "On the '86 gig, I was playing all these MIDI synth parts, and I didn't want to do that on this trip, so I called Adam Holzman to play all the synth parts. And there was like a monsoon for three days. That's why when you look at the video of that concert, you'll see all this plastic covering on the stage. You know, we felt like we were in a cage."

Throughout their set, they ran down Steps Ahead favorites such as "Ooops" and "Self Portrait" (both from *Modern Times*, 1984) and "Beirut" (from *Magnetic*, 1986). Michael also performed a stunning EWI rendition of Duke Ellington's "In a Sentimental Mood," accompanied only by Mainieri on keyboards. Their kinetic set closer, Mainieri's "Trains" (from *Magnetic*), had Michael blowing with such incredible ferocity on an endless string of ideas that it even amazed his bandmates. "Michael played this solo that was just fucking unbelievable!," Mainieri recalled. "And we were supposed to do what we usually did at the end of 'Trains,' where we hit the last note and walk off stage, and then Gadd would come back out and play a drum solo, then we'd all come back out on stage again, and everybody would go nuts. But when I walked off stage, I see Mike, and he says, 'I think I broke my back.' I thought he was kidding because he was laughing when he said it. Then he says, 'No, I really think I broke my back.' And I'm like, 'Really? We gotta go back on!'

"Meanwhile, I know that Gadd was exhausted because it was a long set, so we skipped the drum solo and just came back out and reprised the ending part of 'Trains.' And that was it. We hung out in Tokyo for a night, but Mike went back to New York immediately."

"Mike's back was hurting before the gig," said manager Darryl Pitt. "As I had back surgery twice by that point, I knew about all the stretches and routines you had to do, so we did that at the hotel spa in the effort to create relief. And Mike made it into a game as to when he felt better and when he didn't. So, by the time we made it to the concert, he was feeling a bit better. But then by the end of the show, it wasn't right. Something was very wrong with Mike."

# 12

# THE ARC OF THE DISEASE

Before the debilitating back pain that he endured at the Steps Ahead reunion in Tokyo, Michael had experienced other unrelated back issues while on tour. Near the end of 2000 when his quartet with Adam Rogers, Larry Goldings, and Clarence Penn had a four-night engagement at the Jazz Alley in Seattle, Mike couldn't make the first two nights due to a back injury. As guitarist Rogers recalled, "We played organ trio for two nights, and Josh Redman came by and sat in with us one night. And Goldings kept making the joke on mic to the audience that Mike couldn't be with us because he injured his lower back lifting his discography."

Bassist Chris Minh Doky recalled similar incidents in 2003. "Once when we did a gig in Europe, and his back got so bad that the next morning, he actually had to have a wheelchair. Another time we were going do a gig in Louisiana, and I was in the car heading to the airport, Mike called and said, 'Man, my back is just hurting too much. I can't make the gig. But you guys go ahead and do the gig as a trio.' And I'm like, 'Mike, we can't! They're coming to hear you.' And he said, 'No, I insist. Go ahead; play the gig.' I knew he had back issues, but I didn't know it was that bad."

Mike would invariably laugh off these back issues, saying, "Ah, I'm just getting old." As Susan Brecker acknowledged, "Mike occasionally threw his back out. This was not a chronic problem at all. He saw a chiropractor sometimes and worked out regularly. He had back problems on and off, but mostly off. And he dealt with it."

But what happened to him in Tokyo at the Steps Ahead reunion in late August 2004 was something very different. Mike flew back home from Japan and though he was still experiencing some back pain, he put off having it looked at for a few days in order to attend a ceremony on September 3, 2004, at Boston's Berklee College of Music, where he

received an honorary doctorate of music degree for his outstanding contributions to contemporary music. Back in New York, Michael's friend
and former road manager Jerry Wortman picked him up in Hastings-
on-Hudson and took him to Columbia Presbyterian Hospital, where an
MRI revealed a cracked vertebra. It was later repaired, and Mike was
told that he could resume his busy schedule of performing, composing,
and recording after a period of recuperation. But as Darryl Pitt noted,
"When a bone breaks without any associated trauma, red flags go up."

Michael's injury sidelined him through the month of September,
forcing him to cancel five nights at Moscow's Le Club September 18–22
with The Brecker Brothers. As his brother, Randy, recalled, "I had been
going to Russia with (Russian tenor saxophonist) Igor Butman probably
five or six times by then, and it was always Igor's dream to bring both
of us over to play. So here it was, the gig was booked, and we were
supposed to leave on Monday. Then I got a call from Mike over the
weekend saying, 'I can't go. Something's the matter with my back. It
really hurts.' And I said, 'Well, look, man. Just get over there, and we'll
deal with it then.' And he said, 'No, I can't do it.' So, he didn't come. We
had a really good band with Victor Bailey and George Whitty, Rodney
Holmes, Mitch Stein on guitar. And my wife, Ada Rovatti, really rose to
the occasion by filling in for Mike on tenor sax. But Igor was mortified.
He thought he was being bullshitted because he had already sent the
money to Darryl Pitt for both Brecker Brothers, and suddenly there's no
Mike. But we worked it out with him, and Igor eventually understood
that it was for real, that Mike had a broken vertebra."

Michael's back issues were especially concerning to his sister, Emily
Brecker-Greenberg, because their mother, Sylvia, also had a history of
back problems. As she told Philadelphia's *Jewish Exponent*, "Our mother
had died from a disease known as multiple myeloma, a bone-marrow
disease that affects your skeleton and causes bones to break easily. So,
when Michael fractured one of his vertebrae, I feared the worst."

By October of 2004, Emily's fears were confirmed when Michael
was reexamined and diagnosed with myelodysplastic syndrome, a
pre-leukemic bone marrow disorder. "They looked more closely at his
bone marrow, because when someone breaks a bone that is not the
result of a trauma, there is usually something going on in the marrow,"
explained Susan Brecker. "So they did a bone marrow biopsy and discovered the MDS."

Said bassist John Patitucci, "In the past, when Mike started saying something about his bad back, I just thought, 'Well, he's tall. A lot of my friends that are tall have that thing. And he's not a kid anymore. He's not old, but he's not twenty-five either.' I knew he had been struggling with residual things that were there from his past, but I never had any inkling of a disease like that."

And as Dave Liebman recalled from their Saxophone Summit gig at Birdland the year before: "He had back trouble all week. And I do have a picture in my mind of that last night . . . of him walking to the garage across the street and making me look like I'm an Olympic walker by comparison. I mean, it was really obvious that he had pain in his back, and he was walking so gingerly to his car. Of course, we all have back trouble from time to time—pulled muscle or whatever. But this was something else. And when the news came later on that it wasn't his back but something much worse, it was a big-time shock."

After getting the diagnosis of MDS, Michael canceled a two-week tour through Belgium, Italy, Ireland, Norway, and Sweden with his quartet that was scheduled through the end of October 2004. He recuperated through all of November, and by mid-December he felt well enough to return to the scene. As Pitt explained, "MDS is not necessarily a death sentence. There are low-risk and high-risk varietals. Some people are diagnosed with MDS and can have it for decades and die of something else. The high-risk variety that quickly escalates into AML [acute myeloid leukemia] is what Mike had. About 40 percent of MDS cases ultimately result in AML.'"

Susan speculated that Michael's MDS may have been triggered by the interferon treatments he underwent in 2000 and again in 2001 (during the initial Directions in Music tour) to combat a hepatitis C condition. "I believe there is a correlation, and so does his sister, Emmy," she said. "The doctor would tell you no, but in the fine print of interferon, it said it could lead to leukemia. But nobody talked about it then."

Drummer Bill Stewart recalled Michael being on interferon during the Pat Metheny/Michael Brecker Special Quartet tour of 2000, and Herbie Hancock also remembered Michael's interferon treatments during the first leg of the Directions in Music tour of 2001. "When Mike was on the interferon, it made him sick," said Susan. "Not sick like he didn't feel good; it was like a chemical change in his body. He got weirdly sick. Like, he turned ashen gray. He had done a first round, and then a second round of interferon, a pegylated version, made him so sick that he stopped after six weeks."

Susan added, "I don't think they thought it was a risk at the time. More recently, they're realizing the risk of interferon and chemotherapy is that it could lead to another cancer. With Michael, you couldn't see the hep C. He was treated for it because his counts were bad. And this is like my lifetime regret, but we never should've treated him then. He wasn't having any symptoms, but the doctor said, 'Well, you're going to have symptoms, so let's get under it quick. Your counts are horrible.' Michael wasn't feeling bad, but at the time doctors treated people with his counts with interferon. And we got a second and third opinion, but that's just what they did. Now there's a pill [Harvoni] you can take for hep C. Let's just say the best hypothetical is if we hadn't treated it with interferon, he'd live long enough to get the pill. And the pill would've knocked out the hep C, and everything's hunky dory. But, of course, what happened is just what happened."

Guitarist Mike Stern, who was also suffering from hepatitis C at the same time as Michael, had an entirely different reaction to the interferon therapy. "Mike was a little ahead of the game with the interferon treatments than I was, so he's telling me what to expect. He said, 'You're going to get really depressed, it's going to really fuck with you mentally. Watch out for that.' So, I'd check in with Mike from time to time. Actually, I was calling all the time because I got so obsessed and neurotic about this, and I know I must've been driving him and Susan fucking crazy. But Mike did tell me, 'Well, first month it's not so bad; it's like the flu. But it's gonna get worse.' So, I'd call him back a month later and say, 'Well, weirdly enough, I'm not feeling too bad.' But he kept saying that it was going to get worse, and it was going to depress the hell out of me. Three months later I called him again and told him, 'Mike, I'm actually feeling much better.' So, the interferon somehow worked for me, which I was certainly grateful for. But for Mike, the interferon was like taking poison."

Added Wortman, "I think there might've been a predisposition there in Michael's DNA because his mom had leukemia. So, there's no question that the interferon might've kicked in the MDS twenty years earlier than it otherwise would've."

Persevering through his illness, Michael returned to the scene in triumphant fashion as a guest with iconic Philadelphian saxophonist

Odean Pope and his Saxophone Choir in a three-night engagement at New York's Blue Note. Recorded live on December 13–15, 2004, and later released in March 2006 by Half Note Records as *Locked & Loaded: Live at the Blue Note*, it features Michael and fellow saxophonists Joe Lovano and James Carter on two tracks each. Michael locks horns with Pope on an intensely cathartic romp through Trane's "Coltrane Time" and is showcased on the positively scorching Pope original, "Prince Lasha," featuring a powerful tenor-drums breakdown with Craig McIver that finds him unleashing his signature tenor chops, doubling the tempo at will, and wailing in the altissimo range with ease—a classic Breckerian display. Both exhilarating performances by Michael made one forget for a moment that he had ever been sidelined.

Michael next performed with his Quindectet on January 19, 2005, at Carnegie Hall's adjunct space, Zankel Hall, then commenced a six-week Directions in Music tour on February 3 with Herbie Hancock and Roy Hargrove, this time with Scott Colley on bass and Terri Lyne Carrington on drums. On their Stateside tour, this third incarnation of Directions in Music since its inception in 2001 began incorporating the necessary technology to create surround-sound concerts in every venue on the road. As Colley recalled, "Early on in that tour, we were watching a movie on the bus, which was outfitted with an incredible surround-sound system. So, at some point, I kind of jokingly said to Herbie, 'Man, we should do our concerts in surround sound!' That night he started making phone calls to Apple and got them to send a couple of G4 towers, the newest Apple product at the time. Then Monster Cable sent us a lot of cable, and somebody else provided a bunch of speakers. And we converted our shows to surround sound. Our sound guy Bill Wynn would run cables through the house, up into the balcony, and put speakers in the back of the theater. It was an amazing amount of work for Bill, and he'd have to do this at every new theater on the tour."

Michael was especially thrilled by the new high-tech system for those Directions in Music concerts. "At that time, Mike was experimenting a lot with the EWI," said Colley. "He was coming up with all these new and different sounds like native instruments and other beautiful, organic-sounding things. And Herbie, of course, had a lot of MIDI keyboards, Roy had a pedal or two, even Terri and I had some pedal effects. So, we'd start every concert with maybe twenty or thirty minutes of just pure soundscapes, and then Bill, at his discretion, would move the sounds around the theater to get the full effect of the surround-sound setup. It was really amazing. And Herbie and Mike, both being tech guys with exploring minds, were so into it. Herbie would just open up every bank of sounds that he had until his computer would crash, and then he'd just go to the piano and just kill with that."

The downside of going high-tech on this Directions in Music tour was the huge amount of time needed to do sound checks at each new venue. "I remember the sound checks going for three hours and up, recalled Colley, "because everybody would have to get their individual electronics together and then be able to test the surround-sound things. And I remember Mike being really present for all of them. He definitely didn't need to be there the whole time. He could've just come in and checked his own sound and split, but he was always experimenting with different sounds for his EWI and constantly looking for new ways of working through things. It was incredible to see how dedicated he was, even after a long night on the bus."

Colley also remembered Michael experiencing severe pain in his pelvis and lower back on that tour. "He would never say anything about any pain that he was feeling, he never complained. But then things began to manifest, mostly in his back. So, he would struggle with long tones a lot, and also playing ballads, where he'd have to hold notes for a long period of time. Because that would put a lot of pressure on his abdomen and create a lot of pain in his back. And he only took ibuprofen on the road because he didn't have any other things to relieve the pain."

Through it all, Michael maintained a buoyancy on that tour that defied the disease. "I don't remember him getting dark on the road, honestly, at least that I could have ever seen," said Colley. "And about his dealing with the pain of his illness, I think it was just a general philosophy of his that he just didn't complain about stuff."

The bassist added, "It was an amazing tour for me for a lot of reasons. Aside from all the great music, I spent a lot of time with Mike just talking to him about his process, but also about family and life things. I remember having long discussions with him about his recovery from substance abuse, and the things that he would share with me . . . he was very, very open about that. And for me personally to hear that, because I've struggled with those things myself, was an amazing experience for me. It took some years before I took my own steps towards recovery, but his example was very powerful.

"Michael was also an example of someone who could be a good father and good to his family and still do this thing that we do as musicians—traveling and playing in a different place every night," Colley continued. "The balance between family and the life of a touring musician is very, very difficult, and he did it with such grace. It always stuck with me that he was the best possible example of that."

The Directions in Music tour concluded in Houston, Texas, on March 12. Just eleven days later, March 23, Michael would join his Saxophone Summit partners Dave Liebman and Joe Lovano for a four-night engagement at Birdland. As Lovano recalled, "On our last gig at Birdland, Mike was really not doing well, and he was feeling strange. Each night there were different places in his body that ached and felt weird. He was talking about it a little bit. But it didn't affect his playing at all. His execution and drive were very powerful throughout that whole week."

After that Birdland gig in late March with the Saxophone Summit, Michael and his manager, Darryl Pitt, canceled all of his gigs for the remainder of 2005, including an April tour of Europe with Swiss guitarist Harald Haerter and French trumpeter Erik Truffaz and a swing through Italy in May as special guest with pianist Aaron Goldberg's trio. Chris Potter and Joshua Redman stepped up as replacements for Mike on Stateside Saxophone Summit gigs in June, then Norwegian tenor saxophonist Bendik Hofseth replaced Mike on a European Steps Ahead tour through the summer. The rest of Michael's previously booked appearances in the fall of 2005 with McCoy Tyner, Japanese jazz singer Ryogo Moriyama, Steps Ahead, and Saxophone Summit were all canceled. At that point, it was beginning to seem very likely that Michael's days of performing in public were over.

Beginning in late June of 2005, Michael spent seven weeks at Memorial Sloan Kettering Cancer Center undergoing an intensive regimen of chemotherapy to destroy his unhealthy stem cells before they could be replaced by those of a donor. He was down to 144 pounds and had been physically steamrolled by the disease. He later told the *New York Times* from a bedside interview that took place at the Memorial Sloan Kettering Cancer Center in Manhattan for a story that appeared on August 18, 2005, that he really missed playing and was looking forward to getting back to it, but that dealing with a life-and-death situation took precedence.

Meanwhile, a worldwide search for a donor who was a suitable genetic match for a blood stem cell and bone marrow transplant was underway. Not just a close match, but a nearly identical match was needed. According to doctors, the donor and recipient must have ten genetic markers in common or the marrow is of no use. "Finding a donor is like looking for a needle in a haystack," acknowledged Darryl Pitt, who teamed with Susan Brecker to spearhead an international testing drive. "But if more people get tested, we create more needles."

Pitt added, "It was going to require a superhuman effort to get as many people tested as possible to find a match for Mike. And Susan and I knew that we would have tremendous difficulty getting Michael to agree to go public with this because Mike was such a humble guy. He wouldn't ever want this to be about him. And initially, Mike didn't want anything done on his behalf. Nothing at all. But as I pointed out to him, 'Mike, mathematically, the chances of finding a matching donor for you . . . it's slim. But by being able to put the word out there, we're increasing the donor rolls, which increases the possibility of so many others to find potential donors for them.' And somehow, with Susan's massaging, he went for that. He finally said, 'Fine, just don't make it seem as if it's about me doing this for me.'"

With Michael's approval, Darryl and Susan kicked off a significant bone marrow donor campaign that led to tens of thousands of people being tested in this country and abroad. Donor tents were set up at summer jazz festivals across the United States and Europe. And because Michael was of Ashkenazi or Eastern European Jewish descent, synagogues (including Michael's, Temple Beth Shalom in Hastings-on-Hudson, and the Reform Congregation Keneseth Israel in his hometown of Elkins Park, Pennsylvania) were especially key in finding a potential match, as was the Red Sea Jazz Festival in Israel, where hundreds participated in onsite testing.

By September 1, 2005, following an official press release sent out by Susan about her husband's illness, word spread on websites, in magazines, across the airwaves on jazz radio stations and at jazz festivals throughout the country that Michael was in urgent need of a bone marrow donor with a close genetic match in order to save his life. "We had drives all over the world and raised hundreds of thousands of dollars," said Susan, "but couldn't find a match."

Finally, in November 2005, Michael received an experimental stem cell transplant at a University of Minnesota hospital in Minneapolis with a donation from his sixteen-year-old daughter, Jess, who was a half-match. "For me it was no question of whether I was going to do it or not," she said at the time. The operation alleviated a lot of pain by killing off large growths of leukemia cells, but it remained to be seen if the half-match would take. Michael and his family spent three months in Minneapolis before learning that the transplant failed to engraft, leaving the disease free to spread again.

From November through January 2006, Michael, Susan and their two children, Jess and Sam, had taken up residence in Minneapolis during Michael's half-match haplo surgery and subsequent hospital stay. "He maintained a sense of humor, but he wasn't glib," said Susan. "He understood the seriousness of his condition. And he didn't complain, except to me. He really was tough about it, but it was not fun. And yet, Michael found a way to be playful with the kids while he was in the hospital. Apps were just coming out then for computers, and he found one of the first ones where you could distort photos. So, he would sit on the edge of his hospital bed and distort selfies with the kids and just be playful and silly with them."

Meanwhile, Michael remained committed to the idea of bringing the new music he had composed to fruition. "He was so ill that he was isolated in his hospital room," said Susan, "but he would get on the treadmill and listen to demos and send e-mails to his engineers about what he was hearing. He always had mixes in his head of this new record he wanted to do. It really kept him alive, in a lot of ways."

Guitarist Adam Rogers recalled seeing Michael in Minneapolis during that time. "He had already done the half-match thing with his daughter, Jess, and I was playing at the Dakota in town with Chris Potter, so I'd gotten in touch with Susan and really wanted to come see him. They were staying in an apartment, and it was the day that they had gotten the news that the half-match from Jess didn't work. So, I went to see him and hung with him. He was dark, man, and I couldn't fucking blame him. They were out there for like three months, living in a test tube to try and see if this thing would take. And it didn't. That whole experience really depleted the hell out of him, as it would anybody. In addition to the physical challenges of having this pre-leukemic condition [MDS] and going through that procedure in Minneapolis, the emotional and psychological effects of dealing with that were almost overwhelming."

At his lowest ebb, Michael felt like giving up. "He got pretty dark at one point," said Mike Stern. "I mean, he really wanted to check out. He said, 'If I had a gun . . . well, I wouldn't know how to use it . . . but if I had one, I'd shoot myself.' It was more of his dark humor. And then he said, 'I don't want to do it. I'm staying alive because of my family.' But he still rose from all that and figured out a way to keep going. He was going to AA meetings online because he couldn't attend in person. So, he was always very committed. That was such an important part of his life. He was still trying to stay sober, so he hated the fact he had to take pain medication. It was really a drag for him, but he had to do it."

In the face of all that suffering, Michael somehow still retained his sense of humor. As Stern recalled, "The last time I saw Mike was in the hospital, I came into the room, and he had a morphine drip by his bedside. He was obviously in severe pain, and when he saw me come in, he reached over and started petting the morphine bag like it was his pet cat, and he had this silly grin on his face, going, 'Mmmmmm . . . morphine!' As sick as he was, the guy was still hilarious."

Michael returned to Hastings-on-Hudson in February of 2006 and resumed another round of chemo treatment at Sloan Kettering in Manhattan. "Jerry told me he picked Mike up at the airport, and said he couldn't talk because he was in such pain," Stern recalled. "It was just awful. You could tell he was really, really suffering."

During his hospital stay, Michael reached out to his former composition teacher, Edgar Grana, who was surprised to receive a call from his star pupil. "He called me out of the blue and he told me how useless all the time up in Minnesota had been," said Grana. "And then he talked about bagels. That was so beautiful. Here he was at Sloan Kettering doing all the horrible things he had to do there, but he found some great bagel vendor there and wanted to talk about it. That's the way Michael was. He would always resort back to just everyday routine life stuff. No great polemic. You didn't get that from Michael."

Grana also related an important anecdote that Michael had laid on him. "He told me that Herbie Hancock had come to the hospital room and taught him how to chant (*nam-myoho-renge-kyo*) and that it brought him some comfort. That's a beautiful gift that was beyond music."

As Hancock explained, "Michael began practicing Buddhism, and he actually joined SGI sometime that summer. And he told me his big regret was, 'Why didn't I start this the first time you told me about it.'"

Stern recalled, "When Mike started chanting, he told me, 'Why not? What do I have to lose?' I know that shit can really be strong and really carry you through . . . not physically so much but just emotionally. So, when Mike started chanting, I thought, 'Cool.'"

Meanwhile, the music remained of utmost importance to Michael. "He still wanted to make this new record he had been planning," said Susan, "but we just didn't know if it was going to happen because we kept having it and putting it off again and again."

By May, Michael's health took a turn for the worse. "He really almost died," said Susan. "And then he sort of bounced back in June. He was sick, but he had moments where he felt better than others. That's the arc of the disease. Finally, we realized that he was going to be well enough to make the record. Or so we had hoped."

On June 23, Michael's health rebounded enough for him to make a surprise appearance at Herbie Hancock's sixtieth birthday celebration at Carnegie Hall. "We had long spoken with Herbie about the possibility of it happening, but it wasn't a sure thing," said Darryl Pitt. "It literally happened at the last minute. And Herbie was so incredibly gracious. He was good with whatever would happen, even until the beginning the show. If it wasn't going to work out, it wasn't gonna work out, and he was cool either way. With Herbie, things could be really flexible in the course of a show. And, so, it worked out kind of perfectly in this regard."

"What I do remember is that we wouldn't know until the last minute whether Michael was gonna be able to feel well enough to do it," Hancock recalled. "So, I didn't know. I came off the stage at some point during the show, and George Wein told me, 'Michael's here! He's gonna do it.' That's when I was able to go out and say that thing to the crowd about, 'This really is supposed to be a quartet song. Are there any saxophonists in the house?' And we had no rehearsal or anything. Michael just walked out on stage, and the audience went nuts. And I don't know why he picked 'One Finger Snap.' That's a fast tune, and he's just coming out of the hospital and hasn't played the saxophone probably in a year. And I'm thinking, 'Why would you pick a fast tune like that?' I mean, I wouldn't have called that tune. I'm not that cruel.

But it was his idea, and so we did it. And I was so thrilled to have that situation, which was honoring me, be the moment when he would come out to the public and say, 'I'm here, I'm back, I'm Michael Brecker!'"

As Susan recalled, "He felt well enough that night. I had gone to Bloomingdale's and bought him a new shirt for the occasion, and it was just so wonderful. You know, I never thought he'd play again. And when he walked out on stage . . . I mean, I just sobbed the whole concert. It was so magical. It was unbelievable. And afterwards, he came upstairs where I was sitting in a box, and he said, 'How did I sound?' He was so exhilarated, and I was so exhilarated. We were both so happy."

"After the concert, Mike was so buoyed by the experience," added Pitt. "Everyone was congratulating him backstage, and he was saying, 'Yeah, let's go out on tour! I'm ready to go out on tour.'"

"When he sat in with Herbie at Carnegie Hall, that was a really great moment for Mike," said Joe Lovano. "He was feeling strong in that moment, and I think that gave him a lot of confidence to carry on and do that *Pilgrimage* session. He had been in isolation for so long when he went through the whole stem cell thing in Minneapolis, but then after he came home, he would have moments of feeling strong. And that night at Carnegie was one of those moments. Throughout that whole period in Minneapolis, he hadn't been practicing or playing like he usually did, but his ideas were all there. In the heat of the moment on the bandstand, when you're feeding off of each other's feelings, you go beyond your physical place, and you go into this very beautiful spiritual place. And Mike went there with Herbie that night at Carnegie."

Later that summer, Michael reached out to his old friend Mike Mainieri. "He called me one day and said, 'You want to go a ballgame? Yankee game?' I said, 'Sure.' I hadn't seen him in a while. Apparently, Paul Simon gave him tickets for his suite at Yankee Stadium. So, we went and enjoyed the game. Afterwards he said, 'Why don't you come back to the house?' At the time he was really not well but was recovering. He had already gotten the half-match stem cell transplant from his daughter, Jessica, and was doing a little bit better, but he was still very weak. His legs were kind of thin, and he had a cane. So, I came over to his house and he said, 'I want to play some stuff for you.' So, we went down to his basement, and he was playing some new material on his computer from an album he was going to make. And he said he had been taking lessons from some Turkish guy in Queens [violinist Entcho Todorov] and he was saying, 'I want to learn how to play all these odd rhythms.' So here this guy is sick, but he's still moving forward musically, still searching."

Just prior to the *Pilgrimage* sessions, Gil Goldstein recruited Michael to play on a track for a Juliette Gréco record he had arranged called *Le Temps d'Une Chanson*. "He was really not feeling well then, but he came in, and he just obliterated the track," said Goldstein. "He played an incredible, amazing solo on a tune called 'Né Quelque Part.' You just couldn't play it any better. Rufus Reid was playing bass, and there was a great orchestra [Orchestra of St. Luke] that was very sensitive to pulse. Mike came in like he was playing with Elvin Jones or something and just killed it."

Shortly thereafter, Michael committed to doing his own project. As Goldstein recalled, "I was in Montreal, and Mike called me, and he goes, 'Gilly, I'm pulling the trigger. We're doing it! Let's get everybody together, and we're gonna do it.' He was ready to go."

By August 2006, Michael assembled his dream team of Pat Metheny, Herbie Hancock, John Patitucci, Jack DeJohnette, Gil Goldstein, and Brad Mehldau at Avatar Studios in Manhattan to begin working on his "comeback record." But as Pitt explained, "It was a record that had to be rescheduled a couple of times because of Mike's illness. And I let all the musicians know that at a moment's notice this whole thing might have to be canceled. And they were OK with that."

Though Michael was weak and not feeling well over the course of those three days at Avatar, he went about the recording with workmanlike determination. "He would go to the studio in the morning, and he'd drive himself into Manhattan, park the car, and walk in with his horns," Susan recalled. "And every morning that he would leave the house, I would be crying, 'Let me drive you, please!' And he'd say, 'No, I have to do what I always do. I drive myself to the studio.' But for that whole session, he could barely walk. There was something life-giving about the music for him, and the sessions were kind of like magic to him. But he was really not well."

"It was amazing," said DeJohnette. "He drove himself to the studio every day on his own, and he offered to drive people home afterwards. At some point during the sessions, he said he couldn't feel his legs, but he never complained. I think he knew that he had limited time, and he wanted to go out doing something creative. And I think everybody rose to the challenge, thinking, 'Maybe this will be his last time, maybe not.'"

Added Patitucci, "For Mike, this was major that we were doing this project, because we had talked about it a lot, and he went through periods where he felt like he wasn't up for it. So, I was so excited that, 'OK, now we're going to do it.' And it was very natural, very real, important and joyful. We cherished Mike, and we grabbed ahold of that moment. And he played like his life depended on it."

The simpatico crew stood in awe of Michael's playing throughout those sessions at Avatar and marveled at the intention behind his every note. "When he played his horn, that was home base for him," said DeJohnette. Added Hancock, "When Michael walked off the Carnegie Hall stage for my little birthday celebration, he was still weak. But by the time he did *Pilgrimage*, as soon as he put the saxophone in his mouth, he was like Superman! He played his ass off! And he wrote all of these impossible arrangements. He told me that he had worked with some Balkan musicians and was listening to a lot of Bulgarian music. So, a lot of what he wrote gave him the platform to explore that territory on that record."

As Patitucci remembered, "He was playing so good even in the rehearsals that Metheny was actually joking with him: 'Oh, man, you're just messing with us. You're not sick.' I mean, Mike was just blowing us out of the room in rehearsals. Here you are in a room with Herbie Hancock, Pat Metheny, and Jack DeJohnette, and they were all just flab-bergasted at how good he was playing."

Said David Sanborn, who continues to play "Tumbleweed" and "Half Moon Light" from *Pilgrimage* in his live sets, "Metheny told me that before Mike did that record, he hadn't played his horn for months and months. And that he walked into the studio and was like, 'Oh, man, I don't know if I can make it. I'm just not feeling well.' And then he proceeded to wipe the floor with everybody. Pat told me he was totally sweating trying to play those tunes. Patitucci said the same thing. So whatever impediments he had due to his health, Mike on half speed is three times as good as everybody else on full speed. So, it's like his illness almost leveled the playing field a little bit, but not quite."

Patitucci was also very aware that Michael was suffering during the sessions. "In the studio he was in a booth next to me, and I'd watch him. He stood most of the time he played. I remember him walking to the control room at one point, and it wasn't so easy for him. I think he was in a lot of pain."

Added DeJohnette, "I'd say, 'How do you feel?' And he'd say, 'You don't want to know.'" During the session, when he was sitting for promotional photos, Michael had to be helped up off a stool by the photographer. He apologized to the photographer and said, "I can't feel my legs . . . but no complaints. At least my lungs are working."

"What Michael did on *Pilgrimage* was just beyond belief," said Jerry Wortman. "Because when I brought him home from the hospital just a few months earlier, he couldn't play at all, he couldn't blow. I couldn't even get him down to his basement studio, though I eventually did get him to play the EWI one day. But the saxophone? He physically couldn't do it."

"It was miraculous that Mike was able to play at all considering how sick he was," added Patitucci. "And I was in constant communication with him, since I lived around the corner from them in Hastings, so I knew more than most how really sick he was. Mike would tell me what was happening with his health, and he would write me e-mails saying, 'Yeah, it's tough right now. Really tough.' And yet, he was able to make these sessions at Avatar, and he really rose to the occasion with some incredibly powerful playing. It was superhuman."

In fact, Michael's playing was so ferocious and focused that in the midst of recording, the crew actually broached the subject of performing together in public. As Patitucci recalled, "We were sitting around on the couch in the studio, and Metheny said, 'Man, Mike, you sound unbelievable! You know, maybe we don't have to go on the road, but how about doing a week in New York?' And Mike was like, 'Absolutely. I'd love to do that.' In that moment, everybody thought he was going to beat it. And he already had his eye on doing that other Bulgarian record afterwards, so he was definitely making plans for the future. And we were all convinced that everything was going to be fine because he was superhuman at that session. We all thought, 'There's no way that he's not going to beat this now because look at what he just did!'"

Added Hancock. "One day when we took a break from recording, we went to a little recreation room they had there, and Michael pulled me aside and thanked me for introducing him to Buddhism. He said, 'I found another purpose in life through this practice.' He was born and raised Jewish, but he said that the disease had made him lose his faith. But he said through practicing Buddhism, 'I found another way. I found something else. And perhaps I'll be able to save the lives of other people with this.' And I almost cried hearing him say that because this is what happens in practicing Buddhism. You find some answers that were there that you couldn't see before. So, he found something else about life that didn't depend on music and his being able to be a musician but rather just him being a human being. He found some value that could be created out of suffering. That's what Buddhism is about. It shows you how to change suffering into mission, to find a way to advance through the suffering and move forward. Michael did that. He did everything that this practice is talking about. That was his Buddhist nature that had evolved at that point, and it comes out on that record."

Hancock continued, "Michael's playing on *Pilgrimage* was unlike anything that he done before on any record that I knew of. I mean, he played great on a lot of records, but there was something else going on here. It was something newer and fresher. It was like next level Michael Brecker on that record."

Though it was indeed a superhuman effort on Mike's part just to make the sessions each day, let alone play with such incredible passion and inspiration, it was sad to watch him shuffle across the spacious studio at Avatar (depicted in the 2011 Noah Hutton–directed documentary film, *More to Live For*, which Susan Brecker coproduced). "He did transcend all that physical pain," said Goldstein. "And obviously, it didn't affect his playing at all, which was kind of miraculous. And I remember Pat during the recording saying, 'Well, this really puts to rest the notion that you have to practice in order to do good,' because Mike hadn't touched his horn in a year. And he played really flawlessly on that record."

Added Pitt, "When Mike was in the studio doing *Pilgrimage*, he somehow found the will and the power to be able to make music, because it was the most precious thing in the world to him that he wanted to spend his last breaths doing. He loved music so much, and being able to perform with these guys, for whom he had so much admiration, was like turning a switch back on, where he was as alive as he had ever been.

"But prior to the moment he walked into the studio and moments afterwards, he was a very, very sick man," Pitt continued. "He literally left it all in the studio on those tapes. And he was totally spent afterwards. He had an awareness on some level that he might die. And it was really important to him to do this record."

Gary Gold, who helped Michael overdub some final EWI pads in the downstairs home studio in Hastings, recalled that the final touch on *Pilgrimage* was one note not played. "He had done this solo for 'Tumbleweeds,' and we were looking for a sound for the solo out, but we couldn't find one. Mike kept trying different EWI things and finally I said, 'Mike, remember the sound that Zawinul played on 'A Remark You Made' [the beautiful ballad from *Heavy Weather*, Weather Report's 1977 album]? And Mike said, 'That's it! That's the sound.' So, he did this whole solo approximating that warm flute-like sound, and then we went in to edit it. I pieced it together a little better, moved a couple of licks around, but the last note was bothering me. Finally, I just muted it and we both looked at each other and went, 'Yes! That's totally it. It's perfect now.' So, it's really ironic or cool or zen-like that the last note that Mike ever played, it turned out, we muted. It was the unplayed note. And it made everything perfect."

As they were packing up from that final overdubbing session for *Pilgrimage*, Gold noticed a CD rack in Michael's downstairs studio that contained ten or so copies of *Back To Back*, the second Brecker Brothers album from 1976. "And I said to Mike, 'Oh, shit! I don't have this on CD. Can I take one of these?' And normally it would have been nothing to him, like, 'Yeah, of course.' But instead, Mike said, 'No, I want Sam to have those.' And he just burst out crying. And that, to me, was indicative of how *Pilgrimage* got made. He was staying alive for his family. And if he's alive, he's making music. That's who Mike is."

"*Pilgrimage* was so essential to him," said Susan. "Somehow it kept him alive. Thank God that record was made. But Michael didn't live long enough to mix it. Thank God for Pat, because he took it on. He mixed the record, and he named it. We weren't going to call it *Pilgrimage*. Mike wanted to call it *This Just In*. And Pat sent me this incredible e-mail after Mike died where he said, 'I think we know the name of the record.' Because one of the tunes was 'Pilgrimage.' And he said, 'I think that's what we should call it.' He was right. I mean, it was perfect."

"That record was made because Pat Metheny persuaded Michael to do it," Susan continued. "Michael had written a bunch of tunes before and going into being not well, and he didn't know which kind of record to make. Some of what he had written was music in the Bulgarian style, and some was in more of a jazz style. So, we invited Pat over, and they sat and listened to the tunes that Mike had demoed, and Pat finally

311

said, 'I think you should make the jazz record now and then make the Bulgarian record later.' So that's what Michael did. But there's a lot of these amazing tunes that he wrote in the Bulgarian style, which I hope to release at some point."

Added Goldstein, "I always believed we were going to make another record after *Pilgrimage*, that he was going to survive, and we would do the Bulgarian record. Mike had played that music for Pat when he was really not feeling well, and Pat said, 'You know, I think this is really beautiful music, Mike, but it's so different from your normal music. I think it would be strange for the audience to hear a completely different kind of record.' And Mike took it really to heart and he said, 'Yeah, maybe.' And then he started writing all these new tunes that became *Pilgrimage*. And some of the songs on that record were originally scheduled for the Bulgarian record, like 'Tumbleweed' and 'Five Months Before Midnight.' But then it became more jazzy in everybody's hands."

Following the recording of *Pilgrimage*, Mike went on a much-needed vacation with his family. "He was doing all right that summer," said Susan. "That's why he made the record, and that's why we took a family vacation. We had actually planned a trip that summer to Thailand, but Mike wasn't well enough to travel that far, so we went to Captiva Island in Florida instead. We had a condo there. Mike wasn't walking well or anything, but we really had a good time anyway."

Sam Brecker's bar mitzvah on September 30 was a proud moment in Michael's life. "He was quite sick for that but was able to come and see his family and friends and be part of this huge moment in our son's life," said Susan. "At that point he was really on the decline, but to have him there for this important occasion just meant the world to all of us, and him.

"He wanted to be there," she continued. "That was important to him. Everything was important for him. He didn't want to go. He wanted to make the Bulgarian record. He wanted to see the flowers the next spring. He loved life. He loved being alive. You know, he once said to me that the only regret he had was that he didn't graduate college. Imagine living a life like that with no regrets. He had none. Everything was an experience. Thank God he lived as long as he did, because, you know, drugs could've killed him earlier; instead, the drugs killed him later. But he was so grateful for his life, and so really he wanted to see

Sam's bar mitzvah. He wanted to be there for everything. He really was squeezing the most that he could out of a life that had been curtailed."

Michael was diagnosed with acute leukemia in October. In subsequent weeks, several colleagues and lifelong friends said their final farewells to him. "I took him out to lunch a few months before he died," recalled Bob Mintzer. "He was walking with a cane, seemed to be in good spirits. He was still talking about music and life. You know, he hung in there to the very end and stayed connected to his art and to his family and his friends. He was really a remarkable person. He was somebody who made you feel like you were his best friend, regardless of who you were or how well he knew you. In addition to being a superhuman musician who worked harder than anybody I know, he was also a very caring soul."

"The last time I spoke to him on the phone was the fall of 2006," recalled Adam Rogers. "My girlfriend and I had moved in together, and I had just leased an Audi, which is a car I had always wanted. So, I called Mike, and he was like, 'What's going on with you?' And I told him about my girlfriend and I moving in together and about leasing an Audi, and he was like, 'Oh, my God! That's unbelievable!' And I said, 'What are you talking about, Mike? You're facing this major thing.' And he's like, 'Fuck that! You leased an Audi!! And your girlfriend and you moved in together! I turn my back for two months, and all this shit happens?' He was fuckin' hilarious."

In an e-mail to his old Indiana University colleague Randy Sandke, dated October 18, Michael wrote, "I entered the hospital today, for 5 weeks. Daunting but do-able. My MDS has morphed into fun blown leukemia, so docs are again fighting it with chemo. Chemo starts tomorrow. Scary stuff, but I'll be OK."

Said Jeff Watts, "He was in the hospital and getting treatments and stuff, so I wanted to send him something. The iPod Shuffle had just come out, and so I bought him one and recorded a bunch of music on it and also put a bunch of comedy routines on there, like some Jackie Mason and Richard Pryor and all this shit. I never got to see him again. But I talked to him a couple of times on the phone after that, and he thanked me for the iPod Shuffle. He was like, 'Yeah, man, I'm shufflin', man! I'm shufflin'! They put me in a wheelchair to take me down for tests, and I got my shuffle on, man!"

"I saw him when he was in quarantine," recalled Stern. "He had just done *Pilgrimage*, and he played me some of that. And he said, 'Listen to Herbie; he played with so much love on this.' He said that record was keeping him alive and how he was just very, very grateful to have been a musician, to have been a father. He was grateful for everything."

Darryl Pitt shared a fond memory of Michael during that stay in the hospital: "He would lie in bed, asleep, smiling as his fingers were flying over imaginary keys of his saxophone."

Pitt also recalled a rare moment in the hospital involving the usually hypercritical tenor titan. "There were only two times that I can remember where Mike expressed an unusual amount of self-satisfaction. One was his first Impulse! record. The only other time was when he was in his hospital bed, and Steve Rodby had just done a Pro Tools fix on something for *Pilgrimage*, and Mike was listening to this. He was really sick at the time, and I was sitting there looking at him. And it was literally as if water was given to a plant in desperate need. He sat up, and he held on to whatever it was that he was listening to, and I was looking at him smiling. He was satisfied with the whole thing, including his playing."

Michael returned home just before Thanksgiving 2006. In an e-mail to Sandke, dated December 7, he wrote, "Yes, they beat the shit out of me. Hospital war stories. I'm home now, but the recovery has been excruciating. I was back to square one but starting to get a bit stronger now. Just takes patience. Not my strong suit. The good news is that there is, for now, no leukemia in my system. I'll be starting a new drug regimen soon that hopefully will buy me some time. Right now, though, every day is a bit of a struggle. Oh, well . . . I'm alive and surrounded by amazing family and friends."

One of those friends, pianist Marc Copland, went up to Hastings to visit Michael around that time. "When I got there, Susan said, 'Mike's asleep downstairs.' So, I go down to his studio, and he's lying on the couch, exhausted. So, I see this, and I'm getting ready to tiptoe back out when he calls out, 'Marky.' I walk over to him on the couch and just patted his bald head, and I said, 'Man, go back to sleep.' And I left. Then about three weeks later we do this little e-mail exchange of jokes or puns, like we always used to do. Two days later, he writes me back and says, 'Marky, I'm beyond sick right now.' So, I just wrote him and said, 'Man, hang in there. I'm hoping for you.' I think he lasted another week or two."

Portrait of Michael Brecker *(Photo by Jimmy Katz)*

Randy Brecker also made a trip up to Hastings for his last visit with his younger brother. "He was pretty frail by then," he recalled, "and at one point he was looking kind of wistfully at me, and he said, 'You know, we were pretty good together!'"

In an e-mail to Sandke, dated December 21, Michael wrote, "I'm at home trying to recover. It's very slow and tedious. I haven't been able to play the sax in months! Oh, well, I am just focusing on other things. Family, friends and computers, etc. Life has taken a huge left for me, but I have much to be grateful for."

By January, Michael was still fighting, but the disease was clearly winning. Four days before he passed, he had OK'd the final mixes on *Pilgrimage*. As Pitt recalled to NPR's Liane Hansen, "He said, 'OK, that's it.' And I said, 'Again, just to make sure there's no fixes here, there's no overdubs,' because there was a discussion about having percussion overdubs. And he goes, 'No, that's it.' That was on a Tuesday. On Thursday he was back in the hospital and feeling fine for someone who's sick; you know, bouncing around in bed, and we're walking around and talking. And on Friday, he was dying. It was a very precipitous ending.

In my mind, there can't help but be a connection of, 'OK, the record is done, and now I am, too.'"

Michael died in a Manhattan hospital on Saturday, January 13, 2007, surrounded by family and friends. Cause of death was leukemia, the result of his nearly two-and-a-half-year struggle with myelodysplastic syndrome (MDS). After Michael drew his last breath, those in attendance clapped; a final round of applause for the loving husband, devoted and selfless father, compassionate friend, and beloved and revered tenor titan. As Pitt said, "When Mike took his last breath, we applauded the end of a life extraordinarily well lived. Mike mastered life, and then a two-and-a-half-year war was over."

And then, suddenly, after the round of applause, Michael began to breathe again. "His heart had stopped beating, but he kept breathing for like . . . it seemed like an eternity, though it must have been only a couple of minutes," said Gold. "And I always found that striking, metaphorically—his life ended, but he was still blowing."

In a piece for the April 2007 issue of *Jazz Times*, I wrote the following about getting the news of Michael's passing at the International Association for Jazz Education conference, a three-day schmooze-athon held in New York City and attended by eight thousand music students, educators, journalists, and assorted music industry cognoscenti from around the globe:

*On the morning of Saturday, Jan. 13, the last day of the conference, we were all drawn a little closer together by the crushing news of the passing of Michael Brecker. I arrived at the conference around 1 p.m. The first person I encountered was vibraphonist Mike Mainieri, Brecker's longtime pal and colleague going back to their hippie days together in the sprawling ensemble White Elephant. I spied him standing alone in the lobby and could see the grief in his face. "Mike passed away this morning," he muttered in somber tones. His words fell like bricks, and I walked around in stunned silence all afternoon.*

*I had just communicated with Brecker the week before, when I sent him a copy of saxist-clarinetist Andy Statman's 'Awakening From Above,' thinking that the healing vibrations of that collection of sacred Jewish music would lift his spirits. On Jan. 3, Brecker sent me an e-mail that read: "Hi Bill, thanks for the Andy Statman CD.*

*He is amazing. I really enjoyed it. And thanks for thinking of me.
I'm still at home fighting the battle. All is well though . . . lots to be
grateful for. I hope you are fine and lotsa love, Mike."*
    *Ten days later, he was gone.*

Looking back on their life together, Susan said that rather than reflect on her husband's dark twist of fate, she preferred to think about the good life they had together. "We were a good team," she said in the comfort of her Hastings home. "We did have twenty-five years together and were married twenty-three years. And some people don't have five minutes of what we had. So, I'm super-grateful about that.

"I really was lucky, and so was he," she continued. "Our lives were fashioned around the music and the family, and that was OK with both of us. I did the house and the children, and he did the music. He had dinner with us every night he was home. He'd come up from his studio, and he would have dinner, and then he'd be with the kids, whether it was bath time, reading books, or doing homework, until it was time to go back downstairs to his studio. And we took family vacations. And he really grew within the marriage, as did I. I learned a lot about myself. I would have to say a lot of who I am today is because of Mike. Because he was wise and he had a way about him that you kind of wanted a little piece of him. And he really was just a great partner for me—very accepting, very loving. My life was really good with him."

Susan recalled driving Michael to chemo treatment every morning, an unfortunate trip but one made lighter by Mike's loving nature. "It's about forty-five minutes to Sloan Kettering from Hastings, and we would listen to the blues show on the radio driving into Manhattan, because we both loved the blues. And one day he turned to me and said, 'I really love this time together.' Here I was driving him to a cancer hospital to do these horrible chemo treatments, and he was able to extract joy out of that. He could look at things and see beauty that other people couldn't see. He was such an artist that way. He was so tuned into something that a lot of people aren't tuned into. I think sometimes it's because he didn't have distractions that other people had. He didn't have to deal with the house or fixing it up or having it maintained. He didn't have to deal with the kids or choosing what summer camp to go to. He used to say about me, 'Honey knows everything. Honey does it better.' And it was true. So, a lot of distractions were gone for him. He didn't have to wake up and think about stuff that a lot of people have to think about in their everyday life. And I was so grateful to be able to give him that because I so valued his work that if I could create an environment for him that he could just create, then how perfect!"

Then she paused and added with a chuckle, "Michael's greatest wish was to get an iPhone. But he died right before the iPhone came out. He used to say, 'I just want to live to see an iPhone.' He never did though. Oh, he would've loved it! He could've done so much with that thing—make his movies, record demos, send messages to everyone. He never would have put it down, ever, ever, ever. He would have divorced me and married the iPhone. Trust me . . . you're laughing, but it's true."

Two weeks after the funeral, saxophonist Tim Ries came by to visit Susan. "She took me down to the basement, and there was Mike's horn sitting on the stand, as he always had it. So, I said to Susan, 'We have to put the horn away, because between the dog, the cleaning person, and whatever, the horn can accidentally get knocked over and get damaged.' So, I brought out the sax case, and I opened it up, and I began taking off the neck and putting it in the case, then putting in the bell, closing up the case, and zipping it. And that was even heavier than the funeral for me. Because you're putting away Michael's main instrument forever. And the moment got to us. We were both weeping like children there in Mike's studio. It was heavy because it was the end."

Several years later, Ries, who had moved away to New Jersey by then, called Susan to check in. "And I told her, 'Susan, these horns have been sitting inside the case, zipped up in some closet somewhere for like eight years. They should really be in the air sometimes because if it's in a really humid environment they can get pitted and start to actually eat away the metal.' So, she invited me up to her house in Hastings, and I opened up all the tenors—three Selmer Super Balanced and three Selmer Mark VIs. And she sat there as I played the horns. And when I played Mike's main Selmer Mark VI, Susan goes, 'You have to play that horn. Take it for a while.' So, I took it, and I ended up bringing it with me on tour with The Rolling Stones right after that. And it's become my main horn.

"So, now I open the horn case every day and look at Mike's tenor, and I say a little mantra to myself: 'OK, motherfucker, you have a duty to play great today because of who played this saxophone.' So, there's not a day that I don't think about Michael. Even without the horn, I do anyway because of how much I learned from him. But, also, that I'm blowing air through his instrument. It's another level of calling, like, 'OK, you have to get it together.' And it's just another level of connecting with Mike, in a way."

*Pilgrimage* was released on the Heads Up label on May 22, 2007, just four months after Michael had passed. The album opens with a burst of up-tempo energy on "The Mean Time," with Michael and Metheny joining on a tricky unison line right out of the gate. DeJohnette swings in his inimitable fashion, and Hancock comps slyly in sparse fashion as Michael unleashes with the same remarkable facility—daring intervallic leaps, nonchalant double-timing, and fluid flights into the altissimo range—like the Mikey B of old. This is not the sound of a sick man. With Patitucci grooving mightily underneath and DeJohnette delivering his typical whirlwind performance on the kit, Metheny and Hancock contribute stellar, flowing solos before the interactive crew returns to the challenging head.

Elsewhere on *Pilgrimage*, Michael reveals heightened expressive powers on the balladic "Five Months from Midnight," with some beautiful contrapuntal accompaniment from Metheny and pianist Brad Mehldau. Mike's solo on the more energized second half of the piece is scintillating and very much in Breckerian mode. "Anagram" is a runaway burner. A ten-minute exercise in turbulent swing with some tight unisons upfront by Pat and Mike, it features the tenor titan unleashing in the open-ended blowing section with multiphonics and Trane-inspired "sheets of sound." This is Michael into going full beast mode. Metheny and Mehldau both deliver spectacular solos here on top of a furiously kinetic undercurrent created by the all-world rhythm tandem of Patitucci and DeJohnette. Jack also unleashes an incredible solo over a full band ostinato near the end of this exhilarating number.

"Tumbleweed" carries an earthy flavor (a trace of Pee Wee Ellis's "The Chicken" changes can be detected in the fabric of this piece) while bits of Bulgarian-inspired time signatures are injected into the proceedings at the 1:37 and 7:23 marks. Metheny leads with a brilliant guitar synth solo here that Michael picks up on to launch into his own heroic tenor solo. They close out in furious fashion with sax and guitar synth screaming at each other in a powerful crescendo.

The tender ballad "When Can I Kiss You Again?" was named for a question asked by Michael's son, Sam, during a hospital visit when physical contact was prohibited to avoid infection. Metheny's solo is a warm, heartfelt offering whereas Hancock's is more probing and slightly pensive. Michael's solo here is imbued with deep feeling as it builds to a dramatic peak, the love for his son fairly oozing out of his horn.

The jauntily swinging "Cardinal Rule" exhibits a high degree of interactivity and virtuosity among all the participants, including a brilliant extended solo from Patitucci and some sparkling, rapid-fire exchanges between Brecker and Mehldau over DeJohnette's irrepressible polyrhythmic pulse. It closes with an exhilarating tenor-drums breakdown between Michael and Jack that is a tip of the hat to the John Coltrane/Elvin Jones matchups of yore that inspired them both.

The more mellow "Half Moon Lane," an engaging number with a memorable hook, has Michael taking his time and telling a story on his sax. Following suit, Metheny starts out slow on his solo, gradually building to dizzying, fleet-fingered flights up and down his fretboard. "Loose Ends" opens as a quirky stop-time funk vehicle with allusions to Eddie Harris's "Listen Here" (a piece Michael had recorded in 2005 on Eddie Palmieri's *Listen Here!* for the Concord label). Michael's solo here is positively Herculean, once again belying his underlying illness. Hancock follows with an expansive solo that is breathtaking in its harmonic inventiveness.

The moving ten-minute title track that closes *Pilgrimage* is bittersweet, considering the profoundly sad circumstances that followed. With Hancock creating a spacious, atmospheric vibe on Fender Rhodes and DeJohnette drumming up thunder on the rubato intro, it segues to a stately theme at the 2:48 mark. Herbie's Rhodes solo is right out of the '70s, conjuring up memories of Michael's own musical beginnings with Dreams and The Brecker Brothers. Metheny's warm-toned legato solo invites the listener in, then Michael follows with a flute-sounding EWI solo before they build to a dramatic conclusion.

Said Randy of his brother's swan song, "How he did it, I have no idea. It's a testament to his strength. And this was his most significant work, by far."

In his *Jazz Times* review of the album, Geoffrey Himes wrote: "How would we have responded to this album if it had been just another release from a healthy Michael Brecker? We certainly wouldn't have associated any of these nine instrumental tracks with sickness and death. There is none of the howling anger or desolate anguish that one might expect from a confrontation with mortality. The album also lacks the stoic fatalism that's sometimes associated with dying. In fact, the disc's strongest tracks are all driven by a sense of quest, as if the composer and his bandmates were seeking the answer to a nagging question. If these compositions had been released by a healthy Brecker, we might have thought the musicians were trying to solve the riddle of a romantic relationship, a philosophical quandary or merely the harmonic challenge of finding the perfect restatement of a theme. No matter what the provoking topic may have been—life-after-death, life-before-death or bridge-after-verse—the urgency with which these musicians chase after the answer is thrilling."

In his *New York Times* review of *Pilgrimage*, Nate Chinen said it represented both a postscript and a pinnacle, referring to the mastery and immediacy of the album and the lucidity and passion that Michael displayed on "Half Moon Lane" and the title track, which he described as "calmly valedictory." And Chinen acknowledged that the poignancy in the album's circumstances was impossible to ignore, but he concluded that its balance of ambition and abandon, serious-mindedness, and ebullience was a crystallization of what jazz, at its best, is all about.

Michael received two posthumous Grammy Awards (his fourteenth and fifteenth) for his stunning swan song—Best Instrumental Jazz Album and Best Improvised Jazz Solo for "Anagram."

In his eulogy at a Michael Brecker Memorial held at Town Hall on February 20, 2007, Pat Metheny described *Pilgrimage* as one of the great codas in modern music history.

Randy gave a beautiful eulogy himself at that moving ceremony. "I remember when Trane died and thinking, 'What are we going to do now?' That feeling is once again upon us," he told the sixteen hundred mourners, adding, "We always had a healthy competition going on. We would spur each other on, although I think we all know who would always come out quite ahead. He was forever probing, never satisfied, was always on the path to something new, groundbreaking and astounding. And during his epic struggle, he fought like hell for over two and a half years."

Darryl Pitt spoke of the "colossal void" left by Michael's passing, which he admitted he was still having trouble processing at the time of the Town Hall Memorial: "Mike bounced back again and again from illness, and then he didn't. And now we're all here. In life, I don't have to tell you, Michael Brecker was a gift to each of us. His loss is surreal. It's so weird, and heartbreaking."

In his eulogy, Dave Liebman addressed the traditional Jewish tenet of *tikkun olam*, or "making the world better." As he said, "There was an unspoken agreement that we should do something good for humanity. Our families both were into the idea of making the world better, and Mike wound up doing that."

James Taylor sent a recorded message of thanks, crediting Michael's intercession in his own addictions with saving his life: "We go back, Michael and I. I've said it a number of times before, but I really have the sense that he saved my life. As my sponsor, he was a role model for me. I identified so closely with Michael that the fact that he managed to turn his life around and go forward made me think that it was possible for me, too. I owe him so much for that. Thinking of him in the world made it easier for me to think of myself in the world, really. There's a huge community of us whose lives were hugely changed and altered by Michael. So those of us who remain and survive, we carry him forward now, and his memory. Along with his music, we are what is left of him in this world."

Randy joined with pianist Joey Calderazzo and bassist Patitucci to perform Calderazzo's "Midnight Voyage," a tune from Michael's *Tales from the Hudson,* while Hancock joined Patitucci and DeJohnette in performing his "Chan's Song," which Michael had played on his 2001 album, *Nearness of You: The Ballad Book,* and for which he won a Best Instrumental Jazz Solo Grammy Award. Hancock and Paul Simon duetted on "Still Crazy After All These Years," the Simon tune that Michael had played on in 1975. Liebman played a solo wood flute version of Michael's "A Gathering of Spirits," title track from the Saxophone Summit's 2004 debut album. And Metheny played a solo acoustic rendition of "Every Day (I Thank You)," a beautiful tune he had written with Michael in mind and that they had played together numerous times, including on Metheny's stellar album, *80/81.*

Metheny assessed Michael's tenor prowess in his Town Hall eulogy, noting that people were blinded by the brilliance and ingenuity and strength of his seemingly superhuman saxophone technique. He further opined that the deepest treasure of Mike's amazing gift was sometimes hard to pick out in the wealth of it all.

Michael's thirteen-year-old son, Sam, recalled high jinks with his father—wrestling on the bed, playing catch in the backyard, riding bikes on weekends, playing basketball—as well as laughing and sharing intimate talks. And Susan delivered a profoundly moving eulogy for her husband:

"Mike was the best person I have ever known, and I know that am a better person for having known and loved him. He was kind, he was gentle, he was generous, he was incredibly funny. He believed that people were good, and he looked for and found the good in everyone. When you spoke with him, you knew that you had his absolute attention and that he was genuinely interested in you and in that moment. Mike had an uncanny ability to make everyone feel special. With his constant smile and willingness to please, he was inside your heart within seconds. He and I fell in love the moment we met. I reveled in his telling that story and saying, 'It was love at first sight with Susan.'

"He was so very grateful for his life, his music, his kids, his friends. This grateful man thanked me for every single meal I ever made for him. In our marriage we rarely argued, partly because he just refused to do so. He always took the high road. He was a wonderful father. With his worldwide acclaim and countless awards, he was proudest of his children.

"Carry him in your heart, because he's in there. He gave us all a piece of himself every time we saw him play or spoke to him or hugged him tight. He was the very best of what we humans can be. And I will forever be honored to be Michael Brecker's wife."

The solemn ceremony concluded with Hancock joining Wayne Shorter and Buster Williams (all practicing members of SGI) and Sam Brecker for a full five minutes chanting *nam-myoho-renge-kyo* as the crowd of colleagues, fans, bandmates, family members, and the greater musical community silently filed out of Town Hall.

# EPILOGUE
## More to Live For

Since Michael's passing in 2007, Susan Brecker has been on a mission to keep her husband's musical legacy alive while also raising awareness of the dreaded disease that took his life. A forceful advocate for cancer research, she has jointly produced, along with Michael's manager, Darryl Pitt, a series of biannual "The Nearness of You" benefit concerts at The Appel Room in New York City's House of Swing, Jazz at Lincoln Center, to honor Michael's memory and help support the research being done at Columbia University Medical Center by doctors Azra Raza and Siddhartha Mukherjee. Beginning in 2015 with Paul Simon, James Taylor, Bobby McFerrin, and Dianne Reeves as main attractions, to 2017's show with Diana Krall, Chaka Khan, Wynton Marsalis, David Sanborn, and the Saxophone Summit with Dave Liebman, Joe Lovano, and Ravi Coltrane, and 2019's show starring Hugh Jackman, Patti Austin, James Taylor, and Harolyn Blackwell, these "The Nearness of You" benefit concerts have raised millions of dollars for cancer research.

"I feel so strongly about funding the research," said Susan, "because each new development, every new drug and therapy they learn about is going to extend somebody's life—until they find a cure. And these doctors—outstanding physicians and human beings—are committed to improving the lives of their patients as well. So, in that spirit, I want to support the work that they're doing, and they're making progress. So now is a very critical time for us to support them with a concert like this to bring awareness to this cause and their need for critical funds."

In 2010, Susan coproduced the documentary film *More to Live For*, which follows the lives of three leukemia patients facing death in search of bone marrow transplants that could save their lives, including Michael Brecker. "We made this film and took it to twenty-five film festivals around the world," she said of the documentary, directed by Noah Hutton. "And every time we showed the film, we tested people for the bone marrow registry. That's how I was able to make fifty-four matches, because we just tested so many people. And people are still making matches from the batch that we tested as a result of the film."

Herbie Hancock mentioned that his drummer, Richie Barshay, initially made a donation to the bone marrow registry with the hope of saving Michael's life. He wasn't a perfect match for Michael, but his donation ended up helping someone else who was in need. "Richie was on tour with me when he told me, 'I saved a boy's life,' and I got choked up," Hancock recalled. "You know, it was phenomenal what Michael did, directly or indirectly, to save so many other lives."

Susan has also donated many of Michael's personal artifacts—handwritten original scores, appointment books and journals from the '70s, hundreds of performance cassettes, more than a thousand unreleased photos, set lists, newspaper clippings, gig posters, business materials, and other personal memorabilia along with his instruments, books, awards, and albums—to the Michael Brecker Archive at William Paterson University in New Jersey. Curated by David Demsey, tenor saxophonist-educator and Mike's personal friend, this generous donation represents a treasure trove for students, fans, and aficionados alike.

Susan is also a cofounder, along with Darryl Pitt, of The Michael Brecker International Saxophone Competition, created to assist in the launch of emerging, exceptionally talented saxophonists. The final round of the inaugural competition, held at the 2019 Red Sea Jazz Festival in Eilat, Israel, was judged by Ron Carter, Eli Degibri, Kenny Garrett, and Donny McCaslin. Alex Hahn won first prize, with Alex Weitz and Artem Badenko coming in second and third, respectively. The second Michael Brecker International Saxophone Competition was scheduled for July 2022 in Vienna, Austria.

"Michael was such a positive guy," said Susan. "He was such a beautiful spirit in the world. And to honor him and to know that something good could be done with such sadness, to me, was just so Mike. He was guiding this. I really felt like he was in the room at these concerts. Because so many people loved him and were there for him, I just felt so loved and supported by everybody there—especially the musicians. They couldn't have been more generous and caring."

She added, "Here am I without him, left here on this earth. And as a testament to him, people treat me like I'm Mike—with so much respect and love. And I'm so lucky, because I've been sort of grand-fathered into the jazz community just because of who I was married to. How many people can say that there's this wonderful community of people that love you just because they loved who you were with. So now I have friendships with these saxophone players like Chris Potter, Ben Wendel, Troy Roberts, Ravi Coltrane, Donny McCaslin, and others. These are my people. And they were my people for so long. I just feel lucky that I didn't have to abandon that entire world. I'm just really fortunate . . . so fortunate."

(Susan Nuestadt Brecker has established the Time Is of the Essence Fund created in Michael's honor. One hundred percent of all donations are used for testing new donor registrants. Tax-deductible donations can be made by calling 800 627-7692, or by going to www.themarrow foundation.org.)

# APPENDIX

## Testimonials to a Tenor Titan

**DAVID SANBORN**

**Grammy Award-winning alto saxophonist and charter member of The Brecker Brothers has recorded twenty-eight albums as a leader or coleader and appeared on recordings by Stevie Wonder, David Bowie, George Benson, Michael Franks, Bob James, Steve Khan, Jaco Pastorius, Randy Brecker, the Paul Butterfield Blues Band, and the Gil Evans Orchestra.**

In terms of just pure technique and musicality, there was nobody who could touch Mike. He had so much more technical ability than any other saxophone player I've ever known or even heard about in my life. To me, the only guy that even comes close today is Chris Potter. And I think Chris would be the first to admit that in terms of absolute control of the instrument, there was nobody better than Mike. He was so good he would do stuff on the instrument that was literally just impossible. He would do these multiphonics, moving through it at 32nd and 64th note speed, and do it with such an ease that you weren't even sure what exactly just happened. I mean, it was stunning, just jaw-droppingly great. And I don't think you could find a musician on Earth that would disagree with that.

The world is diminished by his absence. But his legacy is so powerful and so strong and the vitality and the immediacy of his music lives on. Whatever his personal journey and his personal demons were, he transcended them, as far as I'm concerned. Mike's life, to me, was about art and love.

**DAVE LIEBMAN**

**Saxophonist-composer-educator played on more than five hundred recordings, including two hundred as a leader. The 2010 NEA Jazz**

Master worked with Miles Davis, Elvin Jones, John Scofield, John McLaughlin, and Pat Metheny and in 2003 formed the Saxophone Summit with Joe Lovano and Mike Brecker.

Mike was a saxophone scientist. That was his instrument, and he was going to learn as much as possible about it. And it was a very dedicated search with him. Michael played perfectly. When you hear guys who don't play perfectly—-maybe they didn't put in the amount of finger practice that Mike did on his instrument—it's obvious. A lot of the avant-garde cats didn't take care of cleaning up their act; maybe that's the charm. There's certainly a charm about the rawness of a Dewey Redman, who had that crying kind of sound and used it effectively. And when you put Michael next to Dewey—something that is so polished and something that is so raw—the difference is obvious. But guys like Mike and Sonny, Trane, Joe Henderson . . . this is like supreme technique that is beyond ridiculous. There's no holes there. It's completely in tune, it's even, it's perfect.

Virtuosic technique aside, Michael was the sweetest fucking guy around. He was polite, he was beautiful, he was soft spoken, he was a gentleman. He cared. He took care of people and helped them get out of the alcohol and drug thing after he had gotten out of it himself. Michael is a case of somebody who recovered and became a positive force for those who were in the same situation. As a human being, he was a beautiful cat and he was a serious cat. He knew the secret; he knew the story.

## JOSHUA REDMAN

**Tenor saxophonist-composer has twenty-two recordings as a leader or coleader and has toured and recorded with Elvin Jones, McCoy Tyner, Chick Corea, Dave Brubeck, Roy Haynes, Quincy Jones, Ray Brown, Milt Jackson, Joe Lovano, Brad Mehldau, Roy Hargrove, Kurt Rosenwinkel, Paul Motian, the Bad Plus, and his father, Dewey Redman. He played alongside Michael in 1997 at a John Coltrane tribute in Japan.**

I remember once playing a gig in Tarrytown, New York, and, somehow, I got word that Mike was coming to my gig. And sure enough, when we walked out on stage I looked out into the audience, and there was Michael Brecker with his wife, Susan, sitting front row center. And I remember thinking, "Okay, this is not cool! I'm fucking scared!"

And I was making it through the set OK, but there was a point where I was playing a cadenza on a ballad, and I couldn't stop thinking of the cadenza Mike had played on "Funky Sea, Funky Dew" from *Heavy Metal Be-Bop* (Arista, 1978). That was such a formative moment for me the first time I heard him play that. It was 1985, I was at a high school party, probably stoned, and someone put that on. Mike is soloing, and suddenly the band stops, and he takes this outrageous cadenza in the middle of the tune, and I'm like, "What is THIS?!" And from that point, I made myself aware of everything that Mike did. There was that Steps Ahead record where they did "Pools" [*Steps Ahead*, Elektra / Musician, 1983]. There was the Chick Corea record, *Three Quartets* [Warner Bros., 1981]. There was Pat Metheny's *80/81*, which my dad also played on. But *Heavy Metal Be-Bop* was one that really grabbed me, especially that cadenza on "Funky Sea, Funky Dew." So now I'm on stage in Tarry-town, and I'm playing a cadenza with Michael Brecker himself sitting in the front row. I'm so nervous I cannot open my eyes, and all I can think is, "What am I doing here?!"

Mike was the master of the eight- or sixteen-bar saxophone solo. I remember when that Cameo song "Candy" came on the radio, hearing the sax solo and immediately thinking, "That's Brecker!" You could identify him in two notes. It was one thing to tell a story over multiple choruses on rhythm changes or on "Impressions," but it's another thing to tell an incredible story with a powerful emotional impact over eight bars of funk. So, for me, that was one of his great gifts—this kind of architectural sense, his storytelling ability. I think you can make the argument that Mike was the dominant saxophonist of his generation.

I remember when Mike's first recording as a leader came out in 1987. It was one of those records that you knew the exact release date on. I remember lining up at Rasputin Records in Berkeley early that morning to cop that record. When I was coming up, there was this thing known as "the Brecker clone." In the practice rooms at the Berklee College of Music in the late '80s, you could hear cats shedding, and all down the line you'd hear Brecker lick after Brecker lick. I probably would have become a Brecker clone myself if I were good enough to have been one! But I recognized pretty early on I didn't have the chops or the discipline. So, there was a period of time where I realized I had to stop listening to Michael Brecker because the aesthetic and the conception were so powerful and compelling, I was in danger of being overwhelmed by it.

I was trying to learn this foreign language, the jazz language, and realized to really learn it I had to immerse myself in other sources to really understand how to put this language together.

The first and only time I played with Mike was in 1997 at a Four Tenors Tribute to Trane in Japan [with Dave Liebman and George Garzone]. It was amazing to be around Michael then. I mean, he was a god to so many of us and yet always seemed so dismissive of his own brilliance and genius. He was just such a gentle, humble cat—so intelligent, so thoughtful, so soft-spoken. He had a great dry sense of humor and was very self-effacing, which I really can relate to. I'd like to say he was a friend, to the extent that your masters can be your friend.

## DONNY MCCASLIN

**Tenor saxophonist-composer has more than 150 sideman credits, including recordings with David Bowie, Dave Douglas, Dave Binney, George Gruntz, the Maria Schneider Orchestra, and Steps Ahead, as well as fifteen albums as a leader. He was a judge at the inaugural Michael Brecker International Saxophone Competition in Eilat, Israel.**

As a teenager growing up in Santa Cruz, I remember just being stunned by the absolute beauty in Mike's playing. He had such a compelling sound. I was also into Jan Garbarek in that period of him playing with Keith Jarrett's European Quartet [1974–1979], and I felt like Mike's sound was sort of simpatico with that kind of sound Jan had on the instrument. It was just this kind of overwhelming thing to hear, that sound and the passion that he played with. But also, the depth of the content in his playing—all the ideas behind that sound, the different harmonic concepts and the total integrity behind the choices that he made—was just so incredible and something to aspire to as a young musician. I was just so taken with him, and he had a huge impact on my life.

After joining Steps Ahead in 1994, I remember one time playing this ballad that Mike had recorded with them on [1984's] *Modern Times* [Mike Mainieri's "Self Portrait"], where he plays a beautiful solo at the end. So here I was with Steps Ahead, playing that tune and feeling like, "Man, I'm overplaying, I'm not really making this the way I want it."

So, I went back and listened to Mike's version and it was like so simple and yet so sophisticated at the same time. There was just so much emotion, so much expression. Nothing felt superfluous in Mike's playing. It's just the mark of a genius musician. To say that Mike really captured my imagination is an understatement. He set this high bar of sonic expression on the instrument for all of us to aim for.

## CHRIS POTTER

**Tenor saxophonist-composer has worked with Herbie Hancock, Dave Holland, Pat Metheny, Dave Douglas, Paul Motian, Steve Swallow, Red Rodney, and Steely Dan. Widely regarded as one of the most virtuosic tenor saxophonists in the post–Michael Brecker era, he has appeared on more than 150 recordings and has 22 albums as a leader.**

I first checked Mike out when I was in high school. I was already involved in playing the saxophone at that point, starting to play professionally around the South Carolina area where I grew up. And I remember getting the *Steps Ahead* record from 1983. That was my first exposure to Mike's playing, and I just couldn't believe it. I remember thinking, "Man, this is as far as you could ever go on the saxophone."

The first thing that grabbed me about Mike's playing was the unique sound and the depth of his concept. And when you got into the kind of lines that he was playing, I could recognize that he was kind of taking things that John Coltrane and Joe Henderson had done and just carried it even further in some ways, as far as ways of incorporating false fingerings into his lines and ways of superimposing various other kinds of harmonies on top of the basic harmony.

Mike was extremely inspiring to me as a young saxophonist, and then meeting him and getting to talk to him and just seeing how he approached music and the way he acted in general was a further source of inspiration for me. It's important for all of us of any generation to have people that we can look up to from a previous generation that can help show the way. And Mike was an especially large one for me in that regard. He combined extreme natural ability with the drive and the curiosity to take it as far you can. That's the only way I think that you ever get to that ridiculous kind of level that he was on.

## JOE LOVANO

**Tenor saxophonist-composer has recorded more than 40 albums as
a leader or coleader and another 250 as a sideman. He was a longtime member of the Paul Motian Trio with Bill Frisell and played
with Michael Brecker and Dave Liebman in the Saxophone Summit,
recording *Gathering of Spirits* in 2004.**

I met Mike before I moved to New York, around '75. Billy Cobham's
band came to Cleveland to play the Agora Ballroom, and Mike and
Randy were in the band, so I went down to check it out. I had already
heard Mike on some records with Dreams and Horace Silver and was
captured by his beautiful execution and approach. So, we meet, and I'm
telling him how much I'm digging his playing, and he says to me, "Oh,
man, I've been listening to *you!*" Because the Lonnie Smith record that
I played on had just come out [*Afro-Desia* on Groove Merchant]. That
was my first recording session, and WRVR and those stations around
New York were playing it a lot. So that was a funny first meeting—I was
trying to compliment him, and he ends up complimenting me.

I moved to New York shortly after that and was in Woody Herman's
band from '76 to '79, which was around the same time that Mike and
Randy had Seventh Avenue South cooking. There was a lot of gravity
at that place, man, every night! Because it was open late and people
would come by after their gigs for the hang. That whole scene with all
the studio cats and all those *Saturday Night Live* people, and just the
whole crowd was like some amazing energy. Between that scene and
Bradley's, Sweet Basil, the Tin Palace, Sam Rivers's Studio Rivbea and
Rashied Ali's place, Ali's Alley, New York was happening in those days.
That's when Mike and I kind of got closer. We did a lot of jamming at
his pad on Grand Street and at my loft on 23rd Street, mostly just tenor-
drums duos, switching around. That was always fun. And you could
tell when Mike was on drums that Elvin was really his man. Mike had
a special affinity for drummers, and he hit a groove with whatever the
drummer was doing. You could hear it whether he was playing with
Jack DeJohnette, Steve Gadd, Billy Hart, or whoever.

Mike was a true virtuoso on his horn. I remember being down in his
basement studio in Hastings just trying out these wooden mouthpieces

that Francois Louis, the Belgian mouthpiece maker, had made for him. This was probably around 2004. I drove Francois up to Mike's pad, and we went down in his basement studio, and you should have heard him try these mouthpieces, man. He was like Heifetz or something the way he played the harmonics and the overtone series on the horn from the lowest register to the highest register. And that's how he would practice. He would play from the bottom of the horn to the upper extensions and really feel all the overtones and undertones within that. Mike lived in that world. He was constantly searching, constantly evolving, and he had a deep passion and a lot of love in his playing.

## BILL EVANS

**Tenor saxophonist-composer and former sideman to Miles Davis, John McLaughlin, and Herbie Hancock as well as a charter member of the band Elements, he has twenty-three recordings as a leader or coleader and has toured and recorded with Robben Ford, Randy Brecker, Steve Lukather, Wolfgang Haffner, Steps Ahead, and the Scottish National Jazz Orchestra.**

I first heard Mike on a Horace Silver record, *In Pursuit of the 27th Man*. It was 1976, and I was in college, and this was the most contemporary saxophone playing I'd ever heard in my life. To me, it sounded like a super-hip combination of jazz, funk, and soul with an awesome tenor sound and incredible technique. I thought, "Who IS this guy?! I need to hear more." To hear Mike at that time was something quite unique for me. The way he approached playing jazz was this post-Coltrane, quintessentially New York style of playing tenor. It was fresh, modern . . . contagious.

I finally met Mike sometime in 1979 while I was attending William Paterson University in New Jersey. By that time, he had created his own style. You could tell it was Mike Brecker on saxophone in less than three notes. That's a feat in itself. In 1989, some Japanese promoters put together a presentation called Saxophone Workshop for a big festival called "Live Under the Sky" in Tokyo. It was Mike, Stanley Turrentine, Ernie Watts, and myself playing arrangements by the great pianist Don Grolnick of tunes like Wayne Shorter's "Water Babies," George Russell's "Stratusphunk," Duke Ellington's "It Don't Mean a Thing," and Don's

"The Four Sleepers" and "Pools." At one rehearsal, Stanley Turrentine played some of his classic funk lines, and Mike turned to me and said, "Those last few notes Stanley just played were so influential to me."

I remember another festival in Germany in 2005 where the Soul Bop band (me and Randy Brecker) followed Mike's quartet. Mike, of course, sounded amazing. After his set, he said to me, "I really didn't create much out there tonight, but on the encore, I felt like some real improvisation was happening." And I said, "Are you kidding? You were amazing!" The thing is, to him, some shows were more spontaneous than others. To us, he was improvising ALL the time. And to be so humble while being so awesome on the instrument is just so incredibly rare and inspiring. When I hear saxophone players today playing Mike's lines and emulating his style, it makes me happy to think that people are still thinking about him. I miss the guy being on the planet, and I'll always cherish those memories of cool moments at festivals and clubs we shared.

## RAVI COLTRANE

**The son of Michael's biggest role model and inspiration, John Coltrane, he played alongside Michael at a Trane tribute at Newport in 2004 and later replaced Mike in the Saxophone Summit lineup. Their 2008 recording *Seraphic Light* was dedicated to Michael Brecker.**

When I moved to New York in '91, Michael called me out of the blue, and we'd talk a little bit and he'd end it with, "If there's anything that I can do to help you . . . anything." And it was so honest. I could really see it was sort of in deference to John—his music and influence on Michael's own work. I think he felt compelled to extend that kind of respect to me, and that was the connection that we had throughout my time knowing him.

I remember asking him about the only time he heard John play live, in 1966 at Temple University in Philadelphia. He and Randy had attempted to go another time to hear John's band in 1966, but the way he described it was there was a kind of a militant black audience there that night, and they were literally asked to leave. So, I guess he could have heard John two times, but he only heard him the one time, that night at Temple University.

By the early 2000s, I remember seeing Mike at the Iridium, and we talked again about that concert at Temple. And I asked him, "Do you remember anything about the night?" And he put his hands up to his chest and was beating a little bit and said, "I remember this." That a reference to that moment in the concert where John takes the horn out of his mouth and starts beating on his chest and singing. Rashied Ali described it as him sort of outplaying the horn, that he had exhausted the saxophone and couldn't do anything else but sort of . . . scream. And I said, "You know, Michael, I think we have a recording of that in my mother's closet somewhere." So, the next time I was in Los Angeles, I found the tape, made a copy for Mike and later brought it to him. And he was really excited to hear it. The next day, Michael called me. I wasn't at home, and he left the most beautiful message on my answering machine. He explained that right after his gig he was driving back from Manhattan to his home in Hastings and he put the CD on in his car to basically relive that night in 1966 when he was seventeen years old seeing John Coltrane. And I could tell that he was really moved by reexperiencing that music and also hearing John doing this vocalization that is very powerful and moving.

I think Michael came about at a very unique time in music and was able to really utilize everything coming out of the late '60s and early '70s in the jazz and funk-rock scenes. He absorbed so much at a prime time and just got ahead of the game really quickly because he was a focused musician and very diligent about how he practiced. And clearly, he worked out a ton of shit on the saxophone and was able to kind of take it to another place. He also had a very distinguishable sound. And there was a point in the '80s where that sound became THE sound among aspiring saxophone players. There were so many younger players trying to play like Michael then. We used to call them the Breckerheads. But I always thought Michael's thing always sounded most genuine—because it was his shit! And, obviously, his influences were not only John Coltrane but Joe Henderson as well. But he put a lot of shit together and worked it out, all over the horn, and was able to play in a variety of styles of music with a kind of proficiency that made him one of the best of the best. And I think it was his curiosity and passion and the profoundly deep connection he had to the music that really set him apart from other great saxophone players on a similar technical level.

## BRANFORD MARSALIS

**Tenor saxophonist-composer has thirty albums as a leader and more than a hundred as a sideman, including recordings with Art Blakey & The Jazz Messengers, Miles Davis, Horace Silver, Charlie Haden, Billy Hart, Sting, Bruce Hornsby, Harry Connick Jr., his father, Ellis Marsalis Jr., and his brothers Wynton and Delfeayo Marsalis. He played alongside Michael on "Mr. JJ" from Jeff "Tain" Watts's album *Bar Talk* (2002).**

When I was growing up in New Orleans, I was a horn section guy. I was all about playing the parts that made the song work. That was just an instinctive thing in New Orleans. It wasn't about changing the chord structure to make it sound "hip,"; it was about very faithfully duplicating the horn parts. And I knew all the popular horn sections of the day—Jerry Hey and the West Coast guys had a horn section called Seawind, and Earth, Wind & Fire had a horn section called the Phenix Horns with Louis Satterfield and Don Myrick. And when I heard the horn parts on those Parliament-Funkadelic records from the mid-'70s, I was like, "Man, these motherfuckers are killing!" I didn't find out until later that it was Mike and Randy Brecker on a lot of that shit.

So, my introduction to Mike was all those killing solos he did on Parliament-Funkadelic ["P Funk Wants to Get Funked Up" on *Mother-ship Connection*, Casablanca, 1975; "Getten' to Know You" on *The Clones of Dr. Funkenstein*, Casablanca, 1976] and Cameo records ["Candy," "Don't Be Lonely" and "She's Mine" from *Word Up!*, Atlanta Artists, 1986]. Later on, I also heard The Brecker Brothers. In fact, I wrote out their arrangement of Randy's "Some Skunk Funk" for the band I was in at the New Orleans Center for Creative Arts [NOCCA]. It was me, Wynton, Donald Harrison, Tony Dillon on drums, Anthony Hamilton on bass, and my dad played piano. And we would always end the show with "Some Skunk Funk." That was a fun tune, man. It took me like a week to figure out the first line, and I was excited about cracking the code on it.

Later on, when I was a young kid in New York with no gig, I would hang out at Mike and Randy's club, Seventh Avenue South. The vibe of the place was just totally wild. It was one of my favorite clubs ever in the city. You could come in, buy a coke and hear the music from upstairs because they had a set of speakers at the bar, and you could hear the gig for free. As a musician, I didn't need to see the guys playing, I needed to hear them. That's what made Seventh Avenue South so incredibly cool. While I did hang there a lot, I never heard Mike play there.

I finally got a chance to meet him during the summer of 1985 when Mike and I played together with Buddy Tate at the Madarao Jazz Festival in Japan. It was a festival that George Wein organized, and it was held at a mountain ski resort. That was the most time I spent with Mike, because we were there for a week, and we hung out together every day, just talking about life and a little bit about music. I wanted to just vibe with Mike, and he was awesome—very kind, very funny, very perceptive, very aware of who he was. I got to know Mike and Susan well, and I liked them as people. And they were easy to love because they were just cool. And it was great that he had a wife who was not in the music business. So, her relationship with him wasn't about gigs and hanging and wanting to be on the scene. You know, it was cool. She just dug him, and he dug her.

## JOHN MCLAUGHLIN

**British-born guitar avatar performed and recorded with Miles Davis and Tony Williams Lifetime before forming the Mahavishnu Orchestra in 1971. He has recorded more than fifty albums as a leader with his groups Shakti, One Truth Band, Free Spirits, The Heart of Things, Remember Shakti, Five Peace Band, and The 4th Dimension. On May 1, 2001, he jammed with Michael's quartet in his home base of Monte Carlo, which has been available as a bootleg CD.**

I arrived in New York early January 1969 and found a really good underground scene for young jazz musicians. It consisted primarily of organized jam sessions in various lofts around the city. I recall very clearly the jam where I first met and heard Michael Brecker play. Drummer Barry Altschul had a loft on Bond Street, and I arrived with bassist Dave Holland for the jam. We were in a circle of around eight or nine musicians and basically improvised "round robin" style, one after the other. Michael, who looked no older than nineteen or twenty, was opposite to me, and when he began playing, I was blown away. Even then, Michael had the gift of liberating the listener simply because his playing was already masterful. I really couldn't believe a young player could play with such maturity and elegance. Of course, from that time on, I became one of his greatest admirers.

As time went by, we would run into each other, especially after I'd formed the first Mahavishnu Orchestra, and he and his brother, Randy, had formed Dreams. It took quite a long time before we played together again, but I continued to follow his career and buy his recordings, which were always and without exception masterpieces of playing and improvisation. Now while it's true he was strongly influenced by the master, John Coltrane, Michael was able to integrate this influence into his own style that he had created already by the time I'd heard him at Barry's loft. He was simply amazing.

In 1996, I'd planned a recording called *The Promise*, on which I'd organized a freewheeling composition for Michael and myself called "Jazz Jungle," with one of the great rhythm sections of all time—Dennis Chambers on drums, Don Alias on percussion, James Genus on bass, and Jim Beard on piano. All the musicians played exceptionally well. There was a vibe in the studio that affected every one of us. After this recording, Michael and I became much closer and began spending time together whenever possible. And now, after more than twenty-five years, every time I listen to this track, Michael still blows me away.

My relationship with Michael continued to the end. At the time he entered hospital, I got hit with kidney stones. This is nothing compared to what Michael was enduring, but as we were both incapacitated, we passed the time by exchanging jokes. To this day, I miss Michael dearly. He was from the outset a true inspiration and remained so to the very end.

**TIM RIES**

**Tenor saxophonist-composer-educator and longtime member of the Rolling Stones horn section lived near Michael in Hastings-on-Hudson, where they became practicing buddies. He has recorded eight albums as a leader and is also a cofounder of the Prism Quartet, a saxophone chamber ensemble.**

In the summer of 1982, when I was a student at North Texas State, I went on a tour with the One O'Clock Lab Band playing at all the jazz festivals that happened all over Europe. And we just happened to open for Steps Ahead on most of those shows. I was a kid then, twenty-one or twenty-two, just finishing my undergraduate work. And at that point, Mike was as big a star as it gets in jazz, but I had never seen him live up to that point. So being able to play on the same stage as my hero and then meet him and hang out with him was just like a dream.

So now I'm getting to witness this Heifetz of the saxophone first-hand live every night, sitting right out front. And when I finally saw him live, it was different than hearing him on record, because you're actually seeing his fingers move up close, and you can make those connections on the instrument. It was very exciting to witness. And then to interact with him backstage, at the hotel, on the plane to gigs . . . amazing. And it turns out he was a total mensch—very accessible, very kind, just a nice guy.

Right before leaving for this European tour, my friend and fellow North Texas State alumnus Bob Belden gave me a recording of Trane with Miles in Sweden from 1960. It eventually came out as a CD years later, but at this time, in 1982, nobody had this. But somehow Belden got it and passed along a cassette copy to me and, of course, I was transcribing this stuff. So now Michael and I are on the same plane, leaving the Pori festival in Finland and going to Nice in southern France. And I knew that he was a huge Coltrane fan, so as I board the plane, I slide into an open seat next to him and say, "I think I have something that you might enjoy," and I pull out of my front pocket the cassette of Trane with Miles in Sweden. And he looks at me wide-eyed and goes, "Where did you get this?" We struck up a long conversation on that flight, and from that point on for the rest of that tour, he would sit next to me on the plane, and we'd talk about music. It was just hard to imagine somebody of Mike's stature and genius being that nice to me. And when the tour ended, he told me, "Whenever you get to New York, you can call me up, and we'll hang." It was Michael's way of opening the door to me, this kid playing with the One O'Clock Band, and kind of encouraging me. And I really started shedding a lot at that point, determined to leave Texas and move to the Big Apple.

When I finally did make it to New York, I called Michael and he was, again, just super-nice to me. We talked a lot, and he was very encouraging. Years later, when my first daughter turned two and we were ready to leave Manhattan, Michael said, "You should come up here to Hastings and check it out." We ended up moving to Hastings, and then that began an even closer friendship between us. He'd call me up and say, "Hey, come over. I just got this new sax." Or he'd have me come over to try out mouthpieces while he'd go in the next room and listen to the differences between them. Mike was like an excitable kid about mouthpieces. He was always checking stuff out that way.

Here's a story about Mike that is both a lesson in humility and an example of just how curious he was about everything: One day he's driving back from the city, and he heard something on the radio by this young saxophone player that he liked. He later found out who it was, bought the album, and started transcribing the guy's solo on the tune that caught his ear from the radio. And I'm like, "Man, he's Michael Brecker. Does he need to do that?" No, he doesn't, but it was just about learning more about the language. Whatever was current, whatever was happening, he wanted to know about it. He was an inquisitive, intelligent being that soaked up information. If he didn't know it, he wanted to know. And that kind of encouraged me to keep a curious mind myself.

It was both humbling and inspiring to practice with Mike. I remember the first time I came over to Mike's house, I was like, "What do I do? I'm going to take my saxophone out in front of this guy? That's not a good idea." But it was very natural, just like being around a college kid in the school practice room, just hanging out and woodshedding together. I consider myself very fortunate to have met Mike, gotten to know him really well and hang with him a lot. I just miss being able to call him up and say, "Let's get together and play."

## STEVE SLAGLE

**Alto saxophonist-composer-bandleader-educator toured and recorded with Machito and his Afro-Cuban Orchestra, Ray Barretto, Lionel Hampton, Brother Jack McDuff, Carla Bley, Mike Stern, Dave Stryker, and Joe Lovano's nonet. He has recorded twenty albums as a leader or coleader and appeared on more than forty as a sideman.**

I met Mike during the first couple of weeks after arriving in New York from Los Angeles in the spring of 1977. The Brecker Brothers were big stars then. Their first record had already come out, and it was really popular. And out of nowhere I get a call from Randy to make a Brecker Brothers rehearsal. I guess Sanborn couldn't make it, and they were running down some new charts. So, it was really a kick for me to get this call from Randy. Here I am the new kid in town, and I'm rehearsing with The Brecker Brothers! Sure, I was just subbing, but that was one session I'll never forget. Mike didn't really talk that much then. He seemed kind of reticent at the time, not very sociable. I found out later that he was at the height of his addiction then.

It wasn't until years later, when I was first become a father, that we got to be really close friends. And that Mike was a completely different person from the Mike I met in the mid-'70s. Maybe he made up for lost time by suddenly becoming an extremely good listener to what you were saying and what you were going through in your life, and by really being helpful, whether it was offering advice or just empathy.

Mike and Susan's place in Hastings had an incredible view of the Hudson River, and naturally when you'd see it, you'd be very impressed. But he told me, "When I first moved in here, I used to practice and look out at the Hudson. And then within six months I went down downstairs, set up my stuff in the basement room with no windows, and I've been practicing there ever since. I never, ever look out at the Hudson and play anymore." And I understand that, because as players we come up practicing in these little rooms, whether it was at college or when we were living with our parents. It usually was in the basement or the attic or a bathroom or something, and that's what we got used to. We weren't used to having glorious sweeping views in our practice rooms. As Mike said, "The view just becomes a distraction." Because when you're practicing, it's just purely discipline. You're not really paying attention to the environment that you're in as much as just the way it sounds. So, you can be in a really closed space, and it can sound good. In fact, you can hear even better in a tight scene, which is what Mike preferred.

The other thing that I think is important to realize with Mike is that he was very fortunate—and he'd be the first to say it—to have Randy as an older brother. I remember him once saying to me, "Man, my greatest hero in life is my brother." Even if they had their differences—and what siblings don't have differences?—the closeness that Mike and Randy felt as brothers was awesome.

## BOB MINTZER

**Saxophonist-composer and longtime member of the Yellowjackets is also conductor of the WDR Big Band Cologne. He came up in the Buddy Rich and Thad Jones-Mel Lewis big bands, worked and recorded with Sam Jones, Jaco Pastorius, Tito Puente, Eddie Palmieri, Kurt Elling, Michael Franks, and James Taylor, and has thirty-five albums as a leader, including 2001's Grammy Award-winning *Homage to Count Basie*.**

I related strongly to Mike because of his open-mindedness. He looked far and wide for influence and I felt that way from day one with music. I just was intrigued by every kind of music, its differences, its commonalities. I wanted to play every instrument there was. And Mike was very much the same way. I remember in 1982 picking him up at his loft and driving him somewhere, and I asked him, "So what are you working on?" And he said, "I'm transcribing a Stan Getz solo from the '50s." And that was very telling. You know, here's this modernist cat who doesn't sound at all like Stan Getz, and yet he felt that it was critical for his growth and development to check this stuff out. That's the beauty of this art form. It keeps going, if you so choose.

When playing with Mike I always needed to strategize a little bit because, you know, I am not going to out-note Michael Brecker. It would just be futile to try. So, I would actually purposely play less and leave more space, mainly as a means of contrasting what he did, particularly if we were soloing back-to-back. The tendency is if somebody is playing with that level of ferocity, you sort of feel obligated to respond in kind. But I just thought, "I don't have that kind of facility, nor do I think that way." So, I always went a different way.

Mike and I did have a few occasions to play on sessions together. The first thing was an electric Miles kind of record that Al Foster did [*Mixed Roots*, Japanese CBS/Sony, 1978], where I played soprano on a couple tracks, and Mike played mostly tenor but also soprano on one track. Then there was a Joachim Kuhn record [*Nightline New York*, Sandra Music, 1981], which was very dense, complex music. I remember playing on this tune, which had very intricate harmony with a lot of fast movements through these slash chords. I played the first solo, and I was buried in this chart, trying to make sense of it and really struggling to hear what it was. Mike played second, and from note one it was as if he came out of the womb playing this song. I mean, he knew the harmony, knew the form, knew what to play . . . and he had his eyes closed! He wasn't even looking at the music. He had the ability to scan the map of this solo section and just make it his own, seemingly instantaneously. And to be honest, it pissed me off. I said, "How the fuck do you do that?" And he said, "Ah, man. I was just bullshitting . . . you know." And I said, "The hell you were! You just played some of the deepest shit I've ever heard." And it was all the right notes. That's not bullshitting to my way of thinking.

The third time we played together was in Jaco's Word of Mouth band in 1981. I think this was Jaco's first foray as a bandleader of any significance after he left Weather Report. I remember we did that really fast version of "Invitation," which was pretty psycho . . . a 'we're just holding on for dear life' kind of thing. But I felt super-challenged and inspired and honored to be in Mike's company on that record. Then, in 1983, when I started my first big band at Seventh Avenue South, Mike was in the saxophone section.

The fourth time we recorded together was for a recording of mine called *Twin Tenors* [RCA/Novus, 1994]. By that time, I was fairly comfortable in my role with Mike. We did a version of Trane's "Giant Steps" that was WAY up-tempo. Mike had this sort of machine-gun fire way of playing that I certainly can't do, so I played it very differently—less bebop, more motivically, leaving a lot more space. And I felt it was successful; I thought the contrast worked. I wasn't trying to outplay him or be like him; I was just trying to do my own thing.

Mike's take on saxophone playing was so all-encompassing that it had this big impact on me, to the point where I wound up playing and sounding like him for many years. Plenty of us have gone through phases where we emulated one player or another. But the mistake many of us make, and I made as well, was to not dig deep enough. If you emulate somebody's surface mannerisms, then that's all you're gonna get. Whereas, if you dig deep and sort of take apart what they're actually doing melodically, harmonically, rhythmically, and then put it back together your own way, the focus is not on the mannerisms; it's more on the content. And you can sort of revise that content and be better able to make it your own. That's something I discovered later in my career, but it took a long time.

## ADAM ROGERS

**Guitarist of choice for an array of artists on the New York scene as well as a bandleader in his own right with six albums to his credit. He played in the Brecker Brothers Band Reunion and was a key member of Michael's quartet, quintet, and Quindectet, appearing on *Wide Angles*.**

Mike had this great combination of just a really positive outlook and a beautiful cynicism. And it was informed by having a tremendous amount of experience as a human being and seeing a lot of different sides of life, both positive and negative. He was an incredibly smart, perceptive person who had seen all kinds of shit. So, his sense of what was bullshit or what was real was very strong. And I, as a native New Yorker, felt a real connection with him.

I was always so happy to spend time with Mike and talk about anything. I had so much love and respect for him. He was a really wonderful human being who had a great humility mixed with a strong awareness of who he was. He was an unbelievable virtuoso who was always looking around for something that he hadn't heard before. He was a really unique, really curious and searching spirit who was utterly committed to anything he was doing. And he was hysterically funny. I mean, he's the person who taught me how to do a Scottish accent! I honestly felt when Mike passed, and have continued to feel, that the universe contracted a bit. Because Mike's spirit was so huge. Such a great guy. I fuckin' loved him, man.

## CHRIS MINH DOKY

**Bassist who played in Michael Brecker's touring band from late 1999 to 2004. Mike played on his 1995 Blue Note album, *Doky Brothers*, and also appears on his 2006 Blue Note album, *The Nomad Diaries*.**

I grew up in Denmark listening to The Brecker Brothers, and I remember when Mike's straight-ahead record came out [*Michael Brecker*,

1987], I was like, "This is the greatest shit ever!" So, when I joined Mike's band, I was extremely grateful and honored, but I was also scared shitless because Mike would play the way he did, so powerful and amazing, and the band included Jeff "Tain" Watts on drums and Joey Calderazzo, both amazing players. And the music was really complex. Mike really became a huge mentor to me because standing on the bandstand behind Mike when he was playing would be like standing behind Dr. Livingston. He knows where he's going through the woods, he cuts his way through. Everything's clear and logical when you play right behind him. Everything makes sense. And that was the one of the great things about that band—it was so complex but at the same time so logical. And Mike could just, without saying anything, show in his playing what this is about. We didn't even need charts. In that band we would do something called "the lost vibe," where we were trying to play like we're lost. But we were never lost, especially not behind Mike, because you could just follow him, and he was so clear.

Mike is probably the most influential musician on me. And then, as a person, he inspired me and showed me what it's like to be such a great musician as him and a human being at the same time. Mike was just, to use one of his words, a mensch. Mike means the world to me. He's a large part of who I became, not only as a musician, but as a person, too. I have a picture of Mike on my wall right near a picture of my parents. So, he's with me every day. Not a day goes by where I don't see him with his smirk, like he's smiling if I do something stupid. Another personal thing of his that I really loved was his childlike approach to things. Like when he got excited about something, you could not help but be so completely smitten by his enthusiasm and playfulness around it. I remember one time we played a gig, and Herbie showed up, and to watch the two of them like completely take off in this whole explosion of enthusiasm and childlike playfulness . . . it was so inspiring. He was so much fun, man. We had so much fun.

## BEN WENDEL

**Tenor saxophonist-composer recorded four albums as a leader and another thirteen with the genre-defying ensemble Kneebody. Born in Vancouver and currently living in Brooklyn, he was a judge at the**

**inaugural Michael Brecker International Saxophone Competition at the 2019 Red Sea Jazz Festival in Eilat, Israel.**

I first discovered Michael Brecker through his guest appearances on Joni Mitchell's live *Shadows and Light* and on Donald Fagen's *The Nightfly*. Those two albums are great examples of his power to enhance any project he was on. Such a huge, beautiful sound, so well balanced, such incredible technique. To this day, he is still one of the most fluid players to ever grace the horn. And I still cannot get over how unbelievably strong his time feel was. Many folks know how great he played drums, and I am sure that contributed to it. He really was a force of nature who could propel any rhythm section through the sheer force of his playing on the horn.

Michael was heavily inspired by John Coltrane, but how he took that influence in a completely new direction reveals his real genius. Apparently, he saw one of Coltrane's final concerts when he was a teenager. I love thinking about the energetic line that connects those two incredible artists, how Michael is part of that continuum. I loved the way Michael wrote original music—it really blurred the lines and pointed to a completely new approach. Michael continues to teach me every time I hear him. Like all the truly great artists, his music is eternal.

**CHRIS ROGERS**

**Trumpeter-composer-bandleader and son of trombonist Barry Rogers, who was Michael Brecker's mentor in Dreams. Michael played on two tracks from Chris's 2001 recording *Voyage Home*.**

To me, Michael is like a Beethoven or DaVinci or Mozart or Einstein. I would compare him to the greatest thinkers, the greatest scientists and artists in civilization. The intellectual sophistication and complexity of his music combined with the emotional accessibility just puts him on his own level. And like Trane, he kept evolving. He had the soul of an intrepid explorer. And that quality of searching is maybe the overriding thing that defines his solos . . . every single one.

## DAVID DEMSEY

**Tenor saxophonist-educator, professor of music and coordinator of jazz studies and curator of the Michael Brecker Archives at William Paterson University in New Jersey. He is the author of *John Coltrane Plays Giant Steps* and *Chromatic Third Relationships in the Music of John Coltrane* and is a member of the New Hudson Saxophone Quartet.**

Mike had a true gift, but he combined it with an almost maniacal work ethic. There was one chromatic thing that he used to do, which was combining the chromatic scale with harmonics . . . kind of like chromatic alternating to harmonics back and forth. And I remember he did it superfast in front of me just practicing, and I said, "How the hell did you figure that out?" And he said, "I did it in about two or three weeks." And I said, "What?! That's impossible to figure that out so quickly." And Mike said, "You're not understanding. I mean, that's all I did for three weeks. I'd practice that line twelve to fifteen hours a day. And when I fell asleep, I slept. If I needed to eat, I ate. But I practiced that line all the time." Nobody works like that. It's a superhuman ability to focus.

I remember telling him at one of our first meetings how excited I was to be transcribing his solos. And he said, "That's great, thank you. Stop doing that." And I was kind of taken aback by that comment. Here was my hero, and I'd apparently done something wrong. So, I said, "Oh, I'm sorry." And Mike said, "No, no, what I mean is, if you listen to me, all you're doing is becoming another guy who's copying me. But if you listen to who I listened to, you become my peer." And that's some heavy advice. And I remember in my naïveté saying, "Like who? Like what?" And he just ran the list: All the Atlantic Coltrane stuff up to and including *A Love Supreme*. And he added, "Anything after that, you can listen to it all you want, but don't copy it. The screechy shit will not help you." And then he continued the list with Stanley Turrentine, Joe Henderson, Cannonball Adderley, Phil Woods. And I remember jotting them down and made that my buy list. And I would listen to those records and hear some little familiar snippet of some little gesture and say, "That sounds just like Mike." And of course, it's the other way around. So that piece of advice, "If you sound like me, you're imitating me, so listen to who I listened to" was invaluable. I still use that to this day.

## CHASE BAIRD

**The Seattle native has been called "the future of jazz music and the saxophone" by no less an authority than Randy Brecker. He also had a fortuitous and life-changing meeting with Michael Brecker himself as an aspiring fourteen-year-old saxophonist growing up in Salt Lake City. Since moving to New York in 2011 and graduating from Juilliard in 2014, he has emerged as a potent sideman with the likes of Mike Stern, Mike Clark, Antonio Sanchez, Josh Maxey, and the Mingus Big Band. As a leader, he has three recordings to his credit. And, like Michael Brecker, he doubles on tenor saxophone and EWI.**

When I first heard Michael on record around age twelve, it was one of the most powerful musical experiences of my life. Hearing Michael play in person shortly thereafter was like watching an electrical storm unfold right in front of you. It had such huge contrast—at once violently evocative, bold, and courageous while tapping into a deep spiritual vulnerability. What I heard in Michael's music was somewhat an alternative to the life I was living as a kid growing up in Salt Lake City, Utah. I heard music with passion and vitality and electricity and drive, and I immediately knew I wanted to do that, whatever that was.

I got so deep into Michael's playing that I would spend hours and hours and hours every day trying to copy his sound and musical ideas on the saxophone. Around age fourteen, I got inspired to reach out and try to connect with him personally. I sent a recording and letter to his management and ended up having the opportunity to spend a day with him when he came through Salt Lake City on the Directions in Music tour with Herbie Hancock in 2003. It was an unbelievable experience for me because I was meeting my hero. But more than that, I was seeing the man behind the horn. And what I saw was a beautiful, humble, almost self-deprecating man who really loved music and loved to improve and learn. He was a master musician who at the end of the day believed in a lot of hard work. He talked about the honor of playing your ass off for every gig you ever get, no matter how big or small.

That night at the concert, I sat a few rows back from the stage. At some point, Michael saw me in the audience and nodded his head in acknowledgment, as if to say "keep going and you'll be here, too." I vividly remember that moment to this day.

## RICHIE BEIRACH

**Pianist-composer-educator who gave Michael harmony lessons during the loft jam years of the late '60s–early '70s and coled the Free Life Communication collective with Dave Liebman, who was also his bandmate in the group Quest.**

So, here's the thing: Mike was an unusual person. Besides being amazingly talented, which allowed him to master saxophone in a way that very few people do, he always had the sound, the intonation and the chops and the ideas, from the beginning, from the first time I heard him. When he first came to New York, when he was Randy's little brother and nobody fucking knew him, he had this thing. In his sound he had that quality that all the masters have, which is a sense of humanity, of HIS humanity. And that is universal—with Trane, Cannonball, Lieb, Steve Grossman, Bob Berg. There a lot of cats who play saxophone that are very good, but they don't have that element in their sound. So combined with the fact that he could play amazingly fast, with great time, with great taste, and with that searing vibrato that was his, he had really great basic skills of improvisation, of motivic development. His rhythm was right on the case. He was the perfect package. And the Shakespearean tragedy of it is, he hated the way he fuckin' played. All the time.

We did my record *In Born*, which was a tribute to Chet Baker, with Mike and Randy, John Scofield, George Mraz, Adam Nussbaum, and me. Michael did four tunes on that album, one of which was a duo called "Sunday Song." It's a simple tune—four chords, no polychords. But it's so simple and delicate that it shows your vulnerability, so you've got to really express. And I knew Michael could do it. So, we played, and the first take was spectacular. Everybody in the studio is crying; me, too. It was just beautiful and brilliant and humble, the way Michael was. And I said, "So, Mike, what do you think?" He goes, "It's terrible. I have to do another one, please." Like he just took a dump on the floor, you know?

Meanwhile, everybody's got their mouths open, jaws dropped. This is spectacular shit, and he hates it. But it's my record date, it's my tune,

I'm the leader. So, I said to Michael, "What don't you like about it?" He says, "Everything." He was fucking blind to his level of excellence and his own amazing musicality. He didn't get it. He had a very common problem. A lot of major artists only hear the mistakes or what they think is a mistake. They may hear it a tiny little bit out of tune or an idea that wasn't perfectly developed, and they want to cancel everything. To them, it's terrible, and they hate it. So, I finally said, "Look, man, I wrote it, and I played it, and I think it sounds wonderful. And I love it. But let's do another take." He said, "Oh, thank you." So, of course, we did another take, and that was even better than the first! I ended up putting both takes on the CD.

Michael had this universal lament in his sound, but he also had a fierceness about him. He had the ability to let out a torrent of notes to build up the incredible tension so that it could release, and the audience would have a real experience. And Michael knew how to work the rhythm section. With a lot of old-style cats, they might be really good players, but the rhythm section was basically backup. Michael was able to use and interact with the rhythm section in a way that made it more interesting for the rhythm section, for the cats he's playing with. And it made it a million times more interesting for the people watching.

### RICK MARGITZA

**Tenor saxophonist-composer-bandleader who has toured and recorded with Miles Davis, the Maria Schneider Jazz Orchestra, Maynard Ferguson, Flora Purim, Martial Solal, and the Moutin Brothers Reunion Quartet. A resident of Paris since 2003, he has thirteen albums as a leader for Blue Note, Challenge, SteepleChase, Palmetto, and Le Coq Records.**

Michael's technical mastery set a new standard for what was possible on the instrument. But on a much deeper level, I was and continue to be influenced and inspired by his conception and language, which combined all his influences in such a personal and beautiful way. His sound is unmistakable, and the fact that you can tell it is him within a few notes regardless of the context is something that every true artist strives for.

In my early stages of development, I transcribed everything of his that I could get my hands on and spent years trying to sound like him. As I matured, I realized I had to try to find my own voice and spent an equal, if not greater, amount of time trying not to sound like him. He was incredibly supportive of me, and knowing him as the kind, funny, and generous spirit that he was, he influenced me personally as much as his playing did musically.

Michael's influence spans a huge spectrum of styles and instruments. You can hear it in people's playing regardless of the style of music they are playing. Whether it's an eight-bar rock 'n' roll solo or the most sophisticated acoustic jazz setting, his influence is unmistakable. Just like people are still influenced by the legacies of Charlie Parker and John Coltrane, Michael's legacy will go on as long as there are people playing music.

My first meeting with Michael came in 1980 when my college big band from Wayne State University played at the Montreux Jazz Festival in Switzerland. I saw on the schedule that The Brecker Brothers were also going to be playing, so I was terribly excited about the prospect of meeting him. Our first day there I walked around the town with a stack of Michael Brecker solo transcriptions that I had done in case I would run into him. As luck would have it, I saw him on the street, walked up to him and nervously introduced myself and showed him my transcriptions. He looked at them and said, "Wow, you are really into this shit, aren't you?" And what happen next really blew me away: He asked me if I was free the following afternoon and would I like to come up to his room for a lesson. I know from experience that when I am out on the road and I have a day off, that time is sacred. But he was kind enough to share his free time with me. And when the lesson was over, there was no mention of money. That was Michael—completely gracious and generous.

## MICHAEL ZILBER

**Vancouver-born, San Francisco-based tenor saxophonist-composer has performed and recorded with many jazz luminaries, including Dave Liebman, Miroslav Vitous, Mike Clark, Steve Smith, and Bob**

**Berg. He has recorded seven albums as a leader. His latest, *East West: Music for Big Bands* (2019), includes the Michael Brecker tribute, "The Breckerfast Club," based on a fragment of a tune from Chick Corea's *Three Quartets*.**

As a fourteen-year-old, I was floored by Mike's sax break on "Pleasant Pheasant" from Billy Cobham's *Crosswinds* album. It was instantly clear to me that he played like no one else, and I wanted to understand what he was doing. Fast-forward to Boston 1982. I was attending New England Conservatory, and Steps Ahead came to town. The band—Michael Brecker, Peter Erskine, Eddie Gomez, Mike Mainieri, and Eliane Elias—was killing, of course. But the hallucinating part for me was the ten-minute trio thing that Brecker, Gomez, and Erskine got into on the outro of Joe Zawinul's "Young and Fine" with Michael setting the bar at a level I had never imagined possible: power, precision, pure sound, soul, and imagination.

I moved to New York in 1984, and one of the first gigs I heard there was Mike playing with John Abercrombie's band at the Village Vanguard. Totally starstruck, I walked up to Michael at the break and very shyly said, "Hi, Michael, I just wanted to tell you that you are a musical hero of mine." He just stared at his shoes and mumbled, "Thanks." He was not a fan of praise.

In the mid- to late-'80s, you could not throw a brick in New York City without hitting a Brecker clone. I was never a clone but surely phrased and tongued like him and tried to sound like his mighty searing tone. By 1988–89, I had to go cold turkey and stopped listening to Mike attentively for about a decade. I knew that almost every Brecker disciple sounded like a lame imitation, and I did not want to be one of those. His sound, feel, note choices, phrasing were as distinctive as previous generations had experienced with Lester, Bird, and Trane.

In the early '90s, when I moved to the Bay area, a couple of friends and colleagues, bassist James Genus and drummer Rodney Holmes, were playing in The Brecker Brothers band. So, I would meet up with them at gigs and inevitably find myself alone backstage with Mike, tongue-tied and with nothing to say, still in awe. Finally, the subject of mouthpieces somehow came up, and Mike's face brightened. He got a big smile, and we started talking shop. Once we did that, it became easier to converse.

The best lesson Mike Brecker gave me is that the only Mike I should try to be is Mike Zilber, to play every note like it is your last and play what is true and beautiful for you. That's what he did, and for that alone, the entire sax/music world owes him eternal thanks.

## BOB REYNOLDS

**Saxophonist-composer-educator and member of the Grammy Award-winning band Snarky Puppy is known for his work with John Mayer. He is a prolific composer and recording artist with ten top-selling solo albums to his credit, the latest being *Runway* (2020).**

In the winter of 2003, when I was living in New York, I sat in with Aaron Goldberg's trio at Smoke one night. As I headed toward the stage, a friend at another table stopped me as I passed and said, "Hey, did you see Brecker in the back?" I turned around and scanned the back of the club. Sure enough, sitting in the back booth with his wife, Susan, was none other than Michael Brecker. I nearly fainted. I'm not kidding. I'm actually getting nervous again as I write this, re-living that moment.

So, there I am on stage, putting my horn together, not warmed up, trying to think of possible ways to gracefully exit what seemed like impending humiliation. The saxophone had never felt so foreign in my hands. The trio was now a quartet with me at the front. I looked at Aaron, sending mental messages, "*Please* choose a song I know—an easy one!" To my astonishment, Aaron launched into something, and I had no idea what he was playing. If ever there was a moment in my adult life I was close to wetting my pants, it was then.

Fortunately, I began to recognize Aaron's improvised introduction as the Monk classic, "Evidence." Even more fortunately, I'd taken the Thelonious Monk ensemble at Berklee, and this song was ingrained in my memory. "Great," I thought, feeling a little more relaxed. "I'm going to be OK." Then Eric Harland started playing, and that uh-oh feeling returned. Eric started twisting the beat so the song's upbeats became downbeats (and other rhythmic illusions I couldn't comprehend at the time). And I was lost before we even began.

The next few minutes are basically a blur as I went on panicked autopilot. When it was over, I snuck off stage and put my sax away.

I knew I was about to receive a few fake 'Nice job' condolences from friends, and more than likely, that would be the last time I played with Aaron. This had been the kind of moment you practice endlessly for, working to perfect your craft, and I had just blown it big time in front of New York's jazz elite—*and* Michael Brecker!

I felt sick, disappointed with myself, and depressed. As I was leaving the club, I felt a tap on a shoulder. I turned around, and there was Brecker. "You have a beautiful tone," he said. "Is that a Link you're playing?" (saxophone jargon for Otto Link mouthpiece).

I was in shock. It felt like minutes before I was able to respond. Was he kidding? Playing some kind of cruel joke? Hadn't he heard what I'd just done (or more accurately, hadn't done) up there? He smiled again. I pulled myself together, and we stepped outside and started chatting. It took a moment to really take in, that in the dead of a cold winter night turning into early morning, I was standing on the sidewalk outside a New York jazz club talking mouthpieces with one of my heroes! And bizarrely, it was he who was asking the questions.

He talked about how he used to play Links, the trouble with his throat and how he'd reluctantly had to find alternative mouthpieces for physical reasons, and how he had recently begun experimenting with hard rubber Links again. He was kind, encouraging, and generous with his time, and when we finally stopped talking together, he gave me his number and told me to keep in touch.

Over the next couple years, I did just that. I asked for a lesson, but he said he didn't feel like he had much to offer me but that he'd be happy to get together and just play sometime. I regret that I never got up the courage to take him up on that offer. I was young and just too scared and in awe to play duets with him. I couldn't get past the legend and just engage him as a fellow saxophonist. We saw each other from time to time in the city, mostly at his gigs. He recommended repair guys, introduced me to other legendary players, and he always encouraged me to send him my music.

I sent him the rough mix of my first real studio album, *Can't Wait for Perfect*, and he wrote me the kindest e-mail about how, with his health recently taking a turn for the worse, my music was a boost to his spirits. I will treasure that e-mail forever.

In hindsight, and perhaps because of Brecker's generosity to me, I think I probably sounded better than I thought that night, but certainly nothing near my best. He went out of his way to engage and encourage a young guy starting to make his way in town. And for that, I will be eternally grateful.

## FRANCO AMBROSETTI

**Swiss trumpeter-composer, bandleader, and elder statesman of European jazz who has made twenty-five recordings as a leader. He prominently featured Michael on his 1984 album *Wings* and also on his 1985 follow-up album, *Tentets*. They also played together several times at Ambrosetti's hometown Lugano Jazz Festival in Switzerland.**

I discovered John Coltrane in '62–'63 and was so impressed by his intervallic way of playing, which somehow puzzled me. That began a long search of trying to incorporate some of these Coltrane improvisation phrases into my own playing. The obvious next step was to listen to somebody who had already processed the Coltrane vocabulary and made it new and up to date. And that was Michael Brecker. For me, he was number one of all the saxophone players inspired by Coltrane.

The first thing that struck me about Mike was hearing him play a ballad on a record by Don Sebesky ("Moon Dreams" on the 1975 CTI album, *The Rape of El Morro*). He plays that ballad in a very Coltrane-ian way, laying back a lot so the phrases come not right where they should come in the melody, but they come a little bit later. And he stretches all this. That was the first time that I realized that Michael Brecker was a top guy.

I first met Mike in 1977. He played at the Berlin Jazz Festival in Hal Galper's quintet with Randy, whom I had met back in 1966 when we were both in the Vienna International Jazz Competition. So, we were already good friends. I sat in with that same band in 1978 at the Berlin Jazz Festival, and I remember playing a very difficult song of Mike's called "Uptown Ed," which is a blues but really very much a tenor showcase, which for trumpet is not so easy. We got to hang out together during that festival, and that's when I discovered the fantastic man and brilliant person behind the virtuosic saxophone player. And from then on, we were friends. Whenever he would come to Lugano or Milan, he would call me, and I would go and visit him, and he would invite me on stage to play the last two or three songs of his set.

Both he and Randy were always like part of the family. In fact, my son Gianluca decided that he wanted to play tenor sax after meeting Michael at the 1989 Milano Jazz Festival when he was fifteen years old. So, he started to play tenor, and then he went to Boston to study with Jerry Bergonzi, and now he plays soprano sax. Gianluca completed a master's degree in theoretical physics, and when he wrote his PhD thesis for the Technical School of Switzerland, which is one of the top schools in the world, he dedicated his thesis to Michael Brecker.

But in spite of how great a saxophonist Michael was and what a beautiful person he was, I think he suffered from some inner turmoil. He told me one time that the relation that he had with his father was not so easy. When he was at my house in Lugano, and we were having lunch together, I said to him, "Michael, it must be great to be the best saxophone player in the world." And he said to me, kind of somberly, "Yes, but you don't know the price I had to pay. I became this just because that was the only way I could have a relationship with my father." So the price of being a great saxophone player was tough for him—that whole thing of looking for love and approval from the father.

But this, in a way, made him what he is—somebody who had a great sensibility and sensitivity. You also feel some sadness in his playing, especially when he plays a ballad. Because deep inside he had suffered sometimes in his life. And those feelings all came through his horn when he played.

# ACKNOWLEDGMENTS

This book, a labor of love stretching out over two years, would not have been possible without the help of Randy Brecker; Susan Neustadt Brecker; Darryl Pitt; Jerry Wortman; Steve Khan; Chris Rogers; David Demsey, curator of the Michael Brecker Archives at William Paterson University; and Louis Gerrits, the world's foremost authority on Michael Brecker.

Special thanks to Peter Erskine, Mike Mainieri, Dave Liebman, Joe Lovano, John Scofield, David Sanborn, Dave Holland, John Patitucci, Marc Copland, Gil Goldstein, Will Lee, Adam Nussbaum, Adam Rogers, Joey Calderazzo, Kate Greenfield, James Farber, Tim Ries, Jeff "Tain" Watts, Mike Stern, Randy Sandke, Edgar Grana, Vince Trombetta, and Bob Mintzer.

Sincere appreciation to Herbie Hancock, John McLaughlin, Chick Corea, Jack DeJohnette, Richie Beirach, Gene Perla, Lenny White, Branford Marsalis, Joshua Redman, Ravi Coltrane, Steve Gadd, Paul Simon, Antonio Sanchez, George Whitty, Jason Miles, James Genus, Scott Colley, Dennis Chambers, Dean Brown, Billy Cobham, Chris Parker, Barry Finnerty, Richie Morales, Gary Gold, Bruce Ditmas, Hal Galper, Jack Wilkins, Leni Stern, Christine Martin, Chris Minh Doky, Jay Anderson, Chris Potter, Bill Evans, Steve Slagle, Jerry Bergonzi, George Garzone, Donny McCaslin, Harald Haerter, Franco Ambrosetti, Jacqui Perrine, Jason Olaine, Don Lucoff, Don Giller, Evan Haga, Lee Mergner, Michael Segell, Luke Dailey, Ssirus Pakzad, Bill Stewart, Larry Goldings, Dave Kikoski, Boris Kozlov, Jim Beard, Chris Brubeck, Armand Sabal-Lecco, Dave Fiuczynski, Andy Snitzer, Eli Degibri, Michael Zilber, Rick Margitza, Paul Heller, Melissa Aldana, Walt Weiskopf, Tony Lakatos, Troy Roberts, Ben Wendel, Bob Franceschini, Chase Baird, and Bob Reynolds.

Thanks also to Frank Alkyer of *Downbeat*, Mac Randall of *Jazz Times*, Michael Ricci of *All About Jazz*, Heather Phares for AllMusic, Bret Primack for Jazz Video Guy, Lorne Frohman for "Distinguished Artists," Bill Sagan for Wolfgang's Vault, Brad Bellows at the Leigh Kamman Legacy Project, Jenna Molster at NPR, Vicky Mitchell at the BBC, Tori Donahue and Allen Bush at the Berklee College of Music, Victoria St.

Martin of the University of Notre Dame's Dome, Scott Steele for Mike Mahaffay Productions, Mary Rose Muccie of Temple University Press, Larry Dwyer for the Notre Dame Collegiate Jazz Festival, Susannah Cleveland of the University of North Texas, Jamie Krents at Verve Records, Andy Gotlieb of the *Jewish Exponent*, and Jane Muckle for James Taylor.

Thanks also to photographers Jimmy Katz, Suzanne Nyerges, John Paul Endress, David Arky, Lee Marshall, Judy Schiller, Steve Orlando, Stuart Nicholson, Luca d'Agostino, Rick Laird, Jun Sato, Robert Hoffman, Vince Bucci, Peter Freed, Laura Friedman, Odasan Macovich, Hans Neleman, and John Abbott.

Gratitude as always to Lauren Zarambo for her support and encouragement during the two years of this book project; to my literary agent, Peter Rubie; to John Cerullo, Carol Flannery, Barbara Claire and Melissa McClellan at Rowman & Littlefield/Globe Pequot/Backbeat for their guidance along the way; and to my friend and confidant Jeff Levenson for his wise counsel and hospitality.

# DISCOGRAPHY

**AS A LEADER:**

*Michael Brecker* (Impulse!, 1987)

*Don't Try This at Home* (Impulse!, 1988)

*Now You See It . . . Now You Don't* (GRP, 1990)

*Tales from the Hudson* (Impulse!, 1996)

*Two Blocks from the Edge* (Impulse!, 1997)

*Time Is Of the Essence* (Verve, 1999)

*Nearness of You: The Ballad Book* (Verve, 2001)

*Wide Angles* (Verve, 2003)

*Pilgrimage* (Telarc, 2007)

**WITH THE BRECKER BROTHERS:**

*Brecker Bros.* (Arista, 1975)

*Back to Back* (Arista, 1976)

*Don't Stop the Music* (Arista, 1977)

*Heavy Metal Be-Bop* (Arista, 1978)

*Detente* (Arista, 1980)

*Straphangin'* (Arista, 1981)

*Return of the Brecker Brothers* (GRP, 1992)

*Out of the Loop* (GRP, 1994)

**WITH DREAMS:**

*Dreams* (Columbia, 1970)

*Imagine My Surprise* (Columbia, 1971)

**WITH STEPS:**

*Step by Step* (Better Days, 1981)

*Smokin' in the Pit* (Better Days, 1981)

*Paradox* (Better Days, 1982)

**WITH STEPS AHEAD:**

*Steps Ahead* (Elektra / Musician, 1983)

*Modern Times* (Elektra / Musician, 1984)

*Magnetic* (Elektra, 1986)

*Live in Tokyo 1986* (NYC Records, 1986)

## WITH HERBIE HANCOCK/ROY HARGROVE:
*Directions in Music—Live at Massey Hall* (Verve, 2002)

## WITH SAXOPHONE SUMMIT:
*Gathering of Spirits* (Telarc, 2004)

## WITH HAL GALPER QUINTET:
*The Guerilla Band* (Mainstream, 1971)
*Wild Bird* (Mainstream, 1972)
*Reach Out!* (SteepleChase, 1977)
*Speak with a Single Voice* (Century, 1979)
*Redux '78* (Concord Jazz, 1991)
*Children of the Night* (Double-Time, 1997)
*Live at Berlin Philharmonic* (Origin, 2021)

## WITH HORACE SILVER:
*In Pursuit of the 27th Man* (Blue Note, 1972)
*The Hardbop Grandpop* (Impulse!, 1996)
*A Prescription for the Blues* (Impulse!, 1997)

## WITH BILLY COBHAM:
*Crosswinds* (Atlantic, 1974)
*Total Eclipse* (Atlantic, 1974)
*Shabazz* (Atlantic, 1975)
*A Funky Thide of Sings* (Atlantic, 1975)

## WITH JACK WILKINS:
*You Can't Live Without It* (Chiaroscuro, 1977)
*Reunion* (Chiaroscuro, 2001)

## WITH DON GROLNICK:
*Hearts and Numbers* (Hip Pocket, 1985)
*Weaver of Dreams* (Blue Note, 1990)
*Medianoche* (Warner Bros., 1995)
*The London Concert* (Fuzzy Music, 2000)

## WITH CLAUS OGERMAN:
*Gate of Dreams* (Warner Bros., 1977)
*Cityscape* (Warner Bros., 1982)
*Corfu* (GRP, 1990)

**WITH JACO PASTORIUS:**
*Jaco Pastorius* (Epic, 1976)
*Word of Mouth* (Warner Bros., 1981)
*The Birthday Concert* (Warner Bros., 1995)

**WITH PETER ERSKINE:**
*Peter Erskine* (Contemporary, 1982)
*Motion Poet* (Denon, 1988)

**WITH JOHN ABERCROMBIE:**
*Night* (ECM, 1984)
*Getting There* (ECM, 1988)

**WITH HERBIE HANCOCK:**
*Magic Windows* (Columbia, 1981)
*The New Standard* (Verve, 1996)

**WITH CHICK COREA:**
*Three Quartets* (Warner Bros., 1981)

**WITH MCCOY TYNER:**
*Infinity* (Impulse!, 1995)

**WITH CHARLES MINGUS:**
*Me Myself An Eye* (Atlantic, 1979)
*Something Like a Bird* (Atlantic, 1980)

**WITH ELVIN JONES:**
*The Truth* (Half Note, 2004)

**WITH KENNY WHEELER:**
*Double, Double You* (ECM, 1983)

**WITH MIKE NOCK:**
*In Out and Around* (Timeless, 1978)

**WITH JOANNE BRACKEN:**
*Tring-A-Ling* (Choice, 1977)

**WITH MIKE STERN:**
*Time in Place* (Atlantic, 1988)
*Jigsaw* (Atlantic, 1989)

*Is What It Is* (Atlantic, 1994)
*Give and Take* (Atlantic, 1997)
*Voices* (Atlantic, 2001)

## WITH BOB MINTZER:
*Source* (Explore, 1982)
*Papa Lips* (Explore, 1983)
*Incredible Journey* (DMP, 1985)

## WITH MIKE MAINIERI:
*White Elephant* (Just Sunshine, 1972)
*Love Play* (Arista, 1977)
*Wanderlust* (Warner Bros., 1981)

## WITH ELIANE ELIAS:
*So Far, So Close* (Blue Note, 1989)
*Sings Jobim* (Blue Note, 1998)
*Dreamer* (Bluebird/RCA, 2004)

## WITH RANDY BRECKER:
*Score* (Solid State/United Artists, 1969)
*Toe to Toe* (MCA, 1990)
*Hanging in the City* (ESC, 2001)
*34th & Lex* (ESC, 2003)
*Some Skunk Funk* (BHM, 2005)

## WITH STEVE KHAN:
*Tightrope* (Columbia, 1977)
*The Blue Man* (Columbia, 1978)
*Arrows* (Columbia, 1979)
*Crossings* (Verve Forecast, 1994)

# INDEX

# Index

# Index

# Index